CHARTING THE PAST

CHARTING THE PAST

THE HISTORICAL WORLDS OF
EIGHTEENTH-CENTURY ENGLAND

JEREMY BLACK

INDIANA UNIVERSITY PRESS

This book is a publication of

Indiana University Press
Office of Scholarly Publishing
Herman B Wells Library 350
1320 East 10th Street
Bloomington, Indiana 47405 USA

iupress.indiana.edu

© 2019 by Jeremy Black

All rights reserved

No part of this book may be reproduced or utilized in any form or by any means, electronic or mechanical, including photocopying and recording, or by any information storage and retrieval system, without permission in writing from the publisher. The paper used in this publication meets the minimum requirements of the American National Standard for Information Sciences—Permanence of Paper for Printed Library Materials, ANSI Z39.48–1992.

Manufactured in the United States of America

Cataloging information is available from the Library of Congress.

ISBN 978-0-253-03776-3 (cloth)
ISBN 978-0-253-03777-0 (paperback)
ISBN 978-0-253-03780-0 (ebook)

1 2 3 4 5   23 22 21 20 19

Dedicated to

Bill Gibson

CONTENTS

- PREFACE *ix*
- LIST OF ABBREVIATIONS *xxi*

1 The World of History *1*

2 Purposes, Narratives, Methods *33*

3 A Historical World of Partisan Strife: The Early Eighteenth Century *83*

4 Contrasting Approaches: Burnet and Astell *103*

5 The Unstable Past: Dissenters and History *129*

6 History Suited to Midcentury Struggle *145*

7 From the New Reign to the Crisis of Empire, 1760–76 *169*

8 Empire as Historical Narrative: Gibbon and the Descent of Civilizations *193*

9 History in the Age of Burke *220*

Conclusions: Bringing the Past
into the Present   245

· SELECTED FURTHER READING   259

· INDEX   265

PREFACE

> Thanks to Providence, the sacred monuments of History extend the short contracted span of human life, and give us years in books. These point out the glorious landmarks for our safety, and bid us be wise in time.
>
> *The Craftsman*, London newspaper, March 13, 1727

JOHN ADAMS WAS ANGRY. THE UNITED STATES' FIRST AMBASSADOR to Britain was touring England in 1786 with Thomas Jefferson, who was visiting from his ambassadorial post in Paris. Having surveyed a number of landscape gardens, including the splendors of the stately home at Stowe, with its Temple of British Worthies recording Whig heroes, they pressed on. In his diary, Adams recorded: "Edgehill and Worcester were curious and interesting to us, as scenes where freemen had fought for their rights. The people in the neighbourhood appeared so ignorant and careless at Worcester, that I was provoked, and asked, 'And do Englishmen so soon forget the ground where liberty was fought for? Tell your neighbours and your children that this is holy ground; much holier than that on which your churches stand. All England should come in pilgrimage to this hill once a year.'"[1] The meaning is apparently clear: Adams had found a people ignorant of their past. Edgehill (1642) was the first battle of the English Civil War, and Worcester (1651), Oliver Cromwell's last victory, brought to an end Charles II's attempt to defeat the parliamentarian regime.

But pressing on, Adams continued: "This animated them, and they seemed much pleased with it. Perhaps their awkwardness before might arise from their uncertainty of our sentiments concerning the civil wars."[2] Moreover, the contents of Valentine Green's *History and Antiquities of the City and Suburbs of Worcester*, a work that appeared in 1764, with, after the fashion of the period, a lengthier version published subsequently (in 1796), scarcely suggests a lack of local interest or, indeed, ignorance. Green's work, however, reflected—as did the highly positive response by Worcester's citizens to George III's visit in 1788 (the first by a king since that of Charles II)—a different view than that of Adams: Cromwell's victory was certainly not applauded in Green's history. Moreover, the Civil War had led to damage to the cathedral, which was repaired only in the early eighteenth century.

Indeed, to understand England in the long eighteenth century, it is important to consider its engagement with history, for this was an age that took an understanding of the past very seriously and one that employed this understanding in much of its discussion. England was suffused with history. That, of course, is not how it is presented in posterity. Instead, the themes then are of change, indeed revolution. A plethora of revolutions, a veritable line "to the crack of doom," as if shown to Macbeth by the witches, are found, from the first and most famous, the Industrial, now to include Agricultural, Transport, Financial, Commercial, Consumer, Demographic, Emotional, Sexual, and others. More eighteenth-century revolutions, doubtless, will follow from the fertile keypads of historians. The continuing emphasis is on new ideas, new techniques, new technologies (particularly steam power); on the birth of new sciences, such as economics, sociology, and geology; and on new cultural forms and themes, notably the novel, the landscape garden, and the neo-Gothic. The idea of the Enlightenment, indeed of an English Enlightenment,[3] adds a sense that even the very context of ideas was changing. And secularization theorists suggest that religion was on its way out from the eighteenth century. In such accounts, England appears to be a country propelling itself away from its past and very self-consciously to a transformed future.

Why then see historical writing in the period other than as a branch of belles lettres? Indeed, there was relatively little (although much more than is generally appreciated) then of the archive-based research that was to be highly significant in the age of "scientific history" that was assumed to begin in the nineteenth century. In part, this change in the nineteenth century reflected the methods, as well as the location, of a history that was increasingly pursued in universities. Moreover, in considering the earlier period, it is apparent that the English historians of the eighteenth century did not define the age. Nor were they as influential in cultural terms, at least for posterity, as those writers who developed the novel or the Romantic movement or, arguably, the landscape gardeners of the period.

Yet the society, eighteenth-century England, which more than any created the modern age, was also profoundly historical. This was the case in terms of thought, religion, politics, law, society, literature, art, architecture, music, sculpture, and much else. It was true at all levels of society. Indeed, a sense of history was a unifying social force, a shared interest between mansion and cottage. Because of this, whereas the focus of attention in works on eighteenth-century history is very much on the culture of print and notably on books with "history" in the title, that does not mean that the approach to the subject necessarily should mostly be in these terms, and certainly not entirely in them. The literary, like the academic, approach to historiography poses many disadvantages, as it can lead to a failure to appreciate the full range of engagement with history that was seen in the period and, in practice, in others—what can be termed the historical culture.[4]

Historical writing and consciousness were dominated by the interests and preoccupations of people in the eighteenth century. In this respect, history then was as present-centered as it has been in subsequent centuries. Major topics, such as the character of civil and religious liberties, the nature and legitimacy of the state, the engagement with interests overseas, and the nature of society and civilization, were opportunities for historical writers to connect the past with the present. In order to make that connection, writers had to use argument by analogy; and the use of analogy opened discussion of the validity of the comparison being made.

This method of comparison was one of the major foci of historical writing in the period. So, for example, when historians compared the Glorious Revolution of 1688–89 to the overthrow of Richard III and the succession of Henry VII in 1485, they were beginning or taking part in multifaceted historical conversations about the validity of such comparisons. This drove historical debates toward the complex issues of what were acceptable and justifiable precedents and what was the reasonable and sustainable evidence for them. Consequently, the eighteenth century, building on controversies in the seventeenth century, saw the development of what can be presented as a discipline in historical writing, in the sense that the evidence and judgments would be tested and interrogated, rather than accepted without evaluation.

Present-centered history, which was highly contentious, had to be more defensible than historical writing, which did not pack a contemporary punch. This gave a considerable sophistication to historical writing in the eighteenth century. Present-centered history was not, however, one-dimensional. It reflected the major political and theological arguments for and against the settlement of 1689. But it also explored specific issues of government policy during the eighteenth century so that entanglements in Europe, taxation and government spending, and the extent and nature of the naval and military capability of the country were all subject to examination through a historical lens. In this way, historical comparisons were able to be deployed with reference both to broad and to narrow themes.

Present-centered history was also able to offer alternative imagined futures. Writers like Mary Astell (considered in chap. 4) offered a vision of an England returned to theocratic government and absolute monarchy, far distant from the parliamentary settlement of 1689. Ferdinando Warner (considered in chap. 6) wrote of an alternative, more benign English rule of Ireland. So present-centered history offered possibilities in terms of both counterfactual speculations about the past and different trajectories of future development.

The world of eighteenth-century English historical writing was important for the more general development of history as a practice. This and other points were true of Britain as a whole, but the breadth of the subject means that our focus will be on England, although Scottish historians writing English history (notably David Hume in chap. 7) will be included. When English writers referred to "Britain," they tended to mean a greater England, in terms of character and concerns, and this was certainly shown in their treatment of history. There is also the specific focus in this book on the Church of England and its clerical historians, in part as a deliberate attempt to query attempts to provide an essentially secular reading of the culture of the period.[5]

The local dimension, furthermore, repeatedly emerges as important, and is introduced in chapter 2. While scholars in later periods and, indeed, their present-day counterparts frequently have tended to dismiss local and regional history as amateurish or antiquarian, in the eighteenth century there was a greater regard for it. The tendons and muscles of national and international history writing had considerable connective tissue to the sinews of local and regional history. Indeed, the interests and preoccupations of the eighteenth century accommodated the units of local history—parishes, towns, and counties—better than most later periods of historical writing, with the exception of the county studies of early-seventeenth-century England produced in the late twentieth century. The effects of the Reformation, the English Civil War, and even foreign wars, among other topics, could be seen with considerable clarity in such early local studies.

Moreover, local history benefitted from the interest of well-educated scholars who were often clergymen, lawyers, and even politicians out of office. They became skilled in the use of diverse sources, including buildings, landscapes, and inscriptions, as well as archival material. David Douglas has shown how powerfully local historians in the early eighteenth century opened up scholarly discussions on such topics as the nature of Anglo-Saxon culture, the Norman Conquest, the liberties granted or confirmed by medieval charters, and the use of chronicles. He has also pointed out that such research relied on "the generous support of an educated public"—whom he called "the friends of Clio [the classical muse of history]."[6]

The consumption of local history in the eighteenth century was not differentiated from other forms of history as it is sometimes today. The libraries of the educated public did not treat books on local history as a separate body of work.[7] Larger works, such as Edmund Gibson's 1695 English-language edition of William Camden's *Britannia* (first published in Latin in 1586), could be unapologetic in their development of local history into a national compendium. *Britannia* was remarkably popular, with new and revised editions published in 1722, 1753, 1772, and 1789. It was also widely published in Europe and was regarded as an authoritative work of history. Similarly the *Notitia Monastica, or a Short History of the Religious Houses in England and Wales* (1695), of Thomas Tanner (1674–1735), bishop of St. Asaph, was in effect a national collection of local history. An Oxford friend of Gibson, Tanner compiled much material, proposing, among other tasks he did not complete, an edition of the works of the sixteenth-century scholar John Leland and a history of Wiltshire. As a result of research done for the latter, Tanner provided material for Camden's edition of *Britannia*.

Local history research and writing offered an outlet for the talents of clerical and lay scholars. They also offered opportunities for those Nonjurors and Jacobites who had been excluded from any other role in public life, a theme identified in chapter 2. This delving into the subject of history might have represented an escape from an unpalatable present, but it was also a means of exploring how history had unfolded in the way it had.

The relative freedom to write and publish made Britain an important representation of both the contemporary European situation and one that, in this respect, prefigured the modern West. Moreover, the development of history in the United States was greatly influenced by the situation during the period when the United States had been part of the British world, or, at least, that part of the United States out of which US state and public culture developed after 1776. Compared to such countries as Austria, Russia, Spain, and, to a lesser extent, France, Britain maintained a large entrepreneurial world of publishing, as did the United States. This world ensured that history was actively and relatively freely discussed not only in books but also in a range of publications, including pamphlets, chapbooks, newspapers, plays, and verse. The role of the press is particularly notable. Newspapers do not excite much interest in historiography, but they were important in the eighteenth century. In particular, alongside parliamentary debates, newspapers connected the past to the highly partisan world of political contention. That use of history does not tend to attract much attention, notably sympathetic attention, in the modern discussion of historiography, but it was a use that was very important in sustaining an active polemical, rhetorical, symbolic, and, indeed, practical engagement with the past. This was the case for ecclesiastical and confessional politics as well as secular ones.

Books themselves were quite varied in their tone. Moreover, this contrast was understood. In the preface to the second volume of his *History of England* (1718), Laurence Echard noted, "I have several times deviated and descended from the dignity of an Historian, and voluntarily fallen into the lower class of biographers, annalists, etc." These value judgments of contemporary writers repay examination. This volume included Echard's retelling of the story of Oliver Cromwell's meeting with the devil and Cromwell's agreement to serve him.[8]

Many of the leading British intellectuals of the age, including Henry, Viscount Bolingbroke, Edward Gibbon, David Hume, William Robertson, and Adam Smith, wrote history, or about history, or employed history in their writings. These writers mobilized the supposed lessons of history in pursuit of specific intellectual agendas. In particular, the nature of development through time attracted increased attention as the century progressed. This field captured a tension between what can be seen as enlightened historiography and the broader current of the national engagement with the past.

It can sometimes appear as if a focus on history and on historical writing was transformed by the growth of the Enlightenment. In the same way that reason and materialism came to dominate ideas of causation in science and other disciplines, so history in a conventional form was affected by the same secularizing forces. Indeed, history in the eighteenth century is often regarded as absorbing rational and rejecting providential explanations for historical events. The decline of superstition and folklore suggested that God was written out of contemporary historical reasoning. The evidence we consider here suggests otherwise and matches Voltaire's observations in his *Lettres Anglaises* (1728) on the strength of religious activity in England. Historical writing in the eighteenth century did not reflect a smooth, progressive, upward trajectory of secularization and reason, let alone a modernization of historiography,[9] however that is supposed to be understood.

Instead, historical writing saw fluctuations, rather than decline, in discussion of the role of divine intervention. Hume's *History of England* (1756–61) might have been a consciously atheist work, but it was followed—and explicitly countered (as discussed in chap. 7)—by John Wesley's *Concise History of England* (1775–76), which sought to insert

God back into history. The majority of historical writers in the eighteenth century were not atheists of Hume's type. Instead, they tended to be Christians, or at least well-disposed to Christianity. Even Gibbon, who was ambivalent in his attitude to religion, did not dismiss divine intervention. In chapter 15 of *The Decline and Fall of the Roman Empire*, on "the progress of the Christian religion, and the sentiments, manners, numbers, and condition of the primitive Christians," Gibbon made clear his view that the Christian "insinuation" into the body of the Roman Empire happened under providential guidance.

One reason for the popularity of history that encompassed providential themes was the economics of publishing. Religious works, such as Robert Nelson's *A Companion for Festivals and Fasts of the Church of England* (1704), sold extremely well: 10,000 copies of Nelson's book were printed in four and a half years, and a thirty-sixth edition appeared in 1826. *The Church Catechism Explained by Way of Question and Answer, and Confirm'd by Scripture Proofs* (1700), by the Kent cleric John Lewis, a keen defender of the position of the Church of England, went through forty-two editions by 1812, while William Law's *A Serious Call to a Devout and Holy Life, adapted to the State and Condition of all Orders of Christians* (1728) enjoyed huge sales, as did the republication and abridgement of popular seventeenth-century works, notably John Bunyan's *Pilgrim's Progress*. Many of the historical works discussed in this book should be considered in that context.[10] Laying aside issues of the religious commitment of individual writers, which were often strong, it made sound business sense to publish works that captured the popular religious commitment of the age.[11]

Given that most of the English viewed events in their own age as driven by God, including the Jacobite defeats of 1715 and 1745, the growth of empire, military victories, and even the London earthquakes of 1692 and 1750, it would have been remarkable if they had not expected historical writing also to reflect the intervention of Providence. The idea of Britain (in practice, England) as an "elect nation" and a second Israel, chosen by God, contributed to contemporary exceptionalism and also to a sense of historical exceptionalism. Consequently, British elect status was seen to develop from a long sequence of events that justified God's endorsement. Of course this approach could be traced back to the

Reformation; but it could also be stretched further back into a distant past that included Edward the Confessor (r. 1042–66), who was first claimed to have the power to cure the "King's evil," and even to more mythological but powerful figures like King Arthur. This ambient identification of history with divine sanction meant that historical writing naturally reflected such popular sentiments.

Moreover, this book argues not only for the overwhelming influence of politico-religious interests in shaping views of history but also for the continued centrality of religious perspectives in national identity formations, including by means of historical work. This is significant for the broader question of what the study of English history in this period tells us about the nature of eighteenth-century England as both shaped by and reflected in its use of history.

From a very different direction than the interest in Providence, some of the theoretical historical literature from the 1960s that has been fashionable and consciously innovative in its conceptualization has deliberately set out to contest the value and relevance of Enlightenment ideas of modernity. It is therefore useful to turn to the eighteenth century to see the world and work of its historians.

The book begins with two overlapping chapters, the first on the contexts of historical interest and reading and the second on motivation and methods in historical writing. Chapter 3, on the ideological context of history in the early eighteenth century, establishes the background for a series of case studies. Each is considered in order to indicate the variety of historical work in the period and to illustrate particular themes.

Chapter 4 considers two contrasting historians, Gilbert Burnet and Mary Astell. Burnet's *History of the Reformation* represents a major work of historical interpretation, equivalent to Clarendon's *History of the Rebellion*. It was a decisive historical intervention that greatly influenced the interpretation of the Reformation for the next century and beyond. Burnet has attracted attention from historians in the last decade, with contrasting interpretations of the contribution his work made to the history of the sixteenth and seventeenth centuries. Burnet identified a providential force behind the people of a nation when they united in action. This idea of "popular conciliarity" meant that the popular action of a nation in making concerted and unanimous decisions could be seen as legitimate and binding on a monarch. The idea appeared in Burnet's writing before the events of 1688–89 and, therefore, was not a retrospective attempt to justify the Glorious Revolution. Nevertheless, when published in its final form in 1715, the *History of the Reformation* was clearly an argument for the legitimacy of the Reformation and the Revolution. Burnet also identified qualities that were necessary for rulers. He did this in biographical works on, among others, Matthew Hale and John, Earl of Rochester. In both cases, Burnet argued that leaders of society needed to be pious and devout. And he showed in the case of Rochester how even those lacking virtue could be converted to a strong faith. In planning the education of rulers, Burnet argued that the children of aristocrats and monarchs could be brought to avoid cruelty and to embrace moderation and toleration. In this way, Burnet's historical writing suggested a blueprint for a godly society in which rulers, like those in the Protestant cantons of Switzerland, were thought to be benign and themselves governed by the teachings of Protestantism, but also one in which the people, acting together, could assert some sovereignty in the face of tyranny or oppression.

In contrast, Astell's historical model was derived from a highly conservative and biblically inspired view of the nature of society. In a confident and self-assured attack on White Kennett's account of the Civil War, Astell sought to vindicate Charles I from any blame and to place responsibility for the bloodshed on fanatical Puritans and their leaders. Unlike Burnet, she showed a marked concern about trusting the people, whom she dismissed as easily manipulated, and placed authority in church and state in the hands of the monarch. This High Tory account of the past was also deployed to argue for attacking the nascent rights of (Protestant) Dissenters and for restoring an absolute monarchy based on religious principles. An active female historian, Astell was a pugnacious and forthright writer, who argued for the subjugation of women to their husbands, a position that may only seem paradoxical to those influenced by feminism. Astell represents a strand of historical thought that, though it diminished during the eighteenth century, was a reflection of Jacobite and Nonjuring claims to demand a restoration of hereditary monarchy and the ending of religious toleration.

The third case study in this book, in chapter 5, further demonstrates how radically different interpretations of the seventeenth century made it appear unstable and lack the security of a settled account of the past. Accounts of the seventeenth century created strongly divergent accounts of the Civil War. One of the key debates was the character of the seventeenth-century Puritans, forebears of the Dissenters of the eighteenth century, and the degree to which they were responsible for the Civil Wars. This issue directly connected to consideration of whether Dissenters could be trusted and admitted to a full part in government and society. This branch of historical writing had an immediate consequence for the country. The works discussed—by Samuel Wesley, John Oldmixon, and Daniel Neal—exerted a powerful influence on both accounts of the past and implications for the future. Present-centered history was at its most immediate in such historical writing.

Chapter 6 addresses the midcentury situation, focusing on two historians of the 1750s, Richard Rolt and Ferdinando Warner. The first, a onetime Jacobite, offered a vigorous anti-Catholic patriotism. Somewhat differently, Warner's failure to obtain Church preferment meant that he turned to historical writing in the hope of obtaining money, and perhaps advancement. Considering such writers underlines a theme in this book—namely, a consideration of histories that were widely read but not written by the elite historians. This takes us to the heart of how history was consumed.

Chapter 7 directs attention to John Wesley's commercially successful *History of England*, in part in order to suggest the need to avoid too great a concentration on David Hume's perspectives. Chapter 8 uses Edward Gibbon to indicate how history spoke to the international situation of the period, an issue of great significance to Britain. Chapter 9 assesses the impact of the French revolutionary crisis, notably through the arguments of Edmund Burke and Edward Nares. The conclusions include a discussion of the rise of medievalism.

I would like to thank Nigel Aston, Jonathan Barry, Bruce Coleman, Grayson Ditchfield, Bill Gibson, Jeffrey Smitten, Richard Wendorf, Neil York, and an anonymous reader for commenting on earlier drafts of all or part of the book. I have also benefited from a discussion with David Pearson. It is a great pleasure to dedicate this book to Bill Gibson. Originally we were to do this book together, and Bill wrote the first drafts of chapters 4 and 5 and the section on Warner. In his deciding, however, greatly to my regret, to withdraw due to the pressures of other work, he kindly permitted me to use this draft and subsequently provided great encouragement. I am most grateful for his help, and this dedication marks the continuation of a long and happy friendship.

NOTES

1. J. Adams, *The Works of John Adams*, ed. C. F. Adams (Boston, 1856), 3:394–96; *Papers of Thomas Jefferson*, ed. Julian Boyd, 9:364–65.

2. Adams, *Works*, 3:394–96.

3. R. Porter, *Enlightenment: Britain and the Creation of the Modern World* (London, 2000).

4. D. R. Woolf, "A High Road to the Archives? Rewriting the History of Early Modern English Historical Culture," *Storia della Storiografia* 32 (1997): 33–59; D. R. Kelley and D. H. Sacks, eds., *The Historical Imagination in Early Modern Britain: History, Rhetoric, and Fiction, 1500–1800* (Cambridge, 1997).

5. See also J. C. D. Clark, "Providence, Predestination, and Progress: Or, Did the Enlightenment Fail?" *Albion* 35 (2004): 559–90.

6. D. C. Douglas, *English Scholars, 1660–1730* (London, 1951), 244.

7. See, for example, some of the essays in G. Mandelbrote and K. A. Manley, eds., *The Cambridge History of Libraries in Britain and Ireland*, vol. 2, *1640–1850* (Cambridge, 2008).

8. For Cromwell's most famous opponent, the royalist cavalry general Prince Rupert, as diabolical, see M. Stoyle, *The Black Legend of Prince Rupert's Dog: Witchcraft and Propaganda during the English Civil War* (Exeter, UK, 2011).

9. J. M. Levine, *Humanism and History: Origins of Modern English Historiography* (Ithaca, NY, 1987).

10. For a broader critique of the established canon, see J. Black, *Clio's Battles: Historiography in Practice* (Bloomington, IN, 2015).

11. For the extent of the market for sermons, see W. Gibson, "Introduction," in *The Oxford Handbook of the British Sermon 1689–1901*, ed. K. Francis and W. Gibson (Oxford, 2012), 19–23, fn 10. See also S. Rosa, "Religion in the English Enlightenment: A Review Essay," *Eighteenth-Century Studies* 28 (1994): 145–46.

ABBREVIATIONS

Add Additional Manuscripts
BB Bland Burges papers
BL British Library, London
Bodl Bodleian Library, Oxford
CRO County Record Office
EHR *English Historical Review*
NA National Archives, Kew (London)
SP State Papers

CHARTING THE PAST

ONE

THE WORLD OF HISTORY

> When history, and particularly the history of our own country, furnishes anything like a case in point, to the time in which an author writes, if he knows his own interest, he will take advantage of it.
>
> Puff in *The Critic* (1779) (II, i)

THE RIDICULOUS PUFF'S EXPLANATION FOR HIS DECISION TO title his play *The Spanish Armada* in order to draw on public interest in that episode of 1588, following the Franco-Spanish invasion preparations of 1779, captures the decision of Richard Brinsley Sheridan, both playwright and opposition politician, to use this play within a play to satirize the world of the stage as well as the historical purchase of English nationalism. Sheridan also parodied Thomas Kyd's *The Spanish Tragedy* (1592), which had celebrated the defeat of the Spanish Armada as well as providing a murderous play within a play.[1]

History not only provided specific analogies and parallels for those whose main concern was the present but also operated as education, in the broadest sense: the education of a realm and a nation, a country and a society, of individuals and communities. History also served as a survey of memory, as a record of the impact of the decisions (providential and secular, of the past and present), and as a foretaste of the future. Any and all choices on my part in covering these, whether in the space devoted to each, the order in which they are considered, or in the priorities of what is covered, will inherently suggest a significance. That significance may not be intended nor thought out, or may be both but rest unexpressed. That is not the intention here. Alongside consideration of other forms, there is a focus on the culture of print, not least because that created some of the most lasting impressions of the past (lasting, in particular, as books could be read and reprinted for decades and longer) and also was important to the development of a historiographical corpus.

In the eighteenth century, books were preserved in libraries and private collections, rather than discarded. Indeed, that characteristic of the period was far stronger than it is today, when there is a greater tendency for publications to be superseded, even denigrated, by what comes next. Furthermore, in the eighteenth century, both reprints and the deliberate reuse of material by writers and, indeed, by other authors ensured a greater degree of continuity with individual studies and between works. The accretional nature of developments, a deliberately accretional nature, was also readily apparent in other disciplines and in contemporary writings about them, for example law and medicine.[2] It was from print that much ambient culture grew.

However, in focusing on the culture of print, there is a determination here to put, alongside the greats (for example, Gibbon and Hume[3]), other writers who, while popular in their age, have been far less so for posterity. Many of the latter can be seen as hack writers, although this book will establish that that did not mean they were without talent, interest, or significance. This approach matches that taken for Ireland by Toby Barnard. He has emphasized the impact of "histories that were impressionistic and simplistic" and has argued that "what was valued and bought by a select few has tended to dominate reconstructions of the Irish past.... Low rates of survival for the flimsy, cheap and ephemeral, coupled sometimes with a disdain for print that seems trivial have led to the avowedly popular being neglected if not totally overlooked."[4]

Rather than seeing the world of print, however, as a contrast between the greats and the hacks, the lasting and the ephemeral, I would argue that there was a continuum. Moreover, the significance of individual works to contemporaries was far from clear. There was both a ready understanding of some contrasts in goals, means, and achievements and yet also an unfixed character, one in which assessment and classification were far from clear and only became apparent in hindsight. Advertisements and prefaces sought to assert particularity and significance, while reviewers (and competing works) attempted to place particular books and to clarify the field as a whole. Success, however, was limited, in part because there were not the clear means of hierarchical would-be determination seen today, with very few providers such as Amazon and its internet-driven and disseminated reviews.

There will also be a consideration of other aspects of the culture of print, notably newspapers. These reached much of the literate population and were also read aloud, as well as made available in some milieus, notably taverns and coffeehouses. The lapse of the Licensing Act in 1695 was followed by a major expansion in the press. This was centered in London, where the first daily, the *Daily Courant*, was founded in 1702. There was also the development of a provincial press. This ensured that, by 1760, most towns of any size had their own newspapers, while some towns, such as Bristol, Exeter, Norwich, Nottingham, and York, contained competing newspapers. Produced essentially by their editor and printer, frequently the same person, newspapers lacked a staff of reporters and had to respond to reader interests, however perceived. Historical pieces, like their geographical counterparts, provided good copy. More commonly, many items that in no way focused on history nevertheless employed points from it, either to provide interest or to support arguments. This reflected the extent to which the historical frame of reference did not appear redundant with time, which, significantly, was the case both with recent history, notably that of the previous century, and with more distant ages.

History, however, also very much extended beyond printing, let alone books, to other forms and audiences, from architecture to drama,[5] sculpture to opera, taverns to processions, in many respects, far more so than today. It is mistaken to treat engagement with history as an engagement with publications. Indeed, the folk culture of eighteenth-century England was one in which history was the bedrock and the past very much a living presence.

It is best to begin with the beginning. Christening was a religious act and also a means of joining the newborn to an existing family and, in doing so, to establish and assert a range of links. Individuality existed within a context. Whereas the choice of name today is often unrelated to lineage and may reflect names that are liked or associations with popular entertainment or sport, that was not common practice in the eighteenth century. Instead, names very much captured the weight of the past, both secular and spiritual, and its role in establishing identity and carrying it forward. Compared to today, there was an overwhelming use of a small number of names. A political dimension was shown by the use and choice of many monarchical ones, for example, the Hanoverian George and Georgina, as opposed to the Stuart Charles, James, and Henrietta. Family names were crucial at every level of society. There was a tendency to name after parents. Correspondence about naming captured this search for the appropriate association. This correspondence was but a small fraction of the discussion that presumably was part of the process and that doubtless also followed the choice of name as it was explained (both to family members and to others) and commented on (favorably and unfavorably).

EDUCATION

After christening came education.[6] The formal process found much space for history, both sacred and profane, and more so than today. In *Northanger Abbey*, Jane Austen has Catherine Morland complain that historians write "only for the torment of little boys and girls."[7]

The informal aspect of education was also significant. In the family context, oral traditions continued to provide the key historical source,[8] while diaries and letters provided new family history. Oral accounts frequently offered tales of the past, notably those of past members of the family and also of elderly present members. The latter accounts were generally told by or for these members at occasions of sociability. This practice, satirized by Laurence Sterne in his novel *Tristram Shandy* (1759–67), was important to establishing the family as a lineage, and a lineage linked with specific places and experiences. This linkage was a matter, variously, of pride, admonition, and warning, and it was significant in the development of local histories, notably such early county histories as William Dugdale's *Antiquities of Warwickshire* (1656).[9]

Not only literary forms were significant. Eager to be promoted in the peerage, Ralph Montagu, a second son of a peer, was made first Earl (1689) and then Duke of Montagu (1705). In a typical gesture of decorative aggrandizement, he had his coat of arms and family tree carved on his staircase at Boughton House to promote the idea of an unchanging family succession. In his *Itinerarium Curiosum*, the antiquarian William Stukeley described visiting Thomas, Lord Coningsby, Lord Lieutenant of Herefordshire, a committed Whig, in his seat at Hampton Court, Herefordshire, and finding "many of his gallerys and passages... adorned with the genealogy of his family, their pictures, arms." Coningsby also showed Stukeley "four or five vast books in manuscript being transcripts out of the record offices, relating to his manors, royalties, estates, and muniments."[10] However, this research led Coningsby into a series of unsuccessful lawsuits over what he saw as his rights as lord of the manors of Marden and Leominster, rights he believed had been compromised by the tenants. This led Coningsby to print his rights to the Marden property.

Lineage was also a matter of interesting and stirring tales. For the English of the eighteenth century, the Civil War of 1642–46 was particularly significant, not least as it related to places as well as families and because so many had served in it.

Family lineage and lore, which had led to unpublished memoirs (for example by Robert Furse for his son in 1593[11]), developed to become almost a genre of literature by the time of Sir Walter Scott. Inheritance issues were important to family narratives, and this was also seen in the novels of the period, as in Sarah Fielding's *The Adventures of David Simple* (1744), Tobias Smollett's *The Adventures of Roderick Random* (1748), and Horace Walpole's *The Castle of Otranto* (1764). Fatherhood shifted in its meaning and presentation, but both traditional notions (of preserving and commemorating lineage) and developing ones of the culture of sensibility[12] encouraged an explanation of the past.

More generally, in the pre-Romantic period, those who were long-lived were regarded as of particular merit, and the cults of the young and of modernity were less prominent than in modern society. Individual and collective memory, and their expression, were the prime drivers of historical practice. The law gave weight to the memory of old members of the community. For example, the oral memory of the oldest members was important in determining customary rights and practices and in enclosure awards.

Dynasticism, in many senses, was also an important element in autobiography, in that the determination to pass on wisdom and experiences, in order to affirm values, was of significance.[13] Thus, Edward Nares (1763–1841), later regius professor of history at Oxford from 1813 to his death, presented his manuscript autobiography as a history written for the benefit of his children, rather than as a journal written for his own amusement:

> Since life is above all things precarious, and God only knows how long I may live, and as I have at present children so young that though it should please God to spare their lives, I may not live to see them come to maturity; and as it is reasonable to think that when they grow up they will be anxious to know who they are descended from; and yet may have none to tell them. For these reasons, and no other, I have resolved to put together such particulars of my life and connections as may satisfy their enquiries, and serve to inform them who and what their father was, as far as such knowledge can be honestly and correctly communicated by frail man.[14]

The autobiographical approach to dynasticism was seen in many other artistic and literary forms. These included the retention of family correspondence as an aspect of history by heirloom. There was also the commissioning of portraits and the preservation of those of previous members of families. A similar end was achieved by means of commissioning pictures of houses, whereas those of horses more clearly served the memorialization of hobbies.

Family education has left less material than formal processes of education. Some books, however, were written as if part of it. For example, Oliver Goldsmith was very successful with *A History of England in a Series of Letters from a Nobleman to his Son* (1764), while William Russell (1741–93) had a great success with his *History of Modern Europe, in a Series of Letters from a Nobleman to his Son* (1779–84). He explained: "The author's aim was, to strike a medium between the dry chronological method of Pufendorf and the desultory, but captivating manner of Voltaire. For this purpose the epistolary form was chosen, as best calculated to preserve the chain of events, without subjecting the writer to the necessity of omitting, or of throwing into notes, those interesting anecdotes and occasional reflexions, which many consider as the chief merit of history."[15] Russell added: "Modern History not only furnishes the principal subjects that find a place in polite conversation, but also the knowledge of those which enable the young nobleman or gentleman, who has studied the ancient Classics, to enter on public business."[16] Russell also published a *History of America* (1779).

Edward Weston (1703–70), a former civil servant and a committed supporter of the Church of England (he was the son of a bishop), published a series of anonymous works as if a country gentleman giving advice. His *Family Discourses by a Country Gentleman* (1768) deployed history in the service of his charge about the threat of papal power to Britain. To many, this was not a threat that had disappeared with the defeat of Jacobite plans in 1746 and 1759, although others disagreed. Controversies over present issues were read back into accounts of the recent and distant past, and discussion of the latter was then used to support and assert positions in these controversies.

History played a major role in the education both of the influential and of the political nation, and its educational value was frequently cited.[17] In 1728, Daniel Dering wrote to his close friend John, Viscount Perceval, concerning the education of the latter's heir, later John, 2nd Earl of Egmont, and a prominent politician: "With his history will it not be proper to read Chronology, and with his English History at large I fancy after every reign it would do well to look over in such an abstract (for instance as Pufendorf's) the contemporary reigns in France and the Empire [Germany]." Two years later, the boy reported to his father: "I have read very near three volumes of Tyrells history of England, and one of Wicquefort, besides a great deal of Livy and another Roman historian."[18]

These letters indicate the need to read very widely in apparently unpromising archival sources in order to establish individual and more general reading histories and patterns. Tutors' accounts are of particular value. In 1731, the tutor of the young Simon, 2nd Viscount Harcourt, noted in Angers: "His Lordship has finished eight volumes of Rapin's *History of England* in French, and I hope will be able to finish also the full history of France this winter. For his reading here has chiefly consisted in history."[19] Harcourt was in France in order to improve his knowledge of French. What was significant was that, in common with other young people, he was reading history. Well aware of their Norman roots, the Harcourt family was also to be friendly with George III.

In 1744, Benjamin Holloway, tutor to John, later 1st Earl Spencer, wrote to Spencer's great-grandmother, the demanding Sarah, Duchess of Marlborough: "A large and comprehensive knowledge of history seems expedient for a person of quality. This contributing to lay a good foundation for a superstructure, not of political wisdom only, but of common prudence also, with great and ready insight into affairs and events public and private. And in order to read the historians, not loosely, as if one was in the regions of fairy-land and romance, but with distinction of place and time, the aids of geography and chronology are to be borrowed of the mathematics."[20]

Holloway, an Anglican cleric and a fellow of the Royal Society, wrote largely on religious themes, including, in 1751, his *Originals physical and theological, sacred and profane. Or an Essay towards a Discovery of the first descriptive Ideas in things, by Discovery of the simple or primary Roots in Words; as the same were, from the Beginning rightly applied by Believers, and afterwards perverted by Infidels.*

As part of his familiarization with Britain, George II's elder son, Frederick, Prince of Wales, himself father of George III, was given history to read as a child, being provided with the works of Clarendon and Burnet. In 1751, Prince Edward, afterward Duke of York, the second son of Frederick, Prince of Wales, sent Simon, 1st Earl Harcourt (the 2nd Viscount mentioned above), the head of the household for Edward and his older brother, the future George III, a series of letters that included comments on his education in which the history was presented in terms of the lives of medieval monarchs:

> I go on very well with my Latin, as well as the history. I read this morning part of the life of King John, and must say, that though a King, he was a very sad fellow in private as well as public life. (22 June)

> I am now in the reign of King Henry the Third, who came to the throne in his minority; and therefore the Earl of Pembroke was Regent as well as guardian to the young King. The Barons were very angry in John's time that they had not got back again that which they had enjoyed under the Saxon Kings; and after Pembroke's death, being disgusted with the behaviour of the Regents, they sent to Rome to have the King declared of age before the usual time; but they were not long satisfied with their master, when they found that he did not pursue the wise and good measures marked out to him by Pembroke. (27 June)

> I am yet in King Henry III, whose life is very long, and I think very tedious. (2 July)
>
> I shall finish the reign of Henry the Fourth tomorrow, whose reign I think very intrigate [sic] (2 August)
>
> I am in the reign of Richard the Second, whose reign I both detest and abhor; firstly, because he gave himself up totally to his flatterers; and, secondly, because he had not the least grain of honour. (25 August)[21]

Similarly, the future George IV was able, as a child, to explain the historical references in the paintings in the royal collection, including of victories over France, which indicates that they had been used to teach him.

In addition, history books written specifically for children appeared. These included Richard Johnson's *History of France from the earliest period to the present time . . . designed for the use of young ladies and gentlemen* (1786). "Small histories" was the term employed for children's books.[22]

The young could also read and be impressed by books owned by their parents, as, indeed, was intended to be the case. Edward Nares owed his interest to the extensive library of his father, a judge: "The first book I ever remember to have read with a view to useful information was the history of England . . . written I believe by Goldsmith. . . . This I not only read but abridged, and in a short time became so interested in the study of history, that the very next undertaking of the kind was to go through the whole of Rapin's History with Echard's Continuation. . . . I began to write a history of England myself."[23]

Clara Reeve (1729–1807), a neo-Gothic novelist, the eldest daughter of a Whig Suffolk Anglican clergyman, was given to read by him, at an early age, Rapin-Thoyras's history of England, Greek and Roman history, Cato's *Letters*, and Plutarch. Her *The Progress of Romance through Times, Centuries and Manners* (1785) sought to fix what was important. Similarly, Catharine Macaulay (1731–91), a child of land and banking interests, read much classical history while being privately educated, and this reading was to be linked to her commitment to liberty.

Frequently, although not invariably, the partisan purpose of a historical education for the young was readily apparent, and there were suggestions of its impact. For example, it was made clear by a comment of 1752 about Henry Digby (1731–93), the son of a landed gentleman and later an MP: "He has during this last year read Rapin, Clarendon and Burnet carefully, and is become the bitterest enemy that the Stuart family have."[24] In other words, Digby was totally opposed to the Jacobites. This implied thought as well as engagement on Digby's part as Clarendon, a Tory, had a different perspective than Burnet and Rapin-Thoyras, both of whom were Whigs.

Partisanship was not the sole setting, theme, or consequence of such education. To a degree, instead, partisanship was an aspect of a broader belief that the lesson of history was that good government originated in the actions of good men. This approach, one that looked to longstanding classical and biblical ideas and stories, linked political and religious themes with questions of individual character and more general morality.

Related to this, there was an engagement with the interest of the past on its own merits, although the two could not always be readily separated. This was a claim repeatedly made at the time. The 1789 edition of Samuel Patrick's *Geographia Antiqua*, a classical atlas that was first published in London in 1731 (with eight London reprints by 1812), was described as "designed for the use of schools, and of gentlemen who make the Ancient Writers their delight or study." The genesis of this book, like that of many others, reflected a more general cosmopolitanism in the engagement with the book. This atlas, by an active classical scholar, a teacher at Charterhouse, was based on a work by the Halle professor Christoph Cellarius (or Keller) (1638–1707) that was originally published in Latin in Jena, Germany, in 1676. Similarly, *A Complete Body of Ancient Geography, Both Sacred and Profane; Exhibiting the Various Empires, Kingdoms, Principalities, and Commonwealths, throughout the Known World, in Fifty-Two Maps, Selected from the Best Authors* (1741) was the translation of a Latin work. In 1757, *Twelve Maps of Ancient Geography Drawn by the Sieur d'Anville*, originally published in Paris in 1738–40 as part of a multivolume study of ancient history, appeared as a single work in London. The title page referred to the value of such a work for understanding modern classical scholarship: "Being useful and necessary for the readers of the several editions of Mr Rollin's *Ancient History*, and all other writers on that subject."

Such references reflected the accumulative nature of historical awareness. This was linked to, but separate from, the accretional character of research in particular fields. In this case, the accumulative nature included the support that the visual—in the form of maps—offered, that of locating places and of explaining developments. It was made more important by the extent to which books did not as a rule include illustrations or maps. Thus, to understand Gibbon, it was helpful to have access to such maps. In contrast, this was far less of an issue for national history, although the extent to which most readers had a firm notion of the bounds of Mercia or the Danelaw can be questioned. Put differently, such knowledge was not crucial for an understanding of most national history.

At the same time, not everyone was convinced of the value of historical education, whether partisan or not. Indeed, Joseph Cradock (1742–1826), a man of letters as well as a patron of the arts and a fellow of the Society of Arts (FSA), published his opinion that "young men are encouraged to take up general history much sooner than they ought. I would have them strongly impressed with moral virtues, before they venture to read so dreadful a detail of crimes and misfortunes."[25] So for Cradock, history was a subject that could only be entered once a moral foundation had been laid. To others, it was a way to teach such a foundation, indeed, an aspect of a virtual catechism. The presentation of history in the arts was also regarded as educational and moral.

WOMEN

Interests were not always lost when school days were long past, including an interest in history. Diaries and correspondence frequently mention the reading of historical works, and, if more diaries and correspondence had survived, then there would have been more such references.

Educated women feature often in this sphere, whether it be the well-born Louisa, Countess of Pomfret, reading James Ralph's *Introductory Review of the Reigns of the Royal Brothers Charles and James* (1744) in 1748; Lady Mary Coke, daughter of the 2nd Duke of Argyle, a widow, finishing John Campbell's life of the Dutch-born Spanish minister Jan Willem van Ripperda, a key figure in the international crisis of 1725–27, and beginning a history of France while at Bath in 1766; or the well-born Elizabeth Montagu (1720–1800), spending six hours daily, in 1775, reading Philip,

2nd Earl of Hardwicke's, *Miscellaneous State Papers from 1501–1726* and Noailles's *Memoires*. Earlier, Montagu suggested, "Most readers want to find history a smart libel on former times and persons."[26] The Shakespeare Ladies' Club that actively promoted the playwright in the 1730s was very much engaging with cultural history.

Female reading is an instructive qualification to the criticism made by some male commentators that women were frivolous readers, a point supposedly demonstrated by their favor for novels and the immorality that offered. Dr. Johnson claimed over dinner on April 29, 1778, that "all our ladies read now." The home was the sphere for such reading, but it was one in which the idea and language of taste left much space for women.[27] In *Northanger Abbey* (1818), Jane Austen has Catherine Morland and Eleanor Tilney discuss history while walking in the country with Henry Tilney near Bath.

The frivolous Catherine prefers novels, disliking history: "I read it a little as a duty, but it tells me nothing that does not either vex or weary me. The quarrels of popes and kings, with wars or pestilences in every page; the men all so good-for-nothing, and hardly any women at all—it is very tiresome; and yet I often think it odd that it should be so dull, for a great deal of it must be invention."

Eleanor replies: "In the principal facts they have sources of intelligence in former histories and records, which may be as much depended on, I conclude, as anything that does not actually pass under one's own observation."[28]

WOMEN WRITING HISTORY

The majority of the historical writers considered in this book were men, and this is especially true of those who wrote works of religious history. Religious history was assumed to be a field dominated by the clergy—Anglican and Dissenting—and therefore by men. However, this was not completely the case. In the eighteenth century, in the same way that writing became socially diversified, so also did the writers, and women began to contribute to this hitherto male preserve. As this chapter shows, some women were keen to restore female figures to historical prominence, as with Sarah Fielding. However, sometimes, as with Charlotte Cowley's

The Ladies History of England (1780), this was largely a presentational and marketing approach, rather than a significantly different one.[29] Women could play an important role in fictional historical works, such as Delarivier Manley's *Lucius: The First Christian King of Britain* (1717), in which Rosalinda, the female lead, is instrumental in the conversion of Lucius to Christianity. The daughter of Sir Roger Manley, a Royalist officer who had published a *History of Late Warres in Denmark* (1670) and (posthumously) *History of the Rebellion* (1691), she also used historical works in the form of fiction in order to pursue Tory politics at the expense of the Whigs, notably in *The Secret History of Queen Zarah and the Zarazians* (1705), *Secret Memoirs and Manners of Several Persons of Quality, of both Sexes. From the New Atlantis* (1709), and *Memoirs of Europe towards the close of the Eighth Century* (1710).

A feature of eighteenth-century England's general historical writing that differed from earlier periods and most other countries was the growth in the number of female historical writers and of the attention they sometimes paid to the role of women in history. Judith Drake (1676–1723) claimed that histories written by women had been suppressed "by the malice of men" so as to blot out any suggestion of men's weakness and claim "a power they still exercise so arbitrarily and are so fond of."[30] Mary Astell (1666–1731), who preferred to reach back to biblical models of society as her ideal, still argued that most history was written by men and with men's interests in mind.[31] Her illustration of this was Clarendon's *History of the Rebellion*, which, nevertheless, she admired.

Astell was right that there were few works that paid attention to "great women" in political histories.[32] Some women writers supported this trend. The importance of women in history was contested by the Evangelical writer Hannah More (1745–1833), for whom women political leaders were often examples of malice and who preferred a form of female activism and Christian womanhood focused on charity and education.[33] The question arose regarding whether history and nationhood were male monopolies or whether both the writing of history and the creation of nationhood were processes in which women could participate. Indeed women were certainly not absent from history. They featured strongly in biblical histories. In histories of early England, Boadicea, an opponent of Roman rule, was first among the female rulers whose martial virtues were emphasized. In postconquest history, Eleanor of Aquitaine, Philippa of Hainault, Eleanor of Castile, and Margaret of Anjou were equally portrayed as military consorts. Elsewhere, Joan of Arc and Isabella of Spain were also examples of martial women. And Elizabeth I, Mary I, and Mary, Queen of Scots, were sometimes seen as powerful women who changed the course of history—the first still recalled in the popular imagination as the model of Protestant womanhood whose accession day, November 17, was marked by the ringing of church bells throughout the eighteenth century.

A key issue in such writing was whether women had contributed to the progress of civilization and the advance of England. "Bluestocking theology" was a part of the conceptualization of women's role in writing history.[34] Some historians, like Astell, Elizabeth Carter (1717–1806), and Catherine Talbot (1721–70), saw women's religious commitment as a vital element in the moral progress of the country, and they regarded religious orthodoxy as important in achieving their goal and historical writing as part of a religious commitment. Women's piety and learning were also held by some to be an element in cultural advancement, and Burnet explicitly endorsed them as such.

It was not only female historians who regarded women as integral to the progress of society from savagery to civilization. Lord Kames's *Sketches of the History of Man*, published in 1774, presented the changing position of women as both the cause and the consequence of the process of civilization. Women's roles in marriage—and the shift from polygamy to monogamy—were, Kames argued, an important element in the moral improvement of society. Women brought self-restraint to men and, through their conversation and refinement, injected a moral element into their interchanges with men. All of this was destined by nature.[35]

Feminine behavior was therefore, to many writers, an important element in historical development. A strand of continuity connected the Roman matron, the Gothic tribeswoman, and the courtly woman in medieval England.[36] Katherine Read's arresting 1770 painting of the historian Catharine Macaulay as a Roman matron lamenting the lost liberties of Rome was in this context highly suggestive.[37] Seven years later, a statue erected in St. Stephen's Walbrook, in London, portrayed her in marble as a pagan Roman woman deity. The sculpture caused a scandal and had to be removed, even though it had been put up by Macaulay's friend, Thomas Wilson, the incumbent of the parish. In both cases, Macaulay's refinement seemed to be attributed to her classical inheritance. Historians regarded republican Rome as a distant example of political freedom and liberal government, which Britain by the eighteenth century had superseded. But Rome, as Gibbon was to underline, was an ambiguous model: it conveyed aspects of taste, refinement, and political ideas, and it also bore elements of savagery, bondage, and decline, which were not always to be emulated.[38]

Female writers sometimes looked beyond Rome for historical models. Women historians developed a "gendered ethnic consciousness," in which Goths, Anglo-Saxons, and Celts transmitted to the eighteenth century a powerful cultural ancestry in which women could enjoy high status and act as examples. This led to an "affective patriotism," which presaged the Enlightenment, and has been described as a "historicisation of womanhood," which increased as the eighteenth century progressed.[39]

Macaulay regarded herself as exceptional among women.[40] Moreover, her historical writing tended to overlook the role of women. The account she gave of the growth of political liberty in England was one in which chance and circumstance played as great a role as any progressive historical forces. Far more than a Whig foil to Hume's Tory approach, she defied categorization as a Whig or Tory historian, notably in her unsympathetic portrayal of Charles I and her sympathetic account of James II. Despite underplaying the general role of women, Macaulay sought to redress the absence of "female worthies" in historical writing by drawing on Roman women as models of "political petitioners, donors and spouses," who had modern counterparts.[41] This represented women as subservient to men. Her examples were Lady Croke, who in 1637 prevailed on her husband, the judge Sir George Croke, to rule against Charles I in the ship money legal case and, perhaps more convincingly, Rachel, Lady Russell. Rachel Russell was the widow of the Whig "martyr" Lord William Russell, who was executed in 1683 following involvement in the Rye House Plot against Charles II and the future James II. For Macaulay, Lady Russell was an example of a woman who had inspired and stiffened her husband's resolve, like Arria, the Roman matriarch.⁴²

Russell was a potent symbol of a woman who inherited her martyred husband's status as a victim of tyranny under Charles II. Though the Rye House Plot was less significant than the Popish Plot of 1678 or the Exclusion Crisis of 1679–81, it foreshadowed the despotism of James II, and consequently Russell and her husband were seen as noble sufferers in the Protestant cause well into the eighteenth century. In 1773 the publication of Russell's letters, transcribed by Thomas Sellwood from the Russell papers in Woburn Abbey, intensified her status in the history of the period, combining her political standing with a piety and emotion that elevated her further in the popular imagination. Her stoicism in the face of widowhood was widely admired; she asserted to a parson that she would "be silent under [my punishment] but yet secretly my heart mourns, too sadly I fear, and cannot be comforted because I have not the dear companion and sharer of all my joys and sorrows."⁴³ In this case, historical writing was charged, as so often with religious sensibility and, as in fiction, with romantic ideas of an idealized marriage. At the same time, politics played a role. The letters were published with an introduction vindicating the character of Lord William Russell against Sir John Dalrymple's *Historical Collections*.

Female monarchs ensured that there had to be an engagement with powerful women. The reign of Queen Anne (1702–14) very much attracted echoes with past female rulers, notably Elizabeth I (r. 1558–1603). This was not simply a case of comparisons made in publications, but was also seen with private individuals. Thus, Sir John Chardin, a Huguenot who had made money trading in Asian jewels and who became a prominent Orientalist, wrote of Anne in 1703: "The reign of the Queen proves as successful glorious and beloved as that of the renowned Elizabeth and England saw nothing like since her in point of reciprocal confidence and love between the Sovereign and the people and her Majesty's reign is like to be as fatal to the King of France as the other to the King of Spain,"⁴⁴ a comparison of Louis XIV (r. 1643–1715) with Philip II (r. 1556–98). Such a diachronic comparison was a well-established one as the cyclical nature of history was probed in terms of strong and personalized threats, and this approach affected discussion of the present.

Women also engaged with history through writing historical novels, which became significant from the 1760s. An important early instance of the genre was Clara Reeve's popular *The Champion of Virtue, a Gothic Story* (1777), which, from the second edition in 1778 on, was entitled *The Old English Baron*, and she also published *The Memoirs of Sir Roger de Clarendon, a natural son of Edward the Black Prince* (1793). Sophia Lee provided a successful historical romance with *The Recess, or a Tale of other Times* (1785), as well as *A Hermit's Tale* (1787), which dealt with the drama of border warfare.[45]

READING

The reading of history was widespread among both men and women, and some, such as Jonathan Swift, wrote marginal comments in the history books they owned.[46] Readers, such as Thomas Turner, a Sussex village shopkeeper and local official, recorded their historical readings in their diary.[47] Some readers, such as Lady Sarah Cowper and the diplomat Horace St. Paul, went so far as to transcribe large sections of what they read.[48] This was an established practice in the reading of the period and in earlier periods, and one that matched the process of writing. Others corresponded about history and/or with a sense that what they were writing about would be of historical interest.[49]

George III set a tone by preferring history as one of a range of serious forms of writing, including sermons and geographies, and preferred them to novels.[50] That contrast, however, was also to pose a false dichotomy, as there were major overlaps between historical works and novels, not least in content and tone. Many novels, notably those of Henry Fielding, as discussed in chapter 2, were presented as histories and employed conventions from historical writing. Conversely, the emphasis on the individual in most historical works had novelistic themes, tone, and style. There was also a common stance in histories and novels, that of moralism. The working out of character flaws was a key means, as, in particular, was hubris. This moralism was presented as both personal and more general, with the latter having social, political, and religious dimensions. The personal dimension was usually an indication of more general problems, although not inevitably so. Moralism lent itself to the use of history in political contention; and this use helped ensure that the coverage of history was not only extensive but also very much brought into the present. The process is most famous in book form, notably the employment of history by Edmund Burke at the time of the French Revolution, as discussed in chapter 9.

NEWSPAPERS

However, it is the press that is most instructive in the presentation of history for contemporary readers, as the press coverage was much more frequent, with most prominent newspapers coming out weekly and some more frequently, either as dailies or as triweeklies. The press provided much of the coverage of history, and newspapers presented themselves as the interpreters of the past. Thus, on March 11, 1727, *Mist's Weekly Journal*, one of the two leading London opposition newspapers, used French history as a way to comment on Britain: "Whoever reads the History of France will see how that kingdom has been impoverished and eaten up by those leeches who hung upon her, and sucked her vitals; and that they were not a little instrumental in taking away that liberty which she once enjoyed, as much as any other country in Europe.... The Princes of France found no means so effectual for that purpose, as loading the people with taxes, which impoverishing the nobility and gentry, brought them all to hang about the court for employments." The habit of presenting the Parlement of Paris as the "Parliament of Paris" contributed to the drawing of parallels. Political contention using historical examples was commonplace. Pamphlets and other formats did the same.

Sometimes the same writer could take different positions in response to developments in his or her own perception, as well as circumstances, and the context of events. This was seen with (Dr.) Samuel Johnson's employment of history in support of war with Spain in 1738 and against another in 1771. In 1738, in the poem *London*, which was explicitly presented in the title as an imitation of the Roman poet Juvenal, Johnson used Elizabeth I's successful stand against Spain in the sixteenth century as an ahistorical tool in an assault on the attempt by the Walpole government to preserve peace:

> In pleasing Dreams the blissful Age renew,
> And call Britannia's glories back to view;

> Behold her Cross triumphant on the Main,
> The Guard of Commerce, and the Dread of Spain,
> Ere Masquerades debauch'd, Excise oppress'd,
> Or English Honour grew a standing Jest.[51]

His attitude was markedly different by 1771, reflecting personal and political circumstances as well as developing beliefs. It is difficult to determine whether the tempering of youthful optimism or changes in the political situation was more important. Johnson had come to be hostile to aggressive war. In his criticism in 1771 of the pressure for war with Spain in the Falkland Islands crisis of 1770–71, Johnson deployed history differently to his use of it in the late 1730s. He now argued, correctly, that attacks on Spanish America might well be unsuccessful, in large part because of the problems of operating in the tropics, a conclusion he ably supported by reference to the unsuccessful British attack on Cartagena (in modern Colombia) in 1741, a humiliating failure.[52]

Aside from deploying the past in political contention, the press, less frequently, also provided news of new historical information, which in turn offered the impression of a developing subject. This could cover documents and archaeological discoveries. For example, the *Newcastle Journal*, in its issue of May 3, 1740, carried a York item of April 22 that reported at length on a Roman inscription that had been found, and also commented on it:

> We can only conjecture that the Emperors meant here were Severus and his son Caracalla, by their long residence at York, or in the island; and that this Nicomedes, a manumised slave of theirs, out of gratitude for the receiving his freedom here, erected this statue, and dedicated it to the sacred genius of Britain. If this may be allow'd as it cannot be very far otherwise, then this stone and inscription bears the age of fifteen hundred years and upwards; and is another argument of the pristine glory of the ancient EBORACUM;[53] in those days the capital city of the province of Britain.

The *Northampton Mercury* of August 20, 1739, included an anonymous letter to the printer:

> The tessellated Roman pavement, which was found at Weldon, in the County of Northampton, in February last, having for some months past been covered up, in order to have a Building erected over it, to preserve it from the Insults of the Populace, is now to be seen in all its Beauty, and is allow'd by the Connoisseurs to be the finest Piece of Antiquity of

the kind that has been discovered in this kingdom: One Part of it is full 102 Feet long, and 10 broad, and adorn'd with a great Variety of Colours and Figures. In the Middle of this long Pavement, on the North Side, was a Door-place, very plainly to be seen, rising up on Step into a little Room; and on each Side of that were other Rooms, two of which (the Work in them being very beautiful) are now built over, as well as the long Pavement. The Colours of the Stones in the whole Work are chiefly a deep Red, very dark inclining to Black, a Sky-blue, Milk-white, and some of a yellowish Cast. The Workmen employ'd to bare the Ground, found amongst the Rubbish a great many Coins, which were mostly of the Emperor Constantine the Great, the first Christian Emperor; from whence it is plain, that this Piece of Mosaic Work must be of at least 1400 Years standing.

Any curious Persons may enquire of Fra. Horton who keeps the King's Arms at Weldon aforesaid; where they may be sure to meet with good Accommodation for themselves, their Servants and Horses, especially if they please to send Notice of their Coming a few Hours before.

Archaeological finds were not restricted to the Roman period. Bryan Fausett (1720–76), a Kent antiquarian and sometime cleric who, as a young man, had Jacobite sympathies, made a special study of the Anglo-Saxon period and was a keen excavator of graves, forming a collection rich in Anglo-Saxon objects, including coins.[54]

Alongside such archaeological findings, there were the surveys and discussion of prehistoric sites, notably Avebury. This was research and discussion in which esoteric beliefs played a role, particularly with William Stukeley (1687–1765), a clergyman and major figure in field archaeology, who focused on Avebury as well as publishing more widely, including *Palaeographia Britannica, or Discourses on Antiquities in Britain* (1743–52).[55]

Archaeological findings fed the interest in antiquities and also in the history of localities. This interest had a number of forms. In particular, history was a topic among the many activities of the local archaeological and other societies that became so significant to British society. The discovery and evaluation of antiquities proved an important aspect of discussions and correspondence and were published more widely.[56]

Newspapers, another source of information, could report the activities of historians in a fashion that reflected not partisanship, or only partisanship, but a more scholarly interest, and items accordingly were not only published in the London press. The *Ipswich Journal* of September 15, 1764, printed an extract of a letter from Paris that discussed Hume and revealed the connivance of Charles II in Louis XIV's schemes against the Dutch in the early 1670s and also Charles's willingness to establish Catholicism in Britain:

> The celebrated philosopher Hume, who is here with the English Ambassador, has, it is said, obtained leave of the Superior of our Irish College to peruse and make extracts from eleven or twelve volumes in folio of the composition of James II. These volumes are all in the handwriting of that King of Great Britain, and contain, amongst a number of very interesting pieces, the copy of a secret treaty[57] between Charles II and one of the greatest monarchs then reigning in Europe, for reestablishing the Roman Catholic religion in Great Britain and Ireland, and also for dividing between them a neighbouring Protestant state.

In practice, Hume does not appear to have gained the access claimed for him.[58] On May 13, 1771, the *Reading Mercury* similarly commented on William Robertson.

Newspapers made direct reference to individual historical books in an attempt to draw out supposed lessons. The danger of a French invasion led the *Newcastle Courant* to publish a lengthy article on November 24, 1744, beginning: "The affair of an invasion from France having given so great an alarm to our government, it may not be improper at this juncture to give an instance how little in such circumstances mercenary forces or a standing army, ought to be depended upon. This we shall do by an extract from the history of the most important invasion ever happened to the English nation, by William the Conqueror, as we find it in Mr Guthry's [sic] History of England, p. 323." The reference was to William Guthrie's *History*, the first edition of which appeared that year. Thus, the events of 1066 were deemed highly relevant nearly seven centuries later.

Newspapers also played a major role in advertising historical works. In general, this was simply a commercial transaction, one, moreover, that frequently reflected the extent to which newspapers were often owned by printers and/or booksellers or distributors. This was true both of the London press and of provincial papers. There could also be a more direct link between newspapers and historical works, as with Henry, Viscount

Bolingbroke's, founding and authorial role in the *Craftsman*, a major London opposition newspaper launched in 1726. A polemical historical writer, Bolingbroke put his own historical pieces in the *Craftsman*. On October 10, 1730, the *London Journal*, a government newspaper commenting on Bolingbroke, complained that in the *Craftsman* "the History of England is racked and tortured." The *Craftsman* also addressed the supposed lessons from classical history, as in

> the famous Republicks of Greece and Rome ... made criminal for any of their members to affect uncommon Popularity, and conciliate too much the minds of their fellow-subjects. Accordingly we find, in their histories, several instances of the most eminent Patriots, who were banished, and otherwise treated as enemies to their country, only for rendering themselves too much beloved by general largesses and donations, or other extraordinary acts of publick beneficence; for which severities, those Nations have been often reproached, by succeeding Ages, with injustice, barbarity, and ingratitude: but if we examine their conduct, in this particular, with candour and impartiality, I believe we shall find that they acted a very prudent and commendable part.... Indeed the histories of all nations, as well as of theirs, abound with so many instances, in which the favour of the people has been most traitorously abused and perverted to wicked purposes, that, to a serious and thoughtful mind, their conduct stands in need of no justification.[59]

The relationship between history and newspapers was quite varied. The London printer Robert Walker used his newspapers as a forum for serializing religious and historical works, such as his *History of the Holy Bible*, which he claimed had been written by a Laurence Clarke, although no clergyman of the name existed. It may be that Walker thought by this method he could avoid newspaper taxes, but he clearly saw that historical works were an inducement to buy newspapers.[60] At the local level, John Price (1773–1801), a Leominster-born topographer who became a bookseller first in Hereford and then in Worcester, published histories of all three places between 1795 and 1799.

In general, links between newspapers and historical writing are suggestive rather than clear. For example, the historian John Banks (or Bancks) (1709–51) wrote a stridently anti-Jacobite *History of the Life and Reign of William III*, as well as lives of Christ, Cromwell, Peter the Great, Marlborough, and Eugene, the last three biographies of figures alive when Banks was young. His *A Short Critical Review of the Political Life of Oliver Cromwell, Lord-Protector of the Commonwealth* (1739) was one of the first favorable treatments of Cromwell. This was an approach that opposition to the Stuarts made possible for some writers despite Cromwell's republicanism and sectarianism. Banks, an opposition Whig, probably wrote the "Present History of Europe" section in Henry Fielding's *The History of Our Own Times* (1741),[61] and he played a major role in two leading opposition London newspapers, *Old England* and the *Westminster Journal*. On February 8, 1746, the latter advertised Banks's *Compendious History of the House of Austria, and the German Empire*, which, it claimed, gave "a more exact and clear idea of the motives and nature of the present war [the War of the Austrian Succession, 1740–48], and what may probably ensue, than is to be met with in any other work."

The use of the term *history* therefore helped validate a particular approach to the politics of the 1740s. History, indeed, was very much something that reached to the present and referred to it. The *Westminster Journal* also employed history in order to criticize the current government, as with the use of Henry VIII and the balance of power in the issue of December 10, 1748. The paper claimed that Henry held "the Balance betwixt the great contending monarchs on the Continent; and every sovereign of these islands, who will avoid being made a property of, or too much meddling in, foreign quarrels, may always gain the same glorious distinction." Conversely, supporters of intervention in Continental politics cited Elizabeth I's backing for the Dutch from 1585 in their rebellion against Philip II of Spain and for the Huguenots (French Protestants) in the French Wars of Religion from the 1560s to the 1590s.[62] The comparison between newspapers and histories was frequent, as on April 23, 1757, when the *London Chronicle* referred to "each compiler" as a "picturesque historian."

THE PUBLISHING WORLD

Planned, but unfinished, historical works included a history of Europe since 1598 by Bolingbroke, a book that would have ensured that he had to write on Louis XIV at length. There was also Burke's *Essay towards an Abridgement of the English History*, a work forestalled by Hume, and the 1702–27 section of James Ralph's history of 1688–1727. John Wilkes promised a history of England from the Glorious Revolution to the Hanoverian Succession, but volume one, published in 1768, consisted solely of a thirty-nine-page introduction, followed by a notice announcing that the reigns of William III and Anne were in the press and would shortly appear. In this, as in so much else, Wilkes disappointed those who trusted him. Robertson laid aside plans to write a history of British and Portuguese colonization of the Americas to match that of the Spaniards and did not produce the continuation of Hume to cover 1688–1714 that he had discussed.[63] William Russell, who died suddenly, did not begin the history of England from 1760 to 1783 for which he was paid. Tom Paine did not write his planned *History of the American Revolution*. Ferdinando Warner abandoned the second volume of his history of Ireland because of a lack of support from the Irish parliament for the project. In contrast, for English local histories, it was easier for the latter to gain the support of subscribers and to pass on unfinished work from one antiquarian to another in what was generally a clearly accretional historical genre.

The world of print included the publication in Britain, notably in London, of Continental works on history. Some were antiquarian in character, but there was also the appearance of more recent works, which set the context for the developments of the present and future. Thus, 1785 saw the first English edition of the *Memoirs . . . on the Turks and the Tartars* by Baron François de Tott, and 1801, the first English edition of the *History of the Principal Events of the Reign of Frederic William II, King of Prussia; and a Political Picture of Europe from 1786 to 1796, containing a summary of the revolution of Brabant, Holland, Poland and France* by Louis, Count of Ségur.

As part of a more generally dynamic publishing world,[64] that arm of, and for, history was very adept at responding to opportunities. This was not only seen in the translation of foreign works. For example, in 1788 appeared Joseph Towers's *Memoirs of the Life and Reign of Frederick the Third, King of Prussia*, in fact, as a result of different ways of numbering the monarchs, Frederick II, the "Great," of Prussia, who had died two years earlier.[65] A Dissenting minister, Towers (1737–99) had been the editor of the volumes of the *British Biography* that appeared from 1766 to 1772. He carried out research for this in the British Museum.

The publishing world was also linked to the major expansion in book purchase and libraries, a combination that affected the potential for research. Historical writing and the way people read history were changed by the surge of printed material that became more widely available from the middle of the seventeenth century. The Civil War and such later episodes as the Popish Plot (1678) and Exclusion Crisis (1679–81) were the subject of an enormous quantity of pamphleteering, on a scale hitherto unknown in England. This explosion of printing encouraged the emergence of a new trend among book collectors and bibliographers, that of cataloguing and listing publications so that the literature was more accessible. Some of these, like the bookseller George Thomason, aimed to collect together political tracts so that they would be of use to historians. By the time of his death in 1666, his collection of so-called Thomason tracts numbered over 22,000 items. Similarly, Narcissus Luttrell (1657–1732), who compiled in manuscript a daily chronicle, "A Brief Historical Relation of State Affairs from September 1678 to April 1714," began collecting books and pamphlets in 1679. One of his greatest achievements was to catalogue all the tracts and pamphlets published in those and later years relating to the Popish Plot. This sort of cataloguing of printed sources was one of the foundations of the systematic organization of information on which historical writers in the eighteenth century relied.[66]

It was not only book collectors who began to provide guidance to historians. Among those who supplied information on where to find manuscript sources was John Strachey, a Somerset antiquarian and cartographer.[67] In 1739, Strachey published *An Index to the Records, With Directions to the Several Places where they are to be found*. This was a guide to parliamentary and legal records for each monarch's reign from the Norman Conquest onward. The *Index* summarized the archival holdings of the Tower of London, Westminster Hall, the Chancery offices, the Inns of Court, and a number of other locations. In just over a hundred pages, he listed each type of record alphabetically with its location. Strachey's preface outlined that his goal was to provide a help for historians who would otherwise "commit great mistakes, by taking things on credit of those who wrote before them, instead of having resource to the originals themselves." Strachey also pointed out that many records "which ought to be in one place" were scattered and that the absence of a proper list of holdings meant that historians had to search in numerous locations—including some of the private libraries that held public records.[68]

One of the most remarkable book and manuscript collectors was Thomas Bowdler II (1661–1738), who inherited his father's collections and in turn became an obsessive collector. Sometimes Bowdler seems to have bought individual tracts in large quantities at the time of publication so that it is almost possible to re-create from his purchases the items on sale on the bookstalls in St. Paul's Churchyard in London in the early years of the eighteenth century. One of Bowdler's great contributions to scholarship was to scribble the name of the author of anonymous pamphlets on the title pages when he bought them. This made his collection an authoritative source of pseudonymous and anonymous authorship.[69]

The early eighteenth century was a golden age of book collecting in England.[70] For example, the bibliophile Bishop John Moore of Ely built up a huge collection of 29,000 books and 1,790 manuscripts and employed his chaplain, Thomas Tanner, as his purchaser and librarian. After Moore's death in 1714, the library was purchased by George I and given to the University of Cambridge. The library of Robert and Edward Harley, one of the foundation collections of the British Museum (later Library), was organized by the librarian Humphrey Wanley, who admitted trusted historians to it (and occasionally even lent items to them) for research.[71]

Smaller, less distinguished libraries were also important for the readers of history. In Appleby Grammar School in 1704, there were about three hundred books in the library. Most were classical texts, but there were a few mostly Tudor works on the history of England, including Polydor Vergil's *Historia Anglica* and John Stow's *Survey of London*. The same year, the bequest of the books of Thomas Plume came to Maldon to provide a town library, with works on religious topics more significant than historical studies, an unsurprising preference for a cleric.[72]

The fragmentary survival of library records occasionally allows a glimpse into the historical reading in this period. The Maidstone parish library, for example, was established in 1716 with just twenty-three works, but it grew quickly. In the second half of the eighteenth century, of 121 borrowers, 26 were women, who were among the most consistent readers. One reader, Miss Weller, borrowed Thomas Salmon's *Modern History* on ten occasions and ten other women borrowed it. It was also borrowed, together with Camden's *Britannia*, by a barge builder, John Cutbush, in 1778. He kept the Camden volume for seven years.[73]

Another parish library, that of Doncaster, saw historical works dominate in the books borrowed by parishioners. Among the most popular were the *Universal History*,[74] Joseph Bingham's *Antiquities of the Christian Church* (1708–22), Rollins's *Ancient History*, and Burnet's *History of the Reformation*. There was clearly something of a fashion in some book lending and reading: forty one loans of the various volumes of the *Universal History* occurred between 1749 and 1753. In nearby Rotherham, from 1735, Rapin's *History* "dominated loans of the next seventy years" and was in constant demand among schoolmasters and clergy in particular, but tradesmen were also regular borrowers of it. The Rapin volumes were lent on 188 occasions (dwarfing the loans of Clarendon and Burnet's works) and were in particularly heavy demand during 1744 when events in Europe concentrated the minds of Rotherham readers on historical themes.[75]

More generally, the past offered a malleable as well as interesting background to the present, as when, alongside treatments of the Port Royal and London earthquakes of 1692 as warnings of God's anger, clerics responded to the great storm of 1703 by referring back to earlier storms, including in Venice in 1343 and in England in 1387.[76] The weather itself was more regularly recorded, notably thanks to barometers, and this process of measurement encouraged a more defined sense of the normal and thus a different historical account of climate.[77]

The human aspect of the past offered a different type of warning as with the unpopularity of poll taxes in the past serving as a warning against another.[78] The past also provided guidance to what was held to be inherent national interests and was thus a way to judge the present. In 1756, Robert, 4th Earl of Holdernesse, one of the secretaries of state, wrote to Andrew Mitchell MP, the envoy in Berlin: "It is not easy to conceive that the Court of France will ever enter into measures for aggrandising the House of Austria, contrary to the uniform system of politics, which they have never ceased to have in view for these two last centuries."[79]

The republication of earlier works served this purpose of providing background and underlined the extent to which the past did not necessarily seem to be without relevance—indeed far from it. In 1772, John Evelyn's *Fumifugium: or the Inconvenience of the Aer [sic], and Smoak of London Dissapated* (1661) was republished, offering the proposal to banish much industry from London in order to improve its air quality.

History as a guidance from the past was given a particular twist with predictions of the future, as in *The Reign of George VI* (1763) (on which see chap. 7), or more specific uses of such work, for example in the debate on Jewish naturalization in 1753. Predictions were more commonly in the form of almanacs, but they were also attacked. A good example was Swift's attack on almanac makers, as in his *Predictions for the Year 1708. Wherein the Month and Day of the Month are set down, the Persons named, and the great Actions and Events of next Year particularly related, as they will come to pass. Written to prevent the People of England from being further imposed on by vulgar Almanack-makers* (1708). Thus, past, present, and future were all subjects for contention. Prediction was an aspect of the public value of the past to which we turn in the next chapter.

NOTES

1. F. Ardolino, "Sheridan's Parody of the Spanish Tragedy in *The Critic*," *Notes and Queries* 261 (2016): 617–19.

2. J. Oldham, *The Mansfield Manuscripts and the Growth of English Law in the Eighteenth Century* (Chapel Hill, NC, 1992); A. Doig, J. P. S. Ferguson, I. A. Milne, and R. Passmore, eds., *William Cullen and the Eighteenth Century Medical World* (Edinburgh, 1993).

3. J. B. Black, *The Art of History: A Study of Four Great Historians of the Eighteenth Century* (New York, 1965).

4. T. C. Barnard, "Writing and Publishing Histories in Eighteenth-Century Ireland," in *Constructing the Past: Writing Irish History, 1600–1800*, ed. M. Williams and S. P. Forrest (Woodbridge, UK, 2010), 112.

5. J. Loftis, *The Politics of Drama in Augustan England* (Oxford, 1963).

6. M. Hilton and J. Shefrin, eds., *Educating the Child in Enlightenment Britain: Beliefs, Cultures, Practices* (Farnham, UK, 2009).

7. J. Austen, *Northanger Abbey* (London, 1818), chapter 14.

8. For a different view, D. R. Woolf, "The 'Common Voice': History, Folklore and Oral Tradition in Early Modern England," *Past and Present* 120 (August 1988): 21–52, esp. 52.

9. J. Broadway, "William Dugdale and the Significance of County History in Early Stuart England," Dugdale Society Occasional Papers, 39 (1999).

10. W. Stukeley, *Itinerarium Curiosum. Or, an Account of the Antiquitys and Remarkable Curiositys in Nature or Art, observed in Travels thro' Great Britain* (London, 1724): 79–80.

11. A. Travers, ed., *Robert Furse: A Devon Family Memoir of 1593* (Exeter, 2012).

12. J. Bailey, "'A Very Sensible Man': Imaging Fatherhood in England c. 1750–1830," *History* 95 (2010): 290.

13. See, for example, the motivation behind the reminiscences that Henry Hutton left behind for his five sons, N. York, ed., *Henry Hutton and the American Revolution* (2010).

14. Nares, autobiography, Merton College Library, Oxford, Manuscript E.2.41.

15. W. Russell, *The History of Modern Europe*, 2nd ed. (1782, 4 vols.), 1:iii.

16. Russell, *The History of Modern Europe*, 1:iv.

17. J. Andrews, *Letters to a Young Gentleman on his Setting out for France* (London, 1784), 126.

18. Dering to Perceval, August 3, 1728, John Perceval to Viscount Perceval, May 24, 1730, BL. Add. 47032 fols. 79, 191. A translation of Pufendorf appeared as *An Introduction to the History of the Principal Kingdoms and States of Europe*, 2 vols. (London, 1705–6).

19. E. Harcourt, ed., *The Harcourt Papers*, 7 vols. (Oxford, no date), 2:7.

20. Holloway to Sarah Marlborough, February 14, 1744, BL. Add. 61467 fol. 133.

21. Harcourt, *Harcourt*, 46–50.

22. T. Fawcett, "Eighteenth-Century Norfolk Booksellers: A Survey and Register," *Transactions of the Cambridge Bibliographical Society* 6 (1972): 5.

23. Nares autobiography, Merton College, Oxford, E.2.41.

24. Sir Charles Hanbury-Williams to Henry Fox, November 22, 1752, BL. Add. 51393 fol. 123.

25. J. Cradock, *Literary and Miscellaneous Memoirs* (London, 1826), 67.

26. D. R. Woolf, "A Feminine Past? Gender, Genre, and Historical Knowledge in England, 1500–1800," *American Historical Review* 102 (1997): 645–79; J. Brewer, "Reconstructing the Reader: Prescriptions, Texts and Strategies in Anna Larpent's Reading," in *The Practice and Representation of Reading in England*, ed. J. Raven, H. Small and N. Tadmor (Cambridge, 1996), 226–45. John Campbell's *Memoirs of the Duke of Ripperda* was published in 1740.

27. A. Vickery, *Behind Closed Doors: At Home in Georgian England* (New Haven, CT, 2009).

28. Austen, *Northanger Abbey*, chapter 14.

29. P. Hicks, "Female Worthies and the Genres of Women's History," in *Historical Writing in Britain, 1688–1830: Visions of History*, ed. B. Dew and F. Price (Basingstoke, UK, 2014), 24.

30. [J. Drake], *An Essay in Defence of the Female Sex...* (London, 1696), 23.

31. Hicks, "Female Worthies," 18.

32. M. Astell, *The Christian Religion, as Profess'd by a Daughter of the Church of England* (London, 1705), 293. She went on to note that if historians were right that when women did take an important role in history they acted "above their sex," perhaps such roles were played by "men in petticoats."

33. H. More, *Strictures on the Modern System of Female Education* (London, 1799).

34. K. O'Brien, *Women and the Enlightenment in Eighteenth-Century Britain* (Cambridge, 2009): 47, 51, 56–57. For female writers, C. Turner, *Living by the Pen: Women Writers in the Eighteenth Century* (London, 1992); J. Batchelor and C. Kaplan, eds., *British Women's Writing in the Long Eighteenth Century: Authorship, Politics and History* (Basingstoke, UK, 2005); S. Staves, *A Literary History of Women's Writing in Britain, 1660–1789* (Cambridge, 2006); G. L. Walker, *Mary Hays, 1759–1843: The Growth of a Woman's Mind* (Farnham, 2006); F. Gordon and G. L. Walker, eds., *Rational Passions: Women and Scholarship in Britain 1702–1870* (London, 2008).

35. H. H. Kames, *Sketches of the History of Mankind* (London, 1774), the sixth sketch and the appendix "concerning the propagation of animals and the care of their offspring."

36. O'Brien, *Women and the Enlightenment*, 111.

37. The painting was engraved in 1770 by an engraver named Williams, London, National Portrait Gallery, item no. D31911.

38. This was not new; John Aubrey in 1687 wrote, "I find there are many connections between the customs of classical Rome and modern England. The Britons imbibed their Gentilisme from the Romans." R. Scurr, *John Aubrey My Own Life* (London, 2015), 351.

39. O'Brien, *Women and the Enlightenment*, chapter 3; and "History and the Novel in Eighteenth Century Britain," in *The Uses of History in Early Modern England*, ed. P. Kewes (San Marino, CA, 2006), 389–405.

40. K. Green, "Will the Real Enlightenment Historian Please Stand Up? Catharine Macaulay versus David Hume," in *Hume and the Enlightenment*, ed. C. Taylor and S. Buckle (London, 2011), 395. For exchanges between the two historians, see *European Magazine* 4 (1783): 331–32.

41. Hicks, "Female Worthies," 25

42. C. Macaulay, *The History of England from the Accession of James I to that of the Brunswick Line* (London, 1763–83) 2:226–27, 356; 3:198–99. On Macaulay, B. Hill, *The Republican Virago: The Life and Times of Catharine Macaulay, Historian* (Oxford, 1992) and R. Minuti, 'Il Problema storico della libertà inglese nella cultura radicale dell' età di Giorgio III. Catharine Macaulay e la Rivoluzione puritan,' *Rivista Storica Italiana* 98 (1986): 793–860.

43. *Letters of Lady Rachel Russell; from the Manuscripts in the Library at Woburn Abbey* (London, 1773), 6–7.

44. Chardin to Thomas Pitt, January 30, 1703, BL. Add. 22852 fol. 115.

45. F. Price, *Reinventing Liberty: Nation, Commerce and the Historical Novel from Walpole to Scott* (Edinburgh, 2016).

46. H. Williams, *Dean Swift's Library* (Cambridge, 1932), 67–78.

47. D. Vaisey, ed., *The Diary of Thomas Turner 1754–1765* (Oxford, 1984), 9, 49, 106, 163.

48. Hertfordshire CRO, D/EP F29-39, 49, 96, Northumberland CRO, ZB11 B2/17.

49. John Dobson to John Mordaunt, MP, May 7, 1752, Warwick, CRO. CR. 1368/5/4.

50. J. Boswell, *Life of Johnson* (Oxford, 1980), 157.

51. [Johnson], *London: A Poem, In Imitation of the Third Satire of Juvenal* (London, 1738), lines 25–30.

52. [Johnson], *Thoughts on the late Transactions respecting Falkland's Islands* (London, 1771).

53. Eboracum was located in what is now York.

54. D. Wright, *Bryan Faussett: Antiquary Extraordinary* (Oxford, 2015).

55. P. J. Ucko, M. Hunter, A. J. Clark, and A. David, *Avebury Reconsidered: From the 1660s to the 1990s* (London, 1990).

56. M. and D. Honeybone, eds., *The Correspondence of the Spaulding Gentlemen's Society 1710–1761* (Lincoln, UK, 2010).

57. A reference to the Secret Treaty of Dover.

58. D. M. Roberts, "The Scottish Catholic Archives, 1560–1978," *The Innes Review* 28, no. 2 (Autumn 1977): 83–84.

59. *Craftsman*, February 17, 1727.

60. D. H. Reed, "Spreading the News within the Clerical Profession—Newspapers and the Church in the North of England, 1660–1760," in *News In An Expanding World, The Transformation of News from the Renaissance to the Age of Enlightenment*, ed. Siv Gøril Brandtzæg, Paul Goring, and Christine Watson (Leiden, UK, 2017).

61. For this attribution, see the introduction by Thomas Lockwood to the facsimile edition (Delmar, NY, 1985).

62. Anon., *Reflections upon the Present State of Affairs* (London, 1755), 14.

63. J. Smitten, "Moderation and History: William Robertson's Unfinished History of British America," in *Scotland and America in the Age of Enlightenment*, R. B. Sher and J. Smitten (Edinburgh, 1990), 163–79.

64. J. Raven, *Publishing Business in Eighteenth-Century England* (Woodbridge, UK, 2014).

65. A. Page, "'Probably the most indefatigable prince that ever existed': A Rational Dissenting Perspective on Frederick the Great," *Enlightenment and Dissent* 23 (2007): 85–130.

66. J. Roberts, "Opportunities for Building Collections and Libraries," in *Cambridge History of Libraries in Britain and Ireland*, vol. 2, 1640–1850, ed. G. Mandelbrote and K. A. Manley (Cambridge, 2006), 41–43.

67. J. B. Harley, "John Strachey of Somerset: An Antiquarian Cartographer of the Early Eighteenth Century," *Journal of the British Cartographic Society* (June 1966): 2–7.

68. J. Strachey, *An Index to the Records, With Directions to the Several Places where they are to be found...* (London, 1739), 1–3.

69. B. Ll. James, *A Catalogue of the Tract Collection of Saint David's*

University College, Lampeter (London, 1975), xiv–xv.

70. G. Mandelbrote, "Personal Owners of Books," in *The Cambridge History of Libraries in Britain and Ireland II*, ed. G. Mandelbrote and K. A. Manley (Cambridge, 2006), 186.

71. C. E. Wright and R. C. Wright, eds., *The Diary of Humphrey Wanley 1715–1726* (London, 1966).

72. William Nicolson, *Miscellany Accounts of the Diocese of Carlisle*, ed. R. S. Ferguson (Carlisle, UK, 1877), 237; D. Pearson, "Thomas Plume's Library in Its Contemporary Context," in *Dr Thomas Plume, 1630–1704: His Life and Legacies*, ed. C. Thornton and T. Doe (Hatfield, UK, 2018). I would like to thank David Pearson for giving me an advance copy. See, more generally, Pearson, "Patterns of Book Ownership in Late Seventeenth-Century England," *The Library*, 7th ser., vol. 11 (2010): 139–67.

73. G. Best, "Libraries in the Parishes," in *The Cambridge History of Libraries in Britain and Ireland*, ed. G. Mandelbrote and K. A. Manley (Cambridge, 2006), 2:339–41.

74. The full title of which was *A Universal history, from the earliest account of time. Compiled from original authors; and illustrated with maps, cuts, notes, &c. With a general index to the whole*. It was published in numerous volumes between 1747 and 1768 and written by a team of six authors.

75. Best, "Libraries in the Parishes," 331–34.

76. E. L. Avery, "The Great Storm of 1703," *Research Studies* 29 (1961): 46–47.

77. J. Golinski, *British Weather and the Climate of Enlightenment* (Chicago, 2007).

78. Nathaniel Cole to James Brockman, August 12, 1756, BL. Add. 42591 fol. 154.

79. Holdernesse to Mitchell, May 28, 1756, BL. Add. 6811 fol. 133. See also, same to same, June 8, 1756, NA. SP. 90/65. He was incorrect.

TWO

PURPOSES, NARRATIVES, METHODS

PURPOSES

Historical works were usually open about their purposes. Declared in dedications, prefaces, and forewords, these purposes were to the fore in the text. Alongside the general value of political history (or, more generally, history that could be seen as political), particular tones—admonitory, exhortatory, exemplary, celebratory, and alarmist—each served a specific purpose. The discussion of history reflected a continuing sense that the past had shaped the present, as well as a concern with organic development that is not always associated with English thinkers and writers of the period. A focus on the historical works produced in the period therefore suggests a different account to the English Enlightenment from that focused on the Scientific Revolution and, with the latter, a measure of secularism.

History, indeed, provided the central source of evidence for political and religious polemics, with religious mentalities of certainty readily transferred to political aspects and counterparts. In this, there was not a change from the previous period but, instead, a continuance of it. Major concepts continued to have prominence, notably that of an ancient constitution, indeed *the* ancient constitution, as a way for the English to define themselves and to locate their national identity in a historical tradition that claimed they were always, by right, a free people. Every ruler on the throne had to deal with the reality of that distant, but contestable, polemical and frequently revised past, and notably so if the "people" felt they were being oppressed.[1]

This was an aspect of the degree to which, in bringing forward the ancient past in order to underpin and define a sense of nationality and purpose, there was the issue of criticism of the present.[2] The continued role of John Sadler's *Rights of the Kingdom; or Customs of our ancestors touching the laity, power, election, or succession of our Kings and Parliaments, our true liberty, due allegiance*... (1649, reprinted 1682) was significant. Sadler (1615–74) had been a prominent supporter of Oliver Cromwell. Both Josiah Quincy and Thomas Jefferson included excerpts from Sadler in their writings.

Other works linked to the idea of an ancient constitution included Edward Wortley Montgau's *Reflections on the Rise and Fall of the Ancient Republics. Adapted to the Present state of Great Britain* (1759) and the *Historical Essay on the English Constitution* (1771), anonymous but attributed to both Obadiah Hulme and Allan Ramsay. The prominent judge William Blackstone believed in the Ancient Constitution, and it was also popular in Britain's North American colonies,[3] as, indeed, was interest in the legacy of classical republicanism.

This was not the sole form or issue of continuity. Indeed, careers, styles, idioms, and patterns of reference spanned chronological divides, and in both national and local history.[4] Thus, in tracing the origins of seditious ideas, English Royalist historians under Charles II (r. 1660–85), such as the doctor and MP Robert Brady, author of *An Introduction to Old English History* (1684) and *A Compleat History of England* (1685–1700), linked Presbyterians, sectarians, and Catholics as opponents of the monarchy.[5] Affirming or rebutting such, and other, linkages remained very important after the Glorious Revolution of 1688–89. Whig or Tory historians could readily be distinguished by their attitudes to the second half of the seventeenth century,[6] a period in which there was great contention about the past. Moreover, to writers and supporters, their differences helped validate their writings. This was a history as declaration or polemic that was different from the tone that English writers and their French philosophe counterparts ostensibly sought to adopt.

From the late seventeenth century, as a separate process, there was a move away from the baroque sensibilities and tropes that had characterized the presentation of rulers and rulership, past as well as present, fictional as well as factual. These sensibilities and tropes had looked back to the presentation of rulers by classical as well as Christian writers, a process brought together anew by Renaissance humanists as they sought to extol past and present Western rulers with reference to classical forbears. From the Reformation and Counter-Reformation, this approach had come with an older, stronger sense of the monarch as defender of the Church. It brought with it the idea of the monarch as the embodiment of the national religion.

However, from the late seventeenth century, in part as a reaction to absolutism,[7] both British and Continental, and in part as a product of a more utilitarian approach to rulership, there was more of an emphasis on specific factors in the assessment of particular rulers. A focus on factual analysis, on observation rather than traditional authority, in line with the intellectual prospectus offered by Francis Bacon and René Descartes, was intended to provide a more realistic account. Linked to this, the understanding and presentation of truth moved from moral precepts to the search for specific facts, and a concern with origins and development led to an interest in change. The idea of constant attributes, very much related to the "humours" of the individual, was replaced by one that provided opportunities to understand change in terms of success and failure and, linked to this, of an interplay of circumstances and character that provided more excitement to the historical record. This interplay was frequently dramatic in tone and theatrical in presentation. The quality of historical writing in this period has attracted scholarly attention.[8]

Later in the eighteenth century, the French *philosophes* in part qualified history but, more clearly, faced problems in using the past. The *philosophes* found that history, as written by the *érudits*, who focused on textual criticism, could not provide the logical principles and ethical suppositions that were required to support the immutable laws the *philosophes* sought to propound.[9] Separately, the *philosophes* disparaged much of the past: the Middle Ages for allegedly being fanatical and the reign of Louis XIV (1643–1715) for its supposed obsession with *gloire* alongside the brilliance of its civilization. Voltaire's *Le Siècle de Louis XIV* (1751) was important for this representation. At the same time, Voltaire's study was impressive for his employment of actual events, rather than presenting simply a parade of facts. This was history as argument, and not as chronicle. As such, it was an important model elsewhere, although it would be mistaken to suggest that this was a new approach.[10] As a very different work, Voltaire, in his *Essai sur les moeurs et l'esprit des nations* (1745–53), produced a world history within a universal context, rather than writing in a Christian or nationalist framework.[11] Voltaire's work was read in England, which he had visited.

As with other branches of eighteenth-century Western enquiry, the development of history as a coherent intellectual project could, however much it in theory revealed divine work and intention, nevertheless leave scant role for direct divine intervention. In France, for example, historians replaced the customary view of Clovis (r. 481–511), the conquering Frank who converted to Christianity in 493, as a miracle-working royal saint with that of Clovis as a royal legislator on the model of more recent monarchs. As such, historical work apparently paralleled the rise of Newtonian science, which, similarly, did not seek to dethrone God but, nevertheless, limited the divine role and certainly so in terms of causing specific events. The approach drew on the distinction between primary and secondary causes of events. This intellectual thrust represented a new form of realism, one clearly, as well as implicitly, separate from direct manifestations of divine action. The ending of the "royal touch" (the cure of the skin disease scrofula by the hand of the monarch) in England with the accession of George I in 1714 was instructive. In contrast, the Stuart, in exile, continued the practice.[12] The move from seeing comets as God-giving portents was also significant,[13] as was the evaluation of miracles.[14]

Linked to this shift, there could be a self-conscious embrace of a historical view on religion that presented traditional ideas on religion as dated and the consequences of indoctrination, a process done in large part by identifying them with Catholicism. This approach, which was more common from the 1770s, represented a conflation of traditional and strong Protestant anti-Catholicism with ideas of cyclical change and notions of progress. In his *Philosophical Arrangements* (1775), James Harris, an MP as well as a writer on aesthetics, presented history in terms of a decline from classical knowledge into "an Age . . . of legends and Crusades," in short the Middle Ages, and "at length, after a long and barbarous period, when the shades of Monkery began to retire, and the light of Humanity once again to dawn, the arts also of criticism insensibly revived."[15] In his *History of Chichester* (1804), Alexander Hay, a local Anglican cleric and schoolmaster, described the papacy as "the patron of darkness and error," which had sought to perpetuate "the shades of night," and described the Lollard John Wickliff in the fourteenth century as entering "the lists against all the powers of darkness."[16]

Nevertheless, however much supported by criticism of Catholic perspectives, the decline of providential views of history and reflections on the present was a slow and very gradual process. Thus, the deaths of many as a result of an explosion of gunpowder at Chester on November 5, 1772, led to the preaching there of a sermon on the theme of "a serious call to regard Divine Providence."[17] More generally, the history written in the eighteenth century retained a strong element of divine intervention, as did reflections on the present. Indeed, the latter were encouraged by the existential nature of the struggle with revolutionary and Napoleonic France.[18] Separately, a sense of divine intervention was linked in the second half of the century to the revival of revelation as an interpretative method. In part, this was in response to Unitarian enthusiasts for reason, who offered a challenge different from earlier Catholic ones based on revelation.[19]

Concerns with the meaning of time were not always to the fore when readers considered the writing of history. In 1729, Philip, 4th Earl of Chesterfield, wrote to his friend Henrietta Howard, Countess of Suffolk, "Little regard is to be had to history, especially to the causes generally assigned by historians for great events."[20] Such criticism of the subject as a whole, however, was less common than taking exception to particular historians. For, in England, as elsewhere, historical work was largely grounded in the controversies of the present and the recent past, notably religious and political struggles. The idea of a separate sphere for scholarship existed, but antiquarianism without apparent relevance excited slight popular support and could, indeed, be seen as tedious. In his *Historical Account of the City of Hereford* (1796), John Price announced that he had responded to the reviewers' criticism of the history of Leominster he had published the previous year: "He has, accordingly, abandoned the recital of superfluous charters, records, lists, etc which only served to swell the volume; though, in the appendix he has confined himself to the locality of matter which may possibly be deemed unworthy of general notice."[21]

There was a long-established habit of employing the past to warn about the present and future, a practice seen at the level of the poor with the many histories of those hanged at London that were published by the chaplain of Newgate prison: 1,242 between 1703 and 1772.[22] The deployment of the examples of Mary I (r. 1553–58) and James II (r. 1685–88) as reasons to support the exclusion of Catholic claimants from the throne were prime instances.

These reasons took precedence over interest in the past itself. For example, the public memorialization and discussion of the traumatic civil wars of the mid-seventeenth century were not primarily concerned with contesting its issues anew but, rather, those of subsequent political and religious settlements.[23] Of course, memorialization was also a means to contest the issues, notably in the shape of their current relevance.

Memorialization could be of very distant episodes. The pamphlet *Letter from a Gentleman in Worcestershire to a Member of Parliament* used the ravages of the Vikings to warn about the need to keep Norway and Denmark out of Russian hands. This was a warning to 1727 from the ninth century, a warning addressed to a specific historical moment, that of the clash between the alliances of Hanover and Vienna, and represented support for (successful) British attempts to have Denmark (which also ruled Norway) in the former. The comparison was somewhat far-fetched, even though naval technology in both cases was that of the age of sail. The *Daily Post*, a London newspaper, in its issue of August 16, 1745, ranged further back, to Charlemagne, who had been crowned emperor in Rome in 800: "When Charles the Great of France had conquered the greatest part of Italy, and made himself master of all Germany, what notions had the people of England of the Balance of Europe? They undoubtedly thought themselves safe enough; everybody fit to bear arms was a soldier; and so they did not dream of making alliances with either the Greek Emperor, or the Saracans, to pull down the Emperor of the West [Charlemagne], lest he should, for want of other employment, pay this island a visit." On November 30, 1734, *Fog's Weekly Journal*, another London newspaper, used French attacks on English merchantmen in the ignominious reign of Richard II (1377–99) as a way to criticize the current government, that of Walpole.

Comments about the relevance of the past, often the distant past, were not only made in print, but also in private, including by senior politicians who had other things to do than reflect on the handsomely bound historical works (often many such works) in the libraries of their stately homes. Edward, Lord Thurlow, the Lord Chancellor from 1778 to 1792, then the favorite minister of George III and a lawyer with scholarly interests, claimed in 1789 in a letter to James Bland Burges, an MP as well as undersecretary of state for foreign affairs, that "every page of the Dutch History" points out the problems of "supporting a remedy for the political instability in the Austrian Netherlands [Belgium] by organising its government on the Dutch basis."[24]

As with many references to history, by politicians and others, this was scarcely a value-free reflection. Instead, it was politically pointed. In this case, Thurlow, a conservative by conviction as well as temperament and one who had strongly opposed independence for the American colonies, was arguing that the outcome for the revolution against rule by the Emperor Joseph II that had begun in 1787 should be the restoration of Austrian control, and not independence on the basis of republican self-government. This was an argument supported by reference to history.

Indeed, history thus offered a vista of possible developments. If that could be a frightening perspective, this aspect could be claimed to be part of its educational value. This value—frequently partisan in practice—was often presented directly in the titles of works, as in the 1713 pamphlet on the overweening ambition of great men: *The Life of Edward Seymour, Duke of Somerset... With Some Parallel Instances to the Case of John Duke of M--h [Marlborough], late Great Favourite [and] the Sudden Fall of... John Dudley, Duke of Northumberland*. This was a direct linkage of the reigns of Edward VI (1547–53) and Queen Anne (1702–14), with the former called in to provide warnings about the latter: Somerset was overthrown and executed, while his nemesis, Northumberland, tried to usurp power in order to keep Mary from the throne, only to fail and be executed in 1553. John, 1st Duke of Marlborough, had been eclipsed in 1711 by a new Tory government determined to bring the War of the Spanish Succession to a close and had gone into exile. Again, there was no foreshortening of the historical frame of reference comparable to that which is more generally the case in modern Britain.

Newspapers stressed the value of history largely so that they might debate current issues. The *True Briton*, a London newspaper, in its issue of

September 9, 1723, argued: "No study is so useful to mankind as history, where, as in a glass, men may see the virtues and vices of great persons in former ages, and be taught to pursue the one, and avoid the other."[25] As will be seen, history was deployed not only to make short-term points about inconsistency and hypocrisy but also to develop, substantiate, and employ the concept of national interests. In turn, opponents were criticized for betraying these interests, and this alleged betrayal was employed to demonstrate their unworthiness. Untrustworthiness was generally substantiated in historical terms.

For opposition newspapers, history provided a safe perspective from which to attack ministers. It also offered the suggestion that the cause of opposition was both timeless and necessary and that evil governments would eventually collapse, and thus that opposition would be vindicated. On May 11, 1728, in an attack on Walpole, the prime minister, the *Craftsman* claimed: "History gives us frequent examples where the best princes have by such ministers lost the affections of the best people; who are naturally disposed to overlook the personal failings or accidental miscarriages of their sovereign, and are never so much irritated as when he endeavors to support a tyrannical over-grown favourite against their general demand for justice." In adopting this approach, the *Craftsman*, then the leading London opposition newspaper and one in which Bolingbroke played a major role, was at once attacking Walpole and making general points both about the nature of rule and regarding the value of history. This approach, which referred back both to classical and biblical models and roots, was the one in which English readers of individual historical works would have been steeped. As a result, these works are best considered in this context.

Progovernment papers were well able to reply. In 1734, the *Daily Courant*, another London newspaper, carried a life of Cola di Rienzi as a warning against popular disorder and pseudopatriotism, both of which the ministry and its supporters linked with the opposition. In 1347, Rienzi (1313–54) successfully persuaded the citizens of Rome to rebel against aristocratic rule, but, after being driven out, he tried again in 1354, only to be killed as a result of a hostile rising. The dangers of factionalism were frequently presented, notably in the press and in Parliament.

For both sides, the use of history in helping to define party identity ensured that history was further employed to defend or attack such claims. This tactic reflected more generally the role of using precedent and tradition even when new ideas were advanced,[26] but also the nature of history as a source for empirical evidence, whether partisan or not.

Contention about history and between historians did not only relate to politics or, differently, primarily to politics. John Whitaker (1735–1808), a writer who was as cantankerous as he was active, found the first volume of his *History of Manchester* criticized in pamphlets of 1771 and 1773 by John Collier, a Lancashire schoolmaster (and son of a cleric), and in the advertisement to the second edition carefully differentiated it from antiquarian local history.[27] Indeed, local history was frequently a topic for contention.[28] Whitaker himself moved on to produce *The Genuine History of the Britons asserted in a ... Refutation of Mr Macpherson's 'Introduction to the History of Great Britain and Ireland'* (1772) and *Gibbon's 'History of the Decline and Fall of the Roman Empire,' in vols 4, 5 and 6 Reviewed* (1791). In turn, Alexander Fraser Tytler, later Lord Woodhouselee (1747–1813), professor of universal history at Edinburgh from 1780, produced *A Critical Examination* (1798) in response to Whitaker's *The Course of Hannibal over the Alps ascertained* (1794). Whitaker was a critic of the American and French Revolutions, which, in their own ways, drove opinions apart as the legacy of the Glorious Revolution had done for previous generations. Such controversies reflected and further encouraged the sense of the discussion of history as an inherently contentious process.

LOCAL HISTORY

While valuable, and indeed central to much in this book and throughout the period, the emphasis on partisanship should not lead to a neglect of the broader basis of the contemporary world of history.[29] This broader basis was not necessarily incompatible with partisanship, explicit or implicit, but it was not dependent on it. A key element was provided by local history, which could be partisan, and in both national and local terms, but was more commonly antiquarian and topographical. The subject is considered here and as appropriate in the chronological chapters. Historians have tended to overlook, or be condescending to, local and county historians as amateurs or "mere" antiquarians who assembled information. Yet paralleling the process with natural history,[30] their work in the eighteenth century reflects some of the important aspects of the processes of historical writing.[31]

There were important seventeenth-century precursors. Robert Plot (1640–96) had offered a prospectus in his *Enquiries to be propounded... In my Travels through England and Wales* (1670), an anticipation of the travels of Thomas Pennant a century later that are discussed in chapter 7. He proposed a systematic study of natural history (notably rocks, animals, and plants) and antiquities, the first to the fore in *The Natural History of Oxfordshire* (1677), which was dedicated to Charles II. Secretary of the Royal Society from 1682 to 1684, Plot became professor of chemistry and keeper of the Ashmolean Museum in 1683. Dedicated to James II, his *The Natural History of Staffordshire* (1686), which followed, included pre-1066 antiquities, and in 1688 he was made Historiographer Royal. A committed Tory, Plot talked of continuing with a coverage of London but did not do so. He did, however, in 1695, become Registrar of the Court of Honour in the Heralds' Office, another form of antiquarianism.

In the eighteenth century, the focus was on urban history, especially of provincial towns. This was a new iteration of the pride of place that was so significant and that was reflected in ritual, sociability, institutions, and politics, including feasts and feast sermons.[32] The development of urban history writing was an aspect of this pride of place but did not replace earlier means. Bristol, for a while the second-largest city in England, had its first complete history, *The History and Antiquities of the City of Bristol*, by the antiquarian and surgeon William Barrett (1733–89), published there in 1789. This work included the hoaxes perpetuated by Thomas Chatterton. In contrast, Andrew Hooke, a progovernment Whig newspaper owner, who had started to publish a history in 1748, could not make it pay. Both writers praised the role of trade and argued that it was a moral as well as practical good, one reflecting virtue and industry.

This theme was more generally true of what might be termed a republican strand of history, one that looked to classical Athens, to Venice, and to the United Provinces (Dutch Republic), finding prosperity, strength, and progress in terms of maritime activity and naval power, a theme that was to be developed by Hume. It was in accordance both with these ideas, those of a thalassocracy (maritime state), and with the conventions of urban history that Barrett argued that trade and navigation caused towns to prosper. He also claimed that urban history was more valuable than its county counterparts, as it demonstrated the value of economic activity. Hooke advanced similar themes. He also presented an account of urban history as linked to that of the nation, with James II (r. 1685–88), the ruler removed in the Glorious Revolution, a threat to the freedoms of both. Bringing such factors into alignment was one of the tasks of writers seeking to shape history and to put it into a pattern with the present. Depth was provided by the reiteration of the longstanding tradition that Bristol had an ancient origin, an approach that challenged that of William Camden. Very differently, Chatterton provided a past for Bristol by his forgeries of purportedly medieval works. Hooke, in contrast, argued from the absence of evidence, an interesting and thoughtful approach. He suggested that early chroniclers were only concerned by the doings of the Church and had therefore ignored trade.[33]

More generally, the argument from absence was less common than the process of putting excessive weight on problematic pieces of evidence. Nevertheless, both this argument and the scrutiny of the latter served to encourage a debate among readers on the nature of evidence and proof. That not everyone took part in this debate does not mean that it was without value. Indeed, the quality of the discussion of historical evidence could be impressive. In this, local history was in no way secondary to or different from national history. As well as overlapping, each contributed to the other.

The range of local history was extensive. There was not simply an engagement with counties and long-established cities, such as Bristol. These could be joined to the wider undertakings, as in the project to make the information from *Domesday Book* (1086) generally accessible. On December 18, 1755, Philip Carteret Webb, a lawyer and MP, read a paper to the Society of Antiquaries that was published the following year as *A Short Account of Domesday Book, with a view to its publication*. This was the start of a major project, finished in 1783, that listed and located such transcripts and printed excerpts of local sections. Local history could have more commercial appeal, as with *An Historical Narrative of the Great and Terrible Fire of London, Sept. 2nd 1666: with Some Parallel Cases . . . [and] An Historical Narrative of the Great Plague at London,*

1665; with an Abstract of... Opinions [and]... Other Remarkable Plagues, Ancient and Modern... with many Observable Passages of History (1769). Printed in one volume, they were compiled from many sources, these often included as sidenotes.

John Collier (1708–86), a schoolmaster in Lancashire, who was a general author and caricaturist, studied the Lancashire dialect, publishing an account of it in 1746 that went through many editions. He also wrote on the history of Manchester, while his eldest son, John, a Newcastle coach maker, published *An Essay on Charters, in which are particularly considered those of Newcastle, with remarks on its constitution, customs, and franchises* (1777).

Town charters and histories very much linked the past to present legal rights.[34] Thus, John Whitaker received the thanks of Manchester in 1793 for his *The Charter of Manchester translated, with Explanations and Remarks* (1787), a work produced in vindication of the rights of the town against the lord of the manor. This was a traditional cause for historical work but one now pursued in print as part of the process of justification and lobbying. Local maps were part of the same process. They became more common in the eighteenth century, both at the county level and for towns. Civic portraiture was another aspect of urban identity, and the retention and preservation of the pictures were significant.[35]

Not all of these local histories were finished, which stands as a reminder of the need to consider unfinished works as part of the range of historical interest. Local histories not finished included William Bingley's history of Hampshire, for which much work was carried out but of which only *The Topographical Account of the Hundred of Bosmere* was published, and then only for private circulation. Whitaker only published two of the projected four books of his *History of Manchester* (1771–75), although a manuscript continuation went up to the end of the Middle Ages. He also never finished his *Private Life of Mary Queen of Scots*, a topic of considerable interest to the public. As an instance of the wide-ranging ambitions of contemporary writers, Whitaker considered but did not produce histories of London and Oxford, as well as a military history of the Romans in Britain.

In ecclesiastical terms, the most significant element was the contribution made by clergy to local historical writing, and notably so outside the major cities. Among them were John Hodgson in Northumberland, Nathaneal Salmon writing of Hertfordshire, Essex, and Surrey, William Borlase of Cornwall, John Hutchins of Dorset, and Joseph Nicolson and Richard Burn of Cumberland and Westmorland. There were also accounts of particular parishes, for example of Upper Boddington, Northamptonshire, by Edward Maynard, rector from 1696 to 1740.[36]

Historical writing was sometimes seen as an analogy to the clerical and other professions. Writing satisfied the scholarly instinct of many of them, while dispossessed professionals turned to it perhaps as a form of consolation. For example, Nathaneal Salmon chose to abandon the Church in 1702 because, on the accession of Queen Anne, he was required to swear the Abjuration Oath—something he had not been forced to do under William III. He lived for a time as a physician but turned to historical writing when he needed money. Salmon wrote a number of local works, including histories of Hertfordshire, Essex, and Surrey.[37] But his reputation was that of a hack writer and a religious partisan rather than a respected scholar. Salmon died in penury as a result. Joseph Nicolson similarly saw historical writing as a refuge from the county and chapter politics, which he found uncongenial in Cumberland. And it was also a consolation when his wife and sister died.

Of course it was not just clergy who could see local history as a refuge from the religious and political contests of the eighteenth century or as a means to foster particular interpretations. James Wright (1643–1713), a Tory lawyer suspected of Jacobitism and even of converting to Catholicism, chose to write history, notably *The History and Antiquities of the County of Rutland* (1684), rather than engage in politics.[38] Sir Robert Atkyns (1647–1711), a lawyer and politician whose Toryism meant that he too was regarded as beyond the pale in 1689, retired to his home county to write the *Ancient and Present State of Gloucestershire* (1712). John Bridges (1666–1724), a successful London lawyer and official and a fellow of the Society of Antiquaries, accumulated extensive material for the history of his native Northamptonshire, including the transcribing of many monuments and records. He died before his project could be brought to fruition. A subsequent attempt to publish them by subscription was cut short by the bankruptcy of the publisher, and the entire work was not published until 1791, with a cleric, Peter Whalley, being given the credit although he did relatively little. Bridges himself had drawn on clerical correspondents.[39] Sir Richard Worsley, an MP, officeholder, and Grand Tourist, may have been encouraged to write his *History of the Isle of Wight* (1781) by his very public cuckoldry, which he was thought to have condoned.[40]

Local historical writing was often complementary to an active clerical life. William Borlase (1695–1772) in Cornwall was clearly a man whose abilities extended beyond the spiritual work of his parish at Ludgvan, and so he turned to writing history. At first, he was limited to the history and antiquities that were nearby, and he was as much interested in natural history as in human history, a frequent pairing. Author of *Cornish Antiquities* (1754) and of a shorter account of the Scilly Isles, published in 1756, Borlase relied on scholarly encouragement from successive deans of Exeter, Jeremiah Milles and Charles Lyttleton.[41] An active traveler within England, Milles recorded in his journals his great interest in the history of the local nobility and in their contact with national history: there were frequent references to monarchs from Edward the Confessor to Henry VIII.

Similarly John Hutchins, the Dorset historian, was successively incumbent of Milton Abbas, Swyre, and Wareham and also a man whose abilities exceeded his position as a parson. His *History and Antiquities of the County of Dorset*, published in 1774, was testimony to his dedication given that his rectory at Wareham was destroyed by fire in 1762 and he only just managed to salvage his papers.

Many of these writers were of course principally interested in the history of the Church, which was particularly significant for some counties. This historical writing was not always sympathetic to the Church. John Spearman's *An Enquiry Into the Ancient and Present State of the County Palatine of Durham; Wherein are Shewn the Oppressions which Attend the Subjects of this County by the Male-administration of the Present Ministers and Officers of the Said County Palatine* (1729) was an attack on the power and privileges of the bishops, who were uniquely powerful in Durham, and especially on the mining rights and administration of the episcopal estates of the bishops. Spearman compared the bishops to the Borgias, an instance of iniquity that was suitably Catholic, papal, Italian, decadent, and scandalous. In practice, the bishops were not that interesting. William Hutchinson's *History and Antiquities of the County Palatine of Durham* (1786) was more establishment in tone.

Financing local histories was problematic, not least as there was not generally the entrepreneurial backing of London publishers, which was so important for historical works published there.[42] Hutchins was fortunate in obtaining subscriptions for his work, which enabled him to travel to Oxford and London for research.[43] But other historians were less fortunate. Edward Hasted, despite inheriting a substantial estate from his father, was arrested for debt in 1795 largely because of the huge costs of his historical research and his decision to abandon his wife. As a result, Hasted resorted to selling entries in his *History and Topographical Survey of the County of Kent* to local gentry families, with larger sums purchasing enhanced and elaborated family histories. While the income from the sale of the first edition of the work was significant, probably between three and four thousand pounds, Hasted estimated that the cost of researching and writing was more than this, and the same was true for the second edition. This was in part due to the huge expenditure on maps and engravings but also because Hasted insisted on visiting every parish in the county for his research.[44] In 1796, Price announced that future work would depend on the success of his new book on Hereford.[45] He went on to tackle Ludlow (1797) and Worcester (1799).

The work could also be laborious. Hutchins wrote of the problems of finding time between church duties, the bad weather, roads that were "deep" (i.e., very muddy), and a horse that was not able to cope with being ridden. Such problems prevented him from undertaking visits to libraries and archives as much as he would have wanted.[46] Consequently, he had to rely on other local clergy for help, especially George Bingham, a Dorset cleric and local archaeologist, and Thomas Rackett, another Dorset cleric who was also an enthusiast for antiquarian research. The purposes of history might easily seem to become unclear when considering the mismatch between Hasted's prodigious work and rather narrow perspective. However, there was a general consensus that such work was valuable as well as necessary.

NARRATIVES

In 1701, a medal was struck at the request of Electress Sophia of Hanover, granddaughter of James I and mother of George I, to mark her being named heiress to the Crown of England. The reverse depicted "Matilda [c. 1156–89], daughter of Henry II, King of England, wife of Henry the Lion . . . mother of Emperor Otto IV . . . Progenitor of the House of Brunswick." This medal grounded the Hanoverian claim on the succession in primogeniture and the history of the House of Guelph, and not on the Act of Settlement passed by Parliament in 1701. It was a claim also advanced by Wesley in his *Concise History of England* in 1775, in which he traced the legitimacy of the Hanoverian succession back to Matilda.[47] History thereby served to establish and strengthen an alternative claim. Pro-Hanoverian English historians, such as Laurence Echard, also focused on this argument.[48] Such dynastic locating was scarcely new, but it remained important. Indeed, dynastic history was not only a traditional theme in England, and one that was crucial to state formulation,[49] but was also pushed to the fore by the related challenge posed by Jacobite claims, or believed to be posed by them.

It is all too easy to forget such conventional uses of history and such established goals of new works when focusing on the new developments in the period. To an extent, much of the historical writing in the eighteenth century was directly (or, more commonly, indirectly) about the royal succession, not least in terms of accounts and images of royal legitimacy, present, recent, or far more historic. This concern encompassed the royal family. George III had a strong sense of historical consciousness, one that can be followed due to his activity as a correspondent, an activity that contrasted markedly with the situation under his predecessors. Historical images were offered to George from an early age. One of the first accounts of George is of his acting at the age of ten the role of the virtuous hero in a children's production of Joseph Addison's noted play *Cato* (1711): George was given a new prologue to speak. Another Whig classic, Nicholas Rowe's *Lady Jane Grey* (1715), an account of exemplary Protestant virtue, was also staged by the future George and his siblings. Rowe had been made poet laureate by George I. In the play, Lady Jane offered a model of Protestant constancy and pathos in opposition to the wiles of the Catholic queen, Mary I.

A keen reader until his eyesight failed, George III was especially interested in works on theology and history.[50] He praised seventeenth-century writers, such as Robert Sanderson (1587–1663), a sermon writer and chaplain to (and a favorite preacher before) Charles I, who lost his living and the divinity chair at Oxford because he refused to subscribe to the Parliamentarians' Solemn League and Covenant.[51] Samuel Johnson both advised on the purchase of books for the royal family and was a beneficiary of George's largesse. When Henry, Duke of Cumberland, married a commoner in 1771, his brother, the outraged and overwrought George, informed another brother, William, Duke of Gloucester, that such a step might threaten civil war, as he claimed that the fifteenth-century Wars of the Roses owed much to the intermarriage of Crown and nobility.[52] And George was reflective when he visited the tomb of the overthrown and murdered Edward II in Gloucester Cathedral in 1788.

George also took a view on legitimacy that made allowance for the cause of the Stuarts, an allowance that extended to providing financial support for "Henry IX," the younger son of James III, who was a claimant to George's throne. George had no time for the false report that "James III," the "warming pan baby," was a changeling. Instead, he saw his position and that of future British monarchs as resting not on dynastic right but on duty. George was mindful of what the Glorious Revolution meant in terms of the rejection of unacceptable monarchy. In his writings as a prince, George criticized James, arguing that the Glorious Revolution had rescued Britain "from the iron rod of arbitrary power," and praised Oliver Cromwell as "a friend of justice and virtue."[53] In 1799, an approach on behalf of Henry IX led George to reflect that he had "ever thought that" the "true solid basis" of Hanoverian rule was that "it came to preserve the free Constitution of this Empire, both in Church and State, which compact I trust none of my successors will ever dare to depart from."[54] George's linkage of church and state would have chimed strongly with such contemporaries as Johnson, Burke, and Nares.

NATIONAL HISTORIES

The close engagement with England, with place, and with the specifics of its past seen in much historical writing was often antiquarian, including the republication and translation of older historical works, for example of Camden's *Britannia* in 1695 by Edmund Gibson, later a leading Whig bishop. An antiquarian approach did not mean that there was a lack of engagement with broader issues. This was especially true of the coverage of urban governance in urban histories.

The same was true with biography, which was a key aspect of historical writing[55] and included works by writers generally known for other types of writing. William Godwin's first book, published anonymously while he was still a Dissenting preacher, was *The History of the Life of William Pitt, Earl of Chatham* (1783), who had died five years earlier. The goals—indeed, the ethos—of biography were readily explained in these works. At the same time, there were subtle differences in emphasis and, more generally, a shift in the general approach from a morality that rested on personal characteristics located in a critique of general mores, for example, a view of aggression, to one in which individual beliefs were brought to the fore. William Coxe, an Anglican clergyman (1747–1828), praised Sir Robert Walpole in the lengthy biography he published in 1798 for his "love of peace." Praising Walpole entailed breaking with the usual pattern of castigating the minister, one in which Tories could unite with opposition Whigs. Instead, complaining in the preface that too many writers had been misled by contemporary critics (who included Bolingbroke), Coxe argued that the sole way to avoid bias was to work on the papers of the politicians on both sides. Indeed, Coxe's work has still much value to modern historians as a result. Two of the three volumes of the weighty Coxe biography were devoted to documents.[56] Private manuscript collections, including those containing the papers of Walpole and his brother Horatio, proved his particular forte, a goal in which he benefited from his excellent connections with aristocrats. An Old Etonian, Coxe had taught the sons of several aristocrats both at Cambridge and as a traveling tutor. This research involved much work, not least because the collections were not organized or catalogued.

The papers of aristocratic families could serve for private manuscript histories, such as that for the Courtenay Earls of Devon. There was also the use of these papers held in other repositories. Thus, Edmund Lodge (1756–1839), who became a member of the College of Arms in 1782, published, nine years later, a selection from the Howard, Talbot, and Cecil manuscripts in the college as *Illustrations of British History, Biography, and Manners in the Reigns of Henry VIII, Edward VI, Mary, Elizabeth, and James I*. The following year appeared his "biographical tracts" accompanying John Chamberlaine's *Imitations of Original Drawings by Hans Holbein*.

Biographies, and histories organized in a biographical fashion, were produced not only of British individuals but also of foreign ones, and the latter could enjoy a European reputation. Robert Watson's *History of the Reign of Philip II* (1777) was translated into Dutch, French, and German, and his sequel on Philip III, posthumously finished by William Thomson and published in 1783, was translated into French. Historical biography was also seen in the theater. Thus, Tobias Smollett wrote *The Regicide: Or, James the First of Scotland. A Tragedy* (1749), a work repeatedly rejected by the theater, much to Smollett's anger.

The biographical, even dynastic, theme was not the only one. There was also an interest in constitutionalism and therefore in the historical dimension of the constitution, which was one based on a reading of history. Henry Lloyd (c. 1729–83), in his *Essay on the English Constitution* (1770), a work that supported Wilkes, made reference to the classics, including the threat from Philip of Macedon to Greece, as well as to British history. The actions of Oliver Cromwell were cited as instances of the danger of expelling MPs; Charles I and James II demonstrated the dangers of attacking Parliament; and favorites under Elizabeth I and James I emerged as a problem. Henry VIII was described as cruel, and Thomas Cromwell was criticized.

A military commander and commentator, Lloyd, in his writings (like Bolingbroke, Hume, Smollett, and many others), showed the extent to which historical works were not simply produced by historians, or, rather, the need for a wide definition of the latter, one centered on being a writer. Smollett's wide-ranging corpus included *A Complete History of England* (1757–58), its *Continuation* (1760–65), and *The Adventures of an Atom* (1769), an account apparently of Japanese history that, in practice, poorly concealed that of Britain in 1752–56.[57] Looked at differently, the definition of a historian was difficult, an issue that remains the case today.

The constitution, like the law, was an aspect of a living past, one in which history very clearly, both in its relevance and in its coverage, was not separate from the present. Writers deployed history to support the constitution, as with *An Historical Essay upon the Balance of Civil*

Power in England, from its first conquest by the Anglo-Saxons, to the time of the Revolution (1748) by Samuel Squire (1713–66). A clerical agent of Thomas, Duke of Newcastle, Squire wrote widely on the Anglo-Saxon English classics and the English constitution, including *An Enquiry into the Foundations of the English Constitution* (1745), which was dedicated to Newcastle, as was the second edition (1753), which included the above essay. Newcastle was the most influential of the Old Corps Whigs, who dominated government between the fall of Walpole in 1742 and Newcastle's own fall from office in 1762.

Moreover, the constitution could readily be linked to politics. Thus, on September 2, 1749, the *Remembrancer*, a London newspaper, noted, "On the ruins of King James the Second's government a new one was established, which undertook not only to perpetuate the liberty of this country, but to restore the liberty of Europe." The title of the paper was itself a reference to the value of the past. In addition, the use of the term *history* reflected this lack of separation from politics, not least with history understood as of the annals of the present. This could be seen not only with political material, but also nonpolitical. An instance of the latter was *The History of the Works of the Learned. Or, An Impartial Account of Books Lately Printed in all Parts of Europe. With a Particular Relation of the State of Learning in each Country. For the Year of 1699* (1699). This work drew heavily on a Rotterdam work, the *Histoire des Ouvrages des Savans* (1687–1709), a product of the Huguenot diaspora.[58] That diaspora helped broaden the range of interest and reference in English historical writing, as seen for recent history with Abel Boyer and for long-term national history with Paul de Rapin-Thoyras, among other writers.

Issues and evidence, goals and methods, together contributed to the question of whether there was purpose in history. This was a question that most could readily answer in the affirmative, not least if it was expanded to cover historians as well as history. Nevertheless, there were caveats. The radical *County Spectator*, in its issue of November 6, 1792, listed "The Democrats Creed," which included the following entry: "I believe that the present age is more virtuous and enlightened than any preceding one, as may be proved from the spirit of reform, which all Europe is introducing into Church and State." Such a rejection of the past, however, was uncommon, as was seen with the discussion in the colonies and Britain, among supporters of the American Revolution, which was largely in terms of a rejection of unwarranted innovations by George III and a defense, instead, of older liberties.

WORLD AND CHRISTIAN HISTORIES

World history represented a very different narrative than that of the nation, but each was a narrative that brought together past themes and present relevance, notably, for many historians, how best to find a wider purpose in national history. In the case of national history, this purpose entailed an engagement with non-Christian cultures, which, as in John Toland's *Christianity not Mysterious* (1696), involved a commentary on Christianity.[59] World history drew in part on classical and foreign models,[60] although there could also be a Christian dimension. Lancelot Addison's historical works, notably *West Barbary, or a Short Narrative of the Revolutions of the Kingdoms of Fez and Morocco, with an account of their present customs, sacred, civil, and domestic* (1671), *The Present State of the Jews* (1675), and *the First State of Muhametism* (1678), contributed to the Church's sense of its historical and geographical location and as one religion in a diverse world. Oxford-educated, Addison (1632–1703), the father of Joseph Addison, was English chaplain in Tangier and from 1671 held a living in England, becoming dean of Lichfield in 1683.[61] There was, indeed, a longstanding Christian approach to world history, one that gave it meaning in terms of a religious underlaying to the rise and fall of empires that had interested classical writers. Thus, the "Remarks on the Conduct of France" that, as an instance of the widespread circulation of news, appeared in the *Cirencester Flying Post* in September 1742 could then state: "When we see an overgrown power ravaging or subduing its neighbours, we ought to be firmly persuaded, that, after a time, God will raise up some other nation to pull down and destroy that, which was only the instrument of his vengeance on others. The sacred writings, nay, profane history, abound with so many examples of this, that it is needless to point out any particular one." Louis XIV was then treated in this context. Christian world history demonstrated the nature of the creator from his creation and also looked to the traditional idea of the present as a decadent product of human sin, notably Adam's fall. In this view, decline was the major cause and narrative.

Thus, in 1741, William Dodwell (1709–85), an Oxford-educated cleric who rose to be archdeacon of Berkshire, preached a sermon before the university. Dodwell was the son of Henry Dodwell (1641–1711), a Nonjuror who returned to the Church and published extensively on classical history, including *An Invitation to Gentlemen to acquaint themselves with Ancient History* (1694). William Dodwell focused on theological works, including *Two Sermons on the Doctrine of Divine Visitation by Earthquakes* (1756). In his 1741 sermon, Dodwell declared: "It is but too visible, that since men have learnt to wear off the apprehension of eternal punishment, the progress of impiety and immorality among us has been very considerable... uncommon heights of wickedness have been attained."[62]

A very different type of world history benefited from the extent to which, alongside exploration, more history of specific parts of the world outside Europe was made available during the century.[63] Thus, John Morgan published, in 1728, *A Complete History of Algiers: To which is prefixed an epitome of the general history of Barbary, from the earliest times: interspaced with many curious remarks and passages, not touched on by any writer whatever*. Morgan went on to publish *The Lives and Memorable Actions of many Illustrious Persons of the Eastern Nations* (1739). The market, however, was less robust than for histories of England, which on the whole enjoyed wider circulation. Simon Ockley (1678–1720), an Anglican cleric who became professor of Arabic at Cambridge in 1711, wrote a two-volume *Conquest of Syria, Persia, and Egypt by the Saracens* (1708–18) that won considerable fame and was used by Gibbon. Nevertheless, the preface to the second volume was dated from Cambridge Castle, where he was imprisoned for debt in circumstances he ironically claimed were more conducive for writing than his parsonage. Ockley died in debt.

A different form of Christian history was provided by sacred music. This made biblical history more attractive and accessible and gave the liturgy a particular resonance. In his *An Essay on Criticism* (1711), Alexander Pope noted:

> As some to church repair,
> Not for the doctrine, but the music there.

Aside from the music appropriate for the liturgical year, there was also music for special occasions, for example, anthems for state ceremonies and thanksgiving services. These in turn provided a form of religious history.[64] Aside from such noted figures as Henry Purcell and George Frederick Handel, other composers of sacred and secular music included William Croft, Maurice Greene, William Hayes, and John Weldon. Greene (1696–1755), the son of a London vicar, was organist of St. Paul's Cathedral from 1718, adding the posts of organist and composer to the Chapel Royal in 1727 and of master of the King's Band of Music in 1735. His *The Song of Deborah and Barak* (1732) was the first oratorio by a native-born Englishman (although not called such by Greene) and was followed by *Jephtha* (1737) and *The Force of Truth* (1744). Handel's oratorios, including *Esther* (1732), *Deborah* (1733), *Athalia* (1733), *Saul* (1739), *Israel in Egypt* (1739), *Messiah* (1741), *Samson* (1743), *Joseph and his Brethren* (1744), *Belshazzar* (1745), *Judas Maccabaeus* (1747), *Joshua* (1748), *Solomon* (1749), *Susanna* (1749), *Theodora* (1750), and *Jephtha* (1752), helped offer an Anglicized choral version of biblical history, also locating modern Britain in terms that provided an attractive parallel to the echoes of Rome offered by classical references. The oratorio texts pressed the need for national unity and the moral value of art.[65]

METHODS

"I have carefully pointed out the sources from which I have derived information." In the preface to his *History of the Reign of Charles V,* the much-praised Scottish cleric-historian William Robertson, principal of Edinburgh University from 1762 to 1793, expressed what had become established conceptual and methodological principles.[66] The stronger emphasis on the reality, verification, and importance of facts was linked to an assertion of their primacy over attempts at expository manipulation. In contradiction to the idea that "scientific history," in the shape of professionalism and archive-based studies, began in the nineteenth century (and notably in the universities then), there were, indeed, crucial earlier developments. In particular, alongside developing ideas of the precise recording of time and its arrangement in a reportable sequence in the shape of journals,[67] the Scientific Revolution of the late seventeenth century and its popularization in the eighteenth were both highly relevant to the development of history. The stress on sources was related to the idea of an impartial enquiry into the past. The consideration of secular historical evidence served both for theological issues and also for the replacement of providential accounts of time, or at least the lessening of their hegemony, not least with the notion that events had causes, whether immediate, remote, or both. At the same time, metaphysical and theological debates were both vibrant and drew on source-based evidence.[68]

Impartiality, like claims to moderation in the politics and religion of the period, implied a credibility based on reason, not emotion, and supported by testimony, rather than opinion. The extent to which historians, both famous and not so famous, appealed to sources is striking. Moreover, this appeal helped to make the use of sources not only the means to proceed with controversy and to make particular works appear worth reading, as with Guthrie, Ralph, and Coxe, but also normative for the genre as a whole, although also raising the question of which sources the historians were to prioritize.

This account builds on the positive view of historical writing, notably in the early eighteenth century, offered by Laird Okie in 1991. In his book, a revised version of a 1982 doctorate, Okie presented a major transformation from the traditionally humanist chronicle of the Renaissance to an essentially modern style of historical narrative—namely, continuous narratives based on what Okie presented as rationalist and critical methods of scholarship. To Okie, history was no longer confined to affairs of state while historians demonstrated a finer understanding than hitherto of historical change, noting key long-term developments, especially the rise of Parliament and changes in land distribution.[69] However, on a pattern frequent with studies of the eighteenth century, his view of pre-Augustan historical works was overly harsh, not least as it implied that previous historians were guilty of irrationalism. This view enabled Okie, by contrast, to portray his subject in an overly favorable light. Nevertheless, Okie correctly captured a discriminating use of sources in eighteenth-century historiography.

Indeed, taking on board seventeenth-century developments, not least an engagement with archaeology,[70] as well as the developing (from the sixteenth century) emphases on the concept and legal practice of the fact,[71] the ideal of such research was clearly stated in repeated title pages and prefaces. Thus, the lawyer Sir Henry Chauncy (1632–1719), in his *The Historical Antiquities of Hertfordshire* (1700), declared that it was "faithfully collected from Public Records, Ledger Books, Ancient Manuscripts, Charters, Evidences, and other Selected Authorities." Chauncy declared that the research took fourteen years. In the preface to the second volume of his *History of England* (1718), Laurence Echard (1672–1730) cited the writers he had read, including "several manuscripts and particular informations that never yet appeared in the world."[72] He also mentioned that he had consulted living and dead authors on all sides. In the preface to the third volume of his *History of England*, a volume covering 1509–1613 and published in 1752, Thomas Carte mentioned the excellent coverage of sources for Elizabeth's reign and notably the large number of papers of William Cecil, Lord Burghley, that had been printed. Indeed, the volume and accessibility of these papers, which contrasted with the situation for Robert Dudley, Earl of Leicester, and for others, made it difficult to achieve a rounded picture of Elizabeth's reign.[73]

Carte referred to the work of Samuel Haynes,[74] a Cambridge-educated cleric who was vicar of Hatfield, the Cecil seat, from 1737. An assiduous transcriber, Haynes published by subscription in 1740 *Collection of State Papers relating to Affairs in the Reigns of Henry VIII, Edward VI, Mary, and Elizabeth, from 1542 to 1570. Transcribed from the Original Letters and other Authentick Memorials left by W. Cecil, Lord Burghley, and now remaining at Hatfield House* (1740). Haynes died in 1752, but an edition by William Murdin that brought the date of the printed papers down to 1596 was published in 1759. This reflected commitment to the project and interest in it. William Oldys (1696–1761), who, in 1738, had turned down Haynes's request that he cooperate, on the grounds that Haynes intended to ignore papers that dealt with Elizabeth's "girlish frolics,"[75] in turn was an antiquarian who eagerly collected manuscripts. Oldys assisted in publications, including a new edition of Sir Walter Raleigh's *History of the World* (1736), to which he appended a lengthy, research-based life of Raleigh. Oldys also played a role in the publication of the *Harleian Miscellany* and the first edition of the *Biographia Britannica*.

Catharine Macaulay drew for her account of mid-seventeenth-century England on tracts from the period. *The Difference between an Absolute and Limited Monarchy; as it more particularly regards the English Constitution*, written by Sir John Fortescue in the 1470s, was first published in 1714, by his descendant John Fortescue Aland, a lawyer who became an MP and then a judge. In the introduction, Aland stressed the need to study early specimens of the law. Similarly, in 1725, Edmund Sawyer, a London lawyer, published *Memorials of Affairs of State in the Reigns of Queen Elizabeth and King James I, collected chiefly from the Original Papers of the Right Honourable Sir Ralph Winwood, sometime one of the principal Secretaries of State*.

The volume of historical publication was impressive. It represented a continuation with the practice of such publication in the seventeenth century, but a marked accentuation of the process. Moreover, this accentuation enabled the pursuit of controversies, as well as scholarship, based on archival sources.

ARCHIVAL SOURCES

The emphasis on sources was also seen in the greatly expanded field of local history. Local historians realized that key sources of information about people and places were monumental inscriptions in churches and graveyards; they were also a source that was prone to erosion and destruction. Consequently the work of eighteenth-century local historians and travelers in recording monumental inscriptions in churches and churchyards has been an enduring and significant source of historical information, one that ensured that there was far more information for historians to address and deploy.[76] Wright's *History and Antiquities of the County of Rutland* is an example of a work that meticulously recorded inscriptions as a source. It is especially significant since a number of the inscriptions were subsequently worn beyond recovery. Sir Thomas Phillipps's 1822 work on the monumental inscriptions in Wiltshire, a work for which he employed his gamekeeper, William Hensley, provides another example of such a case.[77]

Writers realized that an invaluable source for them was the clergy of a locality. Price acknowledged in the full title of his 1796 history of

Hereford that it was "founded on collections given to the writer" by the Reverend John Lodge, author of *Introductory Sketches towards a Topographical History of Herefordshire* (1793). Some, like Atkyns, in his *Ancient and Present State of Glostershire*, published in 1712, pillaged previous clerical writings on the county, almost to the point of plagiarism. Robert Parsons, chancellor of Gloucester, was used so heavily by Atkyns that it was clear that he had reproduced exactly the same information, and in some cases even the wording was closely followed.[78] Though he was not the first to do so, Atkyns also wrote to local clergy to ask for information, which he included in the work, a process encouraged by the longevity of many clergy and their many years of service in one parish. Worsley's *History of the Isle of Wight* also relied heavily on queries he sent to all the clergy on the isle, which he dispatched as a printed questionnaire asking for information about each parish's history, population, and records. Borlase insisted on writing his history parish by parish, a system that made sense to him but which later commentators found problematic. The parochial basis for county histories (one later seen with the monumental *Victoria County Histories*) was not the most interesting, even if it offered comprehension of a type. William Holman, a Nonconformist cleric, did not manage to finish the history he planned, which was designed to be one on each Essex parish arranged under hundreds.

Some local historians' research was extraordinary. Burn, in writing, with Nicolson, *The History and Antiquities of the Counties of Westmorland and Cumberland*, published in 1777, drew on public records cartularies, private family papers, and manuscripts in Scotland also, and his notes filled twenty volumes.[79] Hasted, preparing to write his *History and Topographical Survey of the County of Kent* (a work that ran to more than seven thousand pages), wrote of his use of Dugdale's *Monasticon* as an "attack," and his notes reached a hundred volumes.[80] For his *History of London* (1739), William Maitland drew heavily on sources, such that much of the work reads like a compilation. Another version, brought up to date, appeared in 1756, and demand for it was indicated by its appearing in four editions by 1769, with another larger one following in 1775.

In the first volume of his *The History and Antiquities of the County of Leicester*, a volume, dedicated to George III, that was published in

London in 1795, John Nichols, the printer to the Society of Antiquaries, continued the title with the claim

> compiled from the best and most ancient historians; Inquisitiones Post Mortem, and other valuable records, in the Tower, Rolls, Exchequer, Duchy, and Augmentation Offices; The Registers of the Diocese of Lincoln; The Chartularies and Registers of Religious Houses; the College of Arms; the British Museum; the libraries of Oxford and Cambridge; and other public and private repositories.
>
> Including also Mr Burton's Description of the County, published in 1622;
>
> And the later collections of Mr Staveley, Mr Carte, Mr Peck, and Sir Thomas Cave.

Nichols's preface drew attention to manuscript sources used, for example, those of Samuel Carte, and included "Earl Ferrers has personally condescended to alleviate my labours, by extracts from the original register of Bredon Priory, by copies of deeds and seals in his own archives, and from the most copious pedigree I have ever yet seen."[81] The lengthy first volume included an account of Roman coins and inscriptions found in Leicester, as well as the *Domesday Book* entry for Leicestershire, a translation, and a long essay about *Domesday Book*. The volume closed with a lengthy appendix that included documents relevant to the history of Leicester and of its earls. Nichols evaluated sources. He also provided in the text an account, in his discussion of the early history of the city, that suggested a civilizational value for the subject: "The early years of prophane history have been long since deservedly named the Unknown and the Fabulous. The founders of empires have dropped from the Heavens, or sprung from the Earth, with equal facility.... Researches, however, into the state and situation of our forefathers, when carried on with proper diffidence, and at least the appearance of authority, are ever grateful, because natural, to the mind of men ... European diligence almost everywhere produces, not national only; but even provincial and local history."[82]

It is instructive that such arguments could be seen in local history as well as its national and wider counterparts.[83] The emphasis on sources and on their critical assessment ensured a move by historians away from the "ancients" to their scrutiny and use by more perceptive "moderns."

Thus, in his history of Hereford, John Price started the text by observing, "He who writes the Antiquities of a provincial city, will find his judgment frequently embarrassed, and his progress retarded by the uncertainty of information and frequently by the contradictory accounts which he receives; for, as few authors have recorded much authentic intelligence of this nature, he is obliged to have recourse to tradition, which, though sometimes true, seldom deserves implicit confidence. Nor is this the only difficulty that will occur: the barrenness of events at certain periods will frequently interrupt his narration, and the regular arrangement of detail."[84]

The use of sources was accompanied by their criticism, and such source criticism spanned the range of the past, from ancient origins to recent years. This source criticism made new works more attractive, as well as offering something of special value to the growing popular market for history.[85] The title of George Charles Deering's *Nottingham Vetus et Nova or an Historical Account of the Ancient and Present State of the town of Nottingham* continued *Gathered from the Remains of Antiquity and Collected from Authentic Manuscript as well as Modern Historians* (1751). The introduction began with a direct engagement with the nature of sources: "It is too common an observation that writers of the history of particular places as well as whole kingdoms, are fond of the marvellous, and think they do not sufficient justice to their subject, without tracing the original of their kings, or the first foundation of their cities and towns, so far back, as to be obliged either to have recourse to the fertility of their own brains, for some romantic beginning of them, or else to be beholden to fabulous authors who have done the business to their hands."[86]

Deering pressed on to criticize "monkish authors" for such faults and offered a parallel between history and the enhancement of sight:

> A consistent account gathered from well attested facts, and drawn from a curious and judicious occular inspection, after having duly compared things with things, like a Reading Glass which only clears up the letters but neither magnifies or diminishes them, serves the reader to see the truth in a proper light; but as such a glass the farther the object is removed from its true focus, represents the same the more and more dim: so the farther an author retires into the dark recesses of Antiquity, the more he clouds his subject, and too often renders his veracity in other particulars suspected.[87]

The account of the foundation of Nottingham in 980 BCE in John Rous's *Historia Regum Angliace*, a transcript of which was printed in 1716, was discredited, and Deering, instead, fixed the foundation of the town to the eighth century CE. German-born, Deering was a doctor. In his *History of Chichester* (1804), the Sussex cleric Alexander Hay (c. 1735–1806), noted, "The generality of writers evince a strange propensity to trace the origin of the people, whose annals they have undertaken to transmit to posterity, to the remotest ages of antiquity."[88]

The new sense that history relied heavily on the use of print and manuscript sources was emphasized in William Nicolson's *The English Historical Library* of 1696–99, which was reprinted in an extended edition in 1714; there were later editions in 1736 and 1776. Nicolson (1655–1727), then archdeacon of Carlisle and from 1702 bishop of the same diocese, bemoaned the "deplorable condition of our public records" and their "useless and confused state."[89] *The English Historical Library* was an attempt to list and describe for the first time the principal historical repositories and archives and their contents. He listed them in order of their historical contents and significance, beginning with the Cottonian and Harleian libraries and moving on through the collections of the College of Arms, the Bodleian (Oxford University Library), and Cambridge University Library. Nicolson included cathedral and corporate libraries as well as the libraries of aristocrats and "private persons." The three-volume work was divided, first, into English national and county antiquities and collections, including those covering the Saxon period; the second volume was the collections relevant to the histories of the Church in Britain, including chronicles, cartularies, and registers; and the third volume described government, parliamentary and royal collections, legal records, and also coinage and medals. Nicolson was a scholar of the Anglo-Saxon period, who was both keen to ensure that other scholars would have access to archives and also convinced that in historical records were the roots of precedents that society needed to identify and follow. Although contemporaries, notably political enemies of the firmly Whig Nicolson, such as the Tory cleric Francis Atterbury, pointed out its errors, this was a precious record.[90]

Sources were also highly significant to the coverage of a very different subject and approach by the ever-active Abel Boyer in his *The History of King William the Third* (1702–3) and the *History of the Reign of Queen Anne digested into Annals*, which began in 1703. Boyer drew attention to sources, including the oral and written testimonies of soldiers and conversations with men of public importance.[91]

More widely, writers could advance theoretical ideas from general principles, an approach that was not focused on historical particularities. There was also, however, an engagement with the social context and with the relationship between theory and practice. Both of these provided room for historical investigation and evidence, and thus for affirming or debating values and methods accordingly. Thinkers were as much concerned with discovery, whether through exploration, observation, or historical study, as with speculation, and this tendency was also seen at the populist end. The application of scholarship to issues of political organization involved theoretical discussion and also debate about the historical basis and credibility of contrasting views on how best to govern particular states. Although the nature and closeness of the relationship with such discovery varied by individual and subject, they were crucial to the development and application of Enlightenment ideas.

The turn to sources was an aspect of the more general interest in evidence and classification. Collecting provided an aspect of this interest in sources. This was related to the interest in sensations seen across the range of senses, and more particularly the impact of Lockean sensationalism in ideas of education and maturity. A sense of the transforming possibilities of time invited attention not only to the past, but also to the prospect of future change. In England, for many, this was a theme deployed in and for the past in the sense of the Glorious Revolution and the possibilities for improvement it had created.

The historiography of the period is generally discussed in a top-down fashion and notably in terms of Bolingbroke, Gibbon, Hume, and Robertson, an aspect apparently of philosophy (or at least a strand of philosophy) teaching by example, industry, and method. Their work linked erudition and exposition in order to establish scholarly norms.[92] At the same time, these writers were all dependent on public support, in the sense of the purchase of their publications, and did not rest on an institutional structure. The consequences of that situation were particularly significant in contrast to the role of governmental and ecclesiastical patronage in most Continental states. Most clearly, the impact of the suppression of the Jesuit Order in 1773 on historical writing and other cultural activity in Catholic Europe was not matched in England.

The work of these major writers was and is important, not least because it was grounded in a widespread public interest and in a broad pattern of publication for the public, points worth assessing when considering the situation today. In the eighteenth century, linked to this, relevance and partisanship were generally more to the fore than what might today be presented as detached scholarship. Alongside an emphasis on a wider range of writing than that of those named above, it is valuable, more specifically, to note the significance of particular historians who have been underrated, including Echard, Guthrie, Oldmixon, Ralph, and Rolt.[93]

Whether historians are treated as high and low or philosophical and hack or impartial and partial or belle-lettrists or miscellarians,[94] these and other distinctions risk underrating similarities between them. The similarities arose not only from common conventions and a shared audience, but also from the extent to which the subsequent separating tendencies of university and popular were not to the fore. Instead, although they had important strengths, Oxford and Cambridge were not prominent in their engagement with postclassical history nor, indeed, with topics and work across a range of subjects. An attempt to introduce economics in Cambridge in the 1750s failed.[95]

As a result, as with works on geography published during the period,[96] it was the public forum that was crucial. History writing therefore was a branch of "Grub Street"[97] as much as of the "Republic of Letters," and an eclectic mix of individuals accordingly produced historical works. The son of a cleric, whom himself had published on music, education, and history, Thomas Salmon (1679–1767) gave up keeping a coffeehouse in Cambridge due to limited trade. This took him to London, where he pressed forward the writing that had already taken up some of his time in Cambridge, although he also traveled widely outside Britain. His books indicate the range of work produced by those who lived by their pen. They included *A Review of the History of England, as far as it relates to the Titles and Pretensions of four several Kings, and their Respective Characters, from the Conquest to the Revolution* (1722), *An Impartial*

Examination of Bishop Burnet's History of his own Times (1724), *Bishop Burnet's Proofs of the Pretender's Illegitimacy... compared with the Account given by other writers of the same fact* (1724), *The Characters of the Several Noblemen and Gentlemen that have died in the Defence of their Princes, or the Liberties of their Country. Together with the Characters of those who have suffered for Treason and Rebellion for the last three hundred years* (1724), *The Chronological Historian, containing a regular Account of all material Transactions and Occurrences, Ecclesiastical, Civil, and Military, relating to the English affairs, from the Invasion of the Romans to the Death of King George I* (1733), *A new Abridgement and Critical Review of the State Trials and Impeachments for High Treason* (1738), *Modern History, or the Present State of all Nations* (1739), and *A Short View of the Families of the present English Nobility* (1751). One of Salmon's grandfathers, John Bradshaw, had been a regicide. His books often seemed to avoid the identification of their author, usually referring to him as "Mr Salmon."

Another example of the range of such writers, a range that subsequently led to them being described notably in the *Dictionary of National Biography* as "miscellaneous writers," was John Campbell (1708–75), a talented figure who published on a variety of topics, including current affairs. His historical compilations included *Military History of the late Prince Eugene of Savoy and the late John, Duke of Marlborough* (1736), contributions to the *Modern Universal History* (notably on transoceanic settlements), a *Concise History of Spanish America* (1741), *A Letter to a Friend in the Country on the Publication of Thurloe's State Papers* (1742), and *The Lives of the Admirals and other Eminent British Seamen* (1742–44).[98]

Thomas Salmon's elder brother, Nathanael Salmon (1675–1742), already mentioned, was a Cambridge-educated cleric who became a Nonjuror and a physician. He also wrote widely. His first two books, both published in 1726 on Roman antiquities, became a partwork (a publication released as a series), *A New Survey of England wherein the Defects of Camden are Supplied* (1728–29), which was reissued in 1731. This work showed how history could be used in partworks, which were an important aspect of the publishing world of the period, one seen again more recently. As with his brother's commentary on Burnet, this work reflected an accretional character to history writing that was frequently corrective. Sometimes combative, this approach overlapped with that of history as controversy.

Nathanael followed with *The History of Hertfordshire, describing the county and its ancient monuments, particularly the Roman* (1728),[99] *Lives of the English Bishops from the Restoration to the Revolution* (1731–33) (a Nonjuring work), and *Antiquities of Surrey* (1736) (a work that concentrated on Roman antiquities). In 1739, Nathanael purchased an unfinished manuscript history of Essex, organized by parishes, compiled by the antiquarian William Holman (1669–1730), a Nonconformist cleric whose fieldwork focused on monumental inscriptions. Salmon published this in parts in 1740–41, although nearly half of the county was unfinished when he died in poverty. An adept writer, who was well read and had an eye for the landscape on his travels, Salmon showed the vitality of country history in this period and also its focus on antiquities. Salmon collected material for a history of Staffordshire in addition to Hertfordshire, Surrey, and Essex. Salmon's work was to be new molded and completed by Philip Morant, rector of St. Mary's Colchester, who produced, first, a history of that city (1748) and, then, one on Essex, in which he carefully explained his sources and included the second edition of his history of Colchester.[100] Morant had also produced *The History of England by way of Question and Answer* (1737).

A popular and wide-ranging historical writer of the second half of the eighteenth century was the Reverend John Trusler (1735–1820). Trusler was an innkeeper's son who had been well educated and had got to Cambridge as a sizar, ensuring that he could afford the cost. He had briefly served as parish clergyman but soon realized that he could earn an income from preaching and publishing. Trusler was the author of *Chronology: or, a Concise View of the Annals of England* (1769), which was republished and expanded as *Chronology, or the Historians' Vade Mecum, The Historians Guide* (1773), later published as *The Tablet of Memory* (1782), and *A Compendium of Sacred History* (1797), and the publisher of a history of Surinam and of Francis Bacon's account of the reign of Henry VII. Trusler also wrote many books on topics as varied as the law, animal husbandry, gardening, geography, manners, and money making. His best seller was a set of over a hundred sermons, printed in a newly devised copperplate handwriting form of type, which clergy could pass off as their own.[101] By the late 1760s, Trusler had made sufficient money from preaching and writing that he did not need a parish or other church to make a living, and his full-time occupation became writing and publishing.

One of Trusler's motives as a writer was his hatred of publishers and booksellers, a hatred shared by many writers of the period. Trusler thought they were dishonest swindlers who robbed both the author and the reading public. He urged writers not to let publishers have the copyright of their work and took every opportunity to attack publishers and booksellers. Consequently, Trusler set up his own sales outlet at 62 Wardour Street in London and issued catalogs, which enabled the public to buy his books directly. One of Trusler's techniques was to gradually add to his books as he came across more information, hence he was able to advertise new editions of his work as "enlarged," "extended," and with "revisions"—all of which promoted sales. He claimed his stock was many hundredweights of books and that they would fill seven wagons. His works were unashamedly aimed at a popular market and at the class of people who wanted to educate themselves. Most were sold for small amounts, though some—especially his geographical works—were sold in installments, which could be bound together. His guides to how to carve a joint of meat and to the principles of politeness were clearly aimed at the upwardly mobile. Trusler's books sold in large quantities, many reaching numerous reprintings and revised editions. Part of his success was his use of the postal system for sales. He negotiated an ingenious system for the sale of his sermons so that the post office would deliver his sales literature to every clergyman in the country free of charge, and he would pay the post office a fee for each clergyman who bought one or more sermons from him. For the distribution of his books, Trusler used Pennant's Parcel Post, which was the only service in London and surrounding counties that could cope with his volume of sales and meant that he did not have to pay the exorbitant costs of the London porterage system.[102]

Besides a desire to make money, Trusler claimed that his goal was to educate the public in a range of subjects, including history. His *Chronology*, which, by 1790, had grown into a two-volume work but was also offered in an abridged, small single-volume version, was a list of events in the history of the world, in alphabetical order, with the date attached to each entry. By 1790, it was in its twelfth edition. His *Historians Guide*, sometimes published as *The Tablet of Memory*, was an alphabetical list of historical figures and events with a brief sentence or two about each. Some of these were extremely slight; for example, his entry on Boadiccea read: "Burnt London, and massacred 70,000 inhabitants; soon after being defeated by Suetonius, poisoned herself." The book was "designed for the pocket in order to set people right in conversation." So it was principally a portable historical reference guide. Trusler added all sorts of information to subsequent editions, including such things as annuity rates, places where markets were held, and even stagecoach fares. Consequently, the work became almost an almanac, as well as a historical reference work. His *Chronology or a Concise View of the Annals of England* was a similarly eccentric compendium of historical information on England, which Trusler assembled to be published. It was advertised as "useful to all who are desirous of being acquainted with their own country."

Trusler's autobiography suggests that his interest in history was deeper than simply that of a publisher intent on making money, although he was certainly content that his historical work had made him wealthy. His *Chronology* alone "amply repaid me for my trouble having gone through 15 editions." It was the huge success of the *Chronology* that, Trusler claimed, had earned him the enmity of the London publishers. But his motives were not simply financial. He was convinced that people were improved by self-education; he wrote, "Men are much altered by education and experience." And he endorsed Coleridge's view that "in every man's face was to be found history of the past and prophecy of struggles to come." Trusler saw education as part of his clerical role, not having a parish of his own; he wrote: "To make men happy they should be taught religion and history... in which God is truly manifest." Trusler also asserted that "people like history and details of lives," so he tried to ensure that his historical works were full of biographical information. Children were especially important, in his view, when it came to the teaching of history: Trusler claimed that teaching them history was as important as teaching them manners.[103]

Trusler exemplified a trend in late eighteenth-century popular history writing and publishing. His work was by no means original and was often hastily cribbed from other authors; it also frequently appeared to be padded out with miscellaneous information. The historical works were full of errors and included lore and myths as if they were facts. He verged on sharp practice by recycling the same material under different titles and making claims to revision and extension that were dubious. In his historical writing, as in his sermon sales venture, he occupied the characteristic Grub Street, but not quite respectable ground, of an entrepreneur who was not always concerned about quality.

Nevertheless, Trusler's aims were sincere, and he clearly dedicated his life to educating the public and continued to do so long after his income and fortune might have led him to retire. His works also brought to the lower classes of society glimpses of historical information that they hitherto lacked. Eventually, Trusler did retire to Bath, where he wrote an autobiography so frank and forthright that, when it was met with widespread antipathy, he bought up the remaining stock of the first volume and refused to publish the second. In the latter, Trusler wrote a comment that he said was from Steele's *Guardian*, though it was more probably from Anthony, 3rd Earl of Shaftesbury, asserting that it was sensible to "think with the wise and speak with the vulgar."[104]

Sources appeared of greater significance because of the emphasis on the role of individual motivation. Historical work and references in the period placed an emphasis on individual free will and not on determinism, an approach that brought together a rejection of Calvinist predestination; religious, legal, and political engagements with the role of choice; and a lack of interest in later themes of revolutionary adaptation and historical materialism. This emphasis encouraged an overlap with fiction. *History*, indeed, was a term deployed to suggest truth and in no way was restricted to factual accounts. Henry Fielding insisted that his novels, which were to be influential in the development of the genre, were "true histories" in that they revealed the truth of behavior. This was an approach especially suited to the ironic and confiding voice he adopted as narrator. In the last chapter of his novel *Joseph Andrews* (1742), Fielding wrote, "This true history is brought to a happy conclusion."

The term *history* frequently appeared in the titles of novels, as in Henry Fielding's *The History of Tom Jones* (1749), Samuel Johnson's *The History of Rasselas, Prince of Abyssinia* (1759), Sarah Fielding's *The History of the Countess of Dellwyn* (1759) and *The History of Ophelia* (1761), James Ridley's *The History of James Lovegrove* (1761), Jane West's *The*

Advantages of Education: or The History of Maria Williams (1793), Frances Brooke's *The History of Julia Mandeville* (1763) and *The History of Emily Montague* (1769), and the anonymous *The History of Mr Byron and Miss Greville* (1767) and *Charles Dacres: or, the Voluntary Exile. An Historical Novel, Founded on Facts* (1797). Popular prose fiction could also use the term, as with Defoe's satirical *Political History of the Devil* (1726), the anonymous *History of Autonos* (1736) (an attack on Walpole), and the version of William Cowper's *John Gilpin* that appeared as an illustrated chapbook for children.[105]

The use of history in this fashion in part reflected the extent to which writers as a whole, whether on the page or the stage, sought a voice with which they could influence their readers, a voice with authority.[106] This was seen in the case of Henry Fielding in his condemnation of false values by means of history. In his mock-heroic novel *The History of the Life of the Late Mr Jonathan Wild the Great* (1743), about a noted London criminal, Fielding offered an ironic account of false greatness, one aimed not only at the criminal but also against great conquerors, Alexander the Great being among those condemned[107]: "When I consider whole nations rooted out only to bring tears into the eyes of a GREAT MAN... because he hath no more nations to extirpate, then indeed I am almost inclined to wish that nature had spared us this her MASTERPIECE, and that no GREAT MAN had ever been born into the world."[108] Alexander was a figure represented critically by a number of writers, including Christopher Smart in 1751.[109] History to contemporaries meant narrative, whether the history in question was a novel or a scholarly work. Each genre also offered morality.

Henry Fielding, moreover, employed the term *history* in his journalism, as in "The Present History of Europe," to suggest that he was offering particularly authentic information.[110] This usage was widespread. David Jones, a prolific writer on recent history, produced from 1701 to 1712 twelve annual volumes. The first was titled *A Complete History of Europe: or, A View of the Affairs thereof, Civil and Military, for the Year 1701. Containing all the Public and Secret Transactions therein... Intermixed with Great Variety of Original Papers, Letters, Memoirs, Treatises, etc... With Remarkables of the Year; The Present State of the Imperial, all the Royal Families... Also, a Catalogue of the Nobility,* and *Privy Council of England, Scotland, etc.*[111] Abel Boyer, a Huguenot refugee and former tutor, published *The History of the Reign of Queen Anne digested into Annals*. In 1710, he followed with *An Essay towards the History of the Late Ministry and Parliament Containing Seasonable Reflections on Favourites, Ministers of State, Parties, Parliaments and Public Credit*.[112] Three years later appeared the Whiggish *A Short History of the Parliament*. In 1732, *The Danverian History of the affairs of Europe, for the Memorable Year 1731* appeared, as did, on February 11 in the *Daily Post Boy*, "The History of the Modern Patriots," a criticism of the opposition. In 1743, James Ralph brought out a *Critical History of the Administration of Sir Robert Walpole*. As part of the overlap of news, politics, and history, very recent history could be presented as part of more wide-ranging works. Thus, John Banks's *Compendious History of the House of Austria* (1746) included a discussion of the causes of the War of the Austrian Succession, which had broken out in 1740.

Issues of accuracy were highlighted by the question of the overlap of history, news, and fiction. This question was foregrounded by concerns about forgery[113] and by a belief in secret histories explaining events, as in David Jones's *The Secret History of White Hall from the Restoration of Charles II down to the Abdication of the late King James* (1697).[114] Secret histories looked toward the belief that John, 3rd Earl of Bute, from his resignation from office in 1763 on, was secretly directing court policies and to Burke's concern in the 1790s about conspiratorial support for pernicious ideologies both in Britain and in France.[115]

History was presented in another form with the discussion of recent events in novels, plays, and poems, as well as their depiction on canvas—for example, the highly dramatic death of James Wolfe and the collapse of William Pitt the Elder (the first, in 1759, on the battlefield of Québec; the second, in 1778, in the House of Lords, and a prelude to his death). George II's victory at the Battle of Dettingen (1743) played a role in Tobias Smollett's novel *Roderick Random* (1748) and in Henry Fielding's *Tom Jones* (1749), while William, Duke of Cumberland's victory at Culloden was in part the inspiration for Handel's oratorio *Judas Maccabeus* (1747). Scenes of imperial success were readily depicted, as in Dominic Serres's painting *The Siege at Fort Royal, Martinique* (1769), recording a British victory seven years earlier. Benjamin West, appointed historical painter to George III in 1772, responded to the serious crisis of the late 1770s—not only the War of American Independence but also rising discontent in Ireland and the Franco-Spanish invasion attempt of 1779—by depicting crucial victories from the past: *The Battle of the Boyne* and the *Destruction of the French Fleet at La Hogue*, events that had occurred in 1690 and 1692.

The same was true with the theater. The audience at Drury Lane on January 1, 1785, were witness to *The Repulse of the Spaniards before the Rock of Gibraltar*, an episode from four years earlier. This was part of a process in which British victories were displayed in spectacle.[116] That, however, was not the sole form of history on the stage. In 1794, Samuel Taylor Coleridge and Robert Southey collaborated on *The Fall of Robespierre: An Historic Drama*, an event that occurred that year in France.

While novels sought to be true histories, historical writing was supposed to capture character. In part because biography had not fully emerged as a genre, but, more generally, due to the central role of character in history, "lives" were a division of history. This was a convention that went back to the classical world, as with Plutarch's *Lives*, a work that remained influential. In his thoughtful *Reflections on Ancient and Modern History* (1746), James Hampton (1721–78), an Oxford-educated cleric who produced a major translation of much of Polybius's history of the rise of Rome that was published between 1756 and 1761, praised classical writers because of "that nice discernment of the several lines and features of human nature, which are so strongly expressed in all the characters, throughout their histories."[117]

History did not only offer character out of interest. Instead, there was the presentation of history as a morally exemplary tale, a presentation that brought history, novels, and the theater together. Indeed, across time, this presentation, a key element in narratives, has been the main theme in historical writing and, even more, the historical consciousness—albeit one challenged by modern academic methods and academic culture, each in part aspects of secularism and self-consciously so. In the eighteenth century, whether the stress was on individual free will or a providential intervention linked to behavior, the emphasis, in contrast, was on a world best understood in moral terms.

Indeed, an anonymous work of 1710 presented Oliver Cromwell as having made a pact with the devil, a theme that represented a continuation of mid-seventeenth-century diatribes but one that, in the eighteenth century, increasingly appeared dated. Echard repeated the story in the second volume of his *History of England*.[118]

Far from being differentiated, the relationship of history or politics with morality was strongly focused in monarchical political systems, both because of the obvious importance of a small number of individuals and due to the longstanding notion of kingship and governance as moral activities. This notion went back to the ancient sacral roles of rulers as responsible for their communities to God (and, earlier, to the gods) and of their intercessionary role with oracles who interpreted the meaning of time. Such an approach was encouraged by sermonizing on monarchs, as in William Stephens's *Thanksgiving Sermon* of 1696 in which Elizabeth I's policy was presented positively: "that England should always make itself the head and protection of the whole Protestant interest.... By making all true Protestants, i.e. all true Christians, her friends she enabled England to make good her oldest maxim of state, which was to keep the balance of Europe equal and steady.... Our allies of the Roman communion must allow this Protestant maxim to be truly Catholic, because their safety from the power of France was wrapped up in it together with our own."[119]

Hampton complained in 1746 that "with modern writers everything is either vice or virtue."[120] This was seen very clearly with such works as Wesley's *A Concise History of England* (1776) and notably with the extensive coverage of royal personality, particularly Elizabeth I's rivalry with Mary, Queen of Scots. As discussed in chapter 7, Wesley was very ready to look to Shakespeare for parallels, as well as to assess the coverage of history by the playwright. The latter became more common as Shakespeare was pushed to the fore as the national writer from the late 1760s, in particular with discussion of Richard III, for example in Horace Walpole's *Historic Doubts on the Life and Reign of King Richard the Third* (1768).

As morality appeared timeless, it seemed pertinent to apply admonitory tales in a modern context. This could be seen with the comparisons of Walpole indiscriminately with Sejanus, the favorite of the Roman emperor Tiberius; Cardinal Wolsey under Henry VIII; George, 1st Duke of Buckingham (of the 2nd creation) under Charles I; and Sir Thomas Clifford under Charles II,[121] all of whom were presented as corrupt and villainous and as taking power that should more rightly be that of the monarch. In each case, their overthrow was presented as exemplary. This did not exhaust the list, which, in addition, could be freshened to take note of current targets. In its issue of October 9, 1762, the *Monitor* published an essay on bad favorites, comparing John, 3rd Earl of Bute, the key advisor of George III, with Roger Mortimer (c. 1287–1330), the lover of Queen Isabella, wife of Edward II. This was a pointed comparison that was to be further developed in 1763 in the published dedication to Bute of the play *The Fall of Mortimer*. Mortimer and Isabella were responsible for Edward's overthrow in 1326 and murder in 1327, only, in turn, to be overthrown in 1330 by Edward II's son, Edward III, after which the first was executed and the second imprisoned. Bute was rumored to be the lover of George's mother, Augusta.

There was an equivalent use of historical examples on stage. In Nicholas Rowe's play *Tamerlane* (1701), the protagonist of Christopher Marlowe's 1587 play was reworked to appear as William III, with his eventually defeated rival Bajazet, the Ottoman ruler, as Louis XIV. Not performed during the Tory ascendancy in Anne's last years, the play was staged in 1722 in response to the Atterbury Plot: "The players of both houses being willing to show their loyalty, the Tragedy of Tamerlane was last night acted both at Drury Lane and Lincolns Inn Fields: the character which gives that play its name was drawn from nature for the character of King William."[122]

Belief that history possessed a cyclical quality, as well as an exhortatory purpose, contributed to this process of citing the past, as time was not held to compromise the moral power of historical exemplars. Indeed, the opposite was true, because time captured and revealed the most fundamental moral lessons and warnings. The general stress on personal drives, rather than on social, economic, and institutional factors, was seen in historical works, as well as in newspapers and other sources. This emphasis on the personal both made moral judgments easier and was readily conducive to different styles of morality and feeling. Thus, historians, like novelists, registered the rise of sentiment in the 1760s and 1770s as a key value and means, and the interest in sentimental feeling was reflected both in their work and in its appeal.¹²³ Love intrigues played a role in such novels as Frances Brooke's *The History of Emily Montague* (1769). Novels, history, and gossip all offered accounts of individuals and thus focused on how best to understand and represent individuality, not least with reference to social norms.¹²⁴

At the same time, it was increasingly regarded as important to offer an historical dimension to discussion of social, economic, and institutional issues. Frederick Eden's three-volume, research-based *The State of the Poor* (1797) focused on that topic, but the lengthier title was also instructive. It continued: *or an History of the Labouring Classes in England from the conquest to the present period; in which are particularly considered their domestic economy with respect to diet, dress, fuel, and habitation; and the various plans which, from time to time, have been proposed and adopted for the relief of the poor.* Eden (1766–1809), an Oxford-educated member of a landed family, was an active writer on economic topics.

History was not only written about in a number of forms and to a variety of purposes. It could also be staged. This was more commonly done in popular celebrations and in the theater, but was not only done there. There was staging for posterity in statuary. Most dramatically, instant history was presented by means of the erection of columns to honor heroes and by other similar methods. The resulting statuary of display contrasted with the classical statuary that was commonly displayed for private edification and delight, although columns also appeared in private estates. Erected in 1730, the Column of Victory at Blenheim Palace bore an inscription to John, 1st Duke of Marlborough, written by Bolingbroke:

> the hero not only of his nation, but his age: whose glory was equal in the Council and in the Field: who by wisdom, justice, candour and address, reconciled various and even opposite interests, acquired an influence which no rank, no authority can give nor any force but that of superior virtue, became the fixed, important centre, which united in one common cause, the principal states of Europe. Who by military knowledge and irresistible valour, in a long series of uninterrupted triumphs, broke the power of France: when raised the highest, when exerted the most, rescued the Empire from desolation, asserted and confirmed the liberties of Europe.

Daniel Garrett built a column, dedicated to the Peace of Aix-la-Chapelle of 1748, bearing a statue of the Apollo Belvedere, for

Sir Hugh Smithson at Stanwick Hall. Personalized by such classical writers as the mythical Clio, history itself could be depicted as a figure in funerary monuments, as in that to John, 2nd Duke of Argyll, erected in Westminster Abbey in 1749. This presentation was taken forward to the public by its use in the frontispiece to that July's number of the *Universal Magazine*.[125]

It was easy in such contexts to see echoes and parallels with the classical world, a theme considered in chapter 8. These, indeed, were frequently deployed in historical works, not least in a rhetorical fashion, but these echoes and parallels did not dominate, still less dictate, historical understanding in a developing empire that was very different from those of Athens and Rome. In 1784, John Andrews argued:

> An English gentleman should be particularly versed in history; not only that of his own country, but those of as many others as he can possibly spare the time to read and study. It is chiefly by an application of this kind that he will become of public utility: he will learn what courses to avoid, by contemplating the calamities they have occasioned; and what measures to pursue, by considering the benefits they have produced. Men of rank and fortune in some other countries may doubtless attain the same knowledge; but in them it will prove inactive and fruitless: it is only in states blessed with liberty that such a science is not a dead letter to the possessor. Study therefore history beyond all other subjects. It will bring you most honour and profit: it will enable you to shine in public deliberations, and to act upon necessary occasions. It will, in short, supply the demands of both theory and practice.[126]

NOTES

1. J. G. A. Pocock, *The Ancient Constitution and the Feudal Law: A Study of English Historical Thought in the Seventeenth Century* (Cambridge, 1957).

2. A. Hadfield, *Shakespeare, Spenser and the Matter of Britain* (Basingstoke, UK, 2003).

3. J. P. Reid, *The Ancient Constitution and the Origins of Anglo-American Liberty* (DeKalb, IL, 2005).

4. H. Erskine-Hill, *Poetry of Opposition and Revolution: Dryden to Wordsworth* (Oxford, 1996).

5. J. Roe, "Robert Brady's Intellectual History and Royalist Antipopery in Restoration England," *English Historical Review* 122 (2007): 1287–317.

6. D. Stephan, "Laurence Echard—Whig Historian," *Historical Journal* 32 (1989): 865; D. C. Douglas, *English Scholars, 1660–1730* (London, 1939).

7. P. K. Leffler, "French Historians and the Challenge to Louis XIV's Absolutism," *French Historical Studies* 14 (1985): 1–22.

8. P. H. Reill, *The German Enlightenment and the Rise of Historicism* (Berkeley, CA, 1975); H. E. Bödeker, G. G. Iggers, J. B. Knudsen, and P. H. Reill, eds., *Aufklärung und Geschichte. Studien zur deutschen Geschichtswissenschaft im 18. Jahrhundert* (Göttingen, 1986).

9. C. Grell, *L'Histoire entre Érudition et Philosophie: étude sur la connaissance historique à l'Âge des Lumières* (Paris, 1993).

10. D. Carrithers, "Montesquieu's Philosophy of History," *Journal of the History of Ideas* (1986): 61–80.

11. K. O'Brien, *Narratives of Enlightenment: Cosmopolitan History from Voltaire to Gibbon* (Cambridge, 1997).

12. S. Brogan, *The Royal Touch in Early Modern England: Politics, Medicine and Sin* (Woodbridge, UK: 2015).

13. S. S. Genuth, *Comets, Popular Culture, and the Birth of Modern Cosmology* (Princeton, NJ, 1997).

14. T. Campbell, "John Wesley and Conyers Middleton on Divine Intervention in History," *Church History* 55 (1986): 39–49.

15. Harris, *Philosophical Arrangements*, in *The Works of James Harris*, 2 vols., ed. James, 1st Earl of Malmesbury (London, 1801), 2:284–85.

16. A. Hay, *The History of Chichester* (Chichester, UK, 1804), 270, 273.

17. Anon., *History of the City of Chester* (Chester, UK, 1815), 103.

18. J. Coffey, "'Tremble Britannia!': Fear, Providence and the Abolition of the Slave Trade, 1758–1807," *English Historical Review* 127 (2012): 844–81.

19. J. Gascoigne, *Cambridge in the Age of the Enlightenment: Science, Religion and Politics from the Restoration to the French Revolution* (Cambridge, 1989).

20. Chesterfield to Howard, July 26, 1729, BL. Add. 22626 fol. 98.

21. J. Price, *Historical Account of the City of Hereford* (Hereford, UK, 1796), 5.

22. P. Rawlings, *Drunks, Whores and Idle Apprentices: Criminal Biographies of the Eighteenth Century* (London, 1992).

23. M. Neufeld, *The Civil Wars after 1660: Public Remembering in Late Stuart England* (Woodbridge, UK, 2013).

24. Thurlow to Burges, December 5, 1789, Bodl. BB, vol. 18 fol. 89.

25. See also *The Citizen*, June 1, 1757.

26. G. Evans, "Partisan Politics, History and the National Interest (1700–1748)," in *Ideology and Foreign Policy in Early Modern Europe, 1650–1750*, ed. D. Onnekind and G. Rommelse (Farnham, UK, 2011), 92.

27. J. Whitaker, *The History of Manchester*, 2nd ed. (London, 1773), xiii.

28. W. R. Powell, "Antiquaries in Conflict: Philip Morant versus Richard Gough," *Essex Archaeology and History* 20 (1989): 143–46.

29. M. S. Phillips, *Society and Sentiment: Genres of Historical Writing in Britain 1740–1820* (Princeton, NJ, 2000).

30. E. Yale, *Sociable Knowledge: Natural History and the Nation in Early Modern Britain* (Philadelphia, 2016).

31. J. Simmons, "The Writing of English County History," in *English County Historians*, ed. J. Simmons (Wakefield, 1978): 1.

32. N. E. Key, "The Political Culture and Political Rhetoric of County Feasts and Feast Sermons, 1654–1714," *Journal of British Studies* 33 (1994): 223–56; J. A. Marino, *Becoming Neapolitan: Citizen Culture in Baroque Naples* (Baltimore, 2011).

33. J. Barry, "Provincial Town Culture 1640–1780: Urbane or Civic," in *Interpretation and Cultural History*, ed. J. H. Pittock and A. Wear (Basingstoke, 1991): 198–235, esp. 211–24; J. Barry, "Chatterton in Bristol," *Angelski* 1, no. 2 (1994): 55–82.

34. R. Brady, *An Historical Treatise of Cities and Burghs* (London, 1690); R. Sweet, "The Production of Urban Histories in Eighteenth-Century England," *Urban History* 23 (1996): 182–84; and R. Sweet, *The Writing of Urban Histories in Eighteenth-Century England* (Oxford, 1997).

35. R. Tittler, *The Face of the City: Civic Portraiture and Civic Identity in Early Modern England* (Manchester, 2007).

36. B. Hornby, "A Place in History through Memoirs," *Northamptonshire Past and Present* 51 (1998): 22–32.

37. Salmon's work included *A New Survey of England, wherein the Defects of Camden are Supplied* (eleven parts, 1728–29), *The history of Hertfordshire, describing the county and its ancient monuments, particularly the Roman* (1728), *Antiquities of Surrey* (1736), and *The History and Antiquities of Essex* (1740).

38. T. Hearne, *Remarks and Collections, Oxford Historical Society*, ed. D. Rainey, vol. 4 (1885), 252.

39. T. Brown and G. Foard, *The Making of a County History: John Bridges' Northamptonshire* (Northampton, UK, 1994).

40. C. McCreery, "Breaking All the Rules: The Worsley Affair in Late Eighteenth Century Britain," in *Orthodoxy and Heresy in Eighteenth-Century Society*, ed. R. Hewitt and P. Rogers (Lewisburg, 2002), 47–61.

41. P. A. S. Pool, "William Borlase," in *Journal of the Royal Institution of Cornwall*, New Series, vol. 5, pt. 2 (1966).

42. H. M. Solomon, *The Rise of Robert Dodsley: Creating the New Age of Print* (Carbondale, IL, 1996).

43. R. Douch, "John Hutchins" in *English County Historians*, ed. J. Simmons (1978), 116.

44. A. Everitt, "Edward Hasted" in *English County Historians*, ed. J. Simmons (1978), 198, 200–203.

45. Price, *Hereford*, 6.

46. *Somerset and Dorset Notes and Queries*, vol. 28 (1960): 187.

47. J. Wesley, *Concise History of England* (London, 1775), 1:189.

48. U. Weiss, "'Inside Was a Parchment, So Beautifully Painted on all Sides.' The Ornate Charters of the Hanoverian Succession," in *Hand and Seal for a Kingdom: The Ornate Charters of the Hanoverian Succession in Great Britain*, ed. M. L. Babin, G. van den Heuvel, and U. Weiss (Göttingen, 2014): 35, 37; L. Echard, *The History of England*, vol. 2 (London, 1718), dedication to George I, p. iv.

49. J. C. D. Clark, "Protestantism, Nationalism, and National Identity,

1660–1832," *Historical Journal* 43 (2000): 274.

50. George III to William Pitt the Younger, February 10, 1800, NA. 30/8/104 fol. 263.

51. J. Boswell, *Life of Johnson* (Oxford, 1980), 157.

52. George to Gloucester, November 9, 1771, RA. GEO/15938.

53. RA. GEO/Add. 32. In his unpublished "Short History of England," George distinguished those in the opposition to Charles I "who not content with removing abuses, were for removing foundations," 32/193.

54. George to William, Lord Grenville, Foreign Secretary, November 24, 1799, BL. Add., 58861 fol. 64.

55. D. A. Stauffer, *The Art of Biography in Eighteenth-Century England* (Princeton, NJ, 1941).

56. P. Fritz, "Archdeacon William Coxe as Political Biographer," in *The Triumph of Culture: 18th Century Perspectives*, ed. P. Fritz and D. Williams (Toronto, 1972), 211–24.

57. D. Greene, "Smollett the Historian: A Reappraisal," in *Tobias Smollett: Bicentennial Essays*, ed. G.S. Rousseau and P.G. Boucé (New York, 1971), 25–56.

58. H. Bots, ed., *Henri Basnage de Beauval en de Histoire des Ouvrages des Savans 1687–1709* (Amsterdam, 1976).

59. J. Williams, "Sacred History? The Difficult Subject of Religion," in *Enlightenment: Discovering the World in the Eighteenth Century*, ed. K. Sloan (London, 2003): 212–21.

60. K. O'Brien, *Narratives of Enlightenment: Cosmopolitan History from Voltaire to Gibbon* (Cambridge, 1997); T. Griggs, "Universal History from the Counter-Reformation to the Enlightenment," *Modern Intellectual History* 4 (2007): 219–47.

61. W. Bulman, *Anglican Enlightenment: Orientalism, Religion and Politics in England and its Empire, 1648–1715* (Cambridge, 2015).

62. William Dodwell, *Two Sermons on the Eternity of Future Punishment* (Oxford, 1743), 85.

63. G. Abbattista, "The English *Universal History*: Publishing, Authorship and Historiography in an European Project, 1736–1790," *Storia della Storiografia* 39 (2001): 103–8.

64. N. Temperley, *The Music of the English Parish Church*, 2 vols. (Cambridge, 1979).

65. R. Smith, *Handel's Oratorios and Eighteenth-Century Thought* (Cambridge, 1995).

66. J. Black, "The Enlightenment Historian at Work: The Researches of William Robertson," *Bulletin of Hispanic Studies* 45 (1988): 251–60.

67. C. J. Sommerville, *The News Revolution in England: Cultural Dynamics of Daily Information* (Oxford, 1996); S. Sherman, *Telling Time: Clocks, Diaries and English Diurnal Form, 1660–1785* (Chicago, 1996).

68. B. W. Young, *Religion and Enlightenment in Eighteenth-Century England: Theological Debate from Locke to Burke* (Oxford, 1998).

69. L. Okie, *Augustan Historical Writing: Histories of England in the English Enlightenment* (Lanham, MD, 1991).

70. S. A. E. Mendyk, *Speculum Britanniae: Regional Study, Antiquarianism and Science in Britain to 1700* (Toronto, 1989).

71. B. J. Shapiro, *A Culture of Fact: England, 1550–1720* (Ithaca, NY, 1999).

72. Echard, *History of England*, 2:ii–iii.

73. S. Adams, "The Papers of Robert Dudley, Earl of Leicester," *Archives* 22 (1996): 1–26.

74. T. Carte, *History of England*, vol. 3 (London, 1752), p. iii.

75. Oldys, *Diary*, 26. Appended to J. Yeowell, *Memoir of William Oldys* (London, 1862).

76. J. Hodgson, *A History of Northumberland*, pt. 2, vol. 1 (Newcastle, 1827), xi. John Hodgson was a vicar.

77. J. Simmons, "James Wright," in *English County Historians*, ed. J. Simmons (1978), 50; P. Sherlock, ed., *Monumental Inscriptions of Wiltshire, an Edition in Facsimile of the 'Monumental Inscriptions in the County of Wilton' by Sir Thomas Phillipps, 1822* (Trowbridge, UK, 2000).

78. B. S. Smith, "Sir Robert Atkyns," in *English County Historians*, ed. J. Simmons (1978), 66–67.

79. B. C. Jones, "Joseph Nicolson and Richard Burn," in *English County Historians*, ed. J. Simmons (1978), 178.

80. Everitt, "Edward Hasted," 192, 195.

81. J. Nichols, *The History and Antiquities of the County of Leicester* (London, 1795), preface, vi.

82. Nichols, *Leicester*, 1:1.

83. G. Parry, "Rummaging in the Dustbins of History," *Times Higher Education Supplement*, January 5, 1990, 18, on the need to recover antiquarian history from "near-oblivion."

84. Price, *Hereford*, 9.

85. K. O'Brien, "The History Market in Eighteenth-Century England," in *Books and Their Readers in Eighteenth-Century England: New Essays*, ed. I. Rivers (London, 2001), 105–33.

86. G. C. Deering, *Nottingham Vetus et Nova or an Historical Account of the Ancient and Present State of the town of Nottingham* (Nottingham, 1751), 1.

87. Deering, *Nottingham*, 1.

88. Hay, *The History of Chichester* (Chichester, UK, 1804): 5; H. Johnstone and F. W. Steer, *Alexander Hay, historian of Chichester*, Chichester Papers 20 (Chichester, UK, 1961).

89. W. Nicolson, *The English Historical Library in Three Parts Giving a Short View and Character of most of our Historians either in print or Manuscript*... (London, 1714), v.

90. D. C. Douglas, *English Scholars, 1660–1730*, 68, 186; W. Stubbs, *Seventeen Lectures on the Study of Medieval and Modern History and Kindred Subjects* (Oxford, 1900), 381.

91. G. C. Gibbs, "The Contribution of Abel Boyer to Contemporary History in England in the Early Eighteenth Century," in *Clio's Mirror: Historiography in Britain and the Netherlands*, ed. A. C. Duke and C. A. Tamse (Zutphen, 1985), 96.

92. L. Braudy, *Narrative Form in History and Fiction: Hume, Fielding, and Gibbon* (Princeton, NJ, 1970); D. Hay, *Annalists and Historians: Western Historiography from the Eighth to the Eighteenth Centuries* (London, 1977), 184.

93. For this approach, see N. Gallagher, "The Beginnings of Enlightenment Historiography in Britain," in *A Companion to Enlightenment Historiography*, ed. S. Bourgault and R. Sparling (Leiden, UK, 2013), 345.

94. D. J. Womersley, "The Historical Writings of William Robertson," *Journal of the History of Ideas* 47 (1986): 497–506; J. Smitten, "Impartiality in Robertson's *History of America*," *Eighteenth-Century Studies* 19 (1985): 56; E. T. Bannet, *Eighteenth-Century Manners of Reading: Print Culture and Popular Instruction in the Anglophone Atlantic World* (Cambridge, 2018).

95. J. R. Raven, "Viscount Townshend and the Cambridge Prize for Trade Theory, 1754–1756," *Historical Journal* 28 (1985): 535–55.

96. J. M. Black, *Geographies of an Imperial Power: The British World, 1688–1815* (Bloomington, IN, 2018).

97. E. C. Mossner and H. Ranson, "Hume and the 'Conspiracy of the Booksellers': The Publication and Early Fortunes of *The History of England*," *Studies in English* 29 (1950): 162–82.

98. G. Abbattista, *Commercio, Colonie e Impero alla vigitia della Rivoluzione Americana. John Campbell publicist e storico nell' Inghilterra del sec XVIII* (Florence, 1990).

99. S. Doree, "Nathaniel Salmon: Hertfordshire's Neglected Historian," in *Hertfordshire in History*, ed. D. Jones-Baker (Hertford, 1991), 205–22.

100. P. Morant, *The History and Antiquities of the County of Essex* (London, 1768), 1:i; C. E. Cobbold, "The Writing of Essex County History, c. 1600–1768," *Essex Journal* 8 (1973): 2–10.

101. W. Gibson, "John Trusler and the Sermon Culture of Late Eighteenth Century England," *Journal of Ecclesiastical History* 66 (2015): 302–19.

102. J. Trusler, *A List of Books Published by the Revd Dr Trusler at the Literary Press, 62 Wardour Street, London* (London, 1790).

103. Lewis Walpole Library, Yale University, Ms 71, manuscript autobiography of John Trusler, ff. 221, 215, 403, 405, 421. Trusler acknowledged that bookselling was not an easy profession, writing, "The man who makes a shoe is sure of his wages—the man who writes a play or a book is never sure of anything but the snarling of the critics," manuscript autobiography of John Trusler, f. 162.

104. Manuscript autobiography of John Trusler, f. 1.

105. J. C. Beasley, "Portraits of a Monster: Robert Walpole and Early English Prose Fiction," *Eighteenth-Century Studies* 14 (Summer 1981): 406–31; C. Ryskamp, "The First Illustrations to *John Gilpin*," *Notes and Queries* 251 (2006): 211.

106. L. F. Warren, "History-as-Literature and the Narrative Structure of Henry Fielding," *Clio* 1, no. 9 (Autumn 1979): 99–109.

107. H. Fielding, *The Works of Henry Fielding*, 10 vols. (London, 1784), 4:101, 149.

108. Fielding, *Works*, 4:147.

109. M. Wild, "Revisiting Christopher Smart's *Midwife*: Alexander the Great and the Terrible Old Lady," *British Journal for Eighteenth-Century Studies* 27 (2004): 279–92.

110. H. Fielding, *The True Patriot*, ed. M. A. Locke (London, 1965), 23.

111. H. Snyder, "David Jones, Augustan Historian and Pioneer English Annalist," *Huntington Library Quarterly* 44 (1980): 11–26.

112. For his authorship of this anonymous piece, see H. Snyder, "Daniel Defoe, Arthur Maynwaring, Robert Walpole and Abel Boyer," *Huntington Library Quarterly* 33 (1969–70): 148.

113. I. Haywood, *The Making of History: A Study of the Literary Forgeries of James Macpherson and Thomas Chatterton in Relation to Eighteenth-Century Ideas of History and Fiction* (London, 1986).

114. Verse on South Sea Bubble, 1720, Alnwick, Northumberland papers, letters, vol. 114.

115. N. Aston, "Burke and the Conspiratorial Origins of the French Revolution: Some Anglo-French Resemblances," in *Conspiracies and Conspiracy Theory in Early Modern Europe: From the Waldensians to the French Revolution*, ed. B. Coward and J. Swann (Aldershot, UK, 2004): 213–33.

116. S. Valladares, *Staging the Peninsular War: English Theatres 1807–1815* (Farnham, UK, 2015).

117. J. Hampton, *Reflections on Ancient and Modern History* (Oxford, 1746), 25.

118. Anon., *A True and Faithful Narrative of Oliver Cromwell's Compact with the Devil* (London, 1710); L. Echard, *History of England*, 2:712–13.

119. W. Stephens, *A Thanksgiving Sermon* (London, 1696): 15–26.

120. Hampton, *Reflections*, 26.

121. *Craftsman*, December 30, 1726; February 17 and 20, 1727; March 6 and 24, 1727.

122. *The Post-Man and the Historical Account*, November 6, 1722.

123. J. C. Hilson, "Hume: the Historian as Man of Feeling," in *Augustan Worlds*, ed. J. C. Hilson, M. M. B. Jones, and J. R. Watson (Leicester, UK, 1978), 205–22.

124. J. Richetti, *The English Novel in History, 1700–1780* (London, 1998).

125. M. Baker, "Roubiliac's Argyll Monument and the Interpretation of Eighteenth-Century Sculptors' Designs," *Burlington Magazine* 134 (1992): 785–97.

126. J. Andrews, *Letters to a Young Gentleman* (London, 1784), 126–27.

THREE

A HISTORICAL WORLD OF PARTISAN STRIFE

The Early Eighteenth Century

THE GLORIOUS REVOLUTION, THE REVOLUTION SETTLEMENT, the Hanoverian Succession, and the defense of all three against Jacobitism forced an engagement with the relationship between the present and the past, just as the Act of Union did in Scotland. Increased freedom of speech and publication, and their identification with Englishness,[1] ensured both the opportunity and need to present the past, addressing issues and using genres employed in earlier decades.[2] Recent events were the most significant source of dispute as they were most readily relevant to current issues.[3]

CONTESTING THE REVOLUTION SETTLEMENT

The varied character and tone of partisanship was indicated by *State-Amusements, Serious and Hypocritical, fully exemplified in the abdication of King James the Second* (1711). This work claimed to have been published by the "booksellers of London and Westminster" and appears to have been evasive about its origins, since its contents were intended to be a source of serious embarrassment to a number of leading people. The first dozen pages briefly described the reign of James II (1685–88) with a distinctly Whiggish tone. The intention of the publication was to expose the fawning collusion of some with the tyrannical king. The author claimed that the king, during his reign, had received nearly seven hundred petitions and addresses from various bodies, most of which were written in the most "extravagant" language.[4] An example of these was reproduced in full in the form of an address from the town of Scarborough on the

83

occasion of James II's proclamation of the first Declaration of Indulgence in 1687. It referred to the king's reign as "perfection," claimed that the town "thanked heaven" for the king's "patrimony of immortal happiness," and continued in long and exaggerated phrases. The town hoped for a male heir for James and described the declaration as a "Magna Carta" to "reasonable" creatures, itself an annexation of history to current political purposes. The author of *State-Amusements* called the petition an "artful amusement."[5]

There followed a list of the *London Gazette* entries relating to the confinement of Queen Mary of Modena (second wife to James II) and the birth of James Edward, Prince of Wales in June 1688, by 1711 "James III" according to the Jacobites. Much of this list was taken up with the congratulatory addresses from foreign envoys who called on the king and queen with their messages. At the end of the section was the list of those peers and officeholders who had signed James II's "deposition" regarding the birth of the Prince of Wales. The declaration was made on November 1, 1688, when William of Orange's invasion was imminent. Its purpose was to dispel the growing rumors and gossip that James Edward was a changeling, or substitute baby, intruded into the birth chamber in a warming pan to ensure that Queen Mary had a healthy child, the queen having previously produced stillborn children. The statement was signed by those who were witnesses to the birth of the child. The list ran to three pages. Many of the peers listed were among those who welcomed William of Orange and later participated in the Convention Parliament that offered him and his wife, Mary (elder daughter of James's first, and Protestant, marriage), the throne in 1689 and then held office under him.

State-Amusements also published a "list of names of the persons of both universities who wrote congratulatory poems in Latin and English on the birth of the Prince of Wales in the year 1688." This was a roll call of some of the men who had become the most distinguished peers, clergy, lawyers, and politicians of the later reigns. The list of names covered eight pages. Among the Oxford poets were Albemarle Bertie (later a Whig MP), Richard Willis and John Wynne (later Whig bishops), Christopher Codrington (the Whig plantation owner), Samuel Wesley (father of John and Charles Wesley), and Edmund Chishull. Those from Cambridge included Humphrey Gower (who opposed the Nonjurors) and such leading clergy and politicians as George Stanhope, Lancelot Manning, John Colbatch, Edward Carteret, Edward Bathurst, and Edmund Keene. That both Oxford and Cambridge had been put under heavy pressure by James to produce the customary collections of congratulatory poems and that most contributors had done so with considerable reservation was not mentioned. The volume concluded with an advertisement for *A Pocket Companion for Members of Parliament; containing an authentick list of all the names of members of each parliament from the year 1640, to the Restoration of Charles the Second: With a correct list of the present House of Lords and Commons by which the reader (by comparing men and things) may readily find who has and who has not chang'd the principles of his Ancestors.* The purpose of the work was to embarrass those who in 1685–88 had reached an accommodation with James II and to point out that some of these were the same people who, after the Glorious Revolution of 1688–89, supported the new regime of William and Mary and Anne. This was the hypocrisy referred to in the title.

The publication of *State-Amusements, Serious and Hypocritical* was stimulated by a number of circumstances. It came out a year after Henry Sacheverell's trial, which underlined some of the problems with holding apparently contradictory political views. Sacheverell's paradoxical position seemed to have been that the revolution of 1688–89 was of dubious morality and legality but that Queen Anne legitimately held the throne. Secondly, it was produced at a time when identifying shifting opinions and reversals of principles had become almost an historical cottage industry. A considerable amount of writers' energy went into claiming that one or other person had previously held opinions diametrically opposed to their current views. An example was Gilbert Burnet who in 1711–14 was, with some reason, repeatedly accused of changing his position on the issue of obedience to the monarch[6] from the 1670s. There were also those clergy who had attended James, Duke of Monmouth, an unsuccessful rebel against James II, on the scaffold in June 1685 and urged him to denounce resistance to the monarch, including Bishops Thomas Ken and Francis Turner, who later defied James II and stood trial themselves in 1688 for their passive resistance to him.

Such an instance of exposing a change of principles was the case of Offspring Blackall. In 1709, Blackall, the new Tory bishop of Exeter, preached before Queen Anne, arguing that civil power came immediately from God and that sovereigns were responsible only to God: "There is no power but of God." Rulers were ministers of God, and "none upon earth had the right to question or resist them."[7] The sermon surprised its listeners because of the apparent reversal of a position held earlier by Blackall. In 1704, at St. Dunstan's Church, London, in a sermon on the queen's accession, titled *The Subject's Duty*, Blackall had advanced a different view. Then he had said government had been established by God from whom its authority was derived, but the exercise of this authority and the type of government were left to mankind. Blackall argued that in England the subject owed obedience to the Crown in Parliament. Indeed, Blackall had explicitly claimed as his objective "to give ease and satisfaction to the consciences of those" who had doubts and scruples about the succession of Queen Anne. Blackall concluded that the Act of Succession established by the revolution of 1689 was "valid and binding."[8] Such a moderate Whig position had been excoriated as Lockean republicanism in *An Essay upon Government: wherein the Republican schemes reviv'd by Mr Locke, Dr Blackall etc are fairly considered and refuted* and the less reasonable *Dr Blackall's Offspring*, both published in 1705.

Blackall may well have felt he was being encouraged to take a High Church position by his appointment to the diocese of Exeter in 1707 by Anne, who had followed Archbishop Sharp's advice and ignored her ministers in appointing him. Though Blackall was careful to avoid suggestions that the divinely instituted civil power implied a hereditary monarchy, with all that that suggested for the legitimacy of Queen Anne's position, many saw that Blackall had altered his ground to views that struck at the heart of the legitimacy of the Glorious Revolution and the principles of government founded in 1689. This sparked a furious pamphlet war between Blackall and Benjamin Hoadly.[9] Catching people out on their apparent inconsistencies encouraged a searching of recent history and its contesting. There were also complaints in the opposite direction: Whig writers commented on how many Tories had been happy to get rid of James but were now chafing at the consequences.

Such issues were serious because of context and ideology. Moreover, the idiom of national threat lent itself to a moral approach. A clear religious theme was seen with many other writers. Religion was a key element in national history and identity, the two being closely linked, while the point of history was demonstrated by the need to show that it offered evidence of the requirement for eternal vigilance. The feeling that the national position, its constitution, liberty, international security, and religion were all under threat accounts for the presentation of history's didactic purpose by Richard Rolt (see chap. 6), John Wesley (see chap. 7), and other writers. History could serve to reveal the threats challenging the nation and the fate that would befall the people if vigilance was lost and Providence was defied. Struggle was a central theme: struggle against vice, both international and domestic, political and religious. Liberty and religion seemed to be dependent upon the moral caliber of the people, and this caliber was threatened by subversion encouraged by poor governance. The Revolution Settlement was no more than a stage upon the road, as the Glorious Revolution of 1688–89, a testament to divine favor, had to be defended, not least if the country wished to be ensured the support of Providence. This defensiveness accorded with the belief that Anglo-Saxon liberties had been overthrown by the Norman Conquest in 1066.

The embarrassment of some people about their own commemorations or their forebears' role in past historical events was not simply a political matter. Religious groups were also vulnerable to discussion. Principal among these were those Protestant Dissenters who'd embraced James's Declaration of Indulgence and were persuaded to support him. Some Dissenters' narrative of the revolution was that they had been staunch supporters of the resistance to James and that their reward for their role in getting rid of him had come in the form of the Toleration Act. There was certainly evidence of strong support by Dissenters against the king, but this was not the whole picture. There were Dissenters who moved to support James when he wooed them in 1687–88. The suggestion that large numbers of provincial Dissenters had been drawn to James and especially those from the Dissenters' heartland of the West Country was damaging, which was why the "Taunton Letters," Tory propaganda of 1701, were so potentially explosive. They had many secrets to keep from the Taunton electors, including the secret support of James II by some Dissenters and the involvement of Whigs in the plots against William III. The "Exeter Queries" were malicious questions that suggested that

Dissenters shared an interest with Catholics and had collaborated with them.[10] In this way, allegation and satire could become history and present the past for a popular readership. Such local rifts and resonances, most carrying forward seventeenth-century issues,[11] contributed greatly to the continually echoing nature of historical controversy.

Works on local history also provided much that was relevant to the general narrative.[12] Thus, the text of Sir Henry Chauncy's *Historical Antiquities of Hertfordshire* (1700) began with a bold statement: "When the Saxons had subdued the Britains [*sic*], and made themselves masters of this land, they endeavoured to extinguish the religion, laws, and language of the ancient inhabitants; therefore destroyed all marks of antiquity that nothing might remain, which could discover to the people of future ages, that any other but themselves were the first inhabitants of this country; they gave new names to all towns, villages and other places."[13] This represented a true "death of history," to use a later term,[14] and one that Chauncy could seek to overcome by his work on antiquities. He was also very critical of the harshness of Norman conquest and rule, his language echoing that of Jacobite propaganda: the Normans were condemned for "continually load[ing] the people with heavy taxes, that they might have so much business to get their living, they might not be able to rebel."[15] Thus introduced to the subject, the reader could consider the lengthy explanation of the feudal system.

Alongside new works on local history came the republication of older works that both reflected interest in such history and also threw light on national topics. In 1689 appeared *London's Flames Reviv'd: or, an account of the several informations exhibited to a committee appointed by Parliament, September the 25th 1666. . . . By all which it appears that the said fires were contrived, and carried on by the Papists.*

At a different scale, both chronological and geographical, histories of England were an important format for the partisan engagement with the past. Alongside new works, there were newly published ones. In particular, although finished in the 1670s, Clarendon's *History of the Rebellion and Civil Wars* was published in 1702–4. From a different political perspective, Thomas Lediard (1685–1743), a writer, surveyor, and diplomatic agent, not only produced a continuation of Paul de Rapin-Thoyras's history of England, a Whiggish work, but also *The Naval History of England*

(1735) and a life of John, 1st Duke of Marlborough (1736). The last, which claimed to draw on manuscript sources, criticized Marlborough's dismissal by the Tories in 1711, while the former, covering the period from 1066, presented the revival of naval success after the Glorious Revolution as looking back to a national tradition. History also proved particularly suitable for political satire, as with John Arbuthnot's *History of John Bull* (1712).

LAURENCE ECHARD

National history provided a way to give a longer perspective to the discussion of more recent politics and also a way to make views on the latter appear more authoritative. Moreover, national history attracted those who were already active in other fields. Laurence Echard (1672–1730) was a prime example. Graduating from Cambridge, he published geographical works, before producing a major and successful study, *The Roman History from the Building of the City to the Perfect Settlement of the Empire by Augustus* (1695), which had gone into ten editions by 1734, delivering an easy narrative that provided convenient morality and favored Caesar and Augustus at the expense of the tribunes.[16] Echard followed on with an abridgement of Sir Walter Raleigh's *History of the World*, and with a general ecclesiastical history, before publishing a three-volume history of England, the first of which, covering to 1625, was dedicated to a prominent Tory, James, Duke of Ormonde, while the second and third, tracing up to 1689, published in 1718, were dedicated to George I. This dedication, which earned the clergyman, a moderate Tory, three hundred pounds from the king and two additional clerical livings, offered a paean to George:

> It would have been improper to have dedicated a work of this nature to a prince of Your Majesty's great knowledge, experience and courage, were not the History filled with so many remarkable events, as are sufficient to add wisdom to the most knowing, information to the most experienced, and caution to the most valiant Prince that ever wore a Crown.
>
> England in an especial manner has been such a mighty and distinct scene of action, in the latter ages of the world, that during the compass of this History, there appears a greater variety of changes, governments and establishments; and there seems to have been more visible and signal

> instances of judgements and punishments, mercies and deliverances from above, than perhaps can be paralleled in any other part of the Western world.
>
> Accordingly we find, on the one hand, the most notorious examples of oppression, tyranny and bloodshed; and on the other, the most amiable instances of mildness and moderation... in short, such exalted degrees of virtue, and such monstrous deformities of vice; with such surprising consequences resulting from both, as may be sufficient to excite, and at the same time to satisfy, the highest curiosity, and afford matter for the noblest information and admonition.

Echard presented the Glorious Revolution as "wonderful and providential." The text of the book as a whole was very clear that "Divine Providence" played a key role, not least due to the lapsed nature of mankind.[17] The Restoration was described accordingly as "the most free and exalted expression of a delivered and overjoyed nation, triumphantly restored, without one drop of blood, by the All-merciful and powerful Hand of Heaven."[18]

PAUL DE RAPIN-THOYRAS

A key work, which, in Nicholas Tindal's translation, superseded Echard, was that of a foreigner who spent most of his life abroad. Paul de Rapin-Thoyras (1661–1725), a Huguenot (Protestant) born in France, came to London in 1686 after the Revocation of the Edict of Nantes the previous year, and, subsequently, landed with William of Orange at Torbay as part of his invasion force in 1688. Fighting for William in Ireland, he was later wounded. Living at The Hague in the early eighteenth century, Rapin-Thoyras wrote a history of England, which was published in ten volumes between 1723 and 1725. Written in French, this history was essentially designed to present England, past and present, for foreigners and did so by seeing a standard Aristotelian tension between popular privileges and Crown prerogatives, a tension that, at its best, produced a balance that guaranteed liberty. The Saxon witan and the post-1688 Parliament were presented as the prime instances of this balance, and there was a ready reading, and forward and back, from one to the other.[19]

Rapin-Thoyras's work was also very influential in England, where, although there were significant tensions over history between Whig writers,[20] it served as a staple of Whig history, once it appeared in a translated edition in 1725–31, a second following in 1732–33, and a third in 1743. There were also continuations. The first, published in 1734, was by David Durand, a Huguenot cleric in London, but was written in French. This was followed by the first English continuation, that by Lediard, published in 1737, and then, in 1744–45, by a two-volume continuation covering 1688–1727 by the translator Nicholas Tindal (1687–1774). Subsequently, Tindal's Rapin-Thoyras appeared in an *Abridgement* (1747) and a *Summary* (1751).

Tindal was an Anglican clergyman who also produced a *History of Essex* (1732) and *A Guide to Classical Learning* (1764).[21] He placed his work on Rapin-Thoyras carefully, dedicating the translation to Frederick, Prince of Wales, and the *Continuation* to Frederick's brother, William, Duke of Cumberland. The dedication to Frederick claimed that the work would be useful to a future king. Prefiguring Bolingbroke's presentation of the Patriot King, a clear prospectus was outlined:

> Here then, as from a faithful monitor, uninfluenced by hopes or fears, Your Royal Highness will learn, in general, that to a prince nothing is so pernicious as flattery; nothing so valuable as truth: that proportionable to his people's liberty and happiness will be his glory and strength: that true valour consists not in destroying, but protecting mankind; not in conquering kingdoms, but defending them from violence: that a prince's most secret counsels, motives and pursuits, will probably one day be published and rigorously judged; and, however flattered whilst living, yet when dead, he will be treated as his actions have deserved, with honour or reproach, with veneration or contempt.
>
> More particularly, Your Royal Highness will here perceive, that foreign acquisitions and conquests were generally fatal to England; all increase of empire burdensome to her, except that of the Ocean, which can never be too extensive, as it enlarges and protects her trade, the principal fountain of her riches and grandeur.
>
> But above all, you will here see the origin and nature of our excellent constitution, where the prerogatives of the Crown, and privileges of the subject are so happily proportioned, that the King and the People are inseparably united in the same interests and views. You will observe that this Union, though talked of by even the most arbitrary princes with respect to their subjects, is peculiar to the English monarchy, and the most solid foundation of the Sovereign's glory, and the people's happiness.

Accordingly, you will here constantly find, that in the reigns where this union was cultivated, the kingdom flourished, and the prince was glorious, powerful, trusted, beloved. On the contrary, when, by an arbitrary disposition, or evil counsels, it was interrupted, the constitution languished, mutual confidence vanished, distrust, jealousy, discord arose; and when entirely broken, as was unfortunately sometimes the case, confusion and civil wars ensued.[22]

Rapin's work sought to balance views, as he did in the account of Anglo-Scottish and Anglo-French medieval conflicts. This was an issue he discussed in the preface as he also considered the problems of writing the history of the Anglo-Saxons: "the History of the Anglo-Saxons being like a vast forest, where the traveller, with great difficulty, finds a few narrow paths to guide his wandering steps."[23] The significance of the book encouraged criticism, as with the anonymous *Defence of English History Against the Misrepresentations of M. de Rapin-Thoyras* (1734).[24] However, for a generation, Rapin-Thoyras apparently set the benchmark for Whig history. It was cited widely, for example by Deering in his 1751 history of Nottingham.[25]

Benchmarks might inhabit library shelves, but, in practice, there were various strands in Whig history, not least because of rivalries, tensions, and differing interests, whether political, religious, generational, or personal. Thus, the historical works associated with the Patriot opposition to the Walpole regime moved from Bolingbroke's essentially political arguments in the late 1720s to a more cultural critique in the late 1730s. The latter focused on Frederick, Prince of Wales, and linked to an imaginative engagement with national myths and history, an engagement that saw interest in the reign of Elizabeth I as well as what has been termed a Patriot Gothic.[26]

GEORGE LYTTELTON

Alongside the formal histories, such as those of Echard and Rapin-Thoyras, there was much discussion of history in other works. A classic instance was the early work of George Lyttelton, a politician who later published a formal work: *The History of the Life of Henry the Second, and of the Age in which he lived, in five books: to which is prefixed a History of the Revolutions of England from the Death of Edward the Confessor to the Birth of Henry the Second* (1767). Lyttelton (1709–73), the Oxford-educated eldest son of a landowner, Sir Thomas Lyttelton, was interested in history from early on, writing a manuscript "Observations on the Reign and Character of Queen Elizabeth" in 1730. In 1735, Lyttelton published *Letters from a Persian in England to his friends at Isaphan* (1735) and became an MP. In the *Letters*, there was a lengthy account of English history, one prefaced by a complaint about the historians: "Past transactions are so variously related, and with such a mixture of prejudice on both sides." Lyttelton noted that they differed most in the ancient power of the Crown and that of the Parliament. "The celebrated Gothic Government" was discussed, as well as its role in producing a Saxon system of limited royal power. This is then presented as surviving the Norman Conquest only for a division to open up between the "nobles" and "the People," with the former a burden to the latter. The reign of Elizabeth is greatly praised with the government then coming "to an equal balance, which is the true perfection of it." An organic account was offered: "She was the head of this well-proportioned body, and supremely directed all its motions." In contrast, James I sought to make himself "absolute" and to do so began "a struggle for power with his people" in which he exploited luxury to sap the spirit of the latter. Charles I continued James's "designs," governing "as despotically as the Sophi [ruler] of Persia." The reaction led to the Civil War, only for an eventual restoration of a sickly monarchy. In turn, as a result of the Glorious Revolution, "the government was settled on a new foundation, agreeable to the ancient Saxon principles from which it had declined." Progress was discerned by Lyttelton: "Thou wilt therefore observe this difference between the government in the reign of Queen Elizabeth, and the state of it since the Revolution; that Elizabeth chose to rule by Parliaments, from the goodness of her understanding; but princes now are forced to do so from necessity; because all expedients of governing without them are manifestly impracticable."[27] An opposition Whig and ally of William Pitt the Elder, Lyttelton was part of the reconfiguration of Whig politics from 1744, becoming an officeholder until 1756 when he was promoted to the Lords. It is frequently problematic to draw close links between political allegiances and historical arguments, but Lyttelton's arguments represented a bridge from the support, in the seventeenth century, for the Ancient Constitution and Elizabeth I, to the development in the latter half of the century of a renewed medievalism. The latter was, in part, a product of the broadening out of distinct and competing partisan narratives of national history in the 1750s and 1760s into a reconciled national account that encompassed the range of most political opinion, even though there were still differences on matters of historical interpretation, such as the character of Richard III or the relationship between Elizabeth and Mary, Queen of Scots.

Aside from politics and the constitution, another major aspect of controversy in this period was provided by the tension between Churchmen and freethinkers. This tension was seen in the consideration of classical texts and the history of the Reformation, as well as in the discussion of the current ecclesiastical situation.[28] This theme is discussed in chapter 5. There was an extensive prehistory for later prominent works, such as David Hume's *Natural History of Religion* (1758). The same was true with disputes between clerics, such as the Bangorian Controversy that was initiated in 1717 when Benjamin Hoadly, bishop of Bangor (and Whig cleric committed to perpetual motion, at least upward for himself), claimed that no type of church establishment rested on scriptural authority, a Whig position that challenged the current linkage of church and state. The controversy saw history deployed in the shape of accounts of Christianity, the Church, and the Reformation.[29]

JOURNALISM

In the meanwhile, the more conventional interplay of history and journalism was another aspect of the period. Pamphlets commented on recent events, as with William Pulteney's *An Answer to one part of a late infamous libel, entitled, Remarks on the Craftsman's Vindication of his two honourable Patrons* (1731), a work that included much discussion of the 1710s. The newspapers themselves made frequent reference to history across a wide range. The classics could be readily deployed. Thus, the *Plain Dealer* of December 7, 1724, announced: "While, like the provinces of the declining Empire of Old Rome, we are fretting, and disturbing ourselves ... the Goths are at our gate.... There seems to be rising near us, that NORTHERN LYON, which has, so often, been prophesied of" (a reference to Peter the Great of Russia). The paper pressed on to argue that past success was no guarantee to the future, with history raided widely to make the point.

The progovernment *Free Briton* of February 11, 1731, replied to the *Craftsman*'s citation of Elizabeth I in favor of isolationism by drawing attention to her willingness to help the Dutch, "in their struggles for Liberty," as she had indeed done from 1585. Conversely, the paper pointed out that James I was "covered with shame for withholding his assistance" to the Palatinate in the early stages of the Thirty Years' War (1618–48), a reiteration of an argument made at the time. The *Craftsman* took a different view of Elizabeth, noting her requirement that England, under the Treaty of Nonsuch of 1585, be put in control of "cautionary towns" so as to control Dutch conduct and adding: "It seems she did not think herself obliged to relieve other states, however distressed, by impoverishing her own; or that the people of this kingdom ought to be mere Knight-Errands, and fight everybody's battles at their own expense."

Newspapers raised wider questions about ideological suppositions, suppositions that were located in both past and present. The *Craftsman* of November 30, 1728, commented: "As I am ready to allow that is scarce possible for a free state to subsist under a Popish Head, so it is plain that a people may lose their liberties under a Protestant Prince. The King of Denmark, for instance, is a very good Protestant; and yet his People are slaves," a reference back to changes made in the seventeenth century and one made more relevant by Britain and Denmark being allies. However, on the whole, it was the standard religious, or rather, sectarian, approach that was taken. Thus, on November 8, 1729, *The Weekly Journal: or, The British Gazetteer* reported the epilogue spoken when the New Theatre was opened in Goodman's Fields, London:

> When Britain first from monkish bondage broke,
> And shook off Rome's imperious, galling yoke,
> When truth and reason were no longer chained,
> In Popish fetters, and by Priests explained,
> Then wit and learning graced our happy Isle.

The hammer-and-tongs newspaper writing scarcely matched the elite critical views on historiography that have attracted much attention.[30] There might be a shared didactic purpose, but the tone was very different.

There was no sense that an exalted status was necessary to judge past "greatness." Instead, the press, like such popular writers as Ralph and Guthrie, emphasized the role of the judgment of the public.[31]

CONTENTIOUS ISSUES

That judgment was provided in another respect in the displays of historical commitment offered by popular commemorations, notably those of the restoration of Charles II in 1660 and of the birth of James III in 1688.[32] The former was a Tory one; the latter, Jacobite. The Whigs, in turn, had their own. Each side also hit at the commemorations by the other. Thus, James III was compared, for example, in *State Songs* in 1715–16, to Perkin Warbeck, an imposter as well as would-be usurper in 1491–96 under Henry VII. Doing this served to delegitimate James III and thus to strike at the Jacobite ideology of divine, legitimate, hereditary right. Popular commemorations were very much a public history that was national from the outset, rather than being international in the shape of an aspect of the broader Anglicization of a classical inheritance.[33]

One aspect of this national history was provided by its being used to respond to the debate between the "ancients" and the "moderns." As an aspect of an affirmation of national over cosmopolitan themes, the moderns came to prevail by midcentury, and historical works allegedly demonstrated this process.[34] It could serve to clarify the Reformation, the Glorious Revolution, or Britain's maritime rise.[35]

The use of history was more complex than suggested by some of the partisan discussion of the past. In emphasizing the moral choices of individuals and the role of Providence, the partisan discussion could underplay the role of circumstance and contingency in order to provide consistent heroes and villains. This point can be seen by contrasting the position of politicians in and out of office. The Whigs, for example, presented themselves as consistently opposed to France during the reigns of James II, William III, and Anne and typecast the Tories as insufficiently stalwart against France. However, the Whigs had taken money from Louis XIV during the Exclusion Crisis of 1679–81 and were to ally closely with France in 1716–31.[36] Views on international relations, indeed, varied. This point extended to contrasting comments on which states and rulers in the past might have been a threat to the balance of power.[37]

In such a context of unfixed rivalry and varying consequences, politicians—or, at least, their polemicists—maneuvered in part through the use of political rhetoric and notably by means of historical examples, which helped to assert identity and to define national interest accordingly, interest that was both political and religious.[38] This process was regarded as important due to the undoubted weight placed upon the influence of the past. Thus, the *Evening Journal* of December 23, 1727, commented: "The dominion of custom is so great over the mind of men that one may venture to say, it hardly leaves them liberty to the thought or freedom to the will.... The generality of people do not consider where they are going, but follow the paths where others have gone before them."

There was a particularly bitter debate over the Peace of Utrecht of 1713, a peace with France made by a Tory ministry that was used by the Whigs, at the time and subsequently, who had supported the War of the Spanish Succession (in which Britain was involved during 1702–13), in order to attack the Tories. In his *The Memoirs of the Life and Negotiations of Sir William Temple, Containing the most Important Occurrences, and the most Secret Springs of Affairs in Christendom, from the year 1665 to the year 1681. With an Account of Sir William Temple's Writings* (1714), Abel Boyer, by then a Whig partisan, used his criticism of Charles II to attack the Tory ministry of 1710–14, arguing a close link between the Secret Treaty of Dover in 1670 and the Peace of Utrecht.[39] The claim of betrayal of Britain's allies and of the Hanoverian Succession was given resonance by suggesting a history of nefarious purposes, with the latter, in turn, employed in order to criticize government policy. This was counterbalanced by the Tory allegation—for example, by Jonathan Swift in *The Conduct of the Allies* (1711)—that the Whigs were excessively pro-Dutch.

The Peace of Utrecht was subsequently employed by the Tories and opposition Whigs in order to suggest that the Old Corps Whig alliance with France from 1716 to 1731 was hypocritical. Tobias Smollett, in the *Briton* of October 9, 1762, in the context of the peace preliminaries with

France at the end of the Seven Years' War, defended the Peace of Utrecht, writing of the Tories: "As soon as their adversaries [the Whigs] had overwhelmed them with ruin, and established their own influence about the throne [of George I], beyond all possibility of reverse, the Treaty of Utrecht, which they had branded as infamous and pernicious, they left unaltered and undisturbed; and instead of producing a fresh rupture in less than one year, it remained in full force very near thirty, a period of tranquillity almost unexampled in the annals of England, during which, she enjoyed, without interruption, every blessing which opulence and security could bestow."

In each case, there were accusations and defenses. In time, subsequent treaties were dragged into the equation and the rhetoric, notably those of Vienna (1725), Hanover (1725), Seville (1731), and Aix-la-Chapelle (1748). Each provided a resetting of the historical discussion.[40]

This argument rose to a facetious height when *Old England*, then the leading opposition essay paper, in its issue of February 8, 1752, turned the arguments of the prominent Whig philosopher, theorist, and office-holder John Locke (1632–1704), specifically his *Essay Concerning Human Understanding* (1689), against the Whig government of the Pelhams (Thomas, Duke of Newcastle, and his brother, Henry Pelham, the First Lord of the Treasury from 1743 to 1754) with reference to peacetime subsidy treaties to foreign powers, a policy the opposition and *Old England* strongly opposed:

> As the disapprobation of foreign subsidies has, we have seen, founded itself in the sense or understanding of Britain, it will demand our closest attention effectually, to counterveil these operations of nature, or, as Mr Locke would (for this purpose more conveniently) say, these prejudices of education. The structure we are here to raise for the public good will therefore find its basis in that great man's system of no innate ideas . . . the present purpose, which is to make us approve foreign politics, demands no more than that all the books which have been wrote, regarding the particular interests of this kingdom, should be burnt. Polity, History, and Geography, are all the offensive studies. . . . You observe all maxims of policy, all knowledge of men, of the trading interests, and of the advantage of our situation, are utterly lost and dead: For by the wholesome prohibition of speaking, writing, or printing . . . all dangerous communication between father and son, will be effectually prevented.[41]

This account reflected the opposition sense of foreign policy as unreal because it was based on a denial of the national interest. Such a denial was allegedly possible because corrupt self-interest was linked to an active attempt to mislead the public, and the rejection of the specific lessons of history and of the historical consciousness as a whole were presented as central to this malign project. Thus, history was seen both as the relationship of continuity within society and as a benign public project. These two elements were presented as a protection against the authoritarianism of government and against intellectual and institutional remodeling. This Tory paper therefore prefigured Burke's arguments at the time of the French Revolution.

Partisan historical writing was a deliberate source and means of embarrassment and attack. Historical writers used history as a means to prick hypocrisy and expose contemporary pretense. This had always been a function of historical writing and remained so. In his *Miscellanies* (1743), Henry Fielding included his engaging *A Journey from This World to the Next*. This drew on classical models and images to produce a series of loosely related stories in which a spirit-narrator introduced the reader to the moral reflections offered by transmigration. Indeed, metempsychosis proved a valuable satiric device, enabling Fielding to scour history (as he had done in his *Jonathan Wild*) in order to tilt at the universal ills of selfishness and self-regard and their focus in the distorting impact of ambition. Fielding used the work to highlight his theme of the corrupting nature of dishonesty and transformed the details of the historical sources, both in order to pursue his theme and so as to provide an eighteenth-century atmosphere.[42] Fielding had abandoned the stage due to the Licensing Act of 1737, a measure taken by the government to neuter criticism in the theater and one that hit the staging of politically controversial history.[43]

In the eighteenth century, with the widening of the Whig and Tory political divide and with a transition from armed conflict to the political pursuit of disputes, partisan historical writing found continuing energy, not least as figures moved into the past. For example, the reputation of William III proved a particularly significant issue given his role in the Glorious Revolution. Thus, on January 1, 1732, the *Weekly Register*, a London Whig paper, published "An answer to the infamous libel on the memory of the late King William, printed in *Fog's Journal* of Saturday last," an answer that included the justified claim that "he set a bound to the conquests of Lewis the Great" (that is, Louis XIV).

Political speeches frequently made reference to such historical points. Such speeches were not only delivered in Parliament, but were an aspect of charges by judges to grand juries as well as of assize sermons. In March 1744, at a time of justified anxiety about the possibility of invasion from France, the judge who gave the charge at the Grand Inquest in Weymouth expatiated on governmental lenience toward Catholics, adding, "therefore it is the more extraordinary that any of them should ever think of disturbing the peace of a government so indulgent but it is notorious to all the world and he was not afraid to say that it had ever been the restless principle of France to promote and encourage factions here as well as in all the countrys [sic] in Europe to carry on their own perfidious schemes, upon which topic he flourished away with great oratory."[44] Such oratory could also be frequently found on the printed page.

The varied means of discussing the past interacted. Thus, longer historical works sometimes appeared, in part, in newspapers. Sections of Gilbert Burnet's *History of My Own Time* (two volumes, 1723-34), a prominent Whig work (see chap. 4), were published in *Read's Weekly Journal*, a progovernment London newspaper, but the *History* was attacked in 1723-24 by *Mist's Weekly Journal*, the leading Tory paper, and also criticized in *Historical and Critical Remarks on Bishop Burnet's History of His Own Time* (1725), by the Jacobite Bevil Higgons (1670-1736). This criticism was countered in the Whig *London Journal* on January 30 and February 6, 1725, which led Higgons to a second edition in 1727 that rebutted the paper's defense of Burnet. Higgons also published *A Short View of the English History; with reflections on the reigns of the kings, their characters and manners, their succession to the throne; and all other remarkable incidents, to the Revolution, 1688* (1723), which refuted Burnet's claims of the Pretender's illegitimacy. As a reminder of the range of media across which history was asserted, Higgons was the author of *The Generous Conqueror* (1702), a play defending the Jacobite claim to the throne. The prosopography of historical writing was both complex and simple.

NOTES

1. D. Cressy, *Dangerous Talk: Scandalous, Seditious, and Treasonable Speech in Pre-Modern England* (Oxford, 2010).

2. K. Sharpe, *Rebranding Rule: The Restoration and Revolution Monarchy, 1660–1714* (New Haven, CT, 2013).

3. H. T. Dickinson, "The Eighteenth-Century Debate on the 'Glorious Revolution,'" *History* 61 (1976): 28–45.

4. *State-Amusements, serious and hypocritical, fully exemplified in the abdication of King James the Second* (London, 1711), 12.

5. *State-Amusements, serious and hypocritical*, 13–15.

6. *A Vindication of the Bishop of Salisbury and Passive Obedience, with Some Remarks upon a Speech which goes under his Lordship's Name* (London, 1710); *The Clergy and the Present Ministry Defended. Being a Letter to the Bishop of Salisbury, Occasioned by His Lordship's New Preface to His Pastoral Care* (London, 1713).

7. The sermon was published at the queen's command as *The Divine Institution of Magistracy and the Gracious Design of its Institution* (London, 1708).

8. O. Blackall, *The Subjects Duty, A Sermon preach'd at the Parish Church of St Dunstan in the West on ... March 8th 1704 being The Anniversary of Her Majesty's Accession to the throne* (London, 1709), 11.

9. W. Gibson, *Enlightenment Prelate: Benjamin Hoadly, 1676–1761* (Cambridge, 2004).

10. *The Exeter Queries* (London, 1701); W. Gibson, *Religion and the Enlightenment 1600–1800, Conflict and the Rise of Civic Humanism in Taunton* (Oxford, 2007).

11. P. D. Halliday, *Dismembering the Body Politic: Partisan Politics in England's Towns, 1650–1730* (Cambridge, 1998); W. Gibson, "English Provincial Engagement in Religious Debates: The Salisbury Quarrel of 1705–15," *Huntington Library Quarterly* 80 (2017): 21–45.

12. For background, see S. Mendyk, *Speculum Britanniae: Regional Study, Antiquarianism and Science in Britain to 1700* (Toronto, 1989).

13. Sir Henry Chauncy, *Historical Antiquities of Hertfordshire* (London, 1700), 1.

14. F. Fukuyama, "The End of History," *The National Interest* (Spring 1989): 2–18.

15. Chauncy, *Hertfordshire*, 9.

16. R. T. Ridley, "The Forgotten Historian: Laurence Echard and the first History of the Roman Republic," *Ancient Society* 27 (1996): 277–315.

17. Echard, *History*, II:1.

18. Echard, *History*, II:910.

19. H. R. Trevor-Roper, "A Huguenot Historian: Paul Rapin," in *Huguenots in Britain and their French background, 1550–1800*, ed. I. Scouloudi (1987), 3–19.

20. I. Kramnick, "Augustan Politics and English Historiography: The Debate on the English Past, 1730–35," *History and Theory* (1967): 33–56.

21. A. Shell, "Antiquarians, Local Politics and the Book Trade: The Publication of Philip Morant's *History of Colchester* (1748)," *The Library*, 6th ser., vol. 21 (1999): 223–46.

22. P. de Rapin-Thoyras, *History of England*, trans. Nicholas Tindal, vol. 1, 2nd ed.(London, 1732), dedication.

23. Rapin-Thoyras, *History of England*, iii.

24. For different views, see *Daily Gazetteer*, September 11, 1735, and, critically, *Craftsman*, January 10 and 31, 1736.

25. Deering, *Nottingham*, 241.

26. C. Gerrard, *The Patriot Opposition to Walpole: Politics, Poetry, and National Myth, 1725–1742* (Oxford, 1994).

27. G. Lyttelton, *Letters from a Persian in England*, 4th ed. (London, 1735), 179–200.

28. J. A. I. Champion, *The Pillars of Priestcraft Shaken: The Church of England and its Enemies 1660–1730* (Cambridge, 1992); S. Ellenzweig, *The Fringes of Belief: English Literature, Ancient Heresy and the Politics of Freethinking, 1660–1760* (Stanford, CA, 2008).

29. A. Starkie, *The Church of England and the Bangorian Controversy* (Woodbridge, UK, 2007).

30. J. Levine, *Humanism and History: Origins of Modern English Historiography* (Ithaca, NY, 1987); J. Levine, *The Battle of the Books: History and Literature in the Augustan Age* (Ithaca, NY, 1991).

31. Guthrie, *A General History of England* (1747), 2:i.

32. J. P. W. Rogers, "John Oldmixon in Bridgewater, 1716–30," *Somerset Archaeology and Natural History* 113 (1969): 93.

33. H. D. Weinbrot, *Britannia's Issue: The Issue of British Literature from Dryden to Ossian* (Cambridge, 1993).

34. D. Spadafora, *The Idea of Progress in Eighteenth-Century Britain* (New Haven, CT, 1990).

35. J. T. Burke, "The Iconography of the Enlightenment in English Art," *Australian Academy of the Humanities: Proceedings* 1 (1970): 55.

36. J. Duke-Evans, "The Political Theory and Practice of the English Commonwealthsmen, 1695–1725" (D.Phil. diss., Oxford, 1980), 150.

37. Anon., *The Balance of Europe* (London, 1711), 5, regarding Charles V.

38. T. Claydon and I. McBride, eds., *Protestantism and National Identity: Britain and Ireland c. 1655–c. 1850* (Cambridge, 1998).

39. G. C. Gibbs, "Abel Boyer 1710–15: A 'French Dog' Seeks New Masters," *Proceedings of the Huguenot Society* 28 (2005): 395.

40. Anon., *French Influence upon English Counsels Demonstrated from an Impartial Examination of our Measures for Twenty Years Past* (London, 1740); J. Black, *Debating Foreign Policy in Eighteenth-Century Britain* (Farnham, UK, 2011), 94–96.

41. *Old England*, February 8, 1752.

42. H. Fielding, *Miscellanies*, vol. 2, ed. B. Goldgar and H. Amory (Oxford, 1993).

43. R. D. Hume, *Henry Fielding and the London Theatre, 1728–1737* (Oxford, 1988).

44. Richard Tucker to his brother John, an opposition Whig MP, March 10, 1744, Bod. MS. Don. C. 107 fol. 17.

FOUR

CONTRASTING APPROACHES

Burnet and Astell

BURNET AND THE DEFENSE OF A NEW ORDER

One of the themes in this book is the wide range of historical writing in the eighteenth century. At the "top end" of the market for historical publications were the works of Gilbert Burnet (1643–1715), including his *History of the Reformation* (three volumes, 1679, 1681, 1715), a work of national importance, for which both houses of Parliament voted him thanks. It was made more accessible from 1728 by the publication of a series of abridged versions in single volumes. The work remained in print well into the nineteenth century. Besides *Foxe's Book of Martyrs*, Burnet's *History of the Reformation* established the dominant interpretation of the religious history of the sixteenth century.[1] As such, it was a powerful force in eighteenth-century thought.

Taken together with Burnet's other writing, principally biographical studies of Mary II (the wife of William III), John, Earl of Rochester, and others, the *History of the Reformation* presents an implicit historical argument for the contract theory of government. In the *History of the Reformation*, Burnet suggested that the people as a whole, when acting in unity, could legitimately claim a measure of sovereignty and thus defend the new order after 1689. Correspondingly, Burnet's other work addressed something of the duties and obligations of rulers and leaders in society. As a body of work, Burnet's historical writing argued for principles of religious tolerance and moderation, which, as much as political principles, were the guarantees of liberty.

Burnet's third volume of the *History of the Reformation* came soon after the publication of the *Ecclesiastical History of Great Britain* (two volumes, 1708, 1714), by the Nonjuror Jeremy Collier (1650–1726), which claimed that the Church was a divine institution as much as the state and that the two were independent. This was standard Tory High Church fare, but Collier's well-referenced work was much more polemical: he defended monasticism, softened the image of Mary I (the persecutor of Foxe's *Book of Martyrs*), and claimed to see much in common between the Church of England and Roman Catholicism. Collier also attacked Luther and Calvin, the founders of Continental Protestantism. Contemporaries regarded Collier's goal as arguing for the succession of the Catholic Old Pretender, James III, and as criticizing the Hanoverians. Best known today for his attack on the nature of contemporary English drama, which he compared unfavorably with that of ancient Greece and Rome, Collier's works also included *The Great Historical, Geographical, Genealogical, and Poetical Dictionary* (1701, 1705), which was partly a translation of an Italian work, and translations of the works of the Roman emperor Marcus Aurelius.

Burnet's third volume of the *History of the Reformation* reflected his delight at the Hanoverian succession of 1714. His trump card was the Providence that he claimed was evident in a long sequence of historical events, including Henry VIII's break with Rome, Mary I's foreshortened reign (1553–58), Elizabeth's successful reign, the Glorious Revolution, the Toleration Act, and the Hanoverian Succession. In response to Burnet, Collier defended himself from the claim that he had been too kind to Mary I and Mary, Queen of Scots, and charged Burnet with anti-Catholic bigotry.[2] But, helped by political success, and thus the nature of the governing system, it was Burnet whose history set the agenda for the coming years. In identifying Deism and unrestrained High Churchmanship as the problems for Anglicanism, he established the principal targets for Low Churchmen for the following three decades.

By 1678, Burnet had reached the view that resistance to the lawful monarch was justifiable. His *History of the Rights of Princes in the Disposing of Ecclesiastical Lands*, published in 1682, claimed that Catholics had lived peaceably with Protestants in England until the 1670s, when they became restless and provocative. The Popish Plot of 1678 strengthened Burnet's view of the historic danger from Catholicism.

Burnet viewed contemporary religious and political events from a European standpoint. This charged his providential view of history with a particular perspective: it was not simply in England that God endorsed and supported Protestantism; it was in Europe as a whole. The deliverance of England from the clutches of Catholicism was, to Burnet, part of a divine liberation of Europe, which saw Louis XIV pushed back by an alliance of Protestant powers. Burnet had an apocalyptic view of the struggle between Protestantism and Catholicism. The evidence that Catholicism was the false church was borne out in what Burnet saw as the persecution of its opponents. In his view, such persecution of Protestant Dissenters and such coercion, when practiced by the Convocation of the Church of England, placed High Church Anglicanism in the same mold as Catholicism,[3] a parallel made for very different ends than that offered by Collier.

Burnet's political testament, written when he was under threat from James II's government of kidnapping and trial for treason in 1687, is instructive. In it, Burnet clearly showed that he saw historical events in Europe and in England as part of the same providential process. He claimed that the "Roman authors have been my constant companions and I formed my mind by the frequent reading of them." From them, Burnet developed "a love of my country." More specifically, from rejecting the example of Thraseas (the Roman senator who openly defied Nero and appeared before the Senate to do so, only to be put on trial and executed), Burnet claimed that self-preservation, rather than a gallant death, was a reasonable form of action.[4]

Burnet sought, after 1688–89, to make the case that the Glorious Revolution was more than simply an ejection of James II, and, instead, a deeply rooted shift in both English and European history. On the one hand, Burnet saw events as divinely determined and God as the moving force of history so that the Reformation was a miraculous event, a key event in the workings of Providence, with the historian deploying a deus ex machina in the style of the opera. On the other hand, Burnet saw that he could shape events and could determine the outcome of political activity through his own writing and intervention. The resolution of this paradox was that God used him, and others, as instruments.

Part of God's "agenda" was to recover the Reformation from the Fall, again through human action, and the mining of history for analogies was a valuable support.[5] This approach prefigured, albeit to very different ends, the later political one that saw the Glorious Revolution and the Revolution Settlement as compromised by malign government and the corruption of society by luxury.

BURNET, NATIONHOOD, AND POPULAR CONCILIARITY

Burnet frequently wrote about "the people," the term he used to mean the nation as a whole. Burnet regarded the people as having a natural freedom; he referred early in the *History of the Reformation* to the way in which Henry VII's agents invaded the "liberties of the people," adding, "when ministers by the king's orders were condemned and executed for invading the liberties of the people under cover of the king's prerogative, it made the nation conclude that they should hereafter live secure under the protection of such a prince."[6]

Burnet drew on long-established ecclesiastical conciliar theory to underpin his understanding of the nature of "the people." Conciliar theory, based on the view that the Church as a whole was "the body of Christ," argued that the Church, as a body of all the faithful (and not just of the clergy), could speak for God and would be guided by divine wisdom. This corporate view of the nature of ecclesiastical authority was easily transferred by Burnet into the civil sphere, and gave validity to the idea of "the people." When acting as a whole, and without sectarian or partisan objectives, Burnet believed that the people of England acted with a specific authority, could claim to be sovereign, and could restrain temporal authorities, such as the monarch. This popular conciliar theory did not only apply to England. Burnet, in discussing Scotland and France, made clear that he took this to be a universal principle. In Scotland, for example, the "slavery" of the people under the Catholic influence of Mary, Queen of Scots, was especially reprehensible.[7] Conciliarism was also significant in the religious and political thought of the United States' founding.[8]

Nevertheless, Burnet did not endorse democracy as a system of government, for the people were subject to the sovereign. Burnet often referred to the people as "the king's people" and, under Mary and

Elizabeth, as "the queen's people."⁹ When monarchs ruled justly and properly, they were owed the affection and submission of the people. One of Burnet's measures of the legitimacy of the Reformation was its focus on, and advantage for, the people. In describing the publication of the English Bible in 1537, Burnet referred to "the people" six times in one paragraph: Thomas Cromwell exhorted the people not to dispute difficult passages; clergy were to instruct the people; the people were urged to undertake acts of charity; the people were to be taught the dangers of idolatry and the foolishness of relics; and the people were to be dissuaded from praying to saints. This rhetorical repetition was designed to show the providential character of the English Bible and the Reformation and that these were served and legitimized by the people. In April 1540, when Henry VIII sent a message to Parliament, Burnet emphasized that "there was nothing the king desired so much as an entire union" of his people in the issue of religion.[10]

Individuals and groups of people, however, could be led astray and, in discussing the rebellions that followed the beginning of the Dissolution of the Monasteries in 1536, notably the Pilgrimage of Grace, Burnet made clear that sectarianism and direct action by groups of people did not represent what he saw as "the people." This was in part because, when they acted singly or in smaller groups, men and women were easily manipulated and could not claim the sanction of divine conciliar legitimacy. Consequently, Burnet portrayed rebels as divided and often in disagreement with each other, to demonstrate that the absence of unanimity marked them as distinct and different from the people. In this, he saw resistance to the Reformation as analogous to the "deluded pilgrims" who were wrongly led by the superstitious claims of corrupt Catholic practices, such as relics and miracles and the claims of Catholics on behalf of transubstantiation.[11] To confront these challenges, messages had to be simplified, and one of the reasons why Henry VIII required all people to read the new litany in English was that this would lessen error and division.[12] Burnet saw the Dissolution of the Monasteries as a restoration of the Magna Carta (and thus of the Ancient Constitution), which had confirmed the property of the Church for "the purposes for which they were at first intended," rather than the ends to which the Church later turned them.[13]

Despite the historical principle of popular conciliarity, Burnet sometimes found himself in difficulty on the issue of the legitimacy of popular action. When it came to the "forwardness of the people" in destroying some images in churches "without authority" under the Protestant Edward VI (r. 1547–53), he claimed that they were following Mosaic injunctions. Burnet was prone to see the people through his own lenses so that, under Edward, "the people generally cried out for a Reformation, they despised the clergy and loved the new preachers."[14] When it came to Wyatt's rebellion of 1554 against Mary, Burnet argued that it lacked the unanimity required of a legitimate popular conciliar action and failed due to poor leadership.[15] Under Mary, Burnet conceded that people were led back to old ways, but, he claimed, the great majority soon came to be alienated by the cruelty meted out to Protestants, an approach that leaves unclear whether the persecution would have succeeded had it had more time. Burnet identified the people of England as concerned by foreign claims to authority, as well as home-grown persecution, especially when such foreign claims were contrary to the laws of England.[16]

The climax of Burnet's history of the Reformation was the succession of Elizabeth in 1558, which was repeatedly endorsed by his account of the joy and relief of the people. Elizabeth's standing was cemented into place by Burnet through her claims to govern in the interests of all the people and to have been married to her people at her coronation. In this, Elizabeth was a model of a good monarch, who "looked on her people as her children," wrote Burnet. The revision of *The Book of Common Prayer* set people at liberty, and she refused to "lay snares for her people" in the form of tests for heresy and loyalty, only requiring the Oath of Supremacy.[17]

THE RELIGIOUS OBLIGATIONS OF LEADERS

Burnet's view of the people as a repository of historical and national consciousness and a source of authority was complemented by the principle that leaders in society should employ religion and piety to inform their decision making. A society that lacked leadership that was pious and rooted in strong Protestant faith would become both corrupt and wayward. With this in mind, Burnet wrote two biographies that offered models for the right form of social leadership.[18] These were studies of John, Earl of Rochester, and of Matthew Hale, a judge, published in 1680 and 1682 respectively. Both exemplified the value and influence of personal faith on events and, therefore, on history.

Hale was a judge whose reputation rested principally on his ability to command respect from both Royalists and Parliamentarians between 1640 and 1670. Legal adviser to Thomas, Earl of Stafford, and Archbishop Laud, he was even rumored to be the counsel who was to represent Charles I at his trial had the king been prepared to cooperate with the legal process. Under the Commonwealth, Hale remained a judge who reformed the legal system as well as serving as an MP. Support for the Restoration in 1660 meant he was able to obtain the post of Chief Baron of the Exchequer and by 1671 was made Chief Justice of the King's Bench. Hale's legacy was principally that he believed in the impartiality of the law, and, perhaps more significantly for Burnet, Hale placed great emphasis on the English Common Law as the repository of the rights and liberties of the subject. Harking back to ideas about the Ancient Constitution, the Common Law enshrined the idea of rule by the consent of the people.

But Burnet's choice of Hale was designed to show how a man of piety was able to influence the events of his day. The centerpiece of Burnet's biography was Hale's religious conversion in 1629–30 so that he saw himself as an instrument of Providence. Burnet was clear that Hale hated religious division and protected Dissenters from the legal voiding of their marriages, which he considered a right of nature.

Rochester, a very different figure to Hale, as he grew ill, had turned to Burnet for comfort, having read his *History of the Reformation*, and the two men began a correspondence that convinced Rochester of how bad his former life had been.[19] Much of Burnet's biography of Rochester was taken up with an account of how he convinced him to abandon his immoral ways and embrace a life of faith. The account is almost catechetical in tone, with Burnet asking Rochester about his views on God, prayer, worship, and other matters, and generally Burnet supplied the answers for which the earl was searching on a number of topics.[20] Rochester came to the view that those who were convinced of the nature of

God and that he "governed the world," and also those who "acquiesced in His Providence," were the happiest men and had quiet consciences.[21]

When Rochester died, Burnet reviewed his life "with the part of an historian." He considered the "mischiefs" of the life that Rochester had led and their impact on "mankind and human societies." Burnet attacked the sort of dissolute character that Rochester had displayed and argued that such people could not be trusted or loved and that they corrupted others: "What influence [they have] on the nation as a whole is but too visible: how the bonds of nature, wedlock and all other relations are quite broken. Virtue is thought an antique piece of formality; and religion the effect of cowardice or knavery."[22]

Nature had exalted Rochester as an aristocrat, but he was debased by irreligion. Yet "he died a most exemplary penitent."[23] Historically, the lessons of Rochester's life and death were, for Burnet, bound up with the life of the nation. Rochester sought, in death, to make his experience one which Burnet could use for national repentance and reform; and he urged both Burnet and his chaplain, Robert Parsons, not to withhold accounts of his sins and misbehavior if it would help others to abandon their former ways. Rochester had come to recognize that, as a man of rank and status, he had a duty to provide leadership to his country. For Burnet, Rochester demonstrated that, historically, individuals and nations prospered when the leaders of society were pious and led their nations from a position of faith and religious zeal. God's revelation of himself to the poorest in society was designed to provide an alternative conduit through which, in a society in which its leaders were dissolute, they could learn the lessons of religion, but, for Burnet, the ideal society was one in which the king and nobles provided leadership and a moral example.

Burnet clearly regarded the leaders of society as under an obligation to follow "the hand of Providence." In his account of Robert Leighton, archbishop of Glasgow (1611–84), whom Burnet had known in his youth, he discussed Leighton's desire to resign his see and to retire from the world: he resigned as archbishop in 1674. Leighton felt that he was unsuccessful and had worked without achieving anything. Burnet however "thought the labouring without success was indeed a very great trial of patience; yet such labouring in an ungrateful employment was a cross and so was to be born with submission; and that a great uneasiness under that of the forsaking a station because of it, might be the effect of secret pride and an indignation against Providence."[24] So to undertake the work of God was a duty.

Burnet was convinced that, "as there is a dark side of human nature, there is likewise a bright one." The historical challenge for great men and women of any age was to turn to the good. In his funeral sermon for his friend the scientist Robert Boyle, Burnet showed how wisdom and knowledge came from God. Burnet believed that aristocrats, such as Boyle, who, he recalled, was the son of an earl and descended from Irish kings, had a duty to use their "great and noble minds" in the service of God and their country. The measure of Boyle's greatness was not the acclaim he earned but the way in which he used his mind and his money to advance religion.[25]

Burnet's *Thoughts on Education*, written in the 1660s but not published until 1761, underscored the need to teach the sons of noblemen the importance of religion. The nobleman's tutor "must also infuse in him a love to his country and duty to his prince; and that he abhor broils and incendiaries and that he listens not to any tattles against those in authority, especially of the King."[26] It was a principle Burnet was in a position to adopt when, in 1698, on the insistence of William III, he was appointed tutor to William, Duke of Gloucester, William's nephew and the only surviving son of the future Queen Anne. Burnet sought to provide Gloucester with plentiful historical examples of right and wrong government, including Alexander the Great and Julius Caesar. His goal was to teach Gloucester "the incompatibility of true piety with superstition and cruelty."[27] The young Gloucester celebrated the anniversary of Elizabeth I's birthday in 1699 with much pleasure, firing all his guns, but he died in 1700.

The principles that Burnet argued noble sons should learn at the universities were "sound religion, love of country, zeal for liberty, hatred of tyranny." Yet Burnet was not optimistic about the education of young aristocrats: "I have often wondered to see parents, who are to leave vast estates, and who stick at no expense in other things, yet be so frugal and narrow in the education of their children. They owe to their country a greater care in preparing the eldest, to make that figure in it to which he is born."[28]

Perhaps the clearest account of Burnet's view of the importance of historical leadership was his account of William III's wife, Queen Mary II (sister to Anne), a woman whose example to the nation was so great that she "shined in all the parts of it." Burnet piled high the qualities that made Mary a great leader: she reformed what was amiss, disliked idleness, read and studied the Bible, removed all suspicion of immorality from court; she was cheerful, took decisions carefully, submitted to her husband's judgment, and struggled against her own natural melancholy. Burnet claimed that these qualities were derived from her piety and religious observance.[29]

Burnet's ideas of the nature of history, and particularly that of England, were developed in part from his experience of living in Europe. Burnet was perhaps one of the most well-traveled churchmen of his age, having spent much time on the continent both as a young man and in the 1680s when he was effectively an exile. Some of his experiences were contained in letters he wrote in 1685 from Switzerland and Italy to Boyle.[30] Burnet noted the wealth of Zurich, which he ascribed partly to its system of government, based on representative government, but also to the absence of public lewdness and drunkenness and the swift and exact system of justice. Burnet noted a readiness for war and that every man was training to bear arms. There was an implicit regard here for Swiss Calvinism. Elsewhere in Switzerland, Burnet noted the poverty and poor soil, which meant that farming was almost impossible and subsistence was all that could be achieved. Yet "every one lives happy and at ease under a gentle government, whilst other rich and plentiful countries are reduced to such misery... so an easy government though joined to an ill soil and accompanied with great inconveniences, draws or at least keeps people in it, whereas a severe government, though in general ideas it may appear reasonable, drives its subjects even out of the best and most desirable seats."[31]

In the Grisons, there were both Catholic and Protestant communities, but Burnet was impressed by how well they lived together in relative peace. Tolerance was what enabled this to happen: when Catholic processions passed through Protestant areas, they lowered their cross and ceased singing. They both shared the same status in law, and there was respect born of previous conflict.[32]

Burnet's ideas of history were the basis of the way in which he conceived of England as a nation. His emphasis on the consensus of the people was based on God as a source for the reliability of popular views. For Burnet, God inspired the unanimous ideas of the people. But the people alone could not form a moral system of government, for this was an onus placed on kings, aristocrats, and officials. Leaders had a duty to be tolerant and to reduce tensions between religious groups in society. They were to be moderate and not to persecute those who disagreed with them. Like the Swiss, they had a duty to enable people of different religious beliefs to live peaceably side by side. They were expected to defend the natural liberties of the people and the Common Law that had grown up in the judicial process, which cemented consent between the rulers and the ruled. Such leaders were obliged to use their advantages and education for the benefit of the people over whom they were set.

In spite of admiration for some aspects of the government of foreign countries, Burnet presented Henry VIII's rejection of papal judicial sovereignty as an example of the way in which domestic authority and rule was not just preferable to that from overseas, but also natural and legitimate, whereas alien rule intruded itself between the natural consensus of the ruler and the ruled. Burnet's prescription for England was that a society and a political system that had learned the lessons of the past could be one that was both at peace with itself and guided and protected by Providence.

ASTELL AND HISTORY

Mary Astell (1666–1731) exemplified the diversity and complexity of women's interpretations of the past. Her work influenced a generation of eighteenth-century aristocratic women, including Lady Catherine Jones, Lady Elizabeth Hastings, Lady Mary Wortley Montagu, Lady Mary Chudleigh, and Anne, Countess of Coventry, as well as such scholars and writers as Elizabeth Elstob, Elizabeth Thomas, and Sarah Chapone, and women readers more generally. In part, this was because Astell had such wide-ranging interests that extended beyond history to mathematics and astronomy, as well as education, philosophy, and theology. Men also read her, notably such scholars and divines as Arthur

Charlett, Daniel Waterland, and George Hickes, who commented on her work.[33] Despite the lack of a formal education, Astell was able to step out of the constraint of her social environment, at least to some extent, by a wide reading of historical and literary works. Her library included books by Plato, Virgil, Marcus Aurelius, Descartes, Arnauld, and Locke, and she read works in Latin and French. Astell recognized that what most women read was determined by their relationship with men:

> They allow us poetry, plays and romances, to divert us and themselves, and when they would express a particular esteem for a woman's sense, they recommend History; tho' with submission, History can only serve us for amusement and a subject of discourse. For tho' it may be of use to men who govern affairs to know how their fore-fathers acted, yet what is this to us, who have nothing to do with such business? Some good examples indeed are to be found in History, though generally the bad are ten for one; but how will this help our conduct or excite in us a generous emulation? Since men being the historians, they seldom condescend to record the great and good actions of women; and when they take notice of them, "tis with this wise remark, that such women acted above their sex."[34]

As with other writers, Astell's historical consciousness and writing in large part reflected her environment, family, and upbringing. Growing up in Newcastle, whose economy was dominated by the coal merchants or hostmen who had been strongly Royalist in the Civil War, meant that Astell was imbued with a sense of the injustice done by Parliament and the Commonwealth. Her grandfather, George Errington, had taken up arms for Charles I and had fought the Parliamentarians in the streets of Newcastle. Her paternal grandfather, the lawyer William Astell, may have been more circumspect but remained loyal to Charles. Moreover, Astell's mother, Mary Errington, was from a Catholic family, many of whose members were active in Newcastle in the late seventeenth century. Astell's uncle, Ralph Astell, wrote a long poem, *Vota Non Bella*, welcoming Charles II's Restoration in 1660, and he emphasized that the monarchy and Church were the twin pillars on which society rested.

Remote from London, it was easier in the North to regard the Glorious Revolution of 1688–89 as not very glorious and to be untouched by the revolution of political principles that had taken place in London.

Astell prized social stability and political continuity highly, seeing them as the opposites of doubt and dissention. To her, controversy and argument were destructive forces that caused division and led ordinary people astray.[35]

The memory of Catholic monastic foundations in the north of England lasted longer than elsewhere, and Astell wrote of the charitable support that they had offered to the poor and needy. Her familiarity with Catholicism meant that she did not share the popular contemporary horror of it. She often defended Catholics and Catholicism in her writings and saw the Church of England as much closer to Catholicism than did most of her Anglican contemporaries. In contrast to Burnet, and underlining the variety of histories on offer, Astell tended to see a greater threat to society from heterodox Protestantism and atheism than from Catholicism. In 1694, Astell wrote *A Serious Proposal to the Ladies for the Advancement of their True and Greatest Interest*, which proposed a college in which women could pursue both education and contemplative life, a Protestant community of women (religious) that clearly owed much to Catholic tradition.

ASTELL AND THE ENGLISH CIVIL WAR

Astell's *An Impartial Enquiry into the Causes of Rebellion and Civil War in this Kingdom* (1704) was a response to White Kennett's sermon at St. Botolph's Church in London on the anniversary of the execution of Charles I in 1649. Kennett was the archdeacon of Huntingdon and a Whig Low Churchman of the sort of which Astell disapproved. His sermon was subsequently published under the title *A Compassionate Enquiry into the Causes of the Civil War*. A critic of Collier and other Nonjurors and High Churchmen, Kennett, like other Low Churchmen, saw Dissenters as allies rather than enemies and aimed to encourage them to return to the Church of England. His sermon, therefore, sought to deny that religious dissent was a prime cause of the Civil War, and consequently he looked for explanations elsewhere. He found them in the undue influence over Charles I of the French and Catholics, but he could not sustain this explanation without an implicit criticism of the king who allowed himself to be influenced in this way. The sermon was controversial, and Kennett was subject to numerous attacks for it, although he also attracted the support of Dissenters, such as Daniel Defoe. The other causes were, according to Kennett, "only a chain of effects" leading from those principal causes.

Astell claimed that Kennett's sermon was one of "popular arts, and such as factious men do not fail to make use of in all ages" and argued that it was inadequate in explaining the overthrow of a "good and merciful prince . . . who never proposed to injure his subjects, or to alter the constitution." Astell feared that Kennett's views damaged the nation by presenting a false view of history:[36] views of the past affected the way people viewed the present.

In the place of Kennett's explanation, Astell developed a strong and uncompromising Royalist analysis of the Civil War. She avoided casting aspersions on Clarendon's history, whose general interpretation she followed, though she clearly intended to improve on it.[37] Astell placed all responsibility for the war on "factious and rebellious" subjects, who refused to be satisfied by Charles I's concessions and were "stiff and contending," and, as a result, brought about the ruin of church and state. Worse still, they had put their fellow subjects under a yoke and had abandoned their liberties: "the free born people of England for all their spirit of honour and genius to liberty, even those great fore-fathers whose offspring we are, had the distain of serving in the most slavish manner and of wearing the heavy and shameful yoke."[38] Unlike Burnet, Astell did not regard self-preservation as a good thing. She argued that it was unchristian, because Christ had said that the surest way to save your own life was to be ready to part with it. For Astell, it was the idea of self-preservation and self-interest that had given rise to the rebellion and Civil War.[39] In 1696, she had written of the self-interest of the men who deliberately set out to cause the Civil War as seeking to "supply their pockets like vultures that live upon the carcass and are always watching for a battle."[40] Self-interest was the opposite of the Christian virtues that should motivate leaders of nations. This view was to be seen in the treatment of profiteering in the War of the Spanish Succession in Jonathan Swift's *The Conduct of the Allies* (1711), a castigation of the war.

Astell claimed that Kennett's Whig account of history that emphasized the danger of royal arbitrary power and of slavery was deceiving people. "Uncorrupted English blood and principles" would never allow liberty to be used as a cloak for malice. Such accounts also overturned the divine order, which required men and women to pay due obedience to their rulers "and patiently to suffer evil for doing so." She compared the danger of popery with disobedience to the civil power, which was "one of the worst doctrines and practices."[41]

Astell's account of the Civil War was that hardships had been exploited by Parliamentarians to turn people against Charles I: "poor good natured people to be forc'd to this." She believed in the natural goodness of the English people but saw them as fallible and weak and emphasized this more than Burnet had done. "Doubtless they [the people] never meant such ill effects any more than the King did," she claimed, but John Pym, the Parliamentarian leader, convinced them that Charles was overly influenced by the French and might receive arms and ammunition from France to enslave them.[42] Astell did not deny that there had been problems, such as taxes, ship money, and forced loans, but the king had set these grievances right before the rebellion broke out. However, "crafty men" suggested that Charles was wedded to arbitrary power and tyranny. Kennett had claimed that a ruler had to be "orthodox, regular, free from ambition and sinister ends," and, argued Astell, "the Royal Martyr was all this." The problem was that people were misled and persuaded by Cromwell and others that Charles was a tyrant.[43] This view of "the people" counteracted the emphasis in Burnet's contract theory.

Astell conceded that Charles was perhaps "over-persuaded by a Popish queen and High Church men such as the Laudian faction" and that there had been anxieties about this by "Honest Presbyterians, and the tender and loyal moderate men." She even admitted that there was an onus on rulers to avoid raising any false suspicions among their people that they supported arbitrary power, "to prevent all misunderstanding."[44] Nevertheless, Astell idealized Charles and thought that his status as a martyr conferred upon him a special quality.[45] She also presented James II as sinned against. Astell thus brought a Christian stoicism and pious resignation to her historical interpretation. With Christ as the ultimate authority on earth, Christianity elevated the idea of a cause that was destined to fail, only to be resurrected in glory. In poetic form, she wrote:

> Thus blest, I shall while here below
> Antedate Heav'n, did monarchs know
> What 'tis with God and Cherubims to dwell
> With Charles they'd leave their empires for a cell.[46]

Astell was also keen to examine what constituted "Popery." She argued that the Catholic Church as a whole could not be condemned as Popish and that only its man-made doctrines—"that superstructure of hay and stubble"—could be deemed to be Popery. To understand the nature of Popery, she recommended Henry Foulis's *History of the Wicked Plots and Conspiracies of Our Pretended Saints* (1662) and his *History of Popish Treasons and Usurpations* (1671). From a Parliamentarian family, Foulis was hostile to Presbyterians and Catholics alike.[47] Astell's support for Foulis's views led her to regret that his books were only available in folio and that cheap popular editions did not exist. As a result, she transcribed sections of his books into *An Impartial Enquiry into the Causes of Rebellion and Civil War*.[48]

In contrast, Astell extracted material from Robert Parsons's *Conference about the Next Succession to the Crown of England* (1594) in order to make a critical point. A Jesuit, Parsons, in his work, discussed the possible successors to the throne on the death of Elizabeth I. Parsons, who accepted the papal right to dethrone monarchs, was often viewed as a supporter of the later Whig view that succession to the throne was not always by hereditary descent and that Parliament had a right to determine the succession.[49] Astell's view of Parsons was damning. Noting that his book had been reprinted in 1648 and again during the Exclusion Crisis, she regarded his work as reprehensible because it was used by some to justify "king killing" and claimed that use of his work by Whigs was an example of the way "Protestants make lawful prize of Popish doctrines as well as Popish altarpieces."[50] Astell asked where in the Bible was there an endorsement of abandonment of the hereditary descent of the throne.

Astell's view of the Civil War was also hostile to political ideology. She argued that "principles, how good soever, are neither infallible in their judgements, whether of things or persons, nor exempt from the passions of human nature." It was, after all, political principles that brought a king's head to the block. In their place, Astell placed Church teaching, which she implied could not be bent to men's corrupt ends. She cited the Anglican homily "against disobedience and wilful rebellion"—and noted that it was Elizabeth I who had ordered the homilies to be read in churches.[51] Moreover, Astell held the view that the monarch was to be entirely in charge of the direction of government.

Astell concluded her work by refuting the accuracy and interpretation of Kennett's account. For example, tonnage and poundage were not, as he claimed, first introduced by Charles I but had been taken by previous monarchs without the sanction of Parliament; Queen Henrietta Maria was "joyfully received" by the people, rather than being seen as a dangerous foreign influence; the Catholicism of James II was a result of the Commonwealth having driven the royal family abroad; and Astell argued that anti-Catholic agitation was as much directed at the Church of England as at Popery and was therefore not what it seemed: "The true and principal cause of that Great Rebellion and the horrid fact that completed it, and which we can never enough deplore, was this: some cunning and self-ended men, whose wickedness was equal to their craft, and their craft sufficient to carry them through their wickedness, these had thoughts and meanings to destroy the government in Church and State and to set up a model of their own invention, agreeable to their own private interests and designs under the specious pretences of the people's rights and liberties."[52]

Far from conceding that Charles might have been responsible for overreaching his prerogatives, she suggested that he did not sufficiently follow the example of Elizabeth I: "there were many causes that contributed to the felicity of Q. Elizabeth's reign, but her magnanimous resolution and stout exertion of her just authority, were none the least of it."[53]

Returning to Kennett's sermon, Astell was keen to link the events of the 1640s to the circumstances of her own day. She reminded her readers that it was by act of Parliament that January 30 was the day to be observed as the anniversary of Charles's martyrdom. Astell claimed that there was a danger of a rebellion, not due to any animus against Queen Anne but on the grounds of party strife and the desire for office. Such rebellious men told the public that power came from the people and that rulers were responsible to them. Astell feared that if they would have "some lucky opportunities" to persuade the people of dangers, that strife and civil war would come again.[54]

Like Burnet, Astell placed great emphasis on the English people. She wished that "the good natur'd English people had not been seduc'd into an unnatural rebellion." She saw them as perennially prey to this fault: "If the causes of the war are represented by halves, and all the calumnies that the Martyr's [Charles I's] greatest enemies could throw upon him are either industriously reckoned up or cautiously intimated, what could plain and honest hearers, who understood only downright sense, being strangers to nice turns and fine expressions, softnings and meanings ... what could these honest men think, but that the true meaning was, to throw all the odium of this reproachful rebellion on the King, as if he suffered nothing but what he brought upon himself?"[55]

Astell argued that such honest hearers would be offended to find that the account of the Civil War that they had been taught struck at the root of the Reformation, the Bible, and morality. Finally, Astell gave a warning to her readers that "there is still a party, and that a restless and busy one, who act by those very principles that brought the royal martyr to the block."[56] To prevent this, it was necessary to hold to Church principles.

Astell's writing, like that of other historians of the period, was laced with conspiracy theory. She spoke of "Commonwealthmen" who were "like moles always working underground," where they could not be seen. These were the men who had undermined James II and "are now at the same work again." This was also a theme that appeared in the Dissenters' histories discussed in the next chapter. Astell claimed that such unscrupulous men were prepared to make alliances with both the supporters of the restoration of James II and the supporters of William III in order to "have no king at all." They would make the same claims about burdensome taxes as were made under Charles I and would argue also that the French were the cause of England's problems again. Such men would never be at rest and would intensify the war with France in order to achieve their aims. Their preference, Astell claimed, was to have a new king as often as a town had a new mayor—and with as little power.[57]

ASTELL AND AUTHORITY

Astell's account of history was one that clearly endorsed the divine right of kings. It was rooted in an explanation for authority that was derived from God and not from humankind, and with rulers primarily answerable to God.[58] This account also reflected a marked dissatisfaction with the present, in which the monarch ruled by the will of Parliament and, therefore, politicians controlled the government of the country. Astell echoed Robert South's view that men and women were not as good spouses and neighbors in the 1670s as they had been before the Civil War. She believed that the natural order of society had been damaged and could not easily be put right again.[59] It is likely that Astell derived some of her views of the natural order of society from friendship with Archbishop William Sancroft, whom she got to know well when she moved to London in 1686. Sancroft encouraged Astell to see her own identity as that of a champion of the Church.[60] Besides Sancroft, she was friendly with the Nonjurors George Hickes and Henry Dodwell and with Francis Atterbury, who was a High Church Tory, all Stuart sympathizers.[61] Sancroft's view of the hereditary and divine nature of kingship led him to refuse to swear the oaths to William and Mary in 1689, and consequently he was ejected from the archiepiscopate and the Church.

In her letters, Astell demonstrated an elevated view of God and the intrinsic sinfulness of humankind.[62] Her view of authority had a direct connection with the life of ordinary men and women, as she advanced a precise analogy with monarchy. A woman, she claimed, "elects a monarch for life" in the form of a husband "and gives him authority which she cannot recall however he might misapply it."[63] Drawing on the views of Sir Robert Filmer in his *Patriarcha* (1680), husbands were therefore "absolute sovereigns" over their wives.[64]

These views of marriage were clearly advanced with one eye on the debate on whether James II had been legitimately dispossessed of the crown in 1688–89 and whether, therefore, William and Mary were rightful monarchs. As a woman, Astell was not in a position to swear the oaths of obedience and abjuration, but her position was clearly that of a

Nonjuror, if not a Jacobite. What Astell was seeking to do was to reverse the principle established in 1689 that government was by consent of the people, and she held that the same was true of marriage: wives could not reject the authority of their husbands. Only God could purge a bad husband or an unjust monarch. This was the interpretation that Astell read back into her historical narrative of the Civil War and forward into her remedy for the future development of England.

ASTELL AND PRESENT-CENTERED HISTORY

Astell returned to a historical account of the Civil War in her tracts on Occasional Conformity. The proposals by Tory MPs to outlaw Occasional Conformity in a series of bills presented to Parliament from 1703 to 1705 were designed to exclude Protestant Dissenters from any place in public life. The bills would do this by closing a loophole in the Test Act of 1673, which permitted Dissenters who took communion once a year in the Church of England to qualify for public office. In a series of proxy contests, a number of Whig-inspired workhouse bills had permitted Poor Law guardians to be exempt from the Test Act and therefore seemed to sanction the admission of Dissenters to public office. But the proposed Occasional Conformity bills would close the loophole by preventing any people from technically qualifying by taking communion in the Church of England and then worshipping in a Dissenting meeting house for the rest of the year. In effect, the bills aimed to reassert the Anglican monopoly over public office.[65] What was especially exasperating for High Church Tories like Astell was that the bills were repeatedly frustrated by the opposition of Whig bishops who voted against them in the House of Lords, where the bishops played a significant role.

Astell was drawn into the debate by a tract written by the Dissenting minister James Owen, *Moderation a Virtue, or the Occasional Conformist Justify'd from the Imputation of Hypocrisy; Wherein is Shewn, the Antiquity, Catholick Principles, and Advantage of Occasional Conformity to the Church of England* (1703), which claimed that moderation and reasonableness were on the side of the Dissenters. Astell's response was *Moderation Truly Stated: or, A Review of a Late Pamphlet Entitul'd Moderation a Vertue; With a Prefatory Discourse to Dr. D'Aveanant Concerning His Late*

Essays on Peace and War (1704). *Moderation Truly Stated* also took aim at Charles D'Avenant's *Essays Upon Peace at Home and War Abroad*, which had defended the war with France and argued for greater toleration of Dissenters. D'Avenant was a former Tory writer who had been persuaded that religious toleration was reasonable, and so he attracted more than usual ire from other Tories. D'Avenant argued that the time was right for Whigs and Tories to put divisions aside and support the war against France. He also suggested that Occasional Conformity would erode the boundaries between the Church of England and Dissent and eventually lead to the reunion of Anglicans and Dissenters.

Astell's response to D'Avenant was mocking and dismissive, charging him with a historical relativism that she clearly disliked. The crux of her argument was that absolute monarchy was reasonable and natural. D'Avenant had claimed that arbitrary power would always produce rebellion. Astell's response was that this was not the case: Henry VIII had arbitrarily changed the whole nation's religion without being toppled, and his daughters, Mary and Elizabeth, both wielded power without restraint and neither was overthrown. Britons were far from being an independent and self-determinant people, claimed Astell: they depended on the Church and state as much as children depended on parents. The institutions of the Church and state were the only protection people had, and this state of subjugation brought with it the obligation of obedience and passivity. As with Kennett, she corrected D'Avenant's factual inaccuracies, both on the Civil War and on ancient history. Historical precision was used to demonstrate the legitimacy of her argument. Astell had clearly read widely to produce *Moderation Truly Stated*, since she cited over 180 works. Her historical views on religious moderation and whether Occasional Conformity was legitimate were rooted in biblical teaching, including the views of King David and the injunction of St. Paul regarding obedience to rulers. In this respect, she again drew on "deep history" to challenge the politics of the day.

Written and published soon after *Moderation Truly Stated*, Astell's *A Fair Way with Dissenters and Their Patrons* (1704) was a rebuttal of Defoe's *More Short Ways with Dissenters*, itself a follow-up to his 1702 satire *The Shortest Way With Dissenters*. Defoe had inflamed Tory opinion in *The Shortest Way With Dissenters* by ironically advocating the gallows for Dissenters, parodying what Defoe saw as the hysteria of the High Church Tory attitude. In *A Fair Way With Dissenters*, although Astell claimed to be writing in a moderate vein, she made no bones of her goal: "the total destruction of Dissenters as a party," since they were intent on ruining the Church of England. They were, in Astell's view, entirely responsible for the Civil War. She took her readers carefully through a historical account of the Civil War, demonstrating mastery not just of Clarendon's history but also of works by Tacitus, More, Milton, Dryden, Baxter, Foulis, Bastwick, Stillingfleet, and others. In doing so, she drew on Dissenters' own writings, which argued for the destruction of the Church of England—not the charity toward it that Owen had claimed marked Occasional Conformity. *A Fair Way With Dissenters* drew plaudits from such Tory allies as Charlett and Hickes.[66]

Astell argued that, though the names had changed from Roundhead and Cavalier to Whig and Tory, and from Royalist and Rebel to Malignant and Fanatic, or Churchman and Dissenter, the sources of the divisions of the 1700s were the same as the 1640s—namely, the work of schismatics and demagogues. The people of England, therefore, were to be treated with caution since they were so prone to be drawn to fanaticism and division by agitators and men of extreme views. These were the views of writers like Sacheverell, Atterbury, and Leslie, for whom, like Astell, political views were largely a function of religious principle.[67] It was the same with historical writing. The view of the past taken by Astell was principally conditioned by her religious views.

ASTELL AS A HISTORIAN

Recognizing that history was made up of facts and of interpretations, some more contentious than others, Astell was precise in her approach to facts. She claimed that Defoe misquoted Clarendon: "Bless me! What hideous spectacles prejudice and prepossession are upon a reader's nose! But when our brother *Short-ways* has laid these aside, has wiped his eyes and is willing to see clearly, I would then advise him to another perusal of that excellent and useful History."[68]

In *The Christian Religion, As Profess'd by a Daughter of the Church of England* (1717), she observed "woe be to me" if she claimed that the

Magna Carta was a forgery or that William the Conqueror was an invention: facts were intractable; opinions were pliable.[69] Yet Astell's views were not influenced by means or processes, like the idea of moderation; she wrote history based on absolute morality: Occasional Conformity was wrong and therefore should not be permitted. It was wrong because it disturbed the natural order of things, and "order is a sacred thing."[70] To Astell, history was a process determined by the interaction of sinful humankind and providential God. She rejected ideas of nobility of birth and poverty as motives for human action in history: what determined good action from bad was the degree to which a person in the past was following divine ordinances or biblical examples. Astell devoted scant attention to economic conditions or social status in the unfolding of historical events as neither was instituted by God.

At the root of Astell's view of history was a moral heroism that was based on faith: Christopher Columbus "had not the thousandth part of the evidence for another hemisphere that Christians have for another life after this," and he might have been seen as a credulous fool if he had not persuaded Queen Isabella of Spain to pawn her jewels to fund his voyage to the New World. Columbus was a hero for his "great act of faith."[71] However, she was silent on how to determine which acts of faith were inspired and which were foolhardy.

Believing that authority was divine, Astell argued that the actions of the Parliamentarians in the previous century were impious and in violation of religious tenets. A desire to return to a past that did not have the messiness of parliamentary politics, with the factions and strife that it entailed, was attractive to those, like Astell, who were disaffected with the post-1689 system of government. But the attempt to turn back the clock to a time of divine political authority in church and state was futile. The Revolution Settlement of 1689 was not one that was reversed; and the succession of 1714 and the events of 1715 and 1745 showed that there was little popular appetite for the sort of regime that Astell would have preferred. Nor was there a golden era of divinely inspired monarchy that Astell wanted to return to, and Queen Anne's attempt to deploy religious iconography had only limited success.

Nevertheless, such feelings about the certainties of authority and power in the past were an important element in historical writing.

Astell's historical lens was also affected by the sense of a godless, sinful present, which was another common theme in historical writing. For Astell, the way to redress such sinfulness was to have pious rulers who would punish political and religious defiance. Astell's writing existed in a border between more conventional Tory history, such as Clarendon's *History of the Great Rebellion*, and the more polemical views of the past contained in Jacobite and Nonjuror works by such writers as Charles Leslie (1650–1722). The emphasis on piety was to look toward George III, although he was more moderate in his attitudes than those Astell had attributed to the Stuarts.

NOTES

1. For a very different modern perspective, E. Duffy, *Saints, Sacrilege, and Sedition: Religion and Conflict in the Tudor Reformations* (London, 2010).

2. J. Collier, *An Answer to Some Exceptions in Bishop Burnet's Third Part of the History of the Reformation &c. against Mr. Collier's Ecclesiastical history: Together with a reply to some remarks in Bishop Nicholson's English historical library, &c. upon the same subject* (London, 1715); A. Starkie, "Gilbert Burnet's *Reformation* and the Semantics of Popery" in *Fear and Exclusion: Roger Morrice and Britain in the 1680s*, ed. J. McElligott (Aldershot, UK, 2006), 138–54; A. Starkie, "Contested Histories of the English Church: Gilbert Burnet and Jeremy Collier" in *The Uses of History in Early Modern England*, ed. P. Kewes (San Marino, CA, 2006), 329–47; A. Starkie, "Henry VIII in History: Gilbert Burnet's *History of the Reformation* (v.1) 1679," in *Henry VIII and History*, ed. T. Freeman and T. Betteridge (Aldershot, UK, 2012), 151–65.

3. T. Claydon, "Latitudinarianism and Apocalyptic History in the Worldview of Gilbert Burnet, 1643–1715," *Historical Journal*, 51 (2008): 577–97.

4. J. J. Hughes, "The Missing 'Last Words' of Gilbert Burnet in July 1687," *The Historical Journal* 20 (1977): 221–27.

5. T. Claydon, "Gilbert Burnet: An Ecclesiastical Historian and the Invention of the Restoration Era," *Studies in Church History* 49 (2013): 181

6. G. Burnet, *A History of the Reformation of the Church of England* (London, 1903), 2.

7. Burnet, *History of the Reformation*, 214.

8. M. D. Breidenbach, "Conciliarism and the American Founding," *William and Mary Quarterly* 3rd ser., vol. 73 (2016): 467–500.

9. Burnet, *History of the Reformation*, 87.

10. Burnet, *History of the Reformation*, 116–17, 131.

11. Burnet, *History of the Reformation*, 107, 112, 224–25. Burnet noted the frequency with which traitors and those condemned to execution exhorted the people to obey the king. Burnet, 264.

12. Burnet, *History of the Reformation*, 141.
13. Burnet, *History of the Reformation*, 182.
14. Burnet, *History of the Reformation*, 184, 189.
15. Burnet, *History of the Reformation*, 312.
16. Burnet, *History of the Reformation*, 40, 296.
17. Burnet, *History of the Reformation*, 364–69, 374.
18. For the background, see K. Sharpe and S. N. Zwicker, eds., *Writing Lives: Biography and Textuality, Identity and Representation in Early Modern England* (Oxford, 2008); A. Walkden, *Private Lives Made Public: The Invention of Biography in Early Modern England* (Pittsburgh, 2016).
19. G. Burnet, *Lives, Characters and an Address to Posterity* (London, 1833), 21.
20. Burnet, *Lives*, 205.
21. Burnet, *Lives*, 205.
22. Burnet, *Lives*, 258.
23. Burnet, *Lives*, 260.
24. Burnet, *Lives*, 297. For Burnet on himself, see M. Greig, "A Peculiar Talent in Writing History: Gilbert Burnet and his *History of My Own Time*," *Archives* 32 (2007): 19–27.
25. G. Burnet, "The Character of a Christian Philosopher in A Sermon Preached January 7, 1691/2 at the Funeral of the Hon. Robert Boyle," *Lives*, 326–76.
26. G. Burnet, "Thoughts on Education," in J. Clarke, *Bishop Gilbert Burnet as Educationalist* (Aberdeen, 1914), 67.
27. Clarke, *Burnet as Educationalist*, 142–43.
28. Clarke, *Burnet as Educationalist*, 151, 158.
29. Burnet, *Lives*, 321–24.
30. G. Burnet, *Some Letters Containing an Account of What Seem'd most remarkable in Switzerland, Italy etc, Written by G. Burnet DD to THRB [the Hon Robert Boyle]* (Rotterdam, 1686).
31. Burnet, *Some Letters*, 43.
32. Burnet, *Some Letters*, 70–75.
33. Bodl., Ballard Mss, 62 f. 85.
34. M. Astell, *The Christian Religion, as Profess'd by a Daughter of the Church of England*, 292–93.
35. She certainly valued stability more highly than the opinions of the people. For an examination of the claim that Astell had any democratic tendencies, see J. Nadelhaft, "Englishwoman's Sexual Civil War, 1650–1740," *Journal of the History of Ideas* 43 (1982): 555–79.
36. M. Astell, *An Impartial Enquiry into the Causes of Rebellion and Civil War* (London, 1704), 5–6.
37. Astell, *Impartial Enquiry*, 16–17.
38. Astell, *Impartial Enquiry*, 9–10.
39. Astell, *Impartial Enquiry*, 11
40. M. Astell, *Six familiar essays upon marriage, crosses in love, sickness, death, loyalty, and friendship, written by a lady* (London, 1696), 73.
41. Astell, *Impartial Enquiry*, 12.
42. Astell, *Impartial Enquiry*, 13.
43. Astell, *Impartial Enquiry*, 14–15.
44. Astell, *Impartial Enquiry*, 19–21.
45. R. Perry, *The Celebrated Mary Astell: An Early English Feminist* (Chicago, 1986), 11, 42, 60–61, 162–69. William Sancroft was also fixated on martyrdom.
46. M. Astell, "On Solitude," in *Early Modern Women's Manuscript Poetry*, ed. J. S. Millman and G. Wright (Manchester, 2005), 189.

47. M. Goldie, "Restoration Political Thought," in *The Reigns of Charles II and James VII and II*, ed. L. K. J. Glassey (Basingstoke, UK, 1997), 12–35.

48. Astell, *Impartial Enquiry*, 24–27.

49. P. Kewes, "The Puritan, the Jesuit, and the Jacobean Succession," in *Doubtful and Dangerous: The Question of Succession in Late Elizabethan England*, ed. S. Doran and Kewes (Manchester, 2014), 47–70.

50. Astell, *Impartial Enquiry*, 29.

51. Astell, *Impartial Enquiry*, 31–35.

52. Astell, *Impartial Enquiry*, 42.

53. Astell, *Impartial Enquiry*, 51.

54. Astell, *Impartial Enquiry*, 17.

55. Astell, *Impartial Enquiry*, 52.

56. Astell, *Impartial Enquiry*, 57.

57. Astell, *Six familiar essays*, 73–76.

58. M. Astell, *A Serious Proposal to the Ladies for the Advancement of their True and Greatest Interest* (London, 1694), 4. For a discussion of this work as a history, see C. Barash, "'The Native Liberty of the Subject': Configurations of Gender and Authority in the Works of Mary Chudleigh, Susan Fyge Egerton and Mary Astell," in *Women, Writing, History 1640–1740*, ed. I. Grundy and S. Wiseman (London, 1992), 67.

59. B. Hill, ed., *The First English Feminist* (New York, 1986), 39.

60. E. Major, *Madam Britannia, Women Church and Nation, 1712–1812* (Oxford, 2012), 126, 275.

61. Perry, *Celebrated Mary Astell*, 42. M. Zook, *Protestantism, Politics and Women in Britain, 1660–1714* (Basingstoke, UK, 2013), 189–96; Hill, *First English Feminist*, 7; G. Paston, *Lady Mary Wortley Montagu and Her Times* (New York, 1907), 12–13.

62. M. Astell, *Letters Concerning the Love of God between the author of the Proposal to the Ladies and Mr John Norris wherein his late discourse, shewing that it ought to be intire and exclusive of all other loves, is further cleared and justified* (London, 1695).

63. M. Astell, *Some Reflections upon Marriage Occasion'd by the Duke and Duchess of Mazarine's Case which is also consider'd* (London, 1700): 103, 106, 109.

64. Astell, *Some Reflections*, 115.

65. W. Gibson, *The Church of England 1688–1832: Unity and Accord* (London, 2001), 75–85.

66. Bodl., Ballard Mss, 62, fol 85. For a critical view, see P. Springborg, ed., *Astell: Political Writings* (Cambridge, 1996), 83–86.

67. Zook, *Protestantism, Politics and Women*, 194.

68. M. Astell, *A Fair Way with Dissenters and Their Patrons* (London, 1704), 24.

69. M. Astell, *The Christian Religion, As Profess'd by a Daughter of the Church of England* (London, 1717), 22–23.

70. M. Astell, *Moderation Truly Stated: or, A Review of a Late Pamphlet Entitul'd Moderation a Vertue; With a Prefatory Discourse to Dr. D'Aveanant Concerning His Late Essays on Peace and War* (London, 1704), 59.

71. M. Astell, *An enquiry after wit: wherein the trifling arguing and impious raillery of the late Earl of Shaftesbury, in his Letter concerning enthusiasm, and other profane writers, are fully answer'd and justly exposed* (London, 1722), 95–96.

FIVE

THE UNSTABLE PAST

Dissenters and History

RADICALLY DIFFERENT INTERPRETATIONS OF THE PAST removed the security of a settled account and made the past appear unstable. In particular, the long shadows of the seventeenth century created a strongly polarized account of the Civil War, a recurrent theme in this book. That polarization did not simply create incremental differences in interpretation; it led to starkly contrasting accounts of the past—indeed, on occasion, diametrically opposed accounts. Perhaps the only comparable issues on which historians in the eighteenth century disagreed so completely was on the guilt or innocence of such historical figures as Richard III and Mary Queen of Scots, an issue that allowed no middle path. In the religious accounts of the past, one of the dominant preoccupations was the character of the seventeenth-century Puritans, forebears of the Dissenters of the eighteenth century, and their guilt or innocence for causing the Civil War. Debates on the culpability of the Puritans related to discussion of the degree to which Dissenters could be trusted or admitted to a full part in government and society: the historical account had an immediate consequence. For these reasons the works discussed here by Samuel Wesley, John Oldmixon, and Daniel Neal exerted a powerful influence both on accounts of the past and on implications for the future. Present-centered history was at its most immediate in such historical writing.

THE SURVIVAL OF THE GOOD OLD CAUSE

In contrast to the legitimist historicist approach of Catholics,[1] Dissenters were keen to develop historical accounts that legitimized legal toleration, which was both recent and precarious,[2] and their role in society. Preoccupied by the events that had shaped their world, many historians of the overshadowing past, for example, Mary Astell, regarded the Puritans as responsible for the Civil War and thus as a malign force. Moreover, Dissenters in the eighteenth century were often seen as the direct descendants of the Puritans and were regarded as prone to the same factionalism and dangerous political ideas as their Puritan predecessors. Consequently, history became a battleground for Dissenters and their opponents to advance claim and counterclaim about the dangers Dissenters might represent in the eighteenth century and the degree to which they had been mischaracterized in the past. If Puritans had been wrongly cast as fanatics and extremists in the seventeenth century, the Dissenters could hardly have inherited these features in the eighteenth century. However, the fear of many was that the "Good Old Cause," of radical republicanism and antimonarchism, was dormant and likely to burst back to life and overthrow the Church and state, as it had done in the 1640s.

In the first decade of the eighteenth century, moreover, there was some evidence that the Good Old Cause was not dormant but was being secretly fostered in the Dissenters' academies. This came to light in a furious pamphlet war between Samuel Wesley (1662–1735), a Dissenter who had conformed to the Church of England, and Samuel Palmer (c. 1692–1732). Wesley had not sought to provoke an attack on the Dissenters, but at some point between 1691 and 1693, he had attended, in the company of some his former Dissenting friends, a meeting of radical Congregationalists and Presbyterians in London. The meeting was, in Wesley's view, so seditious and profane that he walked out. Later that night, Wesley wrote to a friend with a detailed account of his experiences as a student in a Dissenting academy. Wesley's fellow lodger, a printer and bookseller, Robert Clavell, obtained a copy and, in 1703, when the issue of the danger of Dissent was becoming more prominent, published the letter anonymously as *A Letter from A Country Divine to his friend in London concerning the Education of Dissenters in their Private Academies in Several Parts of the Nation*. The publication coincided with the debates in Parliament on whether to close the loophole that allowed Dissenters to hold public office by occasionally conforming in the Church of

England. Wesley's *Letter* made a forthright attack on Dissenting academies, claiming that the students reviled Charles I, for whom Wesley felt a special regard, and, in their conversation, attacked the Church of England and the universities.

Palmer's reply to Wesley accused him of malice and recounting tittle-tattle, and he contradicted many of Wesley's stories. He pointed out that, even if Wesley's accounts were true, they had happened more than twenty years earlier, in the context of the Church's persecution of Dissent under the penal laws of the Clarendon Code, and should no longer be seen as valid. Palmer also provided a strong contrast to Wesley's account by describing the academy he had attended, under Dr. Kerr, as an exemplary institution. Wesley replied to Palmer in *A Defence of a Letter Concerning the Education of Dissenters in their Private Academies, with a more full and satisfactory account of the same and of their morals and behaviour towards the Church of England; Being An Answer to the Defence of Dissenters Education* (1704), in which he repeated his claims that the Dissenters lacked loyalty to the Church and state, and blasphemed the memory of Charles I. The pamphlet war between Wesley and Palmer continued. In 1705, Palmer published *A Vindication of the Learning, Loyalty, Morality and Most Christian Behaviour of the Dissenters towards the Church of England*, and, in 1707, Wesley responded with *A Reply to Mr Palmer's Vindication of the Learning, Loyalty, Morality . . .*

Wesley's altercations with Palmer attracted the attention of Wesley's schoolfellow Defoe. Defoe had already published the ironical satire *The Shortest Way With Dissenters* (1702): pretending to write as a High Churchman, he claimed that the country had harbored Dissenters like a viper in its bosom. They had butchered one king (Charles I), deposed another (James II), made a mockery of a third (William III), and now expected to hold public office under Anne. So subtle and ironic was Defoe's writing that it was not immediately recognized as a satire. In 1703–04, Defoe published other scurrilous works and, in 1704, was sentenced to Newgate Gaol, from which he entered the Wesley-Palmer debate in *More Short Ways With the Dissenters*. Defoe denounced Wesley as "a mercenary renegardo," who was blackening Dissenters' education, though "guilty of many crimes in his youth." He also made the defense of Dissenting academies that they would not exist if only the Church of England would allow Dissenters entry to the English universities.

What emerged from the Wesley-Palmer dispute was that, whether or not there was any truth in Wesley's accusations, there were plenty of people willing to believe that Dissenters were still prone to revert to their old republican ways and who saw the past as a warning to the present. Not only were they vulgar and profane, but also politically dangerous, as their forebears had been. For most of the people who reached this conclusion, political and religious heterodoxy went hand in hand.[3]

This association was questioned by Whigs and their allies ready to see the Church and Dissent as aligned. For the prominent Dissenting minister Samuel Chandler, who was very friendly with Archbishop William Wake of Canterbury and other bishops, and who saw the Church and Dissent as allies, rather than competitors, the battle against Catholicism, instead, was central to national identity, culture, and interest. Moreover, to Chandler, this battle linked human and sacred history, as the Catholic Church, in his view, imposed its own authority over that of the scriptures. In 1731, he wrote a preface to a translation of a history of the Inquisition, stating:

> There being, as I apprehend, no way so proper to expose the doctrine and practice of persecution, as by a fair representation of the unspeakable mischiefs that have been occasioned by it; nor any other method so likely to render it the universal abhorrence of mankind, as to let them see, by past examples what miseries they must expect, if God should ever, for our sins, subject us again to the yoke of ecclesiastical power; which, wherever 'tis not yet under strict restraint, will usurp upon the authority and dignity of princes, and trample underfoot all the civil and religious liberties of mankind.[4]

Chandler also published, in 1766, a life of King David, a central figure from the Old Testament, who was an instance of the overlap of history with religion.

JOHN OLDMIXON AND THE UNSTABLE PAST

Wesley's attack on Dissenters emphasized the significance of historical writing. By depicting the past, historians could represent Dissenters as an enemy within or could vindicate them in similarly extreme ways.

John Oldmixon (1673–1742), a Dissenter who turned late in life to writing history, grew up in a world steeped in Whig resistance to James II, having been raised in Somerset and, as a boy, saw the preparation for the Battle of Sedgemoor in 1685. His family friends and relations were a roll call of West Country opponents of James II.[5] With an income from his family's mercantile business, Oldmixon was able to spend time writing and by 1710 was established as a Whig pamphleteer and journalist, had already written some works of history, and notably had contributed significantly to John Hughes's compilation of sources that was published as *A Complete History of England* in 1706. In the aftermath of the Hanoverian Succession in 1714, Oldmixon turned first to biography and then to writing history. In the 1720s, he established himself as a major Whig historian with *The Critical History of England* (1724 and 1726), *A Review of Dr Zachary Grey's Defence of our Ancient and Modern Historians* (1725), and *Clarendon and Whitlock Compar'd* (1727). The *Critical History* was an especially strong attack on what Oldmixon saw as Tory misrepresentations of the past. He dismissed Clarendon and Echard as apologists for the sort of arbitrary rule that, he stated, was embodied by Charles I and James II. Oldmixon claimed that Clarendon's *History of the Rebellion* had stirred up anti-Dissenting feeling that had fueled the disturbances during the Sacheverell trial in 1710.[6]

In 1729 Oldmixon published a *History of England, during the Reigns of the Royal House of Stuart*, which, although not inexpensive, sold extremely well. Sales were so good that Oldmixon claimed that alone his work would put an end to Jacobitism.[7] Oldmixon was completely uncompromising about the Stuarts so that even Charles II was lambasted as an enemy of the English constitution, who did not care what happened to the country after his death. Oldmixon also added to the emerging cult of Lord William Russell by his hagiography of the "godlike Russell," who was "one of the most virtuous, innocent and beloved Lords who ever lived."[8] Oldmixon had no time for Whig ideology—he did not even mention Locke and gave Shaftesbury short shift—which made for a fast-paced narrative that drove the reader forward.

Oldmixon's claim, without strong evidence, that the Oxford editors of Clarendon's work had falsified it and amended the original text was controversial. Of the original Oxford editors, Henry Aldrich and George Smalridge were dead, and Francis Atterbury was in exile in France, but

Atterbury denied the claim,[9] and it was dismissed convincingly in John Burton's *The Genuineness of Lord Clarendon's "History of the Rebellion"* (1744).

The allegation that writers had doctored or changed historical accounts was also advanced by Oldmixon about Bulstrode Whitelocke's *Memorials of the English Affairs*, first published in 1682, at the height of the Exclusion Crisis. Whitelocke's *Memorials* were written as a Whig response to the strongly Royalist accounts of the writings of Sir William Dugdale and John Nalson, but their Whig credentials were not clear, and they were edited for posthumous publication by Lord Anglesey, whose politics were opaque but who, according to Oldmixon, had rewritten sections to pursue a feud with the Earl of Ormonde, who the *Memorials* implied was disloyal to Charles I in 1645.[10] These claims demonstrated a form of historical instability in which printed sources and published works could not be relied on: editors and revisers could change a version of the past and make it say the reverse of what the original author had intended. History, therefore, was volatile and unreliable, with its controversial dimension emphasized as a result.

Oldmixon's historical writing was charged with the potency that he had been an eyewitness to some of the events he discussed. He had witnessed the wholesale butchery by Colonel Kirk after Sedgemoor in 1685 in which rebels' quartered bodies were hung from trees all across Somerset.[11] Oldmixon was not averse to writing in the first person, which emphasized his opinions and also his testimony as someone who, though young, lived through the events he examined. Unlike writers and journalists like Joseph Addison, Daniel Defoe, Edward Ward, and Richard Steele, whom in part he resembled, Oldmixon amassed huge quantities of source material and undertook research into manuscripts when he traveled around the country. At the same time, he reviled other writers for doing what he did: writing partisan and highly prejudiced accounts of the past.[12]

Oldmixon's popularity lay in part in the fact that he came close to, but always stopped short of, embracing the Good Old Cause of seventeenth-century republicanism.[13] He championed and defended the Independents and Puritans of the Civil War and denied the popular view that they were a rabble—in fact Oldmixon argued that the Puritans were the respectable middle-class supporters of Parliament against the Royalist multitudes. He defended the Levellers from the charge of being opponents of private property who would have established a form of communal property ownership, a Royalist, then Tory, caricature which bore no resemblance to reality.[14] Moderate Whig historians like Kennett, Burnet, and Rapin would not go as far as Oldmixon, and this represented a distinction between moderate and radical Whig history. Oldmixon's work was generally anticlerical in tone and viewed the Church of England as part of the Tory establishment, and crucially so both before and after 1688–89. At the same time, he presented events in a providential perspective, acknowledging that God interposed to ensure the survival of Protestant liberties in Britain.[15]

James Ralph argued that Oldmixon's popularity was a result of booksellers' keenness to promote controversial works of history, which would draw public attention. Ralph, a Tory, claimed that when books were patronized or funded by subscription, they had to adopt a tone that was moderate and restrained. But when, as happened with Oldmixon, an author was entirely dependent on sales, the booksellers stoked up sensational and provocative works.[16] This represented a doubt about commercialism and the market that was typical of much Tory thought.

DANIEL NEAL

A contrast to Oldmixon in method, if not objective, was Daniel Neal, whose *History of the Puritans* was, after Burnet's *History of the Reformation*, the best-selling work of religious history in the eighteenth century. It was a four-volume work published between 1732 and 1738, with an expanded version in five volumes, edited by Joshua Toulmin, appearing from the 1790s. Neal's original work ran to over twenty editions in the eighteenth century with editions published in London, Dublin, Bath, and New York. Neal's work became part of the lore and identity of Dissent, taught to children and widely owned by ministers and laity alike.[17]

A leading Congregational minister in London, Neal had been educated at Thomas Rowe's Dissenting academy and at the University of Leiden in the Calvinist Netherlands. His first venture was a *History of New England*, published in 1720, which earned him an MA from

Harvard. He praised New England's religious toleration and contrasted it with the continuing religious intolerance in Britain. A history of the Puritans had been planned for some time. The Dissenters John Evans and Edmund Calamy had both planned to write such a history and had collected sources and materials for them. Calamy had begun by writing an account of the life of Richard Baxter but was distracted from pursuing his plans by writing a defense of his father and grandfather.[18] Evans had started to lay down a plan to write a first volume up to 1640 and leave the period from 1640 onward for Neal to write. However, Evans died in 1730, and Neal found himself with the whole task.

The period during which Neal was writing his history was one in which the position of Dissenters was in question. There were strong campaigns to repeal the Test and Corporation Acts, which excluded Dissenters from public office—and a petition was presented to Parliament for the repeal in 1732. Further attempts at repeal were made in 1736 and 1739. These initiatives were led in a well-organized campaign by the Dissenting Deputies.[19] The climax of the campaign was reached in 1736 when Walpole was prevailed upon to seek to remove the obligation on Quakers to pay tithes who were routinely imprisoned for failure to do so. In this tense political atmosphere, Neal wrote the *History of the Puritans*. Neal made the case for the repeal of the Test and Corporations Acts in the preface to the work, arguing that the Dissenters were among the most loyal subjects of the Crown and unfairly excluded from participation in public life. Neal took the customary position among Low Churchmen and Dissenters that there was no reason to exclude Trinitarian Protestants from public life but that Catholics were too dangerous to the state to be admitted to full citizenship. It was a position that placed Neal firmly on the side of Whigs and Low Churchmen.[20]

Neal's work was, then, one of present-centered history. It advanced the view that, from the start and throughout the seventeenth century, the Puritans were advocates of liberty and toleration. The freedoms enjoyed by all in the eighteenth century, suggested Neal, were due to the advocacy and suffering of the Puritans in the previous century. Indeed, Neal argued that liberty had been defined by the Puritans as religious individualism. He asked, what was religious conscience if it was not the same as political principle? These views led Neal to charge Elizabeth I with intolerance and persecution in her treatment of Puritans. If this was not sufficiently controversial, Neal blamed James I for setting in train the economic and religious problems that followed and argued that Charles I's Laudian sympathies meant that, by 1640, most people in England were in reality Puritans who only tolerated episcopacy. Neal also argued that Puritans were reacting to forces beyond their control, that there was no Puritan project but a defensive reaction to royal intolerance and persecution. Thus Puritanism by 1640 represented religious and political liberty from oppression by the Crown. Neal claimed that Charles I's execution was not due to the Puritans and that the real culprits were the army officers, influenced by their own political zeal and desire for self-preservation. Neal, who distinguished between different types of Puritan, pointed out that the Westminster Assembly of Divines had called for the release of the king. This interpretation seemed to turn conventional history upside down. Although praising Cromwell as a representative of the independent spirit of the Puritans, Neal had misgivings about him because he relied so heavily on the power of the army to keep him in government.

Neal claimed credit for the Glorious Revolution for the Puritans and attacked the Tories of the 1670s and 1680s as allies of tyranny.[21] Under James II, the Dissenters emerged as heroes who were willing to forego James's blandishments in the Declaration of Indulgence—however insincere it may have been—in order to support Protestant allies in the Church of England. Neal wrote that, while Dissenters had played their part in the revolution with honor, the Tory High Churchmen were "inconsistent and dishonourable": first staunchly loyal to James and then prepared to resist him when their own sectarian interests were threatened. Here too, Neal challenged the received wisdom that the Church had been in the forefront of evicting James in the interests of Protestantism as a whole.

Neal brought the *History of the Puritans* to a close on a note of acrimony. He claimed that in 1689 "stubborn churchmen" had failed to redeem their debt to Dissenters by refusing to grant comprehension and only grudgingly agreed to the Toleration Act under extreme pressure from William III. The Dissenters were therefore the real sufferers of the revolution of 1689, who had a claim on the country that had not been paid.[22] In the light of Neal's revisions of the past, Puritans, often dismissed as fanatics, were no longer a cross to be borne by Dissenters but a glorious people of whom they should be proud and whose activities could give them confidence and self-assurance.[23]

Neal's attack on Elizabeth I and defense of Cromwell were bound to be seen as provocative. The first attack on Neal's work came from Isaac Maddox, himself a former Dissenter, in defense of Elizabeth: *A Vindication of the Government, Doctrine and Worship of the Church of England during the Reign of Queen Elizabeth, against the injurious reflections of Mr. Neale, in his late history of the Puritans. Together with a detection of many false quotations and mistakes in that performance* (1733). Maddox defended Elizabeth from Neal's charge of being a persecutor and suggested that Neal's real aim was to create a Geneva-style theocratic state. Maddox also claimed that Neal's work was littered with factual errors—he provided sixty-five pages of misquotations and factual errors—and that he used private Puritan sources and tended to ignore the public documents of the period. Above all, Maddox saw Neal's history as divisive and felt that it had the potential not to generate support for repeal of the Test Act but to promote discord between Anglicans and Dissenters, of which Catholics and others would take advantage.

The substantive work of attacking Neal fell to Zachary Gray, a Cambridge historian and clergyman, in *An Impartial Examination Of The Third Volume Of Mr. Daniel Neal's History of the Puritans* (1737), *An Impartial Examination Of The Fourth Volume Of Mr. Daniel Neal's History of the Puritans* (1739), and *A review of Mr. Daniel Neal's History of the Puritans. With a postscript, in which the exceptions of that author, to the . . . Lord Bishop of Worcester's Vindication of the government, . . . of the Church of England, . . . are impartially consider'd* (1744). It is likely that Gray's and Maddox's attacks on Neal were orchestrated by Bishops Gibson of London and Sherlock of Salisbury. Gray had a record of successfully attacking Dissenters, having published the ironically titled *A Century of Eminent Presbyterian Preachers* in 1723 to show the sort of extreme sermons some Puritans had preached during the Civil War. Gray's technique was to compare Neal's assertions with those of other historians, sometimes reproducing them side by side, to suggest that Neal's judgments were unbalanced and erroneous and that the weight of historical opinion was against Neal. But it was not Neal's technique that Gray principally targeted. Gray was concerned that Neal's historical account of the Civil War sought to justify the death of Charles I and the overturning of the monarchy. Gray's view was that if those events were not seen as horrifying and uniquely malevolent, there was a danger that people could be led to repeat the same mistakes. So Gray aimed to show that, far from being a moderate, reasonable force arguing for religious liberty, the Puritans were willful, extreme, and destructive. The starting point for return to radicalism and extremism was, in Gray's mind, the attempts to repeal the Test and Corporation Acts.

Neal had accentuated a fault line in the interpretation of the past that continued to trouble historians. Hume had it both ways by at one point agreeing with Neal that the Puritans were the people who carried religious liberty forward but on the other hand seeing them as fractious and prone to fanaticism. In contrast, Catharine Macaulay sided with Neal, as did the following generation of Whig historians.[24]

Neal's achievement was not so much in the accuracy, or otherwise, of his identification of the character of Puritans in the seventeenth century but lay in reclaiming a history in the eighteenth century that could justify and promote the coherent identity of the Dissenters in his own time.[25] The Dissenting identity that emerged in the eighteenth century drew on the history of the Puritans to create a conscience and a rationale for involvement in public life. This identity was not the same as that of the Puritans, but Neal's work gave Dissenters confidence that their forebears had played an honorable role in the shaping of the history of England and that they could also play such a role.

It was exactly this sense of historical confidence that mainstream Anglicans disliked. Sherlock, defending the Test Act in the House of Lords in the same year that the first volume of Neal's *History of the Puritans* was published, cited the book as a reason not to concede the repeal of the act. He attacked the Puritans for having been in the forefront of the regicides and also argued that it was ironic that those Puritans who had claimed religious freedom in England left for North America, where they turned persecutors of those who wanted freedom there.[26]

What made Neal's work such a best seller was that it represented, in a clear and explicit way, how people understood that their present political circumstances were rooted in the interpretation of the past. The issue was multifaceted: Could the writing of history be assigned to Dissenters who had a vested interest in sanitizing and rewriting the past, or should it be left to those who might be hostile to them? Was the past a prescription for the present? In other words, did the Puritan commitment to freedom and liberty that had come to fruition in 1688–89 earn them a greater share in the public life of the country? Was making that claim, alone, a divisive and contentious act? Did history legitimize the present? Moreover, Neal, though he clearly adopted a providential view of history in which God was present in all sorts of events, wrote of the agency and activity of individuals, such that they could change the course of history and thereby create the future.

In these debates, there were echoes of changing religious aspirations. For the High Churchmen, there was the waning of the hope that they could completely eradicate Dissent and return to a gilded past when all men and women were Anglicans, and the Church of England could be a single national church. For Low Churchmen, especially Hoadly, hopes that the Church would broaden its bounds and comprehend different forms of Protestantism so that it could bring the Trinitarian Dissenters back into the fold were fading.

Neal, however, did not simply have to defend his work from Anglicans. There were groups of Dissenters who felt that he had mischaracterized them, notably the Baptists and Anabaptists. To counter Neal's view, Thomas Crosby wrote *The History of the English Baptists* (1738–40) in which he argued that Neal, "from whom we might have looked for more Christian treatment, have made it their business to represent the Anabaptists, as they are pleased in contempt to stile them, in odious colours, and to write many bitter things, even notourious falsehoods concerning them, nay, to fasten doctrines upon them, which they never approved."[27]

When Joshua Toulmin, a Baptist as well as a Unitarian, revised Neal's work in the 1790s, he incorporated large sections of Crosby's work into it to balance what he seemed to concede was a flawed work. Crosby argued that Neal had ignored the information that he had supplied to him and consigned the role of the Baptists to just five pages, and that they were five pages written with considerable partiality. Part of Crosby's complaint was that Neal had mistakenly lumped together all the Baptists and Anabaptists and only saw the issue of adult or infant baptism as a theologically significant element in their traditions; in doing so, he had ignored the German and Dutch traditions and a rich diversity of religious opinions. Moreover, Crosby complained that Neal was willing to portray the Baptists and Anabaptists in the way Dissenters had been traditionally viewed, as tending to be radical and lowborn.

DEEP HISTORY AND SCHISM

Adopting John Foxe's claim that Wycliffe was the "Morning-Star of the Reformation,"[28] Neal had reached further back than the seventeenth century to claim the legitimacy of the Dissenters. By endorsing Wycliffe as the first Protestant, a view Burnet had advanced in his *History of the Reformation*, Neal was making a claim that had been strongly contested by High Churchmen. Laudians, like Peter Heylyn, looked on Wycliffe as a troublesome individual who threatened the peace of the Church. After 1689, Wycliffe was attacked by Nonjurors like Jeremy Collier and Matthew Earbery. Collier and Earbery disliked the fact that Wycliffe endorsed the power of the state over the Church. It was the power of the state over the Church that had dispossessed the Nonjurors from their bishoprics and parishes in the wake of the revolution.[29] So Wycliffe could be viewed as either a forerunner of the sixteenth-century reformers or a dangerous schismatic.

Among Latitudinarian Anglicans, however, Wycliffe remained a heroic figure who spoke truths about the power of the Church and the need for reform. This was especially controversial in the early years of George I's reign when the Bangorian Controversy addressed precisely this issue. If, as Hoadly claimed, Christ had left no institution on earth to act for him, the Convocation could not legitimately discipline churchmen for their views.[30] Wycliffe seemed to point to the same conclusion: the powers of the Church were too great, had been abused, and should be curtailed. In his *The History of the Life and Sufferings of the Reverend and Learned John Wickliffe, D.D.* (1720), John Lewis, Latitudinarian vicar of Margate, regarded Wycliffe as an early reformer for exactly this reason.

So Neal's praise for Wycliffe represented the hope of Dissenters that history could provide a lesson that would be learned in the 1730s: being separate from the Church was not necessarily to be in the wrong. Wycliffe was a figure who legitimized Dissent. This controversy affected the response to the Methodists. George Whitefield was attacked by Nonjurors and Anglicans for being too much like Wycliffe and for being very positive about him: George Lavington, bishop of Exeter, for example, attacked the Methodists as modern-day Lollards. In contrast, Wesley was favorable about Wycliffe. He translated Johann Lorenz Mosheim's ecclesiastical history into English, the work including extensive footnotes in which Wesley endorsed Mosheim's favorable assessment of Wycliffe.

Like Wycliffe, the Donatists were reclaimed by historians in the eighteenth century to justify or attack separation from the Church. They were named after Donatus Magnus, who led a group of fourth-century Christians who refused to accept the legitimacy of those Christians who had been forcibly, or otherwise, converted to Roman paganism under Diocletian. Donatists formed their own line of bishops and, despite formal recognition by the Church and state of those Christians who returned from paganism, insisted on separation from the Church. Thereafter, Donatists were held up as the brush with which any group was tarred if they separated from the Church. Catholics regarded—and attacked—Protestants as latter-day Donatists; Puritans and Dissenters after 1662 were also anathematized as Donatists because of their separation from the Church.[31] In the Restoration period, writers such as Thomas Long and Samuel Parker repeatedly attacked Dissenters as schismatic in the same way as the Donatists had been.

The high point of this was Gray's *A Short History of the Donatists. With an Appendix, In Which the Proud and Hypocritical Pharisee and Schismatical Donatist are Compared with the Rev. Mr. George Whitefield and the Methodists* (1741). He added another ingredient, claiming that Dissenters were like Donatists in being prone to such heretical views as Arianism. In this way, it was not simply that Dissenters were rebellious and rejected the Church's authority. They also represented a danger to the Church because—among other things—they questioned the divinity of Christ and were next door to freethinkers. Gray also broadened the attack on Dissenters to include other groups that seemed to undermine the Church, such as Methodists. Like Neal's use of Wycliffe, Gray reached back deep into history to reclaim an instance by which he could challenge those who deviated from the Church of England. His purpose was to employ history to demonstrate the danger and peril that the toleration of separation represented for the Church and the state. To permit Dissenters to share in the full civil life of the country—as was proposed by the repeal of the Test and Corporation Acts—would be to release an enemy within the Church and the body politic that would ultimately destroy it. By implication, Gray used history as a means to argue for conformity to the Church, as a political as well as a religious necessity. This approach to history was widespread.

NOTES

1. A. Shell, *Oral Culture and Catholicism in Early Modern England* (Cambridge, 2007).

2. A. Walsham, *Charitable Hatred: Tolerance and Intolerance in England, 1500–1700* (Manchester, 2006).

3. W. Gibson, "Samuel Wesley's Conformity Reconsidered," *Methodist History* 47 (2009): 77–84.

4. P. Limborch, *History of the Inquisition* (London, 1731), xv.

5. P. Rogers, "Two Notes on John Oldmixon and His Family," *Notes and Queries* 215 (1970): 293–300; P. Rogers, "Oldmixon, Francis Gwynn and the Prideaux family" and "John Oldmixon and the Family of Admiral Blake," *Notes and Queries for Somerset and Dorset* 29 (1968–73): 54–57, 185–88; P. Rogers, "Sir John Bawden, John Oldmixon's Uncle," *Notes and Queries for Somerset and Dorset* 30 (1974–79): 357–62.

6. J. Seed, *Dissenting Histories, Religious Division and the Politics of Memory in Eighteenth Century England* (Edinburgh, 2008), 22.

7. L. Okie, *Augustan Historical Writing: Histories of England in the English Enlightenment* (Lanham, MA, 1991), 77.

8. M. Zook, "The Restoration Remembered: The First Whigs and the Making of Their History," *The Seventeenth Century* 17 (2002): 223.

9. F. Atterbury, *The Late Bishop of Rochester's Vindication of Bishop Smallridge, Dr. Aldrich, and himself, from the scandalous reflections of Oldmixon, relating to the publication of Lord Clarendon's History* (London, 1731).

10. B. Worden, "The 'Diary' of Bulstrode Whitelocke," *English Historical Review* 108 (1993): 122–33.

11. S. A. Timmons, "Executions Following Monmouth's Rebellion: A Missing Link," *Historical Research* 76 (2003): 286–91.

12. P. Rogers, "The Dunce Answers Back: John Oldmixon on Swift and

Defoe," *Texas Studies in Literature and Language* 14 (1972): 33–43.

13. Zook, "The Restoration Remembered," 219.

14. E. Vallance, "Reborn John: The Eighteenth Century Afterlife of John Lilburne," *History Workshop Journal* (2012): 1–26.

15. Okie, *Augustan Historical Writing*, 82.

16. [J. Ralph], *The Case of the Authors by Profession or Trade Stated, With Regard to Booksellers, the Stage, and the Public* (London, 1758), 3.

17. B. V. Hill, "Suffering for Their Consciences: The Depiction of Anabaptists and Baptists in the Eighteenth-Century Histories of Daniel Neal," *Baptist History and Heritage* 49 (2014): 39–67; N. H. Keeble, "The Nonconformist Narrative of the Bartholomeans," in *"Settling the Peace of the Church": 1662 Revisited*, ed. N. H. Keeble (Oxford, 2014), 209–32.

18. E. Calamy, *An Historical Account of My Own Life with some reflections on the times I have lived in (1671–1731)*, ed. John Towill Rutt, 2nd ed. (London, 1830).

19. N. C. Hunt, *Two Early Political Associations: The Quakers and the Dissenting Deputies in the Age of Sir Robert Walpole* (Oxford, 1961); N. C. Hunt, *Sir Robert Walpole, Samuel Holden and the Dissenting Deputies* (London, 1957).

20. L. Okie, "Daniel Neal and the Puritan Revolution," *Church History* 55 (1986): 458.

21. Okie, "Daniel Neal and the Puritan Revolution," 463.

22. Seed, *Dissenting Histories*, 56.

23. B. Worden, *Roundhead Reputations: The English Civil Wars and the Passions of Posterity* (London, 2001).

24. Okie, "Daniel Neal and the Puritan Revolution," 464.

25. R. E. Richey, "The Origins of British Radicalism: The Changing Rationale for Dissent," *Eighteenth Century Studies* 7 (1973–74): 186.

26. Seed, *Dissenting Histories*, 62–63.

27. Crosby, *History of the English Baptists* (London, 1738–40), 1:i.

28. Neal, *History of the Puritans*, 1:3.

29. J. Collier, *An Ecclesiastical History of Great Britain, Chiefly of England: From the First Planting of Christianity, to the End of the Reign of King Charles the Second* (London, 1708), 1:564. Earbery's views were expounded in his translation of A. Varillas, *The Pretended Reformers: Or, the History of the Heresie of John Wickliffe, John Huss, and Jerom of Prague*, ed. and trans. M. Earbery (London, 1717), xiii–xix.

30. A. Starkie, *The Church of England and the Bangorian Controversy, 1716–1721* (Woodbridge, UK, 2007).

31. J. Hoover, "'They bee Full Donatists': The Rhetoric of Donatism in Early Separatist Polemics," *Reformation and Renaissance Review* 15 (2013): 154–76.

SIX

HISTORY SUITED TO MIDCENTURY STRUGGLE

BRITAIN WAS UNDER THREAT IN MIDCENTURY. ITS PARTICIPATION in the War of the Austrian Succession, in which Britain fought France from 1743 to 1748, was eventually followed by the Seven Years' War (1756–63). In 1744, a French invasion attempt was only thwarted by a storm in the Channel. In 1745–46, a French-backed Jacobite invasion came close to success. In 1745–48, the French overran much of the Low Countries, with the MP Philip Yorke noting in 1745, "I think their progress in the Netherlands this campaign has been greater than any of old Lewis's except that of 1672," thus commenting on the clear reference point of the reign of Louis XIV.

Fighting resumed in 1754–55, with the French inflicting defeats in North America in both years. In 1756, war was declared, there was another invasion scare, and the British colony of Minorca was conquered after the Royal Navy had been humiliated; while, in 1756–57, there were fresh failures in North America, and Britain's European ally Frederick II, "the Great," of Prussia, was put under great pressure. Searching for an historical parallel, Horace Walpole compared Britain to isolated Venice in 1509: "would not one think we were menaced with a League of Cambrai."[1] A sense of crisis repeatedly came to the fore, one matched by a political breakdown in 1756–57 as the Pelhamite system collapsed, a weak ministry replaced it and, in turn, collapsed, and it proved very difficult to construct a replacement.

Historical writing responded, notably to the crisis of 1745. The threat posed by Catholicism was to the fore. There were frequent references to the Marian persecutions of 1553–58, and, to that end, a forty-part edition of Foxe's *Book of Martyrs* was printed. In the wake of 1745, Catholics appeared everywhere. Bishop Lavington of Exeter even argued that Methodists were crypto-papists in *The Enthusiasm of Methodists and Papists Compar'd* (1749).

The debate was more widespread, with the Church of England presented as being under a broader philosophical attack. John Chapman (1704–84), archdeacon of Sudbury and an author of classical studies, including of the numbering of Roman legions, published *Popery the true Bane of Letters* (1746), a claim that there was a Jesuitical plot to undermine the Reformation by means of criticism of scripture and ecclesiastical history, which was followed by *The Jesuit Cabal further opened* (1747). Chapman pressed on to publish in favor of the miraculous powers of the Church (1747) and of "Primitive Christians" (1752).

At the same time, some commentators argued that only political history could provide necessary insights. The *Test*, a prominent London newspaper, claimed on February 12, 1757,

> The mechanism of government is too intricate and subtle, in all its various motions, for a common eye to perceive the nice dependencies and the secret springs, that give play to the complex machinery; and, in consequence the generality of people while the great political movements are passing before them are full of undiscerning astonishment, and only gaze on in expectation of the event. Afterwards indeed when the historian gives his narrative of facts, when he rejudges the actions of the great, and, from the ends which they had in view, and the means by which they pursued those ends, ascertains the colour of their characters, then the minds of men are opened, and they perceive honour and conquest, or disappointment and disgrace, naturally following one another, like necessary effects from their apparent respective causes.

Throughout the period, the press continued to make frequent historical references. Foreign policy played a major role in this and was often linked to constitutional matters. On August 29, 1752, *Old England* took aim at the Hanoverian interests of George II and the interventionism of his British ministers, in the person of Edward III (1327–77) and his pursuit of French titles and territories in the Hundred Years' War: "The grand fault of his reign was the unhappy passion he indulged to foreign acquisitions" and that he too late realized "that an island cannot extend itself beyond the waves which confine it. Britain he found was to be enriched but not extended." The *London Chronicle* of April 5, 1757, referred back to the 1660s to comment on the ministerial instability of 1756–57: "In the course of Sir William Temple's negotiations at The Hague, in the reign of Charles II, the Pensionary De Witt often complained to him, that the counsels of England were so fluctuating, that it was impossible to act in concert with our Crown, or to place any dependence on it."

At the time of national humiliation in the early stages of the war, the *Monitor*, a leading London newspaper, in its issue of November 26, 1757, asked: "Who can forget the days when Elizabeth [I] out of her cabinet gave laws to all Europe." Critical of the commitment of British troops to Germany in 1758, the issue of March 11 had to confront the fact that Elizabeth had sent an English army to the Low Countries in 1585; but this commitment was presented as a form of forward defense for England and thus as different to the role of Hanoverian commitments under Georges I and II. Alongside William Pitt the Elder, the *Monitor* became committed to interventionism: in its issue of October 16, 1762, it was to criticize George III's abandonment of his alliance with Frederick II by making reference to Edward III and Henry V (r. 1413–22), who had allied with the Dukes of Burgundy against France during the Hundred Years' War (1337–1453).

The *Monitor* observed on August 23, 1755, "The preservation of property being the chief end of men's uniting themselves into commonwealths," but this was not the direction of most historical work. Instead, it was a belief that the national position, its constitution, liberty, international security, and religion were all under threat that energized much of the historical writing of these years. It could be seen, for example, in books by Richard Rolt (1724–70) and Walter Harte (1709–74), two very different individuals.

ROLT AND THE DEFENSE OF NATIONHOOD

Allegedly a Jacobite sympathizer in 1745, Rolt became a writer in the opposition Whig circle around Frederick, Prince of Wales, and then, after the death of the latter in 1751, an opposition Whig journalist in the early 1750s. A prominent writer of hack history, Rolt adopted a clear, polemical style and a didactic method.

Oppressed by a corrupt present and by threats of future hazard, Rolt, like other writers, looked back both in contrast and for inspiration to a glorious past, especially to the reign of Elizabeth I. In 1756, when he jointly edited *The Universal Visiter and Memoralist*, Rolt published a poem in it, beginning, "Illustrious Raleigh! Britain's noblest friend." Sir Walter Raleigh had played a major role in maritime opposition to Spain. Elizabeth was greatly praised in Rolt's work for her defense of Protestantism, her vigorous foreign policy, and the challenge to Spain's position in the Americas. Unlike the Hanoverian dynasty, Elizabeth was English, a key molder of the Church of England, and had apparently ensured that foreign policy served national goals. Elizabeth was also sufficiently historical to prove, on the whole, both uncontroversial and malleable, without being so ancient as to offer only tenuous parallels to the present, as was the case with heroic pre-Reformation monarchs, such as Edward III, let alone Alfred and Arthur. However, as Wesley and others were to demonstrate, Elizabeth's treatment of Mary, Queen of Scots, was a cause of much controversy.

Rolt argued that history revealed the threats challenging the nation and the fate that would befall the island if vigilance was lost. The crisis—or rather, crises—of the Seven Years' War, notably up to the invasion scare of 1759, brought his earlier writings to a new focus and energy. In the preface to his *An Impartial Representation of the Conduct of the Several Powers of Europe Engaged in the late General War* (1749–50), Rolt had presented France as a state that had once enjoyed a constitution and "happiness" similar to Britain but was now a sinister and resilient threat: "It will eternally be the employment of France, to forge manacles for the free part of Europe, which she will never fail to make use of, whenever her strength and opulence shall enable her to violate the most solemn treaties, and scatter every pestilence of war to accomplish her destructive purposes."[2]

According to Rolt, France was responsible for the anti-British actions of other powers, such as Spanish opposition to the British commercial penetration of her empire, a theme that justified British opposition to

Philip V, the French candidate in the War of the Spanish Succession. Rolt claimed that periods of Anglo-French peace were simply used by the French to prepare for the next conflict so that peace could not be based on Anglo-French cooperation. This was a theme that had been very much taken by opposition critics of the Walpole ministry. In his biography of the bellicose John, 20th Earl of Crawford, published in 1753, Rolt presented France as "eternally aspiring at universal monarchy," and as the "natural enemy" of Britain, and called for a revival of ancient virtues, such as those represented by Crawford.[3]

Rolt argued that national strength depended upon the liberty and religion of the people, rather than on the size of the armed forces or other criteria. This was a theme that went back to the resistance of classical Greece to Persian invasions and a discussion that linked political ideology, the classical legacy, and civilizational accounts. Liberty and religion were, in turn, according to Rolt, dependent on the moral caliber of the people, and this was allegedly threatened by subversion encouraged by ministerial corruption. Just as the Saxons had been "effeminated" by Catholicism,[4] so could the modern British be by a variety of factors. Indeed, in the *Memoirs of Crawford*, Rolt bewailed, in particular, the nobility's loss of martial skills.

In common with many writers, especially those of an opposition or critical disposition, Rolt regarded 1688–89 as no more than a stage along the road. The Revolution Settlement could not prevent threats, and the price of political and religious liberty was eternal vigilance. In a different context, this thesis was to attract American critics of George III.

Rolt drove his points home, whether writing for children, as in *A New History of France; by Question and Answer* (1753) and in *A New History of England* (1757), a partwork published in numbers, or for adults: "It was not the true intent of history so much to load the memory of the reader with a copious collection of public records, as it is to elevate his thoughts and enrich his understanding."[5] Other works by Rolt included *A New and Accurate History of South America* (1756) and a biography of William, Duke of Cumberland (1766), published soon after the death of the latter. Posthumous works included *The History of the British Dominions in North America* (1773) and *The History of the Isle of Man* (1773).

Anticlericalism, xenophobia, the inseparability of liberty and religious freedom, and the focus on the present were all seen in Rolt's works, notably *The Lives of the Principal Reformers, Both Englishmen and Foreigners, Comprehending the General History of the Reformation: From its Beginning in 1360, by Dr John Wickliffe, to its Establishment in 1600 under Queen Elizabeth. With an Introduction; Wherever the Reformation is amply vindicated and the necessity fully shown from the Degeneracy of the Clergy, and the Tyranny of the Popes* (1759). In this, Rolt ended his account of the life of Archbishop Cranmer, burned as a Protestant under Queen Mary in 1556, by stating that her reign "ought to be transmitted down to posterity, in characters of blood, as her persecution was the most terrible that raged since the time of Diocletian [r. 284–305]."[6] This classical reference called forward the persecution of early Christians under the Roman Empire, as did Handel's oratorio *Theodora* (1750). Following his operas on classical themes, Handel's oratorios covered a number of biblical and classical stories, offering a sung history focusing on morality.

The Lives was a brilliant example of the linkage of history with current political events. As Rolt explicitly presented the position of Protestantism vis à vis Catholicism as one of continuing struggle, it is scarcely surprising that the Seven Years' War became, for him as for others,[7] a conflict between the forces of light and darkness. Frederick was extolled as a Protestant champion, "the Gustavus [Gustavus Adolphus] of the present age ... the appointed guardian-angel of truth and liberty." Moreover, a religious teleological explanation of recent history was advanced. The year 1688 was termed a religious revolution, just as the Reformation was stated to have established "liberty. ... The mind was no longer chained down in intellectual darkness."[8] Protestantism had to be fought for. That was Rolt's conclusion, and it was one suitable for an embattled nation.

OTHER MIDCENTURY DEFENDERS

In the same year as Rolt's *Lives* was published, 1759, Walter Harte's *History of the Life of Gustavus Adolphus* appeared. The son of a Nonjuror, Harte was an Oxford academic who became a country cleric. Like a number of historians, most prominently William Coxe, he had also acted as a traveling tutor, a role that offered most a jaundiced experience of

Catholicism. Gustavus, the king of Sweden killed in 1632 at Lützen fighting Austrian forces, captured both the sense of an embattled Protestantism and of a heroic, self-sacrificing response. He appeared to prefigure the successful warrior Protestantism of Frederick II and thus to provide another instance of an international Protestant martial virtue that could be linked to the "Patriot poets' valorization of the northern and the Gothic" in England.[9]

Other writers also offered exemplary classical comparisons. *Owen's Weekly Chronicle* compared Frederick to Scipio Africanus (victor over Carthage in the Second Punic War) on September 23, 1758, and to Julius Caesar on October 7 and December 16 that year. Thomas, Duke of Newcastle, referred to Frederick as "our modern Alexander,"[10] a reference to Alexander the Great.

The specifics of Britain's current alignments could also be addressed. Frederick, like Gustavus, fought Austria, a Catholic state that was a past ally of Britain but now the ally of France. The *London Evening Post* of June 23, 1757, carried an article on Austrian persecution, cruelty, and ambition that began "That great man Sir Henry Wootten, in his *State of Christendom*, gives the following account of the rise of the House of Austria; the publishing of which may open the eyes of British subjects, who are well-wishers to that house," and ended "This was printed in the year 1667. Have they altered for the better since that time."

The tone of hostility was clear whatever the comparison. Newspaper references to the classical world continued to be frequent and relevant. Thus, the *Monitor* of December 24, 1757, referred to the Punic Wars when calling for a more vigorous strategy of amphibious attacks against France: "A fleet is our best security: but then it is not to lie by our walls; nor be confined to the navigation of our own coasts. The way to delivery Rome from the rivalship and hostilities of the Carthaginians was to carry fire and sword upon the African coast [i.e., to attack Carthage itself]. Employ the enemy at home, and they will never project hazardous invasions."

At the same time, as a reminder of the continuing complexity of the past and the possibility of many readings, supporters of Continental interventionism also referred back, as with the claim that "the first maxim of the Roman Republic was to be faithful to its allies."[11]

Britain was a country under threat believing in its destiny, a notion that certainly was on offer from the historians. In the dedication of 1760 to the fourteenth edition of his *A New History of England*, the prolific writer John Lockman (1698–1771) "endeavoured to set the whole in such a light as may inspire the readers with an ardent love for our pure religion, and its darling attendant, liberty; and, on the other hand, with a just abhorrence of popery, and its comparison, slavery."[12] British commentators used the term *slavery* in reference to the situation in Britain, not across the empire—in short, political control, not the brutal use of labor for economic purposes. Lockman's remarks captured the clear ideological framing of a sense of distinctive nationhood. This framing took place in large part in opposition to apparent threats, which reflected the extent to which responses to challenges—past, present, and future—were crucial to national identity. That year, Lockman also published *A History of the Cruel Sufferings of the Protestants and others by Popish Persecutions in Various Countries*.

The period also became history, and in some troubling ways. In 1788, Charles, Lord Hawkesbury, an influential minister, received a letter from Maurice Margarot, who was subsequently during the French Revolutionary crisis to attract legal attention as a radical:

> The following account may merit the attention of government. I am desired by a gentleman in Paris to engage with a bookseller for the printing and publishing the genuine narrative of all the transactions in the year 1745 written by Prince Charles himself, together with *all* his correspondence relative to that affair and a facsimile to be taken from the original letters of different noblemen to the Prince ... such a publication can do no good—it may in many families cause uneasiness and perhaps worse—I apprehend money to be the object the publisher has in view, and his terms I believe might be brought within the compass of government economy—if government should think it proper to quash such publication.[13]

A much swifter revenge of history had been offered by the political changes of midcentury Britain. They led to a determination to justify past conduct as a means to defend present position, both governmental and among writers. The government certainly thought it appropriate to finance writers who produced not only favorable journalism but also history. Thus, William Guthrie (1708?–70), a Scot who lived in London from about 1730 to his death, was a parliamentary reporter who, from 1745, received a pension (an annual government grant) that was renewed in 1762. His historical works included a *History of England from the Invasion of Julius Caesar to 1688* (1744–51). This was valuable for its use of parliamentary papers, a use that reflected Guthrie's career as a parliamentary reporter. James Ralph (c. 1705–62) produced *A History of England during the Reigns of King William, Queen Anne, and King George I. With an Introductory Review of the Reigns of the Royal Brothers Charles and James. By a Lover of Truth and Liberty* (1744–46), a work that took forward Rapin-Thoyras's work in terms of his use of documents.

Guthrie was not alone in producing such works. Thus appeared the first volume of *A General History of England* in 1747. It was dedicated to the Duke of Beaufort, a prominent Tory with Jacobite leanings, and written by Thomas Carte (1686–1754), a Jacobite and Nonjuror, who described himself as "an Englishman," and thus, by extension, not pro-Hanoverian. This volume covered the period to the death of King John in 1216, a choice Carte linked to the issue of sources:

> This volume brings the History of England down to the time, when the two famous charters of English liberties were granted; and authentic copies of the most considerable acts of our kings, in the course of their government, began to be enrolled and kept on record. It is chiefly by authorities drawn from these last, that we must be guided in our judgment of the disputes that arose afterwards, as well about several articles of the former, as in relation to various branches of our constitution, the prerogatives of the crown, and the liberties of the subject...
>
> An historian cannot, with justice to himself or the world, abate the least of this care and caution till he comes to the age of public records; when all the civil acts of government were enrolled and committed to writing in a regular and authentic manner, and most of the military and political transactions of the same time may be verified in a great degree by those unerring authorities... the ends of History: which, with the knowledge of past transactions, conveys to us the experience of former ages, the examples of our ancestors, and the just characters of persons, who have deserved either well or ill of their country. It treats of the secrets of state; the actions of princes; the conduct of ministers; the condition and behaviour of the people; the forms of their police, customs, and constitution; the wisdom of their laws; the methods and rulers of their justice; the maxims of their politics; the arts or mistakes of statesmen;

the causes of the grandeur of a nation in some ages, and of its decline in others; the virtues which raise it at one time to the height of glory, and the vices which at another sink it into contempt, and pave the way to its ruin. In a word, it lays before our eyes the vicissitude of all human affairs, the fate of kingdoms and states, the variations of religion and government, the occasions and causes of revolutions, with the pretences made use of by such as have projected, and the ends proposed by such as have favoured them; the means whereby they have been brought about, and the effects which they have been found to produce.

To relate these with a proper choice of their important circumstances, and accompanied with just reflections, without favour or prejudice to parties or persons; and without any bias.[14]

Carte himself used his prefaces to reflect on the nature of history. For the third volume (1752), he wrote: "The characters given of the several princes or the great men, who made a figure in the reigns comprised in this volume, are drawn from their actions, the surest rule for judging of their qualities. The order of events is necessary for the clearness of relations, as chronological dates are for a guard of truth, and the refutation of falsehoods: great exactness hath been used in both these respects."[15]

The fourth volume was clear on how to present the regicide of Charles I, one described in strongly religious terms:

The world was struck with astonishment and horror at a scene of action not to be paralleled in all the histories of nations since the creation.... All hearts were full of grief.... [He] died a martyr for the liberties of his people, and the rights of the church of England.... It can hardly be supposed that an iniquity of so enormous a size, as the murder of a rightful sovereign, whose virtues and piety entitled him to a crown of glory, should pass unattended by some divine judgment: and in this enquiry the following rule may serve to direct our judgment. The natural tendency and effects of actions being settled in the very constitution of things, and their relation to each other, by the wise and almighty Author of Nature, we are as reasonably and as surely justified, in deeming the calamities, which are the natural consequences of any unlawful action, to be the judgments of God upon it, as we are in imagining, that our eyes were given us to see with.[16]

Carte went on to claim that the regicide was responsible for the irreligion, immorality, and divisions of the nation to the present day and thus that it repeated in human time the Fall, that is, Adam's sin. More specifically, Carte argued that the regicide led to the future Charles II and James II going abroad, with all the detrimental consequences that followed from their being educated by Catholics.[17] In short, Catholicism and Calvinism were joint threats. Carte himself had worked on James's papers in the Collège des Ecossais in 1740–41, and he removed most of them to England.[18]

Carte's work reflected not only lasting themes in Toryism, but also what it represented in midcentury. The integration of Toryism into a national political culture and language in midcentury is an established theme in scholarly work over recent decades.[19] This can also be seen in the case of the historical writing of the period, albeit with there also being continued Jacobite leanings in some of the works.

DEDICATIONS AND FORMS OF WRITING: THE WORK OF FERDINANDO WARNER

A key theme in this book is the development in the eighteenth century of the market for historical writing. With the growth of consumption of historical writing came a decline in the traditional models of publishing and bookselling. Speculative publishing and production for both mass market items and for the educated "middling sort" led to a shift away from the established publication practices. Publishing by subscription continued, but it declined as a share of the overall market. Writers who sought to produce historical works had to find other ways of securing sales. One method was to associate a work with a leading figure, aristocrat, or member of the royal family through the dedication.[20] Another was to experiment with forms of historical writing in the hope that writing in dialogue or in biographical form would attract public attention. Ferdinando Warner (1703–68) was such a writer. Disappointed in his hopes for Church preferment, he turned to historical writing and sought dedications to leading figures who would patronize and thereby promote sales of his work. He also experimented with the form of historical writing. His work, however, is a case study of an unsuccessful writer or, at least, of one whose success did not match his effort.

In the 1750s, Warner published several works of theology, including *A System of Divinity and Morality*, a five-volume anthology published in

1750, which was a collection of 133 sermons by distinguished churchmen, and his strongly anti-Catholic *A Rational Defence of the English Reformation and Protestant Religion* (1752). This edited "the sentiments and reasonings of our most eminent divines."[21] The goal of the book, to point out the errors of Rome and the dangers of Popery and to vindicate the Protestant Reformation, was one that could not be objectionable; Warner pointed out that such views were of "much moment and importance"—especially in the wake of the Jacobite rebellion of 1745.[22]

From the mid-1750s, perhaps aware that he was unlikely to obtain ecclesiastical preferment, Warner turned to writing history with *Bolingbroke or A Dialogue on the Origin and Authority of Revelation* (1755), *Ecclesiastical History to the Eighteenth Century* (1756–57), *Memoirs of the Life of Sir Thomas More* (1758), *The History of Ireland to the Year 1171* (1763), and *The History of the Rebellion and Civil War in Ireland* (1767).[23]

Each of Warner's works was dedicated to a patron or a potential patron: the *Rational Defence of the English Reformation* was dedicated to Archbishop Herring; his *Bolingbroke* to Alexander Hume Campbell, MP for Berwickshire; the *More* to Sir Robert Henley, the Lord Keeper, later 1st Earl of Northington, whose chaplain Warner became; and the *Ecclesiastical History to the Eighteenth Century* to George II, as was the revised version, which was titled *The History of England as it Related to Religion and the Church* (1759). His *History of Ireland* was dedicated to George III, and *History of the Rebellion and Civil War in Ireland*, to the Duke of Northumberland, the Lord Lieutenant of Ireland in 1763–65.

Warner claimed that, had More lived under the benign regime of George II, he would not have met his end on the scaffold, the sort of ahistorical point and diachronic comparison that was very common in historical writing of the period, although often implicit rather than explicit. But, according to Warner, More had the misfortune to have been born in an age of ignorance and superstition, and hence—as a Catholic—he was prone to "heresy and cruelties"; had he been born later, he might have had a "perfect character." For Warner, religious toleration and rational Christianity—in other words postrevolutionary Low Churchmanship—were solvents for even the most hardened Catholic martyr.[24] Warner's view that More, the ideal of a Catholic who died for his faith and for allegiance to Rome, would not have been so fanatical or cruel had he lived in an age of reason and toleration, was a strong statement of the power of those two ideals to wash away even the most deep-seated Catholic principles. Thus, the case of More could enable Warner to attack those people in public life who lacked his sense of duty and integrity.

Warner's *Ecclesiastical History of England to the Eighteenth Century* was a large two-volume work, which ran to over 1,300 pages. The first volume claimed to provide "what no other impartial history affords,"[25] namely, an account of the two principal directions of religious history in England: "from liberty to servitude and servitude to liberty again."[26] The fulcrum of this account was the Reformation, which represented the breaking of Catholic servitude and thus a return to past probity. Like Burnet, Warner placed great emphasis on the goodness of the English people and claimed that, before the Reformation, it was the "artifice of the Court of Rome" that made "an effectual resistance ... impractical."[27] In contrast, for Warner, the progress from servitude to liberty reached its climax in the revolution of 1688, from which all the liberty of the eighteenth century flowed. Warner also claimed that he had drawn on a wide array of sources to show errors and miscarriages as well as the "mistaken measures" of a number of princes.[28]

Warner's view of monarchy was bleak: a number of kings had acted "contrary to reason and law." Warner contrasted George II with "the miseries that have been inflicted upon other ages, under other princes," referring to the "many instances of tyranny." Warner's skepticism about monarchy led him to urge George "to deliver down to your descendants" the liberty of his subjects along with the Crown.[29] He also asked the king to pay attention to the growth of irreligion and indifference to Christianity among the aristocracy and the progress of Popery and enthusiasm among the poor, a combination that could turn liberty to licentiousness and degrade faith into superstition. Far from seeing any inevitable progress, Warner's view of the historical ebb and flow of servility and liberty led him to warn that the flow might be in the wrong direction: "Under this alarming apprehension, to which the breast of no good man can be a stranger, I thought I could not acquit myself of my duty to Your Majesty, and my country, in a work of more utility ... than to lay open the errors, the mischiefs and iniquities of Popery, in a clear and true detail of its tyranny and usurpation over the English Church."[30]

The second volume of the work linked the themes of the liberties of the English nation with the growth of religious liberty and the advancement of learning. Warner compared the instances of "popular clamour" in history with the instances of it at the present. Government in the past had been sometimes "disfigured" by popular clamor, which brought ruin on the nation. The prime example was the Civil War, which forced Charles II, the "Father of the Country," into exile.[31]

Warner's planned two-volume *History of Ireland*, the first volume of which was published in 1763, was another work that would have run to well over a thousand pages had it been completed. There was no commitment to short works. Warner wanted to give a general account of the history of Ireland, to draw out the acts of the king's ancestors, and "to serve the cause of liberty by an instructive history of the consequences of its abuse." Thus far, Warner's goal was comparable with his objective in writing the *Ecclesiastical History of England*. Liberty was so precious that its history had to be told and retold as an inoculation against the tendency to erode it—what Warner called "fatal politicks." Warner claimed that the heroes of Ireland were little known in England, a country "remarkable [for] its good sense and benevolence" but which nevertheless looked on Ireland "with an eye of prejudice and contempt." He claimed that there was no extant history of Ireland on which the ill-informed could draw. Warner aimed to show to his readers that Ireland was "a province of far greater importance and utility to this nation" than the rest of the British Empire.[32]

Writing such books was "arduous," claimed Warner, and the publication was "painful and expensive."[33] These comments sprang partly from the fact that he had traveled to Ireland in 1761 to work on original manuscripts in Dublin. He had also hoped to obtain support for the project. He received some from the Dublin Society, but the Irish House of Commons was not willing to grant him financial assistance, and he abandoned the project with the first volume ending in the year 1171. Nevertheless, while in Dublin, Warner had gleaned a good deal of material on the seventeenth century, and it seemed a pity not to use it. So he set himself the task of writing a single-volume work on the period. The subsequent *History of the Rebellion and Civil War in Ireland*, which, exceptionally for Warner, ran to a second edition, was published in 1768. Warner added a general comment that was a commonplace of Whig views, especially the Old Corps of establishment Whigs—namely, that history provided many instances of when liberty and freedom gave way to "popular error and frenzy" and ended in "illegal despotic rule."[34]

Warner experimented with the form of how he wrote history. His first historical book, *Bolingbroke or A Dialogue on the Origin and Authority of Revelation* (1755), was written as a dialogue in conscious emulation of classical writers, whom Warner admired. It was a risk, because as Warner conceded, dialogue was a style that had fallen into disuse in the eighteenth century and was "much neglected."[35] Warner laid the decline of dialogue as a historical written form at the door of Antony, 3rd Earl of Shaftesbury, who had claimed that it could lead to "falsehood" and made reading for more than an hour dense and unsustainable. Shaftesbury also argued that dialogue was problematic because no one liked to see exactly what they had said, and so the author of a dialogue had to decide whether to make it unnaturally polite or unacceptably authentic. Warner rejected Shaftesbury's views, claiming that there was nothing inauthentic about dialogue and that it could accommodate the "civility of people of politeness and good breeding." For Warner, there was another reason to persevere with this form of writing: "the author, instead of giving himself any dictating and masterly airs of wisdom, makes hardly any figure at all, and is scarcely discoverable in the dialogue."[36]

Richard Hurd (1720–1808), a clergyman, later bishop of Worcester, followed a similar format in his *Moral and Political Dialogues* (1759). In this work, historical characters discuss issues such as "the Golden Age of Queen Elizabeth." In 1762, Hurd pressed on to publish a sequence, *Letters on Chivalry and Romance*, which offered a defense of medieval knighthood and literature.

While Warner claimed to want to present Bolingbroke and Boyle in their own words, it was quite clear on whose side he was. Bolingbroke had, according to Warner, done "so much violence to his candour and ingenuity, as to dress up arguments against religion, which he must know had all of them been long ago confuted."[37] Warner described Boyle as the "hero of the piece." He was Bolingbroke's equal in social rank, which Warner regarded as important for such a dialogue, but Boyle was also a firm supporter of biblical religion and therefore of revelation.[38]

Warner's *Memoirs of the Life of Thomas More* (1758) was a much more familiar form of historical writing. Warner wrote the book partly because he perceived that historical examples of lives were much more powerful than contemporary biographies, "probably owed, in some measure, to our natural reverence for antiquity; wherein the objects are not familiar to us, but viewed at a great distance in their fairest colours. And if their blemishes and defects are not quite concealed from us, yet, as we are not interested in them, they are greatly shaded in the veneration which we all agree to pay to the illustrious dead."[39]

For Warner, remoteness in time brought an intellectual fairness in which More's qualities could be seen in a balanced view. He aimed to bring him close to the reader and included colorful anecdotes. Warner saw the process of writing history as one in which periodically the reader needed to stop and take stock and also to be guided in how to interpret the events of More's life. So when Henry VII died in 1509, Warner wrote: "As the character of this monarch will serve to illustrate this event of [More's] life, and explain his conduct in it more than the relation of it has done, I shall stop a little to give the reader its proper colours."[40]

Warner's use of sources varied. He quoted phrases and words in the narrative of More's life without explaining where they came from, but also sources that he gave in detail and at some length, so that, in some passages, the book became almost a series of edited accounts from primary material, a pattern also seen with other historians. The account of More's trial for refusal to sign the Oath of Supremacy was largely extracted from More's defense speeches.

Always to the fore in Warner's account of More were his preferred themes of liberty and freedom. He claimed that, as a member of Parliament, More defended the interests of the legislature against the king.[41] He also regarded More's piety as important and argued that his conscientiousness and scruples, while misguided, were undoubtedly authentic. The principal problem that Warner had, as a Whig Latitudinarian, was how to handle More's Catholicism and his refusal to concede the issue of Royal Supremacy. Warner was quite clear that he wanted to be dispassionate in his judgement of More, identifying him as a "patriot minister" of "disinterested virtue."[42] So More had many qualities that Warner admired: "he had a different sense of religion upon his mind, from what courtiers and men of business have in the times we live in." He was pious but not because of the "fashion of the age," which Warner implicitly saw as religiously degraded.[43] Warner wrote of More's exacting management of his family's religious observance: "if we keep [More's] regulation in our eye while we survey the management of families of the greatest part of our modern people of fashion, one shudders at the comparison."[44]

However, Warner had also to present More as a Catholic and made clear that "I must not conceal from the reader what as a great allay to all his virtues, [were] his furious and cruel zeal in the persecution of heretics." Warner concluded that on "this side of heaven" there was no perfection."[45] The imperfection was also clear in More's involvement with the "Holy Maid of Kent" and her claims to visions and prophesy.[46] Warner acquitted More of the charge against him that he denied the Royal Supremacy but noted that he lived in a time of lesser justice. That a jury found More guilty was a "reproach to my countrymen."[47]

The book included a revised translation of More's *Utopia* in which Warner sought to claim More, at least in part, for Protestantism and the Church of England.[48] More's support for Epicurus in *Utopia* was used to show that More was a supporter of the idea that the end of religion was the happiness of humankind—a major theme of eighteenth-century Latitudinarian theology.[49]

Elsewhere, Warner corrected More, as when he claimed that those who had been tortured were happy after death. Warner commented, "How our author came to take up this notion, both so unphilosophical and so irreligious it is hard to say."[50] However, in a footnote in the translation of *Utopia*, Warner defended More explicitly:

> It is plain that when our author [More] wrote this history, he had not bigotry or fiery zeal in his composition. But afterwards, somehow or other, he became devoted to the passions and interests of the popish clergy to a degree of superstition: and even then however, it must be confessed that his zeal carried him rather against the sedition which many run into who favoured the Reformation, than against the doctrines which he taught. For as much attached as he was to the Church of Rome, yet he was not so extravagant in his notions of papal power as some others were.[51]

In this way, a former Dissenter and Low Churchman was able to vindicate a Catholic martyr.

Warner's *Ecclesiastical History of England* was a more conventional form of historical writing. It was subtitled "comprehending a clearer and more connected view of the progress of our Ecclesiastical constitution; the preservation of our rights and liberties; and the rise and declension of the power of the Popes in England, than any other History extant." Warner stated in the preface that history was the best way to persuade people to "private and public virtue."[52]

Warner conceded that he had used Stillingfleet, Inet, Burnet, and Collier but pointed out that none of these authors covered the whole period of which he was writing. He claimed that Collier's work was unduly positive about Catholicism and the pope. Warner claimed that he had undertaken much research for the book: "I have spared neither labour nor expenses in searching all the authors, ancient and modern, of any name, who have wrote of our church history within the period." Warner chose not to insert mention of where he used other authors, partly because "I know of no other end it answers," and it broke up the flow of the reading, but he asserted that every date and fact he gave had been checked against these other authors.[53]

Warner explicitly addressed issues of bias and reliability of evidence. He asked, "Who is able to write the truth?" In some measure, his answer was those who were closest to the events themselves. Warner also added that he tried to write about people as they were, and not to add a layer of interpretation: "this is not only a duty, but in my opinion, is one of the first and chief qualifications of a writer of history." So his aim was to strip history of "legends and fables and false accounts." Consequently, Warner conceded that there might be places where he "contradicts the common opinion or shocks the prejudice of the reader." Where he did this, he did so "on good authority" and with care.[54] His model was Cicero's injunction that the historian should not affirm what is false and suppress what it true and should insert his own judgment sparingly and explicitly. This, Warner claimed, was what Bacon had done for Henry VII and Clarendon had done for the Civil War.[55] Warner warned the reader not to "expect any mirthful and pleasant passages. There was no room for to entertain readers with the eloquence of orators . . . nor with the skill of generals in the field." He was concerned that it was "dry," but he wrote that he had tried not to bore the reader with lengthy accounts of Church councils.[56]

Warner's opinions in the *Ecclesiastical History of England* were clear. Foremost among these was the perniciousness of non-English influences, a repeated theme in general histories that covered the topic. Warner praised the Druids and Celts because he saw them as authentically English, but the Angles and Saxons were not. Those from outside England came to ravish and persecute; St. Augustine came to subdue the native bishops to the pope. Warner's heroes in the early British church were Wilfred, Bishop of Northumbria and Kings Ina, Offa, and Egbert, principally because they defended the English and their interests; while William the Conqueror was condemned for making the Church in England subject to that of Rome and for encouraging monasticism to England's great disadvantage. Henry I was appreciated by Warner for restoring the liberties of the Church of England, but this was short-lived as later rulers conceded dominance to Rome. A good example of the pernicious nature of this was making religious orders exempt from the jurisdiction of English diocesan bishops. Throughout the medieval period, Warner saw the interference of Rome as a source of repeated problems for the Church.

A second theme was that the English clergy before the Reformation learned their cruelty and persecution from Rome and applied it with the same spirit as the papacy. Warner's view of Henry VIII was by no means positive; he saw that Henry was not motivated by religious impulses to break with Rome and questioned the suggestion that Henry was unlawfully married to Catherine of Aragon. But he argued that the Reformation was a happy outcome of these matters. Edward VI was Warner's ideal model of monarchy. Most of the errors of his reign, including the persecution of Anabaptists, were, he claimed, the responsibility of the Lord of the Realm, Edward, Duke of Somerset, and the council. But Edward was clearly a true Protestant who was responsible for the new liturgy and prayer book. As might be expected, Mary was depicted as a persecuting and furious ruler, and Elizabeth, as the fulfilment of the Reformation. Nevertheless, Warner recognized that Elizabeth could also be tyrannical and exceeded her father in the claims she made to royal authority. For Warner, Laud was a greater villain than Charles I, though he censured the king for listening to him too much. When it came to the Restoration, Warner's Dissenting background was evident: Charles II's restoration was not an unalloyed blessing since he ushered in a period of persecution of Dissenters. The revolution of 1688–89 ejected James II, a persecuting king.

A further theme, which also reflected Warner's Dissenting background, was the insufficient maintenance of the lesser clergy. Bishops, Warner felt, were major figures in the Church and state, but the lesser clergy were not treated with sufficient regard. Their widows and children were often left dispossessed when a parson died. Attempts to augment the income of the poorest livings were always treated by Warner as worthy and generous.

The *History of Ireland* was, as Warner conceded, an offshoot of his *History of England*. In writing about England, he found that there was no "tolerable" history of Ireland; indeed, Warner claimed that Ireland was the only European country without its own history. The problem with Irish histories, claimed Warner, was that they were typically written about Ireland's distant past and were replete with fables and legends so that most of them were "mythological" rather than real histories. Warner's principal theme was the low and depressed state that Ireland had been kept in "to the disgrace of letters and the reproach of both nations." He found that English writers were dismissive of Ireland and wrote of Ireland in "opprobrious terms," yet they showed no knowledge of the economy and culture of the land. Irish writers committed an equal error in giving long lists of Irish princes and "speaking of the splendours of their laws and government." Warner said that such views might have elements of truth, but both were partial. The problem was, as Warner saw it, that fewer than fifty English readers would be interested in such accounts of Irish history.[57] Moreover, English writers saw Ireland as alien, like Japan or China, and therefore of little interest.

Warner also identified the location of sources as a problem for writing Irish history. While Dublin contained many "rolls and journals of Parliament," as well as Chancery records and records of the Irish Privy Council, many Irish records had been taken to England and were now only to be found dispersed in private libraries and libraries in Oxford, London, and even Lambeth Palace. Consequently, any historian of Ireland would need to undertake research in both England and Ireland, which was what Warner claimed made his study unique.

In his *History of the Rebellion and Civil War in Ireland*, Warner emphasized his determination to examine the claims about massacres that took place during the Civil War, incidents that he claimed had not hitherto been "fully nor fairly represented."[58] The two writers whose accounts of the Irish massacres had achieved greatest circulation, Sir John Temple in *The Irish Rebellion* (1646) and Edmund Borlase in *Reduction of Ireland to the Crown of England* (1676), had produced both partial and unreliable accounts that emphasized the Irish responsibility for the events. And Clarendon seemed principally concerned to exonerate Ormonde. Warner dismissed accounts by Lords Clanricarde and Castlehaven as too biased toward the Catholics to be reliable.[59] Warner thought that Charles I's responsibility for stoking the Irish problems had been understated. When Warner wrote his account of the massacres in Ireland, he provided two pages of authorities and concluded his account: "whether the account I have given above of this great event in Irish history will satisfy the reader of either party, I don't know; but I have taken great care and pains in the enquiry and I write not to please but to inform; not to irritate parties, but to unite them in the exercise of civil social duties."[60] Warner made a case for his own account of the history with reference to the manuscripts that he had drawn on in Dublin from both official and private papers, including those of Giovanni Rinnuccini, the papal nuncio in Ireland. One of the conclusions Warner drew was that Charles was in collusion with the Catholics in Ireland.[61] Warner wrote that it would "instruct princes to consult the interests and instincts of their subjects, and not to govern by illegal and despotic power." He also warned ministers "that their own passions, faction and ill-humour will produce as much mischief to the public peace ... as the most open villainy." And it would teach the people "not to suffer and assist the folly, the forwardness, the pride and ambition of particular persons to govern the public understanding."[62] Perhaps because he knew how controversial his book might be, Warner did not follow his practice in the *History of England* of not breaking up the text with references to sources. In this case, he littered the margin with original sources for his facts and arguments.

In a defensive conclusion to the preface, Warner wrote that he could not claim that his book was free of errors, but it was free from partiality. He also wrote that "the bigots on both sides, who always have and ever will be the plague of the wise and good," have created in Irish history an "infernal rage," and he had tried to write "without passion or uncharitableness."[63] But Warner hoped that the book would persuade Irish Catholics to turn to religious toleration and loyalty to the government, and Protestants to abandon the vindictive statutes against Catholics—so that they both would come to a peaceful solution to the turbulence that held back Ireland from prosperity.[64]

Warner had his admirers. His *History of England* was a rare example of a work that between the publication of the first and second volume became a work funded by subscription. The subscription list included three members of the royal family, numerous peers, and leading bishops, clergy, and laymen. The libraries of colleges at Oxford and Cambridge and of the Royal Society added their support to the list.

CONCLUSIONS

Warner's work represents the opportunity to consider the ambitions, methods, and prejudices of a minor historical writer in the eighteenth century. As a former Dissenter and Latitudinarian Whig, he found ideas of religious liberty and the overthrow of subordination attractive and compelling. As a consequence, these were the principal narratives with which he concerned himself. Warner was assiduous in seeking out sources, especially manuscript sources, which he saw as valuable because of their proximity to events. His writing was characterized by experimentation with different styles of writing, dialogue, and biography, as well as more conventional history.

The writings of the period were written and read in the shadow of war. The nature of the wars in which Britain was involved threw imperial expansion to the fore, while the drama of crises, notably in 1745–46 and 1756–57, helped make the domestic response, as well as the international challenge, a matter of existential choices. Illuminated by historic examples, national renewal became necessary and, with eventual success, almost self-fulfilling.[65]

NOTES

1. Horace Walpole to Horace Mann, July 11, 1756, *Walpole-Mann corresp.* IV, 570.

2. R. Rolt, *An Impartial Representation of the Conduct of the Several Powers of Europe Engaged in the late General War*, 4 vols. (London, 1749–50), 1:x–xi.

3. R. Rolt, *Memoirs of the Life of . . . John Lindesay, Earl of Crawford* (London, 1753): 432, 86, 12–13.

4. Rolt, *Lives of the Principal Reformers* (London, 1759), ix.
5. Rolt, *Impartial Representation*, 1:x.
6. Rolt, *Lives*, 195.
7. M. Schlenke, *England und das friderizianische Preussen, 1740–1763* (Freiburg, 1963).
8. Rolt, *Lives*, iv, xi, iii.
9. C. Gerrard, *The Patriot Opposition to Walpole: Politics, Poetry, and National Myth, 1725–1742* (Oxford, 1994), 145–46.
10. Newcastle to Andrew Mitchell, envoy in Berlin, May 27, 1757, BL. Add. 6832 fol. 21.
11. Anon., *Reflections upon the Present State of Affairs* (London, 1755), 9.
12. Dedication to J. Lockman, *A New History of England*, 14th ed. (London, 1760). A translator of Voltaire, Lockman's works included histories of Greece, Rome, and Christianity.
13. Margarot to Hawkesbury, March 5, 1788, BL. Add. 38222 fol. 331.
14. T. Carte, *A General History of England* (London, 1747), 1:v, 2.
15. Carte, *History*, 3:iv.
16. Carte, *History*, 4:604–10.
17. Carte, *History*, 4:604–10.
18. E. Corp, "James II and David Nairne: The Exiled King and his first Biographer," *English Historical Review* 129 (2015): 1409.
19. L. J. Colley, *In Defiance of Oligarchy: The Tory Party, 1714–60* (Cambridge, 1982); M. Peters, *Pitt and Popularity: The Patriot Minister and London Opinion during the Seven Years' War* (Oxford, 1980).
20. P. Rogers, "Book Dedications in Britain 1700–1799: A Preliminary Survey," *British Journal for Eighteenth Century Studies* 16 (1993): 213–33.
21. F. Warner, *A Rational Defence of the English Reformation and Protestant Religion* (1752), iv.
22. Warner, *A Rational Defence*, v.
23. Warner also published *Remarks on the History of Fingal and other Poems of Ossian* (1762) and *A full and plain account of the gout... with some new and important instructions for its relief, which the author's experience in the gout above thirty years hath induced him to impart* (1768).
24. More was not canonized until the nineteenth century.
25. F. Warner, *The Ecclesiastical History of England to the Eighteenth Century*, 2 vols. (London, 1756–57), 1:iv.
26. Warner, *Ecclesiastical History*, 1:iv.
27. Warner, *Ecclesiastical History*, 1:iv.
28. Warner, *Ecclesiastical History*, 1:v.
29. Warner, *Ecclesiastical History*, 1:i–v.
30. Warner, *Ecclesiastical History*, 1:vi.
31. Warner, *Ecclesiastical History*, 2:vi.
32. F. Warner, *The History of Ireland* (London, 1763), dedication.
33. Warner, *History of Ireland*, dedication.
34. F. Warner, *History of the Rebellion and Civil War in Ireland* (London, 1768), dedication.
35. F. Warner, *Bolingbroke or A Dialogue on the Origin and Authority of Revelation* (London, 1755), i.
36. Warner, *Bolingbroke*, iv.
37. Warner, *Bolingbroke*, v.
38. Warner, *Bolingbroke*, x–xi.
39. F. Warner, *Memoirs of the Life of Thomas More* (London, 1758), 1–2.
40. Warner, *Memoirs*, 9.
41. Warner, *Memoirs*, 6.

42. Warner, *Memoirs*, 38.
43. Warner, *Memoirs*, 41–42.
44. Warner, *Memoirs*, 45.
45. Warner, *Memoirs*, 67–68.
46. Warner, *Memoirs*, 80–81.
47. Warner, *Memoirs*, 129.
48. Warner, *Memoirs*, 115.
49. Warner, *Memoirs*, 133.
50. Warner, *Memoirs*, 160.
51. Warner, *Memoirs*, 199.
52. F. Warner, *The History of England as it relates to Religion and the Church, From the Earliest Accounts to the Present Century* (London, 1759), i.
53. Warner, *History of England*, iii.
54. Warner, *History of England*, iv.
55. Warner, *History of England*, v.
56. Warner, *History of England*, vi.
57. Warner, *History of Ireland*, v.
58. Warner, *History of the Rebellion and Civil War*, xi–xii. For a modern study, see J. Cope, *England and the 1641 Irish Rebellion* (Woodbridge, UK, 2009).
59. Warner, *History of the Rebellion and Civil War*, xii. Lord Clanricarde's account was contained in his letters, which Warner had read.
60. Warner, *History of the Rebellion and Civil War*, 299.
61. Warner, *History of the Rebellion and Civil War*, xvii.
62. Warner, *History of the Rebellion and Civil War*, xviii.
63. Warner, *History of the Rebellion and Civil War*, xx.
64. Warner, *History of the Rebellion and Civil War*, xxi.
65. M. J. Cardwell, *Arts and Arms: Literature, Politics and Patriotism during the Seven Years War* (Manchester, 2004), 281.

SEVEN

FROM THE NEW REIGN TO THE CRISIS OF EMPIRE, 1760-76

HISTORY WAS A METHOD THAT COULD BE APPLIED TO THE FUTURE as to the past. This was clearly demonstrated in an anonymous work of 1763: *The Reign of George VI*, which dealt with history, but history in the future of the early twentieth century. George VI, an ideal monarch, comes to the throne of Britain at a time of major difficulties. During the reign, there are a series of wars, notably with Russia, whose army attempts an invasion. However, a number of major victories bring peace, prosperity, and growth. By the 1920s, George VI is ruler of France and Mexico, as well as Britain and America.

The 1760s were also important to the writing of more conventional national history. The decade saw the appearance of major works by Robertson and Hume, as well as Gibbon's decision to begin his great history. The decade also saw a new context for national history writing, that of unparalleled victory and apparent imperial destiny. Victorious over France and Spain in the Seven Years' War (1756-63),[1] Britain had clearly become the leading naval power and the dominant force in the North Atlantic. These victories were celebrated in a series of books on the recent war, including Thomas Mante's *History of the Late War in North America* (1772). Ironically, Mante (c. 1733-c. 1802), an officer in that struggle, acted as a spy in the pay of the French Ministry of War in 1769-74. He went on to produce a *Naval and Military History of the Wars of England* (1795-1807), which was heavily dependent on the historical works of Hume and Smollett.[2]

With George III (r. 1760-1820), Britain appeared to have a king who had broken, and consciously so, with the Hanoverian identity of his two predecessors, a king who was happy to identify with Britain. Oliver Goldsmith, a struggling Grub Street writer,[3] produced a *History of Mecklenburg* (1762), to take advantage of interest in the German origins of George's wife, Queen Charlotte; but the king was very much seen in a national light, and interest in the history of Hanover declined.

The decade also saw a strong focus on national cultural interests, rather than cosmopolitanism. This focus led, for example, to great engagement with Shakespeare, notably with the Shakespeare Jubilee in 1769,[4] as well as to the foundation of the Royal Academy to advance British art. Britishness was celebrated as the rise of the "modern," and, to that end, the canon was redefined, even invented.[5] Impressed by James Macpherson (1736–96) and his propagation of stories that he falsely claimed were by a third-century Scottish bard called Ossian, Thomas Percy (1729–1811), a grocer's son who sought to show his descent from the medieval Dukes of Northumberland, published *Reliques of Ancient English Poetry* (1765), an edition of old ballads, which promoted a revival of interest in the subject.[6]

The consequences of the Seven Years' War were clear. This was a decade in which national history was of great interest, but also a national history that looked toward a current state of imperial presence and power. A noble descent was on offer. While party politics were not at the forefront of cultural concerns in the 1760s, 1770s, and 1780s, politics in the wider sense of views on the arrangement and purpose of society remained important.

The habit of referring to the past for partisan purposes, notably to establish a position and as a coin of polemic, continued. Indeed, the lengthy and contentious process of ending the Seven Years' War provided a rich display of such admonition. The *Monitor* claimed on May 10, 1760, that it was clear from the disastrous reign of Henry VI (1422–61), never a good omen for comparison, that Britain must not "make a peace with France upon such terms, which shall restore her to a power to hurt us." Opposition newspapers criticizing Bute and the peace negotiations of 1762 referred to the reigns of Henry III, Richard II, and Edward IV in order to imply that royal favoritism, foreign advisers, bribery, and the determination of evil favorites to introduce arbitrary rule were all again playing a role. The *Monitor*, for example, offered these themes on July 24 and on October 23 and 30, 1762.

Differing forms of polemical relevance were provided on the continuing theme of anti-Jacobitism and the longstanding one of anti-Catholicism, the latter drawing on potent psychological anxieties as well as a clear polemic.[7] In 1764, George, 1st Lord Lyttelton, a prominent Whig politician, moved in the House of Lords the motion that led to the burning "as Jacobitical and violating the Bill of Rights and the Revolution" of Timothy Brecknock's *Droit le Roy. Or a Digest of the Rights and Prerogatives of the Imperial Crown of Great-Britain* (1764). Among the diverse fates of the writers mentioned in this book, Brecknock's was striking. He was hanged in 1786 for complicity in murder. In 1769, the Oxfordshire rector Edward Lewis published *The Patriot King, displayed in the Life of Henry VIII, King of England, from the time of his Quarrel with the Pope till his Death*, a violently anti-Catholic work that very much supported Henry. This historical book accorded with Lewis's anti-Catholic visitation sermon, *Sinners saved by Jesus Christ as preached in Scripture, but Church Fathers and Clergy are no sure Guides to Heaven*, published in 1756, a year of national panic. Edward Weston's *Family Discourses by a Country Gentleman* (1768) used historical references to support his argument that papal power was a threat to Britain.

This general context did not lessen the writing of history that would be contentious, by design or effect. Indeed, the difficulty of history was referred to by the well-read Elizabeth Montagu in 1762: "I imagine no history to be more difficult to write than that of England, as our government is made up of so many different kinds of civil policy and military institutions, altered by the shocks of violence, and the impressions of tyranny at different times, and our writers have been men very inadequate to their subjects."[8] The following day, she added to another friend: "Few people know anything of the English history but what they learn from Shakespeare; for our story is rather a tissue of personal adventures and catastrophes than a series of political events."[9] A new major edition of Shakespeare appeared in 1765. The eccentric MP Edward Wortley Montagu had published *Reflections on the Rise and Fall of the Ancient Republics. Adapted to the Present State of Great Britain* (1759), a change from cheating at cards. His book reflected the two major interests involved in historical writing: classical references and present-day applicability. In a sense, his title made explicit an approach already seen in many works, both books and shorter pieces.

ROBERTSON AND HUME

Several important writers of historical works came to the fore in the 1760s. William Robertson, principal of Edinburgh University from 1762 to 1793, produced the much-applauded *History of the Reign of Charles V* (1764). In his *History of America* (1777), a subject made more challenging by the apparent formlessness and chaos of New World history,[10] Robertson was to go on to offer a parallel to Rome and Britain by considering the Spanish system of colonialization, while also being alive to different historical phases in the latter. Indeed, this approach led Robertson to an emphasis on individuals rather than on some supposed generic system.[11] Such an emphasis indeed appeared justified by the imperial policy of Charles III of Spain (r. 1759–88). Interest in the history of Spanish expansionism led both Anne Plumptre and Richard Brinsley Sheridan to write plays on Pizarro, which were produced in 1799.

A more prosperous and confident country encouraged an interest in national history. It is customary to begin here with David Hume, whose *The History of England, from the Invasion of Julius Caesar to the Revolution in 1688* (1769) was not only a work that attracted ordinary readers but also one that influenced historians, including Gibbon. Hume, moreover, was cited in encyclopedia.[12] He was able to combine proof and narrative in a fashion that saw sources scrutinized. In the first chapter of his *History*, he pressed for putting aside "the fables which are commonly employed to supply the place of true history."[13] Hume used a distinction between primary and secondary sources and applied a branch of probability theory to the assessment of evidence.[14] His ironic humor was conducive to this approach.

Hume's case for philosophy was that it was a means of understanding the world that human beings fashion for themselves, and he then applied this style of reasoning to history. The latter, however, became more difficult than had been anticipated, with Hume feeling that he had to move backward in time in order to explain the turmoil of the seventeenth century, first to consider the decay of feudalism and the concomitant increase of the political power of the House of Commons, as well as the impact of the Reformation, and then all the way back to the Roman Conquest. As a result, it was necessary for Hume to engage with the medieval and earlier legacy, the latter explained with reference to "the curiosity, entertained by all civilised nations of entering into the exploits and adventures of their ancestors." Hume assumed that his ideal reader had already read the standard histories and thus would be impressed by the way he played them off against each other, enabling him to make Tory points against Whig orthodoxy or, seen differently, deploying the historical perspective of the court Whigs while seeking to sever it from its connection with the policies of a particular political party.[15] Indeed, his interest in trade as a factor in national development[16] was difficult to pigeonhole.

Hume did not believe that his argument could be read as Tory in its motivations. To Hume, there was endless constitutional change and no single English constitution.[17] It was not easy for him, however, to shape an account that met the requirements of consistency and avoided what might appear to be unfortunate political allegiances. The drama of individuals also played a major role. Like Wesley, Hume devoted much space to the clash between Elizabeth I and her rival, Mary, Queen of Scots.[18] The *History* made Hume a lot of money, and, for contemporaries, he, indeed, was largely an historian and not a philosopher. He only wrote short and minor pieces during the remaining thirteen years of his life.

Earlier, Hume had offered a very different form of history in a humorous satire against Pitt the Elder. In 1982, it was argued that this hitherto unlocated work was *Sister Peg*, an anonymous publication traditionally attributed to Adam Ferguson. A satirical and accessible allegory of the relations between England (John Bull of Bull-Hall) and Scotland (Sister Peg of Thistledown), this included a historical perspective that discussed the Union of 1707 and the crisis of 1745 before moving to more modern politics.[19]

WESLEY

Alongside Hume, it is instructive to consider at length not Robertson or Gibbon, but Wesley's *A Concise History of England, from the Earliest Times, to the Death of George II* (1776), which was an important instance of the more frequent and populist type of historical publication during the century. Moreover, Wesley's providentialist and moralistic history has received insufficient attention due to the standard focus on the stadial history of the more famous Enlightenment histories and because Wesley, like Milton, is famous for other reasons.[20]

The scholarly coverage of Wesley's lengthy historical work is limited. Aside from a very short piece in 1900 on Wesley's strong and lengthy defense of the reputation of Mary, Queen of Scots, a piece critical of his work as a historian,[21] the *History* was essentially ignored, which is an instance of a more general selectivity in texts. Thomas Herbert did little for the *History* by writing in 1940 that "as a history his book is of course utterly worthless today." This conclusion was somewhat qualified by noting that the work offered many insights on Wesley's views on royal power.[22] More recently, Thomas Smith has provided the first detailed analysis of the work's coverage of medieval England, while also noting that Wesley's study "has received almost no attention from historians to date," despite having sold well at the time,[23] which is an important point about impact. As a reminder of Wesley's range, others of Wesley's best sellers were not religious, notably his *Primitive Physick*.

The neglect until recently reflected a number of factors. These included the nature of the work's composition and the extent to which it is not directly central to Wesley's activities as a religious figure. The writing definitely lacks the flair of a Gibbon. The judgmental tone is more that of a moralist than one of a writer who, like Gibbon, delights in epigraphs, although that preference appears to have matched those of many readers as well as of numerous other historians. The nature of Wesley's composition and writing was one of coming in a tradition, rather than seeking to be known by originality. In his preface, Wesley acknowledged his debt to the comparable work of Rapin-Thoyras, Smollett, and Goldsmith, most particularly to the last. There were also references to Hume and Robertson.[24] Goldsmith's *The History of England, from the Earliest Times to the Death of George II* had appeared, also in four volumes, only five years earlier. It demonstrated the possibilities of such works and also the buoyant market for them, one very much seen in the holdings of the libraries of the period. Goldsmith, in turn, had drawn heavily on Hume.

This pattern of drawing heavily on very recent works acted to demonstrate the value of these works and, in part, established the authenticity, and thus authority, of the new history. Several historians referred to this process as a way to improve their work. Wesley saw the selection and shaping of material as his key role, one that gave this material, including the work of others, meaning.[25] This approach, with its emphasis on continuity, each work in part a gloss on what had come before, arose from an exegetical quality to his writing, a quality also seen with other writers. It was as if history was a text that had to be used to appreciate the divine purpose and the role of Providence. This, indeed, gave the work purpose and affected its tone.

Moreover, a general focus on origins and ancestry affected much of the public understanding and writing of history, with the authority of earlier accounts encouraging an emphasis on new work largely as a continuation of them, gaining and conferring approval, while also favoring what is somewhat unfairly seen as "scissors-and-paste" treatments of the past. That criticism is in many respects a secular and present-minded view. While not without value, it is pertinent to supplement this view with the traditions of presenting general histories as continuations of the Bible, explaining and interpreting current events in the light of the Christian faith, a practice also with dynastic histories, chronicle writing, and customs of legal writing. To take the last, whether Christian canon-law and common-law traditions, Islamic hadith collections or the Jewish Talmud, they were all forms of historiography. Each added a chronological framework, often allowed for change over time, and were instances of studying vice and virtue in the past in order to demonstrate and teach proper conduct. These practices of legal exposition were important in amplifying the use of the past as a sanction of authority. Lengthy and often bitter eighteenth-century debates about copyright, focused in particular on the Copyright Act of 1710 and the House of Lords 1774 case of *Donaldson v. Becket*, were instructive for contemporary attitudes.[26]

Among his endeavors in other forms to the same end, Wesley sought to use the history of the country of his readers as a way to demonstrate the divine role in the affairs of men, the fundamental link that was too readily set asunder, and thus to call his readers to God. Meaning was present and had to be explained. Demonstrating the divine role was his stated goal, and, if he only rarely explicitly addressed this in the text, this role illuminated his work. What might appear a paradox in the last sentence is not one that would have been so apparent to contemporaries as there would have been less of a need for an explicit engagement. Instead, the character of the *History* is somewhat similar to that of the Book of Kings in the Old Testament, the book of the Bible most frequently used as a text for readings and sermons in the Church of England during the century, and notably so in the idea of good and bad kings and in the interplay of free will and divine intervention. The readership would have been well aware of this parallel, and that point underlines the need to consider the strong implicit, as well as explicit, place of the Bible in eighteenth-century historiography. The parallel with ancient Israel of the idea of a chosen people was also appropriate in a culture resonant with such echoes, notably with Handel's popular oratorios. Understandings of the Bible were significant both for spiritual and for secular ends.[27] Far from this lodestar being challenged by science, it was assumed that the study of astronomy would strengthen religious knowledge and awareness.[28]

The purpose of demonstrating the divine role helped ensure a consistent moral goal and tone in Wesley's *History*. These volumes were not part of a project, whether or not crudely classified as Enlightenment, to employ science, including history, in order to analyze humankind outside a Christian framework. Thus, to use the standard language, this was not a "stadial" history, a history of the stages of human development, as presented for example by Adam Smith in *The Wealth of Nations* (1776) and in periodical works, such as "An Historical Account of the Rise and Progress of the Arts and Sciences," published in the *Royal Magazine* in December 1761.

Instead, the engagement was very much with divine purpose in history and time as framed by this purpose,[29] with a Christian society, and with the moral characteristics and choices that had affected its course. In particular, this led Wesley to a focus on monarchs. In part, this focus reflected a concern about great men but also a belief that the choices they made were not only decisive but also provided an opportunity to see morality in action, and a belief that that opportunity had to be grasped in order to understand the past. This was an established approach and one characteristic of much history writing, both at the time and earlier, albeit not always with as explicit a Christian message. In part, indeed, this approach reflected the weight of classical models in the writing of history, for example, the work of Tacitus, although Wesley himself was not particularly interested in classical comparisons.

The focus on individuals and, in particular, on the warnings offered by their faults was one frequently seen in other historical writing. Much of the writing lacked intellectual subtlety and philosophical profundity. It is instructive to consider Wesley in this context. He was essentially a preacher and exemplified the relevance of eighteenth-century and earlier sermon literature to the writing of history. Much of both was presented as directly relevant to the current day. Newspapers offered the same approach, the *True Briton* of September 9, 1723, arguing, "No study is so useful to mankind as history, where, as in a glass, men may see the virtues and vices of great persons in former ages, and be taught to pursue the one, and avoid the other." This was very much the approach taken by Wesley.

Other writers happily adopted the biographical approach, which, in part, was a product of the patristic scholarship (and comparable work by John Foxe) that focused on saints or sinners and martyrs or heretics. It was more relevant to most readers than the stadial, more sociological approach, which again highlights the issue of where best to place the emphasis of scholarly attention.

The combination of relatively recent history, religion, and monarchy ensured that the Reformation in particular, a history that had to be told as a moral tale, could indeed be so. This goal was given particular force during the longstanding confrontation with Jacobitism from 1689, a confrontation very much presented as moral as well as ideological, and individual as well as collective. Wesley had been an active denouncer of Jacobitism. He was also worried that "the senseless wickedness, the ignorant profaneness," of Newcastle's poor and the "continued cursing and swearing, and the wanton blasphemy" of the soldiers would endanger divine support.[30] The Battle of Culloden swept away such doubts, but the effective end of Jacobitism, with the total defeat of the French invasion attempt in 1759, did not close the approach of history as a moral struggle.

The role of royal personality as the focus of history, a role so excitably offered by the treatment of Henry VIII, was shared for most historians by Queen Elizabeth. She, moreover, was seen as an acceptable counterpoint to Henry and to William III. Indeed, those who opposed the erection of a statue to William in Bristol in the 1730s wanted one for Elizabeth. Unlike William, she was English, Anglican, and had apparently ensured that foreign policy had served national (and not Dutch) goals, while her private life was far less exotic and questionable than that of Henry VIII. More particularly, and this can be seen with Wesley and others, however much he searched for earlier moral lessons, Elizabeth had the advantage that she was not so ancient as to offer only tenuous parallels to the present. This was the case, for him and others, with the treatment of most pre-Reformation monarchs, although Edward III and Henry V served their turn in providing a valiant pedigree for bellicose opposition to France.

At the same time, Elizabeth was sufficiently historical to prove malleable. Wesley's fervent and lengthy defense of Mary, Queen of Scots, put him out of the mainstream, not least compared with Robertson's *History of Scotland, During the Reigns of Queen Mary and of King James VI* (1759), and gave an element of his work a proto-Romantic feel. In contrast, Elizabeth served most commentators as a virtuous defender of Protestantism and the key molder of the Church of England. This was somewhat different to the appearance of Elizabeth in Adam Smith's *Wealth of Nations*: she attracted attention there solely as the first person that wore stockings in England.[31]

Wesley was very much in the tradition of history as account of, and call to, virtuous struggle, and it was understandable that he should see the history of England both as a part of his writing on religion and as a morally exemplary tale. Politics and morality were not differentiated by contemporaries. Instead, their relationship was strongly focused because of the obvious political importance of a small number of individuals and because of the notion of kingship and governance as moral activities. As the relationship appeared timeless, it seemed pertinent to apply admonitory tales from the past in a modern context. In a fashion that made sense of Wesley's *History*, the importance of personal drives, rather than of socioeconomic or institutional or geopolitical forces, was a central feature of much history writing, one that accorded with the stress on narrative.

Wesley himself referred to Shakespeare, and notably in his coverage of Richard III, claiming, "It is evident from the conduct of Shakespeare, that the house of Tudor retained all their Lancastrian prejudices, even in the reign of Queen Elizabeth."[32] Wesley was critical of Shakespeare's treatment, although sensibly accepting that it would have far greater influence than that of historians. He obviously was a close reader of Shakespeare for he pressed on to compare *The Winter's Tale* with the events of Henry VIII's reign, seeing Hermione as Anne Boleyn and "the unreasonable jealousy of Leontes, and his violent conduct in consequence" as "a true portrait of Henry the Eighth, who generally made the law the engine of his boisterous passions."[33] The interest in monarchs, role of personalities, and commitment to a national glory that involved both medievalism and a positive portrayal of the Tudor Age, certainly in terms of the Reformation and of Elizabeth, were also seen in paintings and on the stage.

In response to the general moralization of the past, James Hampton complained, in 1746, in his *Reflections on Ancient and Modern History* that "with modern writers everything is either vice or virtue," and wrote of "the common-place maxims, wrong criticism, and perverse jumble of ancient and modern politics, which are so frequent in the men of mere learning. . . . the impertinences of those groveling writers, who, on pretence of explaining every hidden spring and movement of the state, paint the great personages of history after their own vile likeness, and make them speak and act, as they themselves would have done in the same circumstances."[34]

Wesley's writing was very much in accordance with the dichotomy of vice and virtue. This was particularly the case given that each discussion of a monarch included coverage of his or her personality, a discussion in which God played a role. Thus, the section on Edward VI (r. 1547–53) ended, "Such a prodigy of understanding and virtue, was taken unsullied to the GOD whom he loved."[35] This was a strongly Protestant view.

The focus on individual personality was linked to a dramatization of these reigns. Thus, Mary, Queen of Scots, was praised in direct opposition to Elizabeth, and Wesley was highly critical of Elizabeth's treatment of Mary, attributing this to dislike and envy rather than political calculation.[36] This theme was to be taken up in the very pro-Marian *Mary Queen of Scots Vindicated* (1787), a three-volume work by John Whitaker, the historian of Manchester, which was followed in 1790 by a second edition and a volume of additions and corrections. Whitaker subsequently worked on a *Private Life of Mary Queen of Scots*, but it was not published.

So also for Wesley, personal drama was to the fore in the treatment of Robert, 2nd Earl of Essex.[37] In contrast, less attention was devoted to much of the more conventional history of the period. For example, the Spanish Armada of 1588, a topic that did not have a comparable personal drama, received relatively little attention from Wesley; while English domestic history for much of the reign was presented as peaceful, and therefore, "there scarce passed any occurrence which requires a particular detail."[38] This view extended to the absence of discussion of social and economic trends.

The seventeenth century and, even more, the eighteenth provided Wesley with an opportunity to apply his morality to the history of a period that he felt had more to offer of relevance to current readers. Far from seeing a continuity in history, Wesley proposed a fundamental change with James I's reign (1603–25). In contradiction to the king's ideas on the royal prerogative, "new ideas of liberty had for some time been stealing in; and only wanted the reign of a weak monarch to appear without control . . . an emulation took place, to imitate the freedom of Greece and Rome . . . symptoms immediately began to be seen of a more free and independent genius in the nation.[39]

In many respects, the remainder of the *History* consisted of the unfolding of this genius, such that Charles I's failure was attributed to his being unable to accommodate himself to "the genius of the people" and its pressure on the constitution,[40] a view Burnet would have accepted. In a point also made by others, this pressure was a political counterpart to the search for religious liberty seen with the Reformation. The two were linked; Wesley observed of the education of Charles's children, "that turn towards popery which has since been the ruin of that unfortunate family,"[41] a direct reference to the failure and fate of James II (r. 1685–88), who could serve as a moral as well as dramatic counterpart to the monarchs who came after.

The Civil War (1642–46) was correctly seen by Wesley as a fundamental clash reflecting differing views of the country:

> Never was contest more unequal than this seemed at first between the contending parties: the king being entirely destitute of every advantage. His revenue had been seized by Parliament; all the sea-port towns

were in their hands, except Newcastle, and thus they were possessed of the customs; the fleet was at their disposal; all magazines of arms and ammunition were seized for their use; and they had the wishes of the most active members of the nation.

To oppose this, the king had that acknowledged reverence which was paid to royalty. The greater part of the nobility adhered to him.[42]

Alongside the inconstant character of some of Wesley's judgments—for example, about the Civil War, not an easy subject to tackle due to its changing character and consequences—the concern about Popery provided a theme in his work that continued until the defeat of the Jacobite challenge in the reign of George II (1727–60). As another link there was the difficulty in preserving monarchy as an ideal form from the follies of party government, a theme that Bolingbroke in his *The Idea of a Patriot King* (1749),[43] Frederick, Prince of Wales, and George III all outlined. Thus, Wesley thought that James I's "failings were mostly owing to his being too early initiated in the intrigues of parties, who vied with each other to give him wrong notions of government, and to inspire him with a thorough hatred of all liberty, either civil or religious. Had he behaved upon his throne, and towards his subjects, as a plain, country gentleman would have acted towards his tenants upon his private estate, without launching into the subtleties of controversy, or pretending to explore the depth of politics, he would have made a great figure on the theatre of the world."[44] George I was also to be criticized by Wesley for aligning with political factions.

The idealization of a monarch as "a plain country gentleman" acting in a paternalist and patriotic fashion captured the theme of both Bolingbroke and George III, and also the degree of unreality bound up in it, although George was able to present the role.[45] To a degree, this was a Tory rejection of the modern world as in some respects almost inherently corrupt and a call for a return to a simpler society. At the same time, Wesley was willing to offer a more complex version—for example, in praise of James I: "Modern writers have greatly exaggerated some of his failings. His pacific notions, though he carried them too far, were of infinite benefit to his dominions; and posterity has been ungrateful to his memory in not observing that he chalked out, and in many respects filled up the great outlines of commerce, which have raised England to her present pitch of glory and greatness."[46]

While castigating the Stuarts, the Parliamentarians were criticized by Wesley for pushing matters too far in 1641 and for not being sufficiently mindful of the dangers of civil war.[47] Indeed, Wesley delivered a firm attack on republicanism; although, as was normal, without explaining why, on that basis, the Dutch were to escape criticism:

> In the comparison between a republic and a limited monarchy, the balance entirely inclines to the latter, since a real republic never yet existed, except in speculation; and that liberty which demagogues promise to their followers is generally only sought for themselves. The aim in general of popular leaders is rather to depress the great, than exalt the low; and in such governments, the lower ranks of people are too commonly the most abject slaves. Again, in a republic, the number of tyrants are capable of supporting each other in their injustice; while in a monarchy there is one object, who, if he offends, is more easily punishable.[48]

This very much looked back to the classical condemnation of republicanism by writers ready to argue the superiority of Imperial Rome. The same lesson was driven home for the aftermath of the Civil War: "From this period, to the despotic government of Cromwell, the constitution was convulsed with all the agitations of faction, guilt, ignorance, and enthusiasm. The kingly power being laid low, the parliament assumed the rein; but they were soon to submit to the military power, which, like all democracies, was turbulent, transient, feeble and bloody."[49]

Oliver Cromwell, "a great, bad man" with his "fanatic chaplains,"[50] a classic Tory view, was of a piece; and the criticism of the Protectorate government was strong. In contrast, Wesley presented General George Monck as more just. However, in bringing in Charles II in 1660, General Monck led to the Crown going to a ruler who was devoted to pleasure.[51] As with his Stuart predecessors, although for different reasons, he was unable to preserve order and restrain the baser instincts. Charles's personality was seen as a key problem, with his engaging manner and popularity lined to his unsuitability: "His indolence and love of pleasure made him averse to all kinds of business; his familiarities were prostituted to the worst of his subjects; and he took no care to reward his former friends, as he had taken no steps to be avenged of his former enemies."[52]

With a characteristic favor for the Tory pantheon, Wesley presented Charles as initially satisfactory because he was "directed in all things by

Clarendon . . . the king uniformly preserved an air of moderation and neutrality."[53] Nevertheless, Clarendon's support for the laws came to seem objectionable to Charles, who had "never much loved" his "steady virtue."[54] Instead, Charles turned to the Cabal, the ministry, according to Wesley, most "fitted to destroy all that liberty which had been establishing for ages."[55] In supporting the causes of Louis XIV, autocracy, and Catholicism, the Cabal very much represented betrayal from within, an argument repeatedly directed by contemporaries against the Old Corps Whigs and against corruption. There was also, for Wesley, the extent to which Charles was unable to prevent the dangerous and bloody panic of the Popish Plot of 1678.[56] Indeed, Wesley was disgusted: "One can scarce contemplate the transactions of this reign without horror. Such a picture of guilt on each side; a court at once immersed in sensuality and blood, a people armed against each other with the most deadly animosity, and no single party to be found with sense enough to stem the general torrent of rancour and suspicion."[57]

Wesley linked policy flaws to personality: "He [Charles II] was abandoned to all vices. A worse man never sat on the English throne."[58] In turn, the despotic James II was to be swept aside by the "train of providences" in 1688 that enabled William of Orange to effect "the delivery of the kingdom,"[59] and, with the fall of James, the third volume ended. The very organization of the book thus helped mark the significance of events, a common feature among historians of England, and provided Wesley with a pattern of providential intervention. As a member of the Established Church and a Tory, it is unsurprising that Wesley criticized both Popery and fanatical Protestantism, a position also taken by his critics within the Church, such as George Lavington, bishop of Exeter.[60]

In the fourth volume, that beginning with William III's reign (1689–1702), Wesley very much embraced Tory themes and directly related them to the politics of the era. Although he praised William, Wesley was critical of the way in which England lost out in the Nine Years' War (1689–97) and was, he claimed, misused by her Dutch allies. Wesley also condemned public plunder and widespread corruption. These criticisms were accentuated for the War of the Spanish Succession (1702–13), as John, Duke of Marlborough, was presented as profiting from the conflict, themes earlier adopted by Jonathan Swift in his *The Conduct of the*

Allies (1711) and by other Tory writers. A clear religious dimension was offered, with Marlborough's riches seen as "Poor gain, if he lost his own soul!"[61] There was no formal bargain by Marlborough with the devil, as was depicted for Oliver Cromwell, but the subtext was still present, and it was not difficult to read from the case of Cromwell.

In a contrast to the focus on Continental warfare with Marlborough, Wesley advocated the Tory "blue-water strategy," the focus on transoceanic activity that looked back to Drake and Elizabeth I, as well as the Tory case on the end of the war.[62] He continued in this approach in his coverage of foreign policy under George I, who was criticized as overly favorable to Hanover and a king of faction.[63] Wesley thus reiterated the established Tory linkage of Continental interventionism, corruption, and the moneyed interest.[64] Tory skepticism about international alliances was frequently advanced by Wesley: "this was the age of treaties, subsidies, and political combinations. At that time, the politicians of the age supposed that such chains would secure the permanence of dominion; but experience has taught the contrary."[65]

Much of volume four was dominated by war. This confronted Wesley with issues of tone and content. He was no Quaker, but that increased the complexity of his task. Wesley made his preferences clear. War could be noble, but its conduct had to be appropriate. Writing of the aftermath of the Battle of Culloden, where the Jacobites were heavily defeated in 1746, he noted in a criticism of the Duke of Cumberland's generalship: "Civil war is in itself terrible, but more so when heightened by unnecessary cruelty. How guilty soever an enemy may be, it is the duty of a brave soldier to remember that he is only to fight an opposer, and not a suppliant. The victory was in every respect decisive, and humanity to the conquered would have rendered it glorious. But no mercy was shown; the conquerors were seen to refuse quarter to the wounded, the unarmed, and the defenceless; and soldiers to anticipate the base employment of the executioner."[66]

In turn, the conquest of French Canada under George II in 1758–60 was presented as a key means to national greatness, one made necessary by the French threat. Thus, of the 1758 campaign, Wesley observed: "The taking of Fort du Quesne [now Pittsburg] served to remove from their [the British] colonies the terror of the incursions of the Indians, while it interrupted that correspondence which ran along a chain of forts, with which the French had invironed the English settlements in America."[67] General James Wolfe was presented as the hero of 1759, a young man "who, without being indebted to family or connexions, had raised himself by merit. . . . He carried on the war with all the spirit of humanity which it admits of."[68] His heroic death was described, and Wesley presented him in terms that had an allusion to Christ: "it is the lot of mankind only to know true merit, when they are going to lose it," which may have been an autobiographical thought on the part of Wesley.[69] This presentation in print matched that in the pictorial depictions of Wolfe.

Wesley turned from this triumph to the less successful war on the Continent. He observed of the 1757 Convention of Klosterseven between France and Hanover: "Treaties between nations are seldom observed any longer than interest or fear obliges: and among nations that take every advantage, political faith is a term without meaning."[70] Fortunately for the trajectory of the book, Wesley was able to move on via the Battle of Minden in 1759, a "splendid" victory marred by the conduct of Lord George Sackville,[71] to naval triumph the same year:

> The courage and the conduct of the English admirals had surpassed whatever had been read of in history; neither superior force, nor number, nor even the terrors of the tempest, could intimidate them. Admiral Hawke gained a complete victory over an equal number of French ships, on the coast of Bretagne [Brittany] in Quiberon Bay, in the midst of a tempest, during the darkness of the night, and what seamen fear more, upon a rocky shore.
>
> Such was the glorious figure the British nation appeared in to all the world at this time. But while their arms prospered in every effort tending to the real interests of the nation an event happened, which for a while obscured the splendour of her victories.[72]

This was the introduction to the death of George II, which marked the close of the book, a close that was not capped by a conclusion or a postscript. As a result, victory was the theme at the end, a victory that solved the existential issues posed by Catholicism, France, and autocracy.

These challenges played out in terms of a historical narrative that was very much organized in terms of the individual qualities of the monarchs, qualities that sometimes bore an elliptical relationship to the events of the reign but that offered a readily graspable approach to the subject. The model offered was that of Queen Anne (r. 1702–14), according to Wesley, "certainly one of the best and most unblemished sovereigns that ever sat upon the throne of England,"[73] a view that expressed Tory orthodoxy. George III was not a subject covered in Wesley's history, but he both reflected Wesley's views on kingship, notably his favor for Anne, and set an acceptable tone of improving interest in the past.

Wesley's *History*, therefore, accorded well with a strong tradition of history writing in eighteenth-century Britain as well as with an aspect of Tory thought and its continuation after the demise of the Tory party. In particular, Dr. Johnson, both in his criticism of Walpole's government over reluctance to go to war with Spain in the late 1730s and his support of Lord North's government over its reluctance to fight Spain in the Falkland Islands crisis of 1770, offered approaches similar to those of Wesley. For both men, as later for Edmund Burke in his responses to international development, there are issues of inconsistency, but the inconsistencies of these writers capture the difficulties of applying a moral political stance in a complex and changing world.[74]

Wesley is significant as one of the writers who kept Tory thought active. The re-creation of Toryism as a politics of patriotism and nationalism in the 1790s owed much to the ideological and political pressures, issues, and contingencies of that decade but also echoed more traditional themes. The continued expression of these themes was an important aspect of the political thought of the earlier period of George III's reign.

OTHER WRITERS

The moral component very clearly presented by Wesley was far from unusual.[75] Indeed, Wesley's *History* deserves attention precisely because it is not original but reflects so interestingly on a widespread engagement with the moral quality of the past. The same is true with Wesley's emphasis on the role of individuals. For example, in 1769, James Granger published a *Biographical History of England . . . adapted to a Methodical Catalogue of Engraved British Heads. Intended as an Essay towards reducing our Biography to System, and a help to the Knowledge of Portraits*. Individuals were crucial to Horace Walpole's *Anecdotes of Painting in England*

(1762–80), Thomas Warton's *History of English Poetry* (1774–81), and Johnson's *Lives of the Poets* (1779–81). These also represented attempts to establish what was important and fix a canon, as also in Benjamin Victor's *History of the Theatres of London and Dublin from 1730* (1761–71). At the same time, the variety of history was to the fore. Thus, in the 1760s, Guthrie produced a *General History of the World, from the Creation to the Present Time* (1764–67) and a *General History of Scotland* (1767), each Whiggish works in which progress led toward modern Britain. Goldsmith's books included *An Account of the Augustan Age in England* (1759), which dealt with the period of Alexander Pope and Jonathan Swift.

To move the focus to another means and genre of perception, travel provided a further possibility for an engagement with national history. As a result, the greater interest in travel within the British Isles in the closing decades of the century, and its focus on rural areas, ensured that there was a stronger response to the possibilities of national history, one allied to local history. This in particular led to a repositioning chronologically, with the interest being notably in the Roman and medieval past.

Travel was made a common, even normative, experience through travel literature, a generally ignored form of history writing that requires attention. One of the most significant writers was Thomas Pennant, whose *Tour in Scotland*, carried out in 1769, included northern England and was published in 1771, going into five editions by 1790. Pennant (1726–98), a member of the Welsh gentry educated in Oxford, had gone on the Grand Tour but subsequently was an active traveler in the British Isles, who also wrote a *Tour in Wales* (1778) and a posthumously published *Journey from London to the Isle of Wight* (1801). In his tours, he commented on both Roman and medieval remains and on history, earning the description "he was the first who enlivened the dryness of topographical research with historical and biographical anecdote."[76] In the *Tour in Scotland*, Pennant discussed the Lincolnshire Fens: "passed near the site of Swineshead Abbey, of which there are not the least remains. In the walls of a farm-house, built out of the ruins, you are shown the figure of a Knight Templar, and told it was the monk who poisoned King John; a fact denied by our best historians."[77]

On Burlington Quay in Yorkshire, where Charles I's wife, Henrietta Maria, landed in 1642, he commented that the pursuing parliamentary admiral "brutally fired for two hours at the house where she lay, forcing her to take shelter, half-dressed, in the fields. Nor Parliament nor admiral were ashamed of this unmanly deed, but their historian, the moderate Whitelock, seems to blush for both, by omitting all mention of the affair."[78]

This reference to Bulstrode Whitelocke's *Memorials of the English Affairs from the beginning of the Reign of Charles I to the happy Restoration of King Charles II* (1682) reflected the continuation of old controversies and the awareness of long-published works. The second edition of the *Memorials* had appeared in 1732.

Pennant's interests in the landscape of history were shared. Thus, in 1789, George Huntingford, then master of the school at Warminster and later a bishop, wrote to his friend Henry Addington, then Speaker of the Commons and later Viscount Sidmouth and prime minister, who had been traveling in Hampshire: "The old ruins of Beaulieu I know well, and remember with an impression bordering on superstition."[79]

Historians chose sources that tended to conform to their presuppositions. Thus, for the same period, Catharine Macaulay, in her *The History of England from the Accession of James I to that of the Brunswick Line* (1763–83), drew extensively on John Rushworth's *Historical Revolutions*, which appeared in eight volumes between 1659 and 1701, with a second edition in 1721 and an abridgement in 1703. Rushworth (c. 1612–90), an officeholder under the Parliamentarian government of the 1640s and early 1650s, was attacked by Royalist writers, notably John Nalson, for bias.

At the same time, alongside the various aspects of what can be seen as positivism, there was also a skepticism about the ability of historians, irrespective of controversies, to understand causes and thus, more generally, concerning the very value of historical exposition. In his *Thoughts on the Late Transactions respecting Falkland's Islands* (1771), Johnson stressed the unpredictability and volatility of human affairs:

> It seems to be almost the universal error of historians to suppose it politically, as it is physically true, that every effect has a proportionate cause. In the inanimate action of matter upon matter, the motion produced can be but equal to the force of the moving power; but the operations of life, whether private or public, admit no such laws. The caprices of

voluntary agents laugh at calculation. It is not always that there is a strong reason for a great event. Obstinacy and flexibility, malignity and kindness, give place alternatively to each other, and the reason of these vicissitudes, however important may be the consequences, often escapes the mind in which the change is made.[80]

Johnson's cautious sense that developments, both in individuals and more generally, could not be predicted, because they were "irrational," and that therefore foreign policy risked upset if it sought to create a system based on the apparently predictable, indeed measurable, views and interests of others, was therefore based on a historical insight. For Johnson, this insight focused on the flux he also saw in the changing nature of the language. Indeed, this sense of impermanence was a characteristic feature of Tory writers pessimistic about the chances of a well-ordered society, and it was especially notable among Anglicans conscious of the challenges to the position of the Church. Changes in the text of Johnson's massive *Dictionary of the English Language* (1755) reflected his attempt to fix the shifting language, but this was a struggle in which he increasingly doubted his ability. He moved from the confidence of his *Plan of the Dictionary* (1747) to the subsequent resignation of the preface, written after the work on the first edition had ended.[81]

The emphasis on morality did not necessarily produce predictability but gave a dramatic note to history. A sense of improvement owed much to that of better monarchs from 1689 on, to the anchoring of the monarchy in a new constitutional system, and to a conviction that England was forward-looking and had moved forward from its medieval past.[82] It was unclear, however, to the cautious, such as Johnson,[83] and to critics, such as radicals, British and American, that this anchoring had provided lasting success. Meanwhile, as indicated with travel literature, references to history continued to be found across a range of literary types.

NOTES

1. M. J. Cardwell, *Arts and Arms: Literature, Politics and Patriotism during the Seven Years War* (Manchester, 2004).

2. R. C. Cole, *Thomas Mante: Writer, Soldier, Adventurer* (New York, 1993).

3. R. C. Taylor, *Goldsmith as Journalist* (Rutherford, NJ, 1993).

4. M. Dobson, *The Making of the National Poet: Shakespeare, Adaptation and Authorship, 1660–1769* (Oxford, 1992).

5. H. D. Weinbrot, *Britannia's Issue: The Rise of British Literature from Dryden to Ossian* (Cambridge, 1993).

6. B. H. Davis, *Thomas Percy: A Scholar-Cleric in the Age of Johnson* (Philadelphia, 1989).

7. A. Marotti, *Religious Ideology and Cultural Fantasy: Catholic and Anti-Catholic Discourses in Early Modern England* (Notre Dame, IN, 2005).

8. Montagu to Lyttelton, July 15, 1762, HL. MO. 1414.

9. Montagu to Elizabeth Carter, July 16, 1762, HL. MO. 3079.

10. D. J. Womersley, "The Historical Writings of William Robertson," *Journal of the History of Ideas* (1986): 505–6.

11. I. F. Pugliese, "From Antagonism to a Common Fate: Guillaume-Thomas Raynal and William Robertson," in *Raynal's "Histoire des deux Indes." Colonialism, Networks and Global Exchange*, ed. C. Courtney and J. Mander (Oxford, 2015), 168–69.

12. J. Fieser, ed., *Early Response to Hume's 'History of England'*, 2 vols. (Bristol, 2002); *Encyclopaedia Britannica*, 5th ed. (London, 1815), 8:62. With regard to Hume's account of Ethelred's massacre of the Danes.

13. D. Hume, *The History of England*, 8 vols. (London, 1813), 1:2.

14. D. Wootton, "Narrative, Irony, and Faith in Gibbon's *Decline and Fall*," *History and Theory* 33 (1994): 83; L. Okie, "Ideology and Partiality in David Hume's *History of England*," *Hume Studies* 11 (1985): 1–32.

15. J. A. Harris, *Hume: An Intellectual Biography* (Cambridge, 2015), 374; V. G. Wexler, *David Hume and the History of England* (Philadelphia, 1979); N. Capaldi and D. W. Livingston, eds., *Liberty in Hume's "History of England"* (Dordrecht, 1990); D. Wootton, "David Hume: The Historian," in *The Cambridge Companion to Hume*, ed. D. F. Norton (Cambridge, 2009), 447–79.

16. J. Wei, *Commerce and Politics in Hume's "History of England"* (Woodbridge, UK, 2017).

17. A. Sabl, *Hume's Politics: Coordination and Crisis in the History of England* (Princeton, NJ, 2013).

18. W. L. Robison, "Hume and the Moral Historian: Queen Elizabeth I," *European Legacy* 18 (2013): 576–87.

19. D. R. Raynor, *Sister Peg: A Pamphlet hitherto Unknown by David Hume* (Cambridge, 1982).

20. N. von Maltzahn, *Milton's 'History of Britain': Republican Historiography in the English Revolution* (Oxford, 1991).

21. R. Butterworth, "Wesley on Mary Queen of Scots," *Proceedings of the Wesley Historical Society* 2, no. 5 (1899–1900): 111–14.

22. T. W. Herbert, *John Wesley as Editor and Author* (Princeton, NJ, 1940).

23. T. W. Smith, "Authority and Liberty: John Wesley's View of Medieval England," *Wesley and Methodist Studies*, 7 (2015): 1–26. See also W. Gibson, "Tory and Whig: John Wesley and the Concise History of England," http://oxford-institute.org/2013-thirteenth-institute; J. Black, "John Wesley and History," *Wesley and Methodist Studies* 9 (2017): 1–17.

24. For example, J. Wesley, *A Concise History of England, from the Earliest Times, to the Death of George II*, 4 vols. (London, 1776, hereafter *CHE*), 3:34–35.

25. I. Rivers, "John Wesley as Editor and Publisher," in *The Cambridge Companion to John Wesley*, ed. R. L. Maddox and J. E. Vickers (Cambridge, 2010): 146–47, 153.

26. M. Rose, *Authors and Owners: The Invention of Copyright* (Cambridge, MA, 1993).

27. A. Hessayon and N. Keene, eds., *Scripture and Scholarship in Early Modern England* (London, 2006).

28. G. P. Brooks, "Mental Improvement and Vital Piety: Isaac Watts and the Benefits of Astronomical Study," *Dalhousie Review* 65 (1985–86): 551–64.

29. T. A. Campbell, "John Wesley and Conyers Middleton on Divine Intervention in History," *Church History* 55 (1986): 39–49.

30. Wesley to Matthew Ridley, Mayor of Newcastle, October 26, 1745, Northumberland CRO. ZRI 27/5.

31. A. Smith, *An Inquiry into the Nature and Causes of the Wealth of Nations*, ed. R. H. Campbell, A. S. Skinner, and W. B. Todd, 2 vols. (Oxford, 1976), 1:262. For an approach similar to that of Wesley, see W. Goodall, *Examination of the Letters said to be written by Mary Queen of Scots to James, Earl of Bothwell, showing by intrinsic and extrinsic evidence that they are forgeries*, 2 vols. (Edinburgh, 1754); W. Tytler, *An Inquiry, Historical and Critical, into the Evidence against Mary Queen of Scots* (1759; 4th ed. London, 1790).

32. Wesley, *CHE*, 2:139.

33. Wesley, *CHE*, 2:139–40.

34. Anon. [J. Hampton], *Reflections on Ancient and Modern History* (Oxford, 1746): 26–27.

35. Wesley, *CHE*, 2:261.

36. Wesley, *CHE*, 2:327–29.

37. Wesley, *CHE*, 3:13–14.

38. Wesley, *CHE*, 2:337.

39. Wesley, *CHE*, 3:85–86.

40. Wesley, *CHE*, 3:220.

41. Wesley, *CHE*, 3:105.

42. Wesley, *CHE*, 3:180.

43. F. Nibelius, *Lord Bolingbroke (1678–1751) and History. A Comparative Study of Bolingbroke's Politico-historical Works and a Selection of Contemporary Texts as to Themes and Vocabulary* (Stockholm, 2003), 147–61.

44. Wesley, *CHE*, 3:107–8.

45. I. Kramnick, *Bolingbroke and His Circle: The Politics of Nostalgia in the Age of Walpole* (Cambridge, MA, 1968); S. Varey, "Hanover, Stuart, and the *Patriot King*," *British Journal for Eighteenth-Century Studies* 6 (1983): 171.

46. Wesley, *CHE*, 3:108.

47. Wesley, *CHE*, 3:163.

48. Wesley, *CHE*, 3:171.

49. Wesley, *CHE*, 3:199.

50. Wesley, *CHE*, 3:245–46.

51. Wesley, *CHE*, 3:264.

52. Wesley, *CHE*, 3:261.

53. Wesley, *CHE*, 3:262.

54. Wesley, *CHE*, 3:267.

55. Wesley, *CHE*, 3:275.

56. Wesley, *CHE*, 3:285, 289, 298.

57. Wesley, *CHE*, 3:313.

58. Wesley, *CHE*, 3:316.

59. Wesley, *CHE*, 3:346.

60. C. Haydon, "Bishop George Lavington of Exeter (1684–1762) and *The Enthusiasm of Methodists and Papists, Compar'd*," *Southern History*, 37 (2015), 63.

61. Wesley, *CHE*, 4:91. For a modern treatment, see J. R. Jones, *Marlborough* (Cambridge, 1993).

62. Wesley, *CHE*, 4:94–95.
63. Wesley, *CHE*, 4:109–11.
64. Anon., *A Letter from an English Traveller at Rome* (n.p., 1721), 14.
65. Wesley, *CHE*, 4:138–39.
66. Wesley, *CHE*, 4:227–28.
67. Wesley, *CHE*, 4:280.
68. Wesley, *CHE*, 4:282.
69. Wesley, *CHE*, 4:284.
70. Wesley, *CHE*, 4:286.
71. Wesley, *CHE*, 4:289.
72. Wesley, *CHE*, 4:290–91.
73. Wesley, *CHE*, 4:108.
74. J. Black, "Samuel Johnson, Thoughts on the Late Transactions respecting Falkland's Islands, and the Tory Tradition in Foreign Policy," in *Samuel Johnson in Historical Context*, ed. J. C. D. Clark and H. Erskine-Hill (Basingstoke, UK, 2002), 169–83.
75. Lyttelton to ---, April 5, 1772, BL. RP. 2377 ii.
76. T. Pennant, *A Journey from London to the Isle of Wight*, 2 vols. in one (London, 1801), Anon. preface, 1:v.
77. Pennant, *A Tour in Scotland 1769*, 4th ed. (London, 1776), 15.
78. Pennant, *Tour in Scotland*, 17.
79. Huntingford to Addington, September 17, 1789, Exeter, Devon CRO. 152M/C1789/F99.
80. S. Johnson, *Thoughts on the late Transactions respecting Falkland's Islands* (London, 1771), 33–34.
81. A. Reddick, *The Making of Johnson's Dictionary, 1746–1773* (Cambridge, 1990).
82. N. Hudson, *Samuel Johnson and the Making of Modern England* (Cambridge, 2003).
83. J. C. D. Clark, *Samuel Johnson: Literature, Religion and English Cultural Politics from the Restoration to Romanticism* (Cambridge, 1994).

EIGHT

EMPIRE AS HISTORICAL NARRATIVE

Gibbon and the Descent of Civilizations

DESCRIBING THE PENNINES AS "THE BRITISH APENNINES,"[1] William Hutchinson provided an amusing instance of the long pattern of making classical references when deploying historical examples. These examples were not only found in mighty tomes, most famously those by Gibbon. In addition, classical history was deployed and applied in a national context, including on the stage and on canvas and in architecture, statuary, Parliament, and print. These references and settings represented ways to understand and present national history but also increasingly, from midcentury, a new imperial position, one that testified to the continued role of Rome as a point of reference. Classical history was important in part because it was the major form of historical knowledge that was taught in school and also because the notion of cultural continuity was much more significant than in the present age. This use of classical history sat within a context in which writers and readers were well conversant with a Latin tradition,[2] although less assuredly with a Greek counterpart, let alone with other parts of the ancient world. Nevertheless, comparisons were readily made. Antonio Verrio's murals on the King's Staircase at Hampton Court glorified William III as Alexander the Great. The play *Zelmane: or The Corinthian Queen* (1705) presented the protagonist as an able war leader and made a direct comparison with Anne. In contrast, Richard Glover's epic *Leonidas*, its theme drawn from classical Sparta, was forbidden by the Lord Chamberlain under the censorship introduced in 1737, as was Henry Brooke's *Gustavus Vasa: The Deliverer of his Country*, a play based on early sixteenth-century Sweden.

Classical references appeared most appropriate after 1688, not in a republican context, but, rather, with reference to a new monarchical destiny, first with William III and later with George I. Each could be discussed as a new Augustus, a reference intended to suggest that they were a figure who would bring peace and stability after division, conflict, and chaos, as well as to provide fame by comparison, and, in particular, to show that William was no Cromwell. References to the classical world added notions of royal competence to those of legitimacy, an addition that was a valuable response to Jacobitism. A key courtier, John Lord Hervey, published *Ancient and Modern Liberty Stated and Compared* in 1734.

There was a strong moral dimension to the standard presentation. The collapse of, first, the Roman republic and, then, empire offered warnings to modern Britain. In 1747, discussing modern Britain and, more specifically, corruption, Henry Fielding wrote:

> Some degree of corruption always has attended and always will attend a rich and flourishing nation.... Cato himself, the great patron and martyr of Roman liberty, in this sense not only admitted its [corruption] utility, but practised it. He was himself at the head of a subscription to bribe the Romans for their own good, and to keep men out of public trusts, who attacked the liberty of their country, and at last destroyed it, by the same factious methods and by the same popular outcries which are now practised and raised within this kingdom ... let us think of Safety before Reformation.[3]

On March 12, 1748, Fielding wrote in the *Jacobite's Journal* of "Greek and Latin authors, which have been the bane of the Jacobite cause, and inspired men with the love of Athenian liberty and old [Republican] Rome, and taught them to hate tyrants and arbitrary government."

References were not only sought in constitutional and dynastic terms. More specific examples were also advanced, and repeatedly so. In 1722, William, 2nd Earl Cowper, a prominent opposition Whig and formerly a minister, complained about the building of ships by Britain for France. He offered a lot of reasons, including the prescient warning that France, then an ally, could change situation, adding, "Would the Romans have done this for the Carthaginians or vice versa?" He went on, "It would not be permitted to build forts on a frontier, and sell them to a neighbor—ships are our forts."[4]

Cowper's reference to the classical world was typical not only of parliamentary discussion, but also of the printed debates about policy. On April 14, 1727, the *Craftsman*, discussing the right of governments to defend themselves, observed, "The Roman Dictators were never created but on the greatest emergencies.... this power... only temporary... but when once it became ordinary, and the Dictator made himself perpetual, it immediately swallowed up the liberties of that glorious people."

The classical narrative threw national issues into prominence and dramatic relief. The narrative gave them a civilizational resonance and parallel and also encouraged a polarization into exemplary and reprobate, thus offering a secular parallel to religious accounts. It was assumed that listeners and readers were not only knowledgeable about the classical world, but also interested in it. References to the classical world also praised writers and speakers by comparison. Parliamentary speakers could appear the Ciceros of the modern age.[5] In the dedication to Walpole of his play *The History of Saguntum* (1727), Philip Frowde declared: "While you bring the learning and arts of Greece and Rome into the Cabinet; either that to instruct in the depths of reasoning; or these in the rules of governing; no impression can ever be made to our prejudice, from the intrigues or menaces of a foreign power." Other plays on classical themes included Colley Cibber's *Perolla and Izadora* (1706), set during the Second Punic War, Addison's highly successful *Cato* (1715), Charles Beckingham's *Scipio Africanus* (1718), and Richard Glover's *Boadicea* (1753) and *Medea* (1761). The subject and style of historical play was to be very different by the time of the English Romantics.[6]

Other tranches of the arts also had classical parallels. On the completion of its first year of publication, the achievements of the *Tatler* (1709–11) were summed up by Joseph Addison by saying that the periodical was modeled on the "Censors" of classical Rome. Nicholas Rowe, poet laureate from 1715 to 1718 and a critic of Jacobitism, produced little of importance as laureate, bar completing a verse translation of Lucan's *Pharsalia*, a project that testified to the prestige of work on classical texts and the extent to which major (and minor) literary figures were also active as translators. Historians could seem comparable to Tacitus and other classical historians, not least in their own imagination, and they used classical models in their writing, notably in the early part of the century.[7] Bolingbroke's notion that history is philosophy teaching by examples was probably inspired by his reading of Thucydides or of Dionysius of Halicarnassus.

The very setting of the elite was that of a modern classicism or neoclassicism, or, seen differently, an Anglicization of classical forms, techniques, and preoccupations.[8] Most prominently, landscape gardening represented an Anglicization of classical notions of rural harmony, retreat, and beauty. This style was modeled on the classics, specifically imagined Virgilian landscapes mediated through the paintings of Claude Lorrain and Poussin. The presentation of the landscapes of Roman Italy in the paintings of Lorraine influenced the banker Henry Hoare when he laid out the gardens at Stourhead from the 1740s. The same can be said, in particular, with the buildings erected in the landscaped surrounds of stately homes. At Stowe, Richard, Lord Cobham, had a Temple of Ancient Virtue and another of British Worthies with the choice of both offering an exemplary history. The imitation of the Temple of Theseus (or Hephaestus) at Athens designed for the grounds of Hagley Hall by James "Athenian" Stuart in 1758 was the first copy of a Greek Doric temple. These and other buildings referred directly to the classical world, such as Henry Flitcroft's Pantheon at Stourhead, the Temple of Bacchus at Painshill, and the Column and Statue of Liberty at Gibside, the second a Roman Doric column topped by a statue of Liberty dressed in classical drapery and carrying the Phrygian cap, the cap of Liberty. These did not reflect a lack of confidence in British products; instead, they were part of the appropriation of the classical past to contemporary purposes. Statuary set the same tone. Thus, at Studley Royal, in the 1730s, the themes were classical: statues of Hercules and Antaeus, Bacchus, Galen, Priapus, Pan, the Wrestlers, and the Dying Gladiator. At his new country seat, or, rather, palace, at Houghton, Sir Robert Walpole displayed in the vaulted entrance hall the statue of a gladiator given by the Earl of Pembroke.

Similarly, classical ideas and designs came greatly to inform British architecture.[9] In part this involved a re-presentation of the past. Medieval and Tudor stately homes were rebuilt in whole or part as classical, for example, Clandon Park, Dyrham Park, Ickworth, Kedleston, Killerton, Lyme Park, Osterley Park, Studley Royal House, Syon House, the Vyne, Wallington, and Wilton House.

Paintings offered similar contexts when they brought the classical world home in a vivid fashion, offering moral lessons. This process was particularly seen toward the close of the century, notably with the paintings of Benjamin West, as in his *The Departure of Regulus from Rome*,[10] but was also apparent earlier. History painting was an increasingly recognized and important genre. Separately, the standard depiction of travelers on the Grand Tour in classical settings helped intensify this relationship and to suggest a ready transference of values across time.

The classical world provided a context, parallel, and explanation for that of the modern world, one that threw, and throws, light on contemporary attitudes toward time and history. As a result, arguments from the classical world were believed still to be of direct relevance, as in Jonathan Swift's *A Discourse of the Contest and Dissensions between the Nobles and the Commons in Athens and Rome, with the Consequences they had upon both those states* (1701). Cowper could refer to the three Punic Wars between Rome and Carthage, which had occurred in 264–241 BCE, 218–201 BCE, and 149–146 BCE. That Rome only rose on the defeat and destruction of Carthage and had to do so were the lessons that could be drawn, and these lessons were applied to the relationship between Britain and France. By 1793, when Britain entered the French Revolutionary War, it had over a century of experience of conflict with France, as well as a longstanding background of conflict with Spain. In each case, experience was perceived through the perspective of collective and contentious public myths, such as the hopes invested in blue-water strategy. Such myths were given additional weight and resonance by classical references, although it is necessary not to adopt too instrumental an account.

A different point about Carthage was made by William Pitt the Elder when, with his typical capacity to rethink a question that so infuriated many contemporaries, he reversed the comparison in the House of Commons' debate on the Address in 1755: "We have been told indeed that Carthage and that Spain in 88 [1588, Spanish Armada] were undone, notwithstanding their navies—true; but not till they betook themselves to land operations *and Carthage had besides a Hannibal who would pass the Alps*."[11] The last was a critical reference to William, Duke of Cumberland. Thus, Britain had to be a naval power, a lesson Pitt himself had to qualify in 1758 when troops were sent to the Continent.

Comparisons with the classical world could be challenged and, indeed, had to be to make sense of political positions. These challenges could extend to the very process of drawing comparisons. The progovernment *Whitehall Journal* of November 6, 1722, criticized opposition writers: "The state of the Roman Empire, under all its varieties... they are all promiscuously made use of by these authors, to influence and illustrate politics.... By no force of wit... can those words in any one Roman sense be applied to our English constitution." Different classical writers, notably historians, were made use of in order to argue the case for particular political and policy strategies, for example a quasi-Athenian focus on naval strength, which appeared particularly attractive to midcentury Tories critical of Continental interventionism, such as John Shebbeare in 1755–57.[12]

Classical references could, it was assumed, be understood by most readers. Thus, the *St James's Chronicle*, in its issue of August 13, 1765, printed what purported to be an agreement between a newspaper editor and a politician: "I engage to publish a periodical paper in favour of the late Administration, and to assume the name of Anti-Sejanus, that Lord B---[13] may be treated by me as an overgrown implacable favourite like Sejanus, and his –[14] represented as a cruel and vindictive tyrant like Tiberius. For this 10s 6d per paper."

It was instructive that Sejanus was still in play, in this case against Bute rather than Walpole. The classical past provided an acceptable pedigree and cultural context for civic virtues, one located in high-minded and moral politics, and also, in contrast to Christianity, which offered a legacy that was both fluid and open to interpretation that did not fall foul of authority. Moreover, this legacy could serve to discuss Britain's imperial role and the extent to which it was at the forefront of a process of civilizational change. In 1746, Thomas Ashe Lee, an army officer serving in Scotland, wrote after the crushing victory over Highland rebels at Culloden, about the British troops "dispersed through the several parts of this heathenish country, converting them to Christianity, and propagating a new light among them. Some few of them bring in their arms, others skulk in the woods and mountains, but we take care to leave them no sustenance, unless they can browse like their goats." Lee saw the Highlanders as barbarians, compared them unfavorably with the Gauls, and sought a historical comparison with the campaign by reading Caesar.[15] Caesar's *Gallic Wars* was indeed much read, and classical writers proved especially important for army officers, although from midcentury there was a greater emphasis on more recent works. A number of historians translated classical writers, such as William Guthrie's translating Cicero and Quintilian. Major Robert Donkin based his *Military Collections and Remarks* (1777), a call for the reorganization of the British army, on his studies of the armies of the Roman republic. An interest in the classics was not seen as incompatible with one in "modern history."[16]

The interest in the classics was enhanced by the pronounced emphasis on Roman remains and origins in the works of antiquarians and local historians. Thus, Thomas Pennant began his *A Tour in Scotland 1769* at Chester with an account of the city that included its extensive Roman remains.

Moreover, there was a strong crossover between writing on the classical world and that on national history. This was seen both in the idea of translation of empire from Rome to Britain (in Russia the focus was on translation to Russia)[17] and in the works of individual writers. Laurence Echard, later a prominent historian of England, also published *The Roman History from the Building of the City to the Perfect Settlement of the Empire by Augustus Caesar* (1695), a work that had gone through ten editions by 1734.[18] The classical world was also very important in Britain's North American colonies, notably because of its role in education and also because it gave rise to a republican tradition.[19]

The sense of relevance, as well as interest, helped explain the major impact of Edward Gibbon's *Decline and Fall of the Roman Empire* (1776–88). A politician as well as an historian, Gibbon was an MP from 1774 to 1780 and 1781 to 1784, and a member of the Board of Trade from 1779 to 1782. In 1779, at the request of Thomas, 3rd Viscount Weymouth, one of the secretaries of state, Gibbon wrote the *Mémoire Justificatif* against the hostile conduct of France and Spain in the War of American Independence (1775–83). However, it was very much for the *Decline and Fall* that he was known, and, unlike Hume, it was as a historian that he was to be known to posterity.

Gibbon encouraged attention to the rise and fall of empires "from which affecting examples, wisdom forms her noblest precepts."[20] He therefore helped underline the continued significance and relevance of the classics and, in turn, encouraged it. The renewed struggle with France from 1793, indeed, provided new opportunities, leading the writer Richard Bentley to complain in 1798: "We hear of Rome and Carthage every day and in every debate, even to puerility."[21]

Gibbon's theme of the Roman Empire collapsing because of internal political-cultural decay stemming in particular from the collapse of an active civic spirit, rather than external attack, accorded with the eighteenth-century preferences for moral history and history with a meaning, and also for a focus on domestic causes. Similar arguments were made by opposition critics in Britain that century. Gibbon's account was an exemplary tale with an Enlightenment moral, as the customary diatribes against excess and corruption were given depth, direction, complexity, and contentiousness by Gibbon's critique of the impact of monotheism and, specifically, Christianity.

Sir Walter Raleigh had stopped his *History of the World*, written while a prisoner in the Tower in 1603–16, at 168 BCE.[22] However, there was a longstanding interest in the decline of Rome and a willingness to apply it to Britain. In 1764, James Hampton published *Two Extracts from the sixth Book of the general history of Polybius . . . translated from the Greek. To which are prefixed some reflections tending to illustrate the doctrine of the author concerning the natural destruction of mixed governments, with an application of it to the state of Britain*. It is more pointed than Gibbon's history. Gibbon himself wrote against a background of recent works, including Goldsmith's unscholarly *The Roman History, from the Foundation of the City of Rome to the Destruction of the Western Empire* (1769). James Harris, whom Gibbon described as learned, amiable, and a major scholar of Greek literature and philosophy,[23] argued in his *Philosophical Arrangements* that the nature of change had been encouraged by tyranny in the ancient world, which therefore led to the need for exegesis: "In process of time, languages, customs, manners, laws, governments, and religions insensibly change. The Macedonian tyranny after the fatal battle of Chaeronea, wrought much of this kind in Greece; and the Roman tyranny, after the fatal battles of Pharsalia and Philippi carried it throughout the known world. Hence therefore of things obsolete, the names became obsolete also; and authors, who in their own age were intelligible and easy, in after days grew difficult and obscure. Hence then we behold the rise of a second race of critics, the tribe of scholiasts, commentators, and explainers."[24] Gibbon's approach made it possible to avoid a detailed examination of the causal mechanics of the impact of the narrative of warfare and politics he discussed. On the other hand, this approach helped him to range widely, as the level of expertise he required was not that of detailed world history. Instead, he considered empires of the mind, their rise and relationships, especially Christianity and Islam, offering, as a result, an ideological dimension of power. This encompassed not only Rome but also the post-Roman states in the West, most interestingly the Norman kingdom of Sicily, yet also republican Venice, as well as the eastern opponents of Byzantium.

Providing at least an apparently clear parallel for Britain and the purposes, methods, and identity of its empire, Gibbon distinguished between two kinds of international power and relationships: those of defined and civilized states with each other and those between barbarians and civilized states. The constant pressure on settled peoples of migrant, mobile, fluid forces was one of the many themes throughout Gibbon's work, although one in which it was not easy to place modern Britain. There was a moral as well as a developmental aspect. Barbarians, to Gibbon, were closer to the original state of man, and this increased their military potency, the threat they posed, and the interest they offered: "In the state of nature every man has a right to defend, by force of arms, his person and his possessions; to repel, or even to prevent, the violence of his enemies, and to extend his hostilities to a reasonable measure of satisfaction and retaliation."[25] In the marginal habitats of nomadic peoples, it was possible to recover "the first ages of society, when the fiercer animals often dispute with man the possession of an unsettled country." In contrast, "in the civilised state of the Roman empire the wild beasts had long since retired from the face of man and the neighbourhood of populous cities."[26] Robertson had a similar view.[27]

The energy of the barbarians was presented by Gibbon as having a primeval quality, a view that had taken on extra meaning since the Lisbon earthquake of 1755. The "rapid conquests" of Monguls and Tartars were described in terms of "the primitive convulsions of nature, which have agitated and altered the surface of the globe."[28] In his lengthy opening paragraph, Hume had dismissed barbarians: "The sudden, violent, and unprepared revolutions incident to barbarians, are so much guided by caprice and terminate so often in cruelty, that they disgust us by the uniformity of their appearance; and it is rather fortunate for letters that they are buried in silence and oblivion."[29]

To Gibbon, barbarians were difficult to cow: the "apparent submission" of the Caledonians "lasted no longer than the present terror. As soon as the Roman legions had retired they resumed their hostile independence."[30] Indeed, far from identifying emotionally with the armies of civilization and showing deep contempt for their barbarian opponents, as has been argued,[31] Gibbon contrasted the "untutored Caledonians glowing the warm virtues of nature, and the degenerate Romans polluted with the mean vices of wealth and slavery."[32] Neither were Christian at this point.

A warning to his British readers and a rather faint echo of the idea of the "noble savage," this message was driven home repeatedly. Indeed, Gibbon was clearly receptive to the positive reevaluation during the Enlightenment of "primitive peoples"—one, for example, applied in Spain against the Roman conquerors[33] and encouraged by the Ossian cult—but also thought this application pertinent to modern Britain. Gibbon contrasted "the servile adoration of the Byzantine court" with "the freedom and pride of a barbarian" in the case of the Emperor Justin and an Avar embassy. Moreover, in southern Italy, "the superior spirit and discipline of the Normans gave victory to the side which they espoused," and, in Sardinia, "the savage mountaineers preserved the liberty and religion of their ancestors; but the husbandmen of Sicily were chained to their rich and cultivated soil."[34]

For Gibbon, Islam owed much to the military strength of another such "barbarian" people, the Arabs. Their character, he argued, placed a bound to empire, again a warning to modern Britain:

> The arms of Sesostris and Cyrus, or Pompey and Trajan, could never achieve the conquest of Arabia; the present sovereign of the Turks may exercise a shadow of jurisdiction, but his pride is reduced to solicit the friendship of a people whom it is dangerous to provoke and fruitless to attack. The obvious causes of their freedom are inscribed on the character and country of the Arabs. Many ages before Mahomet, their intrepid

valour had been severely felt by their neighbours in offensive and defensive war. The patient and active virtues of a soldier are insensibly nursed in the habits and discipline of a pastoral life.[35]

Although Gibbon was suspicious of theories of environmental determinism,[36] the environment was given a role as with his discussion of the difficulties of Aurelian (r. 270–75) in the eventually successful campaign against Zenobia, queen of Palmyra. To Gibbon, the conqueror pursuing the Arabs found that "his victorious troops are consumed with thirst, hunger, and fatigue in the pursuit of an invisible foe, who scorns his efforts, and safely reposes in the heart of the burning solitude. The arms and deserts of the Bedoweens are . . . the safeguards of their own freedoms."[37] This represented a variant on views of the inherent environmentally based nature of civilizational character and progress, a view seen with classical authors and revived with Montesquieu.[38]

Yet Gibbon also focused on a shift in favor of civilized society, one that Britain was at the forefront of at sea, although that was very much not his concern. Indeed, Gibbon underplayed the maritime dimension of history, both in specifics and more generally. Arguing that civilization had led to science and that "cannon and fortification now form an impregnable barrier against the Tartar horse,"[39] Gibbon in effect claimed that cyclical processes were not at work in the relationship with "the savage nations of the globe . . . the common enemies of civilized society."[40] To Gibbon, either the overwhelming force of a powerful empire was required to control or, at least, restrain barbarians, or, thanks to the capacity of gunpowder to multiply strength, this could be achieved by the smaller forces of individual modern European states, of which Britain was at the fore. More recent historical work directly criticizes Gibbon for arguing that it was gunpowder weaponry that caused the fall of Constantinople in 1453, instead putting the emphasis on the command skills of Mehmed II.[41]

The divided nature of Europe was presented as essential to the quality of governance, the number of independent forces was multiplied, and "in peace, the progress of knowledge and industry is accelerated by the emulation of so many active rivals."[42] In contrast, Byzantium was presented as suffering from a lack of competition.[43] Prefiguring modern ideas of the positive significance of multipolarity (not, of course, a word to be expected from Gibbon), he shared Robertson's view that imitation within Europe was important to the character of the latter and to the ability of Europe to develop.[44] Competition was seen as offering a proto-Darwinian element and to offer the value of multipolarity, to adopt later terms but ones that had meaning in the period.

Gibbon, indeed, offered an account of modernization, one that complemented the account of Britain's development through and thanks to the Glorious Revolution, the account offered by historians of Britain. Shared power and authority were common to both. To Gibbon, modernization referred both to Britain and Europe, and a key aspect of post-Roman European history was its multipolar nature. To Gibbon and indeed the British tradition of the balance of power, this multipolarity had been challenged by attempts to revive aspects of universal empire in the West. To the British of the eighteenth century, the key instance was Louis XIV of France (r. 1643–1715), but history and, therefore, historians gave this attempt resonance, particularly bringing in Philip II of Spain (r. 1556–98) and, underlying both, the universal aspirations of the Catholic Church.

One of Gibbon's achievements was to provide a far longer and broader pedigree of this challenge, a challenge that therefore took on an existential force, and one of a civic purpose that was very different from the classic narrative of Christian existentialism. Gibbon saw the attempt to revive universal empire as a key legacy of Rome, one that therefore complemented the ambitions of barbarian invaders of the world of civilization. Initially, the two were combined in the case of the kingdoms that replaced the Roman Empire. For example, seeking to win the support of the Avars against the Gepids, Gibbon makes Alboin, king of the Lombards, declare that the reward would be "inestimable: the Danube, the Hebrus, Italy, and Constantinople would be exposed without a barrier to their invincible arms."[45]

Those who sought to recreate links with the Roman past based on the position of an emperor did not impress Gibbon, in part because they could not offer the continuity or checks and balance of the responsible government of the contemporary British Empire. This was an argument that could be employed against recent and modern would-be hegemons, most clearly Philip II and Louis XIV. According to Gibbon, Theodoric had qualities but "wanted either the genius or the opportunities of a legislator" and thus failed to create the basis of a lasting power, while Charlemagne similarly lacked "the general views and the immortal spirit of a legislator, who survives himself for the benefit of posterity. The union and stability of his empire depended on the life of a single man," ironically an instructive argument given contemporary North American criticisms of George III. The medieval German emperors were, he claimed, "unworthy successors" of Trajan and Constantine.[46]

In practice, Gibbon seriously oversimplified the political actions and aspirations of these medieval emperors as they did not really seek to revive imperial Rome. In his critique of royal empire, he was very much in accord with the notion of parliamentary monarchy, especially that of the Whigs, but also that of George III. Indeed, Gibbon was very much influenced in his history by his admiration for the British constitution.[47]

For Gibbon, the revival of imperial Rome was no longer an option, for the multiplicity of European states was maintained by a balance of power that matched in the international sphere the necessary disposition and operation of power within communities. Providing historical resonance for a Whig world that was domestic as well as international, Gibbon read the necessity of and preference for the balance back into the past. To him, "the form and equal balance of the Constitution" of republican Rome somewhat confusedly "united" the character of three different elements: popular assemblies, senate, and regal magistrate.[48] Again, "legislative authority was distributed in the assemblies of the people by a well-proportioned scale of property and service."[49] Gibbon presented this achievement as difficult as well as necessary. In contrast to the Roman achievement, Theodoric (c. 445–526), the Ostrogothic leader and king of Italy, failed to join, through balancing, "Goths and Romans."[50] Moreover, in eighth-century Rome, the successful re-creation of the "rough model of a republican government," with its consultation and checks and balances, failed because "the spirit was fled" so that "independence was disgraced by the tumultuous effect of licentiousness and oppression."[51]

International balance was also necessary. Theodoric was praised because he "maintained with a powerful hand the balance of the West ... and although unable to assist his rash and unfortunate kinsman the king of the Visigoths, he ... checked the Franks in the midst of their victorious career.... The Alemanni were protected.... An inroad of the Burgundians was severely chastised."[52] In contrast, in the early fifteenth century, "instead of prolonging the division of the Ottoman powers, the policy or passion of Manuel was tempted to assist the most formidable of the sons of Bajazet,"[53] with fatal consequences for Byzantium.

This instance demonstrated the extent to which the balance was not an automatic process but, rather, one that required appropriate action. This requirement underlined the prescriptive, rather than descriptive, character of the balance and the need for sage leadership. The balance was presented by Gibbon as crucial to the maintenance of multiple statehood in Western Europe. Earlier, Robertson had seen the balance in the same favorable light and thus offered an account of the necessary history of and future for British foreign policy with Britain very much part of a European system. The balance was understood by Robertson as the product of

> political science ... the method of preventing any monarch from rising to such a degree of power, as was inconsistent with the general liberty ... that great secret in modern policy, the preservation of a proper distribution of power among all the members of the system into which the states of Europe are formed.... From this era [the Italian Wars of 1494–1516] we can trace the progress of that intercourse between nations, which had linked the powers of Europe so closely together; and can discern the operations of that provident policy, which, during peace, guards against remote and contingent dangers; which, in war, hath prevented rapid and destructive conquests.[54]

Robertson's book was an important source for Gibbon's thinking on international relations. Gibbon saw "a peaceful system" of sovereign, interbalanced states as essential for the advancement of knowledge, ideas, arts, and sciences. More generally, the balance was central to the idealization of modern Europe by eighteenth-century historians as a peaceful system of interbalanced states. This prospectus served British interests, as it provided a safe background for transoceanic expansion, while also defending British history as the cause of such balance, both international and domestic.

Universal history does not readily lend itself to consistency, and there were contradictions in Gibbon's handling of such questions as the value both of divided authority within a state and of multiple statehood at the international level, problems that faced other writers when they addressed British history. Thus, Gibbon wrote of Italy in the late sixth century as "divided and oppressed by a ducal aristocracy of thirty tyrants," adding that the threat of Frankish invasion led the Lombard dukes, other descendants of "barbarians," to renounce "their feeble and disorderly independence; the advantages of regal government, union, secrecy, and vigour, were unanimously confessed."[55] Gibbon also referred to "the rival principalities of Benevento, Salerno, and Capua ... the thoughtless ambition or revenge of the competitors invited the Saracens to the ruin of their common inheritance." The failure to achieve "a perfect conquest" of southern Italy led to continual calamity.[56] The Muslims of Sicily were also "ruined by their divisions," to the advantage of the Normans,[57] an accurate view.

Moreover, the disunity of Christendom made it fruitless to hope for the recovery of Constantinople.[58] Indeed, offering a justification of the situation of the Church of England as the Established Church, it is instructive to consider the historical position of Christianity in this respect, for, having weakened classical Rome, Christianity was unable to provide the ideological fusion necessary to sustain Christendom as a successful multipolar system in the face of the Turkish advance. Thus, Crusader Acre "had many sovereigns and no government," and was full of lawlessness and vice.[59] Later, the urgings of Pope Pius II (r. 1458–64) for unity and activity against the Turks were foolishly ignored: "Regardless of futurity, his successors and the powers of Italy were involved in the schemes of present and domestic ambition; and the distance or proximity of each object determined in their eyes its apparent magnitude. A more enlarged view of their interest would have taught them to maintain a defensive and naval war against the common enemy; and the support of Scanderberg and his brave Albanians might have prevented the subsequent invasion of the kingdom of Naples."[60] These failings had lasting consequences. While Gibbon was writing, the banners of the Turkish Empire still waved above the walls of Belgrade, having regained the city from Austria in 1739, while the displacement of the Greek and Syrian world by that which was Arabic and Islamic appeared immutable.

For Gibbon, therefore, the value of dispersed power, both within states and in the international system, depended on their political culture and ideology. The attitudes of ruling individuals or groups were of particular importance, as was their ability to command or secure domestic support. In the case of eighteenth-century Britain, with the desire of the ruling group to see themselves as modern Romans, this ability was reflected, in the eyes of contemporaries, in the constitutional system. However, the latter was not necessarily the key element or, indeed, one that was present at all. To Gibbon, "the empire of Rome was firmly established by the singular and perfect coalition of its members. The subject nations, resigning the hope and even the wish of independence, embraced the character of Roman citizens."[61] Thanks to Islam, in Arabia "the hostile tribes were united in faith and obedience, and the valour which had been idly spent in domestic quarrels was vigorously directed against a foreign enemy."[62]

An ideology could be of value not only because it created, animated, and bound together an empire, making it effective, but also if it enabled a multipolar system to operate more successfully. A historian who, on the pattern of the period, engaged with the present, Gibbon adopted such a perspective when considering contemporary Europe:

> It is the duty of a patriot to prefer and promote the exclusive interest and glory of his native country: but a philosopher may be permitted to enlarge his views, and to consider Europe as one great republic, whose various inhabitants have attained almost the same level of politeness and cultivation. The balance of power will continue to fluctuate, and the prosperity of our own or the neighbouring kingdoms may be alternately exalted or depressed; but these partial events cannot essentially injure our general state of happiness, the system of arts and manners, which so advantageously distinguish, above the rest of mankind, the Europeans and their colonies.[63]

It was scarcely surprising, therefore, that Gibbon welcomed the Eden Treaty of 1786, an Anglo-French commercial agreement that lowered tariffs, removed prohibitions, and reflected an optimistic assessment of the possibilities of encouraging international understanding. This treaty was a requirement of the peace settlement in 1783 at the end of the War of American Independence. Gibbon wrote to his friend John, 1st Earl of Sheffield: "As a citizen of the world, a character to which I am every day rising or sinking, I must rejoice in every agreement that diminishes the separation between neighbouring countries, which softens their prejudices, unites their interests and industry, and renders their future hostilities less frequent and less implacable."[64]

Accordingly, in the *Decline and Fall*, Gibbon condemned the disruptive character and impact of irrational emotionalism and "the wild democracy of passions":[65] the preference for self over society, the quest for glory. In terms of foreign policy, he was aligned with the caution of the administration of William Pitt the Younger, which had negotiated this treaty, rather than with the xenophobic criticism of the treaty by the Whigs under Charles James Fox. The latter argued that rivalry between Britain and France was immutable, earlier the thesis of the historian Richard Rolt.

History served to demonstrate the value of prudence and could be employed to do so. Gibbon clearly thought highly of the Roman emperor Marcus Aurelius (r. 161–180), who detested war, "as the disgrace and calamity of human nature," except when in "the necessity of a just defence."[66] Furthermore, the failure of Julian the Apostate's Mesopotamian expedition against the Persians in 363 led to a fine section contrasting the fate of the expedition and the hopes of its bellicose supporters: "They entertained a fond persuasion that the temples of the gods would be enriched with the spoils of the East; that Persia would be reduced to the humble state of a tributary Province, governed by the laws and magistrates of Rome; that the barbarians would adopt the dress, and manners, and language of their conquerors; and that the youth of Ecbatana and Susa would study the art of rhetoric under Grecian masters."[67]

The Byzantine emperor Justinian, to Gibbon, sought fame in "the poor ambition of titles, honours and contemporary praise." He had "the cold ambition which delights in war, and declines the dangers of the field," while Tamerlaine, a quintessential "barbarian" conqueror, "followed the impulse of ambition."[68] Gibbon's general perception of history in terms of the personal views of rulers ensured that he adopted a moralistic attitude to their use of power; and this attitude was extended to republics. He wrote of Venice: "Their zeal was neither blind nor disinterested; and in the conquest of Tyre they shared the sovereignty of a city, the first seat of the commerce of the world. The policy of Venice was marked by the avarice of a trading, and the insolence of a maritime power; yet her ambition was prudent: nor did she often forget that, if armed galleys were the effect and safeguard, merchant vessels were the cause and supply, of her greatness."[69] For Gibbon, true fame lay elsewhere.

For both past and present, Gibbon adopted the *philosophe* approach that national interests, if correctly understood, were naturally compatible and that war arose from irrational causes, such as religion, and the irresponsibility and self-indulgence of leaders. These views were echoed in Gibbon's thesis that territorial expansion was dangerous, not only for prudential reasons—namely, that the state might become overextended as a force within the international system—but also because it posed a threat to the character and culture of the governing order. Thus, Augustus's skepticism about the value of distant conquests was praised, as was the prudent cession of territory by Hadrian.[70] This cession was a response to the ambitious overextension of the empire under his predecessor Trajan.

More generally, according to Gibbon, "the decline of Rome was the natural and inevitable effect of immoderate greatness,"[71] which, indeed, was a conventional view of the period, one related, in a somewhat uncritical fashion, to cyclical ideas of history, both religious and secular.[72] Conquest, it was claimed, had a similar effect on the Arabs and the Mongols,[73] a theme that was far less developed in the literature. The notion that conquest could lead to a dangerous overexpansion and then to implosion was a common one and matched ideas about the corruptibility of human society. It was applied by British writers concerned about the consequences of British colonial gains, which were seen as dangerous both in practical terms and in their moral counterparts. This argument was also seen in the discussion of foreign powers, such as by Samuel Whitbread, a Whig, when speaking in Parliament about Russia in April 1791.[74]

This standard view of past, present, and future, one that can be characterized as enlightened, had, however, its major limitations. Other than in terms of reprehensible ambition, this view offered scant understanding of dynamic elements in international relations, the scope of change, and the attempt by certain powerful rulers to match diplomatic developments to their growing power. This approach was essentially a static one. Thus, Montesquieu has been seen as displaying "a fearful resistance to change."[75] Gibbon, indeed, offered little guidance to the processes at work in international relations, contemporary or past, and his view of the balance of power was clearly that its maintenance was a necessary reactive task. Aside from the balance, international order was to be maintained because "in war, the European forces are exercised in temperate and undecisive contests," while the dissemination of gunpowder weaponry ensured that the European powers "stood on the same level of relative power and military science."[76]

These bland statements did not describe the international relations of the period. Indeed, while Gibbon was writing his masterpiece, the First Partition of Poland (1772), a measure decried by most international commentators, had suggested that the European international system appeared to be in a state of collapse, with nothing to prevent the partitioning powers from making new gains. There was widespread concern that this approach would continue and possibly accelerate. Indeed, the early 1780s saw the development by Russia of the "Greek Project": the carving out of a new Eastern Roman Empire from the Turkish dominions in favor of Catherine the Great's second grandson.

Given Gibbon's argument, an established view, that a multipolar state system represented a major improvement on universal empire and that the balance of power was fundamental to the maintenance of this system, it is striking how far he, like Robertson, neglected the actual developments of the 1770s and, more generally, the deficiencies of the European international system in which Britain was involved, however indirectly. There was far more attention given by other historians to the supposed failings of the national political system. Concern about what the international system could mean for Britain was increased by the fact that France was aligned, at least in part, with the partitioning powers as a result of its alliance with Austria. In contrast, Britain had no alliance with any of these powers. Moreover, because France did not join Austria against Prussia in the War of the Bavarian Succession (1778–79), Britain remained isolated and was unable to benefit from the possibility of improved relations with Prussia. As it turned out, the partitioning powers divided: Austria and Prussia went to war in 1778–79 and came close to it in 1784 and, even more, 1790, while Prussia (then allied with Britain) and Russia came close to war in 1791.

As a different critique of Gibbon, the international system collapsed not due to the partitioning powers, serious as their goals and methods were, but as a consequence of the French Revolutionary and Napoleonic Wars. Successive coalitions against France were defeated; the territorial and constitutional nature of the Low Countries, Italy, Germany, and Switzerland were totally remolded; the interests of third parties were arbitrarily handled by stronger powers; and, by 1812, France had swollen to rule or dominate much of Europe. In no way did this outcome correspond with Gibbon's portrayal of a benign course for international relations. Instead, there was the destruction of any balance within Europe.

The toxic addition to the practices of the partitioning powers was the new ideology of revolutionary France. Indeed, dining with Gibbon in Lausanne in Switzerland in May 1792, the diplomat John Trevor noted that his compatriot was "more animated than usual," adding, "Even Mr Gibbon who in general voit assez de sang froid [sees things calmly] seems to be alarmed at the temper of the times."[77] The Paris that had lauded Gibbon on his visit in 1777 was swept aside.

The French Revolution vindicated Gibbon's suggestion that the stability and civilization of contemporary Europe might be threatened, although he had minimized and misjudged the source of the threat when he wrote: "This apparent security should not tempt us to forget that new enemies and unknown dangers may *possibly* arise from some obscure people, scarcely visible in the map of the world. The Arabs or Saracens, who spread their conquests from India to Spain, had languished in poverty and contempt till Mahomet breathed into those savage bodies that soul of enthusiasm."[78]

The threat to European civilization appeared remote to Gibbon precisely because of what he saw as the nature of civilizational development both on the world scale and within Europe[79] and because he could not see the "obscure people" in question. Nevertheless, there were indications that Gibbon was already fearful of an ideological threat in the shape of Joseph Priestley's blend of Unitarianism and radicalism. This blend indeed appeared latent in English Dissent.[80]

When the threat from within Europe materialized in the form of the French Revolution and its link with British radicalism, the configuration of assumptions and prejudices that underlay British attitudes and therefore the use of history were focused anew. There were continued references to the classics. Thus, the young Charles, Earl of Dalkeith, later 4th Duke of Buccleuch, a Tory politician as well as landowner and amateur cricketer, thought that the September Massacres of 1792 in Paris outstripped "the massacres of Rome in its most abandoned style."[81]

There were changes, however, to the conception of the present that affected both views to the future and potential approaches to the past. Once atheistic France had been identified with the Antichrist, then Catholics could appear as allies.[82] Moreover, Islamic powers could now be appealed to for cooperation on the grounds that the Revolution was a common threat, its murderous trajectory "unexampled in the history of the most barbarous and savage nations."[83]

Earlier, Gibbon, in the *Decline and Fall*, was optimistic not only about Europe's position regarding Asian "barbarians," but also on the oceanic scale. He argued that the Europeans' "easy victories over the savages of the new world" ensured that in the unlikely event of civilization collapsing in Europe before new barbarian inroads, it would be sustained "in the American world."[84] This point was linked to the issue of naval strength, Gibbon noting that Europe had been earlier protected by the naval weakness of an Asiatic power: "if Chosroes had possessed any maritime power, his boundless ambition would have spread slavery and desolation over the provinces of Europe."[85] Gibbon followed the British tendency to see naval strength as particular to more liberal forces. This approach looked back to the presentation of Athens, Venice, and the Dutch and offered a distinctive strand to European history. This strand was important to the maintenance of a republican tradition, one that was to be significant in the background to North American republicanism.

Gibbon was aware of moral problems with European expansion but was convinced of its general benefit:

> Since the first discovery the arts, war, commerce, and religious zeal have diffused among the savages of the Old and New World these inestimable gifts ... every age of the world has increased and still increases the real wealth, the happiness, the knowledge, and perhaps the virtue of the human race. The merit of discovery has too often been stained with avarice, cruelty, and fanaticism; and the intercourse of nations has produced the communication of disease and prejudice. A singular exception is due to the

virtue of our own times and country. The five great voyages, successively undertaken by the command of his present Majesty [George III], were inspired by the pure and generous love of science and of mankind . . . introduced into the islands of the South Sea the vegetables and animals most useful to human life.[86]

This account was of course Eurocentric in the fashion of the day. Savages were to receive "gifts," and expansion entailed ecological imperialism.[87]

In practice, attitudes similar to those of Gibbon were voiced by those involved in British foreign policy in the 1780s. The India Act of 1784 declared that "schemes of conquest and extension of dominion in India are measures repugnant to the wish, the honour, and the policy of this nation." In addition, in 1786, Charles, 3rd Duke of Richmond, the Master-General of the Ordnance, informed Francis, Marquess of Carmarthen, the foreign secretary, that he had no time for the idea that Britain should acquire more sugar islands in the Caribbean, as they would be "more . . . than our number of people or riches can afford to cultivate. . . . The protection of such distant possessions is always difficult for this country which has so few troops to spare."[88]

Gibbon and the classical world were deployed to urge imperial probity. In 1788, "the luminous pages of Gibbon" were cited by Richard Brinsley Sheridan, a theatrical politician as well as political writer, when declaring that there was no parallel in the classical world for Warren Hastings's exactions and aggression in Bengal.[89] This was a statement that the book scarcely supported. Parallels were also drawn in history, as with the argument in Thomas Maurice's *Indian Antiquities* (1796) that there was an affinity between Druids and Brahmins. Maurice, a clergyman and a friend of Johnson, was a major interpreter of India, not least in his *History of Hindostan* (1795–98).

Despite the longstanding controversy about his views on Christianity, there was little doubt of Gibbon's moral and moralistic concerns.[90] The moral approach of his didacticism was such that he focused on the virtue of prudence and the prudence of virtue, notably on those led by reason. At the same time, Gibbon kept the application of history to specific current events at a distance, a process encouraged by the irony of his authorial voice, though this voice fell foul of clerical commentators who were determined to find explicit religious purpose in history.[91] Gibbon praised Henry Fielding's *Journey from This World to the Next* (1743) as providing "the history of human nature,"[92] and Julian the Apostate (r. 361–63), for whom Gibbon had some affection,[93] was used by Fielding as his narrator in this work.[94] In it, Fielding employed metempsychosis, journey through time, a particular type of history, to make points that would have been direct, pertinent, and barbed to contemporary readers. In contrast, Gibbon did not, for example, criticize the purchase of army commissions or the affairs of the East India Company in his work and thus "ransack antiquity and history"[95] to serve a present purpose that would in practice have dated fast. Gibbon's purpose was loftier.

Yet there were also notable limitations in the *Decline and Fall*. For example, Gibbon did not really address economic and cultural progress, however crucial he thought them to social development.[96] This choice was instructive, as it was argued that modern Western states, by combining naval empire, commerce, and representation, could avoid the fate of Rome.[97] Instead, Gibbon's was essentially a political account. The notions of rulership, governance, and political life as moral activities were such that the sway of empire, both past and present, were seen in that light both by Gibbon and his readers. In this stress, Gibbon corresponded to the more general emphasis and approach of British historians of the period.

Reading Gibbon, it is instructive to consider some of his contemporaries in another longstanding historical tradition, that of Persian works of history, which were produced across the vast Indo-Persian literary realm. In this realm, as with Gibbon, the technique, patterns, and motifs constituting the historical account served to articulate symbolic values, with considerations of rulership "embedded in a wider dynamic of prestige and space that transcended modern notions of centralisation and boundedness."[98] Gibbon's purpose was also moralistic, and his concern similarly was to range across the centuries. Gibbon's critical evaluation of his material was especially impressive, as was his range.

Gibbon demonstrates the significance of John Andrew's reflection in 1784 that history was of general value: "Were you destined to spend your life at a distance from the busy scenes of the political world, still it is highly becoming an individual of condition above the vulgar in this land of liberty, to qualify himself to judge of what passes on the stage of public transactions."[99]

NOTES

1. W. Hutchinson, *The History of the County of Cumberland*, 2 vols. (Carlisle, 1794), 1:i.

2. N. A. Mace, *Henry Fielding's Novels and the Classical Tradition* (Newark, DE, 1996).

3. H. Fielding, "A Dialogue between a Gentleman from London ... and an Honest Alderman of the Country Party," in *The Jacobite's Journal and Related Writings*, ed. W. B. Coley (Oxford, 1974), 31–32.

4. Cowper, notes for parliamentary debate, January 11, 1722, Hertford, CRO., Panshanger papers, D/EP 182 fols 96–104.

5. R. Browning, *Political and Constitutional Ideas of the Court Whigs* (Baton Rouge, LA, 1982).

6. R. Lansdown, *Byron's Historical Dramas* (Oxford, 1992).

7. P. Hicks, "Bolingbroke, Clarendon, and the Role of the Classical Historian," *Eighteenth-Century Studies* 20 (1987): 445–71; P. Hicks, *Neoclassical History and English Culture from Clarendon to Hume* (Basingstoke, UK, 2001); J. Moore, I. M. Morris, and A. J. Bayliss, eds., *Reinventing History: The Enlightenment Origins of Ancient History* (London, 2008); A. Lianeri, ed., *The Western Time of Ancient History: Historiographical Encounters with the Greek and Roman Pasts* (Cambridge, 2011).

8. C. A. Hanson, *The English Virtuoso: Art, Medicine, and Antiquarianism in the Age of Empiricism* (Chicago, 2009).

9. M. Wills, *Gibside and the Bowes Family* (Chichester, UK, 1995): 43–47; G. Clarke, "Grecian Taste and Gothic Virtue: Lord Cobham's Gardening Programme and its Iconography," *Apollo* 97 (1973): 56–67; D. Stillman, *English Neoclassical Architecture*, 2 vols. (London, 1989).

10. R. Alberts, *Benjamin West: A Biography* (Boston, 1978).

11. H. Walpole, *Memoirs of King George II*, ed. J. Brooke, 3 vols. (New Haven, CT, 1985), 2:70.

12. D. Ahn, "From 'Jealous Emulation' to 'Cautious Politics': British Foreign Policy and Public Discourse in the Mirror of Ancient Athens (c. 1730–c. 1750)," in *Ideology and Foreign Policy*, ed. G. Onnekink and D. Rommelse (Farnham, 2011), 129; K. Demetriou, "In Defence of the British Constitution: Theoretical Implications of the Debate over Athenian Democracy in Britain, 1770–1850," *History of Political Thought* 17 (1996): 280–97.

13. Bute.

14. Majesty [George].

15. Earl of Ilchester, ed., *Letters to Henry Fox* (London, 1915), 9, 13–14.

16. James, 1st Earl of Malmesbury, ed., *The Works of James Harris*, 2 vols. (London, 1801), 1:xxiii.

17. S. L. Baehr, "From History to National Myth: *Translatio imperii* in Eighteenth-Century Russia," *Russian Review* 37 (1978): 1–13.

18. R. J. Ridley, "The Forgotten Historian: Laurence Echard and the First History of the Roman Republic," *Ancient Society* 27 (1996): 277–315.

19. C. Richard, *The Founders and the Classics: Greece, Rome, and the American Enlightenment* (Cambridge, MA, 1995).

20. W. Hutchinson, *The History and Antiquities of the County Palatine of Durham* (Newcastle, 1785), i.

21. R. Bentley, *Considerations upon the State of Public Affairs* (London, 1798), 63.

22. N. Popper, *Walter Raleigh's "History of the World" and the Historical Culture of the Late Renaissance* (Chicago, 2012).

23. E. Gibbon, *The History of the Decline and Fall of the Roman Empire*, ed. J. B. Bury, 7 vols. (1897–1901; original published in 6 vols., 1776–88), chapter 52, fns 58, 69. Citations refer to this edition unless otherwise noted.

24. J. Harris, *Philosophical Arrangements* (1774), in *The Works of James Harris*, ed. James, 1st Earl of Malmesbury, 2 vols. (London, 1801), 2:283.

25. Gibbon, *Decline and Fall*, 5:358–59.

26. Gibbon, *Decline and Fall*, 1:93.

27. W. Robertson, *The History of the Reign of the Emperor Charles V*, 3 vols. (London, 1769; 1782 ed.), 1:5–6.

28. Gibbon, *Decline and Fall*, 7:1.

29. D. Hume, *History of England* (1813 ed.), 1:2.

30. Gibbon, *Decline and Fall*, 1:129.

31. L. Damrosch, *Fictions of Reality in the Age of Hume and Johnson* (Madison, WI, 1989), 122.

32. Gibbon, *Decline and Fall*, 1:130. On this passage, see L. Davis, "'Origins of the Specious': James Macpherson's Ossian and the Forging of the British Empire," *The Eighteenth Century* 34 (1993): 132–50, esp. 144–45. See, more generally, J. G. A. Pocock, *Barbarism and Religion: IV, Barbarians, Savages and Empires* (Cambridge, 2005).

33. F. W. Alonso and G. C. Andreotti, "On Ancient History and Enlightenment: Two Spanish Histories of the Eighteenth Century," *Storia della Storiografia* 23 (1993): 91.

34. Gibbon, *Decline and Fall*, 5:3, 23; 6:175.

35. E. Gibbon, *The History of the Decline and Fall of the Roman Empire*, ed. J. B. Bury, 2nd ed. (London, 1909–14), 5:340.

36. C. Roberts, *Edward Gibbon and the Shape of History* (Oxford, 2014), 9. For Gibbon's work in the context of other "enlightened" histories on a grand narrative scale, see K. O'Brien, *Narratives of Enlightenment: Cosmopolitan History from Voltaire to Gibbon* (Cambridge, 1997); J. G. A. Pocock, *Barbarism and Religion: I. The Enlightenments of Edward Gibbon 1737–1764* (Cambridge, 1999) and *II. Narratives of Civil Government* (Cambridge, 1999).

37. Gibbon, *Decline and Fall*, 5:319.

38. R. L. Meek, *Social Science and the Ignoble Savage* (Cambridge, 1976).

39. Gibbon, *Decline and Fall*, 4:167.

40. Gibbon, *Decline and Fall*, 4:164.

41. K. DeVries, "Gunpowder Weapons at the Siege of Constantinople, 1453," in *War, Army and Society in the Eastern Mediterranean, 7th–15th Centuries*, ed. Y. Lev (Leiden, 1997), 343–62.

42. Gibbon, *Decline and Fall*, 4:166.

43. Gibbon, *Decline and Fall*, 1:109.

44. K. O'Brien, "Between Enlightenment and Stadial History: William Robertson on the History of Europe," *British Journal for Eighteenth-Century Studies* 16 (1993): 53–63.

45. Gibbon, *Decline and Fall*, 5:6.
46. Gibbon, *Decline and Fall*, 4:187; 5:285, 307.
47. H. T. Dickinson, "The Politics of Edward Gibbon," *Literature and History* 8 (1978): 194.
48. Gibbon, *Decline and Fall*, 4:160.
49. Gibbon, *Decline and Fall*, 5:263.
50. Gibbon, *Decline and Fall*, 4:187.
51. Gibbon, *Decline and Fall*, 5:263–64.
52. Gibbon, *Decline and Fall*, 4:186.
53. Gibbon, *Decline and Fall*, 7:76.
54. Robertson, *Charles V*, 1:134–35.
55. Gibbon, *Decline and Fall*, 5:14, 21–22.
56. Gibbon, *Decline and Fall*, 5:167–68.
57. Gibbon, *Decline and Fall*, 6:176–77.
58. Gibbon, *Decline and Fall*, 6:207.
59. Gibbon, *Decline and Fall*, 6:364.
60. Gibbon, *Decline and Fall*, 7:207–8.
61. Gibbon, *Decline and Fall*, 4:165.
62. Gibbon, *Decline and Fall*, 5:396.
63. Gibbon, *Decline and Fall*, 4:163.
64. *The Letters of Edward Gibbon*, ed. J. R. E. Norton, 3 vols. (London, 1956), 3:61.
65. Gibbon, *Decline and Fall*, 5:20.
66. Gibbon, *Decline and Fall*, 1:78.
67. Gibbon, *Decline and Fall*, 2:525. See also 5:39.
68. Gibbon, *Decline and Fall*, 4:431–32; 7:75.
69. Gibbon, *Decline and Fall*, 6:382.
70. Gibbon, *Decline and Fall*, 1:2, 7.
71. Gibbon, *Decline and Fall*, 4:161, and re: Trajan, 1:6–7.
72. P. R. Ghosh, "Gibbon's Dark Ages: Some Remarks on the Genesis of the *Decline and Fall*," *Journal of Roman Studies* 73 (1983): 17.
73. Gibbon, *Decline and Fall*, 5:396; 7:19. On Gibbon's sources, see D. O. Morgan, "Edward Gibbon and the East," *Iran* 33 (1995): 88.
74. W. Cobbett, ed, *Cobbett's Parliamentary History of England from 1066 to 1803*, 36 vols. (London, 1806–20), XXIX:181–204.
75. M. L. Perkins, "Montesquieu on National Power and International Rivalry," *Studies on Voltaire and the Eighteenth Century* 37 (1965): 76.
76. Gibbon, *Decline and Fall*, 4:166; 7:82.
77. Trevor to James, Lord Malmesbury, May 28, 1792, Winchester, Hampshire CRO. Malmesbury papers, vol. 169.
78. Gibbon, *Decline and Fall*, 4:164–65.
79. J. W. Burrow, *A Liberal Descent: Victorian Historians and the English Past* (Cambridge, 1981), 63, 113; J. G. A. Pocock, "Gibbon's *Decline and Fall* and the World View of the Late Enlightenment," *Eighteenth-Century Studies* 10 (1977): 287–303.
80. J. G. A. Pocock, *Virtue, Commerce and History* (Cambridge, 1985), 155.
81. Dalkeith to Malmesbury, September 29, 1792, Malmesbury papers, vol. 149.
82. A. Robinson, "Identifying the Beast: Samuel Horsley and the Problem of Papal AntiChrist," *Journal of Ecclesiastical History* 43 (1992): 592–607.
83. Additional Instructions for Robert Liston, envoy in Constantinople, 26 Feb. 1794, NA. FO. 78/15 fol. 47.

84. Gibbon, *Decline and Fall*, 7:82; 4:166.

85. Gibbon, *Decline and Fall*, 5:71–72. "Khosrow" is the preferred modern spelling for Chosroes. Khosrow I, also known as Anushiruwan the Just, was the King of Kings of the Sasanian Empire from 531 to 579 CE.

86. Gibbon, *Decline and Fall*, 4:168–69.

87. A. W. Crosby, *Ecological Expansion: The Biological Expansion of Europe, 900–1900* (Cambridge, 1986), 228–30, 234.

88. B. B. Misra, *The Central Administration of the East India Company, 1773–1834* (Manchester, 1959), 32; Richmond to Carmarthen, March 26, 1786, BL. Egerton Mss. 3498 fol. 235; Alexander, 1st Lord Loughborough, to Pitt, December 9, 1792, NA. 30/8/153 fol. 71.

89. P. Quennell, *Four Portraits: Studies of the Eighteenth Century* (London, 1945), 125.

90. P. R. Ghosh, "Gibbon Observed," *Journal of Roman Studies* 81 (1991): 137n37.

91. N. Aston, "A 'Disorderly Squadron'? A Fresh Look at Clerical Responses to *The Decline and Fall*," in *Edward Gibbon: Bicentenary Essays*, ed. D. Womersley (Oxford, 1997), 253–77, esp. 267–77; J. G. A. Pocock, "Gibbon and the Invention of Gibbon: Chapters 15 and 16 Reconsidered," *History of European Ideas* 35 (2009): 209–16.

92. Gibbon, *Decline and Fall*, 3:384n13.

93. G. M. Young, *Gibbon*, 2nd ed. (London, 1948), 121.

94. B. A. Goldgar, "Myth and History in Fielding's *Journey from This World to the Next*," *Modern Language Quarterly* 47 (1986): 241–43.

95. *Whitehall Journal*, November 6, 1722.

96. J. Clive, *Not by Fact Alone: Essays on the Writing and Reading of History* (New York, 1989), 64–65.

97. J. Scott, *When the Waves Ruled Britannia: Geography and Political Identities, 1500–1800* (Cambridge, 2011).

98. C. Noelle-Karimi, "Afghan Polities and the Indo-Persian Literary Realm: The Durrani Rulers and Their Portrayal in Eighteenth-Century Historiography," in *Afghan History through Afghan Eyes*, ed. N. Green (London, 2015), 77.

99. J. Andrews, *Letters to a Young Gentleman* (London, 1784), 127.

NINE

HISTORY IN THE AGE OF BURKE

> The Frenchman acknowledged that they had been miserable and wretched, but pleased himself with the prospect of what was to come; he said that "the States General ... were forming a constitution preferable in many respects to that of England ... that the Tiers Etat": Here the Englishman interrupted with "D--n your Tiers Etat! Where is your Magna Carta and your Bill of Rights!"
>
> London Chronicle, March 2, 1790

THROUGHOUT THE EIGHTEENTH CENTURY, FRENCH HISTORY served most British commentators as an object lesson in explaining British exceptionalism, while also warning of dangers. The idea of an inherent antagonism between Britain and France was regarded as repugnant by those who can be termed liberals, and they treated this idea as less plausible than reliance on a detailed historical explanation. Indeed, defending the 1786 trade treaty with France, the treaty that Sheffield discussed in the previous chapter, William Pitt the Younger, the prime minister from 1783 to 1801 and from 1804 to 1806, told the House of Commons: "To suppose that any nation could be unalterably the enemy of another was weak and childish. It had neither its foundation in the experience of nations nor in the history of man. It was a libel on the constitution of political societies, and supposed the existence of diabolical malice in the original frame of man."[1]

Nevertheless, an interest in specific historical episodes was not incompatible with a belief in natural differences. In 1785, John Andrews, who, in his search for reasons to criticize, claimed that Cardinal Richelieu in the early seventeenth century had encouraged French literature in order to soften French dispositions politically, described the French as a people "whose restless temper was ever breaking forth in the least excitation. Not, indeed, in those heroic struggles against tyranny; and in favour of that national freedom and felicity which were the objects of our ancestors at that time, but in pitiful wranglings for the private interest of such turbulent grandees. . . . Nothing more clearly proves the difference between the English and French nations than the commotions that disturbed France under his administration."[2]

On a pattern both dating back and continually refreshed, the apparently autocratic political society of France in the eighteenth century was commonly attributed to Louis XI in the fifteenth century, Richelieu, Mazarin, and Louis XIV in the seventeenth, although other causes were mentioned, including the creation of a regular French army to defeat England in the Middle Ages.[3] A prolific writer, Andrews (1736–1809) was a moralist who accepted the notion that history was philosophy teaching by example. His major historical work was the first English history of the American Revolution: the *History of the War with America, France, Spain, and Holland, commencing in 1775 and ending in 1783* (1785–86). Other works included *History of the Revolutions of Denmark* (1774) and *Historical Review of the Moral, Religious, Literary, and Political Character of the English Nation* (1806).

In the eighteenth century, British history was presented as different to that of France in large part due to the Glorious Revolution, although earlier historical periods were also held responsible. In *The New, Impartial and Complete History of England* (1783) by Edward Barnard, the intention of the book was given as "to display the patriotic virtues of our illustrious ancestors and to inspire the present age with an emulation of imitating their glorious examples." This was necessary given the recent defeat of Britain by France in the War of American Independence/American Revolution (1775–83). Barnard argued that "to Edward III we owe the superiority which in his time the English began to obtain over the French, and which, should their councils be directed by wise and honest men, it is hoped they will maintain to the latest posterity."[4]

The Glorious Revolution was, in turn, employed by writers to serve as a basis for calls to particular ends rather than simply a national exceptionalism.[5] This was a longstanding method, one also seen with the supporters of the American Revolution. It was, indeed, a method that could be readily applied to new ends. Thus, the *Leeds Mercury* of November 11, 1788, urged the abolition of the slave trade and praised the events of 1688:

> In order to know the true value of that glorious and important event, which has just been commemorated throughout this island, we should contrast our present state with what it would inevitably have been, had not that triumphant change produced by the Revolution been effected. Bigotry and superstition, despotism and tyranny, would, long ere this, have defaced this fair flourishing Isle, and have so contracted and duped the noble and emulous spirit of Britons, that they would, compared with what they now are, scarce have seemed like men. With liberty, the source and course of every human good would have fled, commerce, industry, every ornamental and useful art, that polish and refine our manners, give pleasure in our social and solitary hours, and bread to thousands. Instead of that free communication we now enjoy, we must have conversed by nods and shrugs, with doubtful and ambiguous looks.

The presentation of calls for change, however radical, in an historical context was longstanding. The anonymous "Thoughts on Levelling with an Account of the Insurrection of Wat Tyler," in other words, the Peasants Revolt of 1381, printed in the *Bristol Journal* on April 5, 1777, claimed: "A consciousness of primitive equality is strongly impressed on the heart of every man; and a desire of recovering their original consequence, joined to the pressure of present inconveniences, has at different times roused the populace of every nation to arms." Somewhat differently, the committee of the Revolution Society in London resolved in 1788 that the principles of the Glorious Revolution should be perpetuated and then interpreted them in a radical fashion:

1. That all civil and political authority is derived from the People.
2. That abuse of power justifies resistance.
3. That the rights of private judgment, liberty of conscience, and the freedom of the press ought ever to be held sacred and inviolable.

That the seventeenth century was a source of controversy was not simply due to the Glorious Revolution. Instead, it was to be underlined the following January, in what was another annual basis for historical recollection, the January 30 sermon before the House of Lords, the commemoration of the execution of Charles I on that day in 1649. In 1755, there was a discussion in the House of Commons about ending the practice, but that had got nowhere. Giving the sermon in 1789, George Pretyman, the cleric closest to Pitt, rejected the High Church cult of Charles I as a martyr and offered some strong criticisms of Charles for trying to make himself "absolute" and for his favor to "Popery."[6] Thus, national history remained highly contentious in a year that unexpectedly saw the start of the French Revolution. Indeed, it had become more contentious due to the need to respond to the disasters of 1775–83.

Rolt's themes of inherent national animosity, themes discussed in chapter 6, were to be revived in response to the French Revolution, and during Britain's wars with Revolutionary and then Napoleonic France, wars that continued from 1793 to 1815 with only two brief intervals, in 1802–3 and 1814–15. The use of history in this period as a whole is most readily discussed not with reference to the French but regarding their opponents. History was a past to be discarded for the French revolutionaries who got rid of monarchy in 1792 and followed with destroying the ancien régime. "History wars" in France meant the end of history. They started the calendar anew, with Christianity deliberately repudiated. The new year was to begin on September 21, the date of the autumnal equinox and of the Declaration of the French republic in 1792. Society was to be regenerated as well as systematized, in part by using time to replicate natural order as well as the traditions of classical republicanism. In newly ordering time, a new collective memory was to be created and thus a new history.[7]

The break with the past was a central part of a wider political stance by the French government, one that offered an example to British radicals. Thus, feudal rights and monarchy were abolished, as opposed simply to replacing the monarch, while secularization entailed a rupture with the role of the Church in education. For these reasons, history was not a prime concern of the revolutionaries, other than in the shape of memorializing their own achievements. For these purposes, there was a stress on instant history in the shape of commemorative ceremonies. The dramatic "texts" produced were paintings, notably the works of Jacques-Louis David, especially his *Death of Marat* (1793), rather than scholarly books. More generally, the emphasis was not on the past, but on a spirit of progress and on uniform modern systems. This emphasis was shown in the Institut National des Sciences et des Arts established in 1795. Moreover, history literally became a museum, notably with the Musée des Monuments Française founded in 1795. The treasures of the despoiled cathedrals and monasteries were placed there.

EDMUND BURKE

The impact of the French Revolution in contemporary historical work was strongest in England not in supportive works but in the case of the hostile reaction to it, which was particularly pronounced in England. The most famous, both for contemporaries and subsequently, was that of Edmund Burke (1730–97), who argued, in his deliberately provocative and immediately celebrated *Reflections on the Revolution in France* (1790), that developments in France were harmful because they were unrelated to any sense of continuity, indeed any historical consciousness. In contrast, at the Restoration of the Stuart dynasty in 1660 and with the Glorious Revolution overthrowing the authoritarian James II in 1688–89, the English, according to Burke, "regenerated the deficient part of the old constitution through the parts which were not impaired. They kept these old parts exactly as they were, that the part recovered might be suited to them. They acted . . . not by the organic *moleculae* of a disbanded people," the latter a reference to contemporary France and to the idea of starting history anew.[8] More generally, with Burke there was an emphasis on the common good, and not on rival assessments that put the stress on the individual.[9]

Burke's praise for the Glorious Revolution helped draw the sting on some of the potential criticism of his work, although criticism was still sustained. Interest in and support for the Glorious Revolution were widely rooted. It was not only seen in publications from London. Thus, in 1788, Hayman Rooke and Samuel Pegge produced in Nottingham *A Narrative of what passed at the Revolution House at Whittington, County of Derby, in . . . 1688*. Produced for presentation "to some Nottinghamshire and Derbyshire friends," it detailed the meeting of the conspirators at a modest inn at Whittington while sheltering from a shower, an inn since called the Revolution House.

Burke's view of relatively recent history was related to a more general interpretation of English history. Citing William Blackstone's 1759 edition of the Magna Carta and quoting from the texts of the Petition of Right (1628) and the Declaration of Rights (1689), Burke claimed: "It has been the uniform policy of our constitution to claim and assert our liberties, as an entailed inheritance derived to us from our forefathers, and to be transmitted to our posterity.... This policy appears to me to be ... the happy effect of following nature, which is wisdom without reflection.... People will not look forward to posterity, who never look backward to their ancestors."[10]

Burke also employed classical history, as in his criticism of Britain in India[11] and in his description of the French revolutionaries as treating France as if conquered, notably with the creation of new governmental units: "They have made France free in the manner in which sincere friends to the rights of mankind, the Romans, freed Greece, Macedon, and other nations. They destroyed the bonds of their union, under colour of providing for the independence of each of their cities."[12] This was an extremely far-fetched comparison, but also one in which Burke sought to deploy his capacity for making comparisons that drew on the heritage of a broad European civilization.

The *Reflections* attracted much attention. For example, John Hatsell, the chief clerk of the House of Commons, wrote to Henry Addington, the Speaker of the House of Commons, who was close to George III: "I have been wonderfully amus'd and inform'd by Burke's Pamphlet. At the same time, much of it might have been spar'd, and to have been, for the credit of the Author. The triumph over Ld. G. Gordon, and The Defence of the Monastick Institutions, were not topicks necessary for Him to insist upon. But his attack upon the two Societies, and his observations upon the proceedings of the French assembly, appear to me full of sound Philosophy, true Politicks, express'd with wit and powers of *Eloquence*."[13]

Burke continued, in his *Appeal from the New to the Old Whigs* (1791), to argue that it was his views that were consistent with the Glorious Revolution of 1688–89, rather than those of Whig radicals such as, most prominently, Richard Price and Joseph Priestley. In his sermon "On the Love of Our Country," preached at a meeting house in London on November 4, 1789, Price, a prominent Dissenting minister, described the French Revolution as "glorious," an argument taking forward Dissenting views earlier in the century, and discussed in chapter 5, that angered Burke. Burke claimed that the French Revolution was compatible not with the Glorious Revolution, as the Whig radicals argued, but with the regicide of 1649, the execution of Charles I, a step that had religious as well as political resonances. Thus, history was not only asserted as a principle by Burke, but also contested as a practice. Burke quoted from the prosecution case against the Tory cleric Henry Sacheverell in order to clarify what Whig principles had been in the reign of Queen Anne (1702–14) and how 1688–89 had been interpreted then.[14] Burke felt that the events of 1688–89 could only be appreciated in the light of the assumptions to which they had given rise, and he did this in order to deny contemporary radical attempts to interpret the legacy.

This quest to understand developments in their appropriate context led to an appreciation of sources. Burke quoted as his "authorities" for the Revolution Settlement "the acts and declarations of Parliament given in their proper words" and also cited sources for his account of the Peasants Revolt of 1381 as an instance when the majority had no right to act. In his *Letter to a Member of the National Assembly* (of France) (1791), Burke argued that "the last revolution of doctrine and theory" previous to the French Revolution was the Reformation, which had produced "principles of internal as well as external division" across Europe, a reasonable view.

As the French Revolution was increasingly radical, so it became easier to deploy the Glorious Revolution against it. Burke's account was also matched by other historians. Thus, William Coxe attacked Price and, like Burke, praised William III and the Glorious Revolution.[15] Meanwhile, British supporters of the French Revolution also became more radical. As such, they had little time for conventional definitions of loyalty and thus scant reason to refer for justification to the events of 1688–89.

Coxe's subsequent work, notably his three-volume biography of Sir Robert Walpole and his three-volume biography of John, 1st Duke of Marlborough, published in 1798 and 1818–19 respectively, also took a view strongly supportive of the Glorious Revolution and of the established narrative. Previous attempts to use Marlborough's papers to produce an authorized biography had failed, but Coxe was equal to the methodical slog required.[16] The Glorious Revolution was commonly presented in England as an essentially peaceful act. This misleading presentation was made possible by a focus on events in England, where indeed there was some bloodshed, rather than their far more violent Scottish and Irish consequences. This approach served as a basis from which to condemn the violence of France. Moreover, whereas William's actions in 1688–89 could be located in a favorable international context, that of opposition to the aggressive Louis XIV, the international context in which revolutionary France was judged, that of proselytism and expansionism by the revolutionaries, was less sympathetic to its cause.

The details of Burke's use of historical example can be challenged, especially in the light of his failure to accept that the events of 1688–89 marked a major discontinuity in English history and were only enforced in Ireland and Scotland after considerable violence. However, the polemical purpose of Burke's philosophical discussion of historical development made such an interpretation necessary. To insist upon Burke's historical errors and the difficulties posed by a belief in direct divine intervention that, however, could not be readily identified[17] may be to miss the point of his understanding of history and his belief in the need to understand history.[18] Moreover, to criticize him for thinking of the past as a divinely intended teleological order is to entail a dismissal of most eighteenth-century history and of the attitudes that illuminated it and gave it both meaning and impact. Burke struck an echo not only thanks to his ability to write powerfully, but also because his understanding and use of history were far from marginal. History was shaped for Burke, as for his contemporaries, including his opponents, by purpose and was far from being an arbitrary assemblage of events.

The same can be said, from a very different political perspective, for Catharine Macaulay, in her *Observations on the Reflections of the Right Hon. Edmund Burke on the Revolution in France* (1790), and for Mary Wollestonecraft, in her *An Historical and Moral View of the Origins and the Progress of the French Revolution; and the Effect It has Produced in Europe* (1794).[19] Recent history from a Dissenting viewpoint appeared in the works of William Belsham, a supporter of political liberty, including the American Revolution. His major works were *Memoirs of the Kings of Great Britain of the House of Brunswick-Luneburg* (1793), *Memoirs of the*

Reign of George III (1795–1801), and *A History of Great Britain from the Revolution to the Accession of the House of Hanover* (1798). In 1806, these works were reshaped and extended into the twelve-volume *History of Great Britain to the Conclusion of the Peace of Amiens in 1802*. Belsham had earlier published works contesting Burke's view of the French Revolution and also pressing for political reform.

Aesthetic and cultural sympathies played a role. Burke was not only a supporter of the Glorious Revolution, but also a writer whose engagement with continuity helped lead to a sensitivity to the Middle Ages and a sympathy with French monasticism. This has been seen as an aspect of Burke as the first of the Romantic historians.[20] While that placing is not without point, it also underplays the longer-term interest in the medieval period as one of the development of Parliament and struggle with France, each of which served to counteract the argument about a Norman yoke introduced with William I's conquest. Indeed, the Anglicization of the Middle Ages and, to a degree, of the Norman yoke was another instance of the continuity and gradual change Burke applauded.

At the same time, reform could also look to the medieval period, as with Robert Southey's epic poem *Joan of Arc* (1796), a work in which patriotically disposed rulers played a role. Southey also gave historical lectures in Bristol in 1795.[21] More generally, national history and culture—for example, the plays of Shakespeare—served to offer an alternative to the classics as providers of a currency of discussion and reference in an age with a more democratic political and cultural language.[22] In so doing, national history and culture could be employed to serve different—indeed, competing—political goals.

The execution of Louis XVI in January 1793 led to the use of the January 30 sermon in Westminster Abbey before the House of Lords in a different fashion from that of Pretyman in 1789. Samuel Horsley, bishop of St. David's and a supporter of Pitt, delivered a powerful attack on political speculation and revolutionary theory. Horsley dismissed the notion of an original compact arising from the abandonment of a state of nature and, instead, stressed royal authority. According to Horsley, the existing British constitution was the product and safeguard of a "legal contract" between Crown and people, while the obedience of the latter was a religious duty. Horsley's forceful peroration linked the executions of Charles I and Louis XVI: "This foul murder, and these barbarities, have filled the measure of the guilt and infamy of France. O my Country! Read the horror of thy own deed in this recent heightened imitation! Lament and weep, that this black French treason should have found its example, in the crime of thy unnatural sons!" The congregation rose to its feet in approval.[23]

EDWARD NARES

The outbreak of war with France in 1793 and the move of the French Revolution that year into the Reign of Terror helped ensure that Burke's arguments had a powerful and continuing public resonance in Britain, one that was far stronger than when the *Reflections* were published in 1790. They were supported by a renewed interest, in revealed theology, in revelation, providentialism, and biblicalism, rather than natural religious truths, as part of an increased critique of reason, heterodoxy, deism, and science.[24] This, however, was not the sole basis for confessional readings of history, not least due to the tensions within the Church of England.[25] Edward Nares (1763–1841), an Anglican cleric and, from 1813 until his death, regius professor of modern history at Oxford as well,[26] took forward themes advanced by Burke, while underlining their religious implications. He combined a nationalistic perspective born of Protestant zeal and hostility toward foreign developments with a strong interest in history. Like Wesley, Nares was very interested in the age of Elizabeth. Indeed, in 1828, he produced a major, three-volume life of Burghley, one in which, in the preface, he declared his determination to link patriotism and Protestantism: "he prides himself upon being an Englishman, an English Protestant, a Church of England man, a Divine."[27]

Earlier, Nares made a powerful case for the value of history in a sermon preached in 1797 on a day of public thanksgivings for a series of naval victories. He presented history as of value because it displayed the providential plan, and he contrasted the historical perspective with the destructive secular philosophy of present-mindedness. Nares came to the reassuring conclusion that British victories proved divine support:

> From the first invention of letters, by means of which the history of
> past ages has been transmitted to us, and the actions of our forefathers

preserved, it has ever been the wisdom of man, under all circumstances of public and general concern, to refer to these valuable records, as the faithful depositaries of past experience, and to deduce from thence by comparison of situations, whatever might conduce to his instruction, consolidation, or hope. Thither the statesman of the present day frequently recurs for the conduct and support of the commonwealth.... Thither... the religious man ... bent upon tracing the finger of God in all concerns of importance to the good and welfare of man, is pleased to discover, in the course of human events, a direction marvellously conducive to the final purposes of Heaven, the constant and eternal will of God: and continually illustrative of his irresistible supremacy, his over-ruling providence, his might, majesty, and power!"

To Nares, there was a clear struggle between the historical and the opposition to history, one related to that between good and evil and, more specifically, the understanding of the providential and the failure to seek such understanding: "the enemy begin their operations on the pretended principle of giving perfect freedom to the mind of man ... the first step to be taken in vindication of such a principle, is to discard all ancient opinions as prejudices.... The great point is to discover the heavenly purposes and these can only be fitly studied in the consequences."[28]

Similar arguments were also made by other clerics in their sermons,[29] although without their matching Nares's other achievement in 1797: eloping with Lady Charlotte Spencer, after her father, George, 4th Duke of Marlborough, had refused to allow them to marry.

Other historians also offered criticisms of revolutionary enthusiasm. In his *History of Greece* (1784–1810), which was much reprinted, Sir William Mitford (1744–1827), a landowner and MP, provided a cautious account of the value of Athenian democracy. He had been encouraged to write the study by Gibbon, a fellow officer in the Hampshire militia, and his commitment to the system included having one son as a captain in the Royal Navy.

The hostile treatment of the French Revolution continued into the nineteenth century with English novelists joining historians in presenting the Revolution as violent, terrifying, and un-English.[30] The Revolution was also played out by historians in terms of British political divisions.[31]

In the meanwhile, the Revolution had given new life, scope, and scale to conspiracy theories,[32] while also affecting the description of recent British history. James, 1st Earl of Malmesbury, who had been a leading diplomat and then a Whig who had switched to support the Pitt government, published in 1801 the works of his father, James Harris (1709–80), a noted writer as well as an MP and officeholder. The dedication to George III itself fixed both ideological framework and recent history: "Whose life and reign have been an uniform practice of religion and virtue. To Your Majesty Europe is indebted for whatever is still preserved to it of social order and legitimate government." Harris was presented as offering the necessary middle way, in an account that captured the view that the Enlightenment, or at least aspects of it, had led to the Revolution: "He detested the gloom of superstition, and the persecuting spirit by which it is so often accompanied; but he abhorred still more the baneful and destructive system of modern philosophy ... almost seem that he foresaw its alarming approach and fatal progress."[33]

Britain had its own equivalents to Napoleon's celebration of success, although, alongside the apotheosis of George III and the constitution,[34] there was less focus on the power of the ruler and no equivalent to the prowess of Napoleon. War with France forced to the fore history of the type seen with earlier conflicts, namely, historical accounts of war that overlapped with journalism. These created an instant celebratory history of the war with France, one that drew on classical images as well as current idioms[35] and that was seen in a variety of genres, including paintings[36] and poetry, for example, William Bowles's *The Battle of the Nile* (1799). There was much demand. For example, published in 1815, Hewson Clarke's *Naval, Military, and Political Events in Europe, from the Commencement of the French Revolution to the entrance of the Allies into Paris, and the conclusion of a general peace* went into a second edition the following year. Cambridge-educated, Clarke was a writer for periodicals, who attacked Lord Byron in the *Satirist* and, in 1832, published *A Continuation of Hume's History of England*, which took it to the accession of William IV in 1830.

At the same time, there was more willingness and ability in Britain than in France to comment adversely on war. For example, Samuel Pratt wrote of the United Provinces in 1795: "With regard to the general history of this country, for many revolving ages, it resembles the general history, alas, of almost every other nation in the habitable globe; a picture of battles lost and gained, cities sacked or besieged, villages buried, burned, or desolated, the fury of men contending with man, and the disasters of human nature aggravated by the ambition and weakness of human creatures."[37]

Burke was not alone among politicians in writing history. During the Peace of Amiens (1802–3), Charles James Fox visited France in 1802, seeing Napoleon and Lafayette but also spending much time in the archives, where he transcribed the reports of the French envoy during the reign of James II. A part of his history of the reign was published posthumously, by Lord Holland in 1808, and focused on the king's attempt to establish a despotism. In 1811, Samuel Heywood, a Unitarian and judge who had been a friend of Fox, published a *Vindication of Mr Fox's History of the Early Part of the Reign of James II*.

Alongside this focus on war and politics, it is necessary to note other voices. These included Jane Austen, who produced a *History of England, from the reign of Henry 4th to the death of Charles 1st, By a partial, prejudiced, and ignorant Historian*. This was a parody of Goldsmith's *History*, but one adding Austen's personal feelings. Austen's work indicated the malleability of history and its openness to personality on the part of the writer.[38] Meanwhile, political engagement was matched by writers claiming impartiality, and the latter came more to the fore after the Napoleonic Wars ended in 1815. Thomas Cromwell (1792–1870) argued in 1822 that distance from the life of Oliver Cromwell made it possible for the historian to be "divested of the partialities incident to a too close inspection of his subject-matter; that the moment was fully come, at which the Historian might avail himself of the valuable labours of writers contemporary with the events he describes, without imbibing their party feelings, or sympathising with their interested or vindictive passions."[39] This did not prevent Cromwell from going on to offer as an appendix a parallel of Napoleon and Oliver Cromwell, one very much to the benefit of the latter.[40] Sympathetic to Oliver Cromwell, Thomas Cromwell was brought up as an Anglican, becoming a Unitarian minister.

LOCAL HISTORY

While much of the history of the period was not written on the national scale, that did not mean that it did not reflect broader questions of the national past and destiny. That can be seen very clearly with the plethora of local histories.[41] For example, William Hutchinson (1732–1814) was a solicitor and topographer, who found time, as clerk to the Lord Lieutenancy of Durham, to write history. In 1781, subscribers were solicited for his two-volume history of Durham to be published by Solomon Hodgson, printer, proprietor, and editor of the *Newcastle Chronicle*. In the end, Hutchinson's *The History and Antiquities of the County Palatine of Durham* appeared in three volumes in 1785–94, leading to legal disputes with Hodgson over the length and to Hutchinson's loss of several hundred pounds.[42] He was able to use material in a range of archives, including that of the bishops.

In 1794, Hutchinson also produced *The History of the County of Cumberland*, published in Carlisle and dedicated to Sir John Sinclair. This was a mature work that discussed the nature of sources, at the same time considering the descent of nationhood from antiquity. Hutchinson started with the Brigantes, the pre-Roman tribe in the north of England. He referred to the problems of sources: "The accounts given by the Romans are, of themselves, confused and contradictory" in "this dark part of history." This led to a discussion of the queen of the Brigantes, Cartismandua or Cartimandua (r. c. 43–69), one in which there was consideration of the role of women:

> In those days, it was no disgrace, to the bravest people, to be governed by a woman; disgustful effeminancies had not then contaminated the sex; the fripperies and insignificancies of the female accomplishment were reserved to a very distant age: even men inured to indefatigable labours and toils, constantly in arms, subsisting chiefly by warfare or the chase, and bred up to feats of valour and the simple rules of native honour, were not ashamed to be led to battle by a woman; and to receive the maxims of their interior police, from the dictates of female judgment; nor is the history of Cartismandua blotted, till, by the intercourse of the Romans, the native virtue of the Brigantes was corrupted.[43]

Hutchinson presented luxury and wealth as bringing corruption and vice. Cartismandua expelled her husband, Venutius, and took his armor bearer, Vollocatus, to her bed: "To the Roman manners we must attribute this most flagrant breach of conjugal duty: it was no new thing with the invaders; but among Britons, before the Roman accession, we do not hear of one instance. The Roman writers presumed to impute to the natives the grossest state of incontinence . . . that the women held a common intercourse with a whole family." [44]

Hutchinson rejected this as incompatible "with the general tenor of the Druid administration, the tenets of which were deduced from moral obligation." Pre-Roman culture was greatly praised by Hutchinson, himself a prominent Freemason, who presented the Druids as an "order of men possessed [of] all the learning of the age" and argued that, as a result, the people were "wonderfully enlightened" with their theology uncorrupted by "idolatry." Indeed, Hutchinson's comments on the Druids and on religion more generally led him to query notions of development and to suggest that the modern world was in a state of crisis. The Druids, who were described at length, were presented as in harmony with the universe: according to Hutchinson, the Druids "taught the adoration of the divine essence, and deduced arguments from examples displayed in the book of nature."[45] In contrast, Hutchinson decried the present state of religious belief:

> In this polite age, we . . . have shaken off all holy veneration for the priesthood and their doctrines, under the detestable applications of enthusiasm, bigotry and superstition . . . the house of prayer is deserted. . . . The vulgar, when not kept in awe, are insolent, and when at liberty, are licentious. When we look back upon the volume of human life, and reflect that the knowledge of mankind was progressive, and that innumerable ages had elapsed, to bring them to the estate of civilisation, in which they now are, we must conceive a most melancholy idea of the first race of men. From the history of ancient states, we are led to determine, that innovations in religion, and contempt of sacred things, marked the advancing dissolution of each empire; disobedience to government succeeded; the bonds of public faith were thenceforth loosened; the compact between citizen and citizen was so far dissolved, then corruption prevailed against private virtue

and the state therefore collapsed.[46]

Hutchinson was also highly critical of the Romans, presenting them as bringing in "nothing but articles of luxury and magnificence" and as insinuating their habits and manners into the life of their subjects.[47] In contrast, and with a look to Gibbon's portrayal of barbarian virtue, in the fifth century, according to Hutchinson, "the warlike and ferocious bands, who possessed the northern regions, from their implacable aversion to the Romans, remaining uncontaminated with their vices, and not become imbecillitated by their luxuries," conquered Roman Britain.[48]

The first volume of John Nichols's *The History and Antiquities of the Country of Leicester* appeared in London in 1795. The son of a London baker who became a printer, Nichols (1745–1826) was a wide-ranging entrepreneur in the culture of print. He was Grub Street as cultural renaissance, as, in a provincial context, was a figure Nichols acted for, William Hutton (1723–1815), a Dissenter, bookseller, writer of verses, and land speculator, who opened the first circulating library in Birmingham (1751) and published a well-received *History of Birmingham* (1781), as well as *The Battle of Bosworth* (1788), *A Dissertation on Juries* (1789), *A History of the Hundred Courts* (1790), *A History of Derby* (1791), and *The History of the Roman Wall* (1802). Popular interest was suggested by republication in new editions of the histories of Birmingham, Bosworth, Derby, and the Roman Wall.

The editor of the *Gentleman's Magazine*, Nichols was also an antiquarian, a chronicler of the book trade, a collector of literary manuscripts, and a publisher of literary works as well as of histories of Canonbury, Hinckley, and Lambeth. Printer for the Society of Antiquaries, Nichols also printed for the government the type facsimile of *Domesday Book*, a work that linked so many historians, and published *The Epistolary Correspondence of Francis Atterbury* (1783), a Tory bishop closely linked to literary circles, who was expelled from England as a result of Jacobite plotting against George I. Nichols's history of Leicestershire was dedicated to George's great-grandson, George III, who was described as "Patron of the Arts and Sciences, And Father of his People." In a historical throwback to Anglo-Saxon days, the dedication referred to the book as an "investigation of the History and Antiquities of a large portion of his extensive Mercian Demesne."

Nichols was very dubious about the legends of early origins for Britain and Leicester. He traced the idea of Trojan origin, only to be highly skeptical, and evaluated the legend of Leicester being founded by King Lear. Nichols concluded on the former in an anthropological fashion: "It cannot be doubted, that Britain was first peopled from the Continent by the Celts, or Gauls. This is proved, partly from the vicinity, and partly from a comparison of manners, religion, and languages."[49] The 1815 edition of *Encyclopaedia Britannica* argued that "We have no accounts that can be depended upon before the arrival of Julius Caesar."[50]

Loyalty to the present establishment was very much the theme of a number of works, with the tracing of local history serving to demonstrate a continuity that was presented as the basis for current conditions. This can be seen in Valentine Green's account of Worcester. Having abandoned legal studies, Green (1739–1813) had become a leading mezzotint engraver, and in 1775 he had been appointed mezzotint engraver to George III. In 1796, Green published *The History and Antiquities of the City and Suburbs of Worcester*, a lengthier version of an earlier work of 1764. This new work included not only a list of subscribers, but also a dedication to George III, whose 1788 visit to Worcester, the first by a monarch since that by Charles II, closed the history:

> The tracing of the steps by which a military station was improved into a metropolis, the feudal seat of a Saxon viceroy transformed into that of arts and opulence, will not, it is presumed, be found destitute of sufficient interest to merit attention. Its church, from the earliest times, has been one of the most renowned for its sanctity and discipline; its prelates revered for the extent of their learning and the eminency of their virtues; its magistrates and citizens honoured for their probity and loyalty, and not less so for their upright administration of justice, and prompt obedience to the laws: zealous to dignity, by exemplary conduct, the character they respectively sustained, each has mutually assisted in elevating the name of their city to the most distinguished height of moral pre-eminence. Thus guided and guarded, by the firmest friends to its peace and its prosperity, Worcester has become a complete illustration of the substantial good which results from a steady adherence to the principles of orderly government, supported by our glorious constitution; under the benign auspices of which, national liberty and social harmony, have not only been permanently secured to Worcester, but to all the classes of a brave, a generous, and a free people, who have the happiness to share in the mild influences of your Majesty's beneficent reign.[51]

The history provided Green with opportunities to make aesthetic and historical points that captured his interests and values. The destruction of altars in the Reformation is regretted, and Green noted: "Hence the incongruous appearance they make in our old churches and more especially in our cathedrals; and hence the unnatural and barbarous conjunction of modern Grecian architectural forms and embellishments, that continually offend our sight, about an altar placed in an ancient Gothic structure." This iconoclastic aspect of the Reformation was criticized indirectly by the remark that such destruction had continued in the 1650s, which Green described in terms of "the puritanical period of the Usurpation."[52] The latter is a description of the Interregnum that followed the execution of Charles I.

The Civil War was referred to by Green in terms of "the horrors of civil commotion." In opposition to John Adams's view when he visited the city in 1786 (a view mentioned in the preface), Worcester's stance in 1651 when Charles II was proclaimed king there was held up as heroic by Green. This was a point made by comparison with the Romans: "a cause now arrived at its last crisis, and to which its citizens, who had been subdued, but not conquered, still attached a truly Roman firmness to support."[53] Charles's subsequent defeat at Worcester was followed in Green's book by the brutal ravages of the parliamentary victors, not a theme generally taken: "The parliament army, now masters of the city, gave way to the most atrocious acts of outrage that the meanness of rapacity could stimulate in the dark mind of a sanguinary puritan: and although ostensible authority for a general pillage was not absolutely given by Cromwell, it is as certain that not the least restraint was put upon the brutal violence of his ruffian troops, who fell to ravaging and plundering without mercy, few or none of the devoted citizens escaping their cruelty."[54]

A similar critical view can be found in the reprinting in Colchester of versions of *A Most True Relation of That as Honourable as Unfortunate Expedition of Kent, Essex, and Colchester, in 1648* by Matthew Carter, a Royalist who had been imprisoned after the defeat at Colchester.[55] Green went on to publish *An Account of the Discovery of the Body of King John in the Cathedral Church of Worcester, July 17, 1797* (1797). The following year, he lost money as the result of French destructiveness in Düsseldorf, where he was engraving paintings in the ruler's collection.

The last example here of local history serving to make general historical points comes from an historian generally known for his writing on the national scale, William Coxe. He published *An Historical Tour of Monmouthshire* (1801) dedicated to Sir Richard Colt Hoare, with whom he had traveled there in 1798 and 1799 and who presented him to the rectory of Stourton. Coxe's interest in archives and his excellent connections were shown in his acknowledgment to Charles, 1st Earl of Liverpool, the chancellor of the Duchy of Lancaster, for granting permission to consult the duchy's archives. The book was of a type that was becoming common. It was "not . . . a regular history of Monmouthshire, but a description of the principal places, intermixed with historical relations, and biographical anecdotes."[56] Individuals appeared in many contexts. Liverpool responded to Napoleon's seizure of power by emphasizing a cultural and intellectual contrast between Britain and France, one in which a particular character was asserted as the goal: "The strange revolution that has happened in France turns almost into ridicule every idea hitherto entertained of free and representative government; it may, perhaps, though unfortunately have the effect of changing the opinions of mankind, from one extreme to another: it will be the duty of the British government to maintain that true mediocrity, which is the support of all due authority, on the one hand, and of true freedom on the other."[57] Liverpool's son made his old college friend Nares regius professor.

Aside from drawing extensively on the work of antiquaries, notably for his discussion of the antiquities of Monmouthshire, Coxe was also keen to judge between other historians. For example, in a footnote on his discussion in the text on the resistance to the Saxon invasion, Coxe commented: "Mr Whitaker has plainly proved, in opposition to the assertions of Gildas, which are adopted by Hume and others, that the Britons did not act with pusillanimity, but defended themselves with great spirit and vigour." This was a reference to John Whitaker's *The History of Manchester* (1771–75), which was also cited by John Duncumb in his history of Herefordshire.[58]

Similarly, regarding Arthur, he claimed: "To repeat the fabulous stories of Geoffrey of Monmouth would be to insult the reader's understanding; and the traditional songs of the bards are too uncertain and unconnected to form the basis of genuine history." Coxe added the reasonable point that, even if the accounts of Arthur's victories were factual, the victories had only retarded the Saxon success.[59] For Coxe, the Saxons were not the worse of conquerors. Indeed, they were contrasted with the less attractive Romans and the Normans. Moreover, on a longstanding pattern,[60] the Saxons were presented as more benign than the Vikings, such that it was the Saxons who defended England against the foreign invasions of, first, the Vikings and, then, the Normans.

This was also seen with other historians, for example, with the major study by Sharon Turner (1768–1847). London-born and a lawyer, Turner was interested in the study of Icelandic and Anglo-Saxon, and he devoted himself to the Anglo-Saxon manuscripts in the Cottonian Library in the Bristol Museum, producing a four-volume *History of England from the earliest period to the Norman Conquest* (1799–1805), a work suffused with detail, which went into a fifth edition in 1828. Turner was to take his history down to 1603 in 1839 and, in 1832, added a *Sacred History of the World as displayed in the Creation and subsequent events to the Deluge*. Turner rejected any idea of kinship between the Saxons and those he termed "the Vandals of Scandinavia."[61] Duncumb, in contrast, wrote of the "unparalleled cruelties" of the Saxon conquest.[62]

Turner's response to the Vikings contrasted with an engagement with them that reflected Romanticism. There was a political dimension, notably a Whiggish association between them and the early cultivation of European liberty, one that was a parallel not only to the commitment to (at times, cult of) Saxon liberties, but also to Gibbon's interest in Caledonian defiance of the Romans in the first century. This response to the Vikings was taken further by travelers to Iceland, notably Henry Holland (1788–1873), the son of a Cheshire doctor, who rose to be Queen Victoria's physician. In 1810, Holland visited Iceland with Sir George Mackenzie and Dr. Richard Bright and contributed to Mackenzie's *Travels in Iceland* the accounts it contained of Iceland's history and literature. Impressed, Holland claimed that during the Middle Ages, brave Norwegians, exiles from the "despotic sway of tyrannical royalty" at home, had settled in a desolate land and made it fertile, bringing with them their mythology. Holland offered a bardic account of winter recitals of forefathers' deeds "from whom they had received that inheritance of liberty, which they now dwelt among deserts to preserve.... Whilst their condition with respect to all the comforts or necessities of life is scarcely superior to the savage state, their moral and intellectual qualities raise them to a level even with the most civilized communities of Europe."[63]

This, however, was a minority position. Benign toward the Saxons, Coxe was highly critical of the Normans, bringing a particular local dimension to the issue:

> The invasion of the Normans [of Wales] was wholly different from that of the Saxons: the conquests of the Saxons being made in the name and with the troops of the sovereign, were annexed to the possessions, and subjected to the jurisdiction of the crown; but the Norman kings, engaged in foreign affairs, and employed in quelling insurrections, were unable to extend their arms into Wales; the great barons therefore were invited to make incursions at their own expense, and with their own retainers; were rewarded with the lands gained from the Welsh ... became despots in their demesnes, awed the crown, when worn by weak princes.... Such was the wretched state of feudal jurisprudence in Monmouthshire, as well as in the other marches of Wales, till Henry the eighth abolished the government of the lords' marchers, divided Wales into twelve shires, and included Monmouthshire among the counties of England; a happy change from the oppression of feudal tyranny, to the just and equal administration of English laws![64]

Writing at this level was not separate from that of national or global history. Instead, the impact of these different types of history interacted, while controversies were played out at many different levels. Coxe and Green contributed to and reflected a widespread, popular patriotic Anglo-Saxonism that was a theme, consistent with the idea of a Norman yoke, throughout the eighteenth century and that continued to play a powerful role in the nineteenth century.[65]

The language of Britishness might be used, but the reality, as here, was of Englishness: a patriotic Anglo-Saxonism meant nothing in Ireland, Scotland, and Wales, just as Roman rule was irrelevant for the first two. This patriotic Anglo-Saxonism was seen throughout the eighteenth century and looked back to earlier scholarship, particularly that of Laurence Nowell and William Lambarde,[66] and earlier arguments, notably about the Ancient Constitution. At the same time, the theme became stronger toward the close of the eighteenth century in part as an English instance of a romanticism that also had a political resonance.

The deployment of sources in local histories was a characteristic that it is too easy to underplay. That would be misleading as the quality and interest of many of the works are notable. Looked at in a broader perspective, historical writing was a continuing aspect of a more general fusion of a quest for and of Britishness and a celebration of the modern. The rewriting of the past in terms of the present, a longstanding process, was one in which the Anglicization of classical traditions increasingly adopted an agenda shaped by the concerns of a commercial society affected by political divisions and contexts that were different from their composition and character in the early decades. Alongside the redefinition of the literary heritage, notably with the positive reevaluation of Shakespeare and Chaucer and the accompanying emphasis on the vernacular, came a lessening of the classical hegemony in historical writing as the emphasis on Britishness was matched by a strong engagement with national concerns.

The "enlightened patriotism" that was to be a consistent theme in the late nineteenth century was already very much in evidence. This was an aspect of a nationalism based on a strong sense of special characteristics and providential purpose. Nationalism in history is frequently focused on the nineteenth century.[67] In England, it was well in evidence already in the eighteenth and evident in the glorification of opposition to France and in particular causes, notably the lead in antislavery from the 1780s. The Napoleonic Wars led to greater state intervention in culture,[68] but the celebration and debating of a national culture was already well developed, and notably so in the discussion of history.[69]

NOTES

1. Cobbett, *Cobbett's Parliamentary History of England*, XXVI:392.

2. J. Andrews, *A Comparative View of the French and English Nations, in their Manners, Politics, and Literature* (London, 1785), 9–12.

3. Cobbett, *Cobbett's Parliamentary History of England*, XII:882.

4. E. Barnard, *The New, Impartial and Complete History of England* (London, 1783), 193.

5. R. B. Sher, "1688 and 1788: William Robertson on Revolution in Britain and France," in *Culture and Revolution*, ed. P. Dukes and J. Dunkley (London, 1990), 98–109.

6. G. Pretyman, *A Sermon preached before the Lords Spiritual and Temporal . . . 30 January 1789* (London, 1789), 13.

7. M. Shaw, *Time and the French Revolution: The Republican Calendar, 1789—Year XIV* (Woodbridge, UK, 2011); S. Perovic, *The Calendar in Revolutionary France: Perceptions of Time in Literature, Culture, Politics* (Cambridge, 2012).

8. E. Burke, *Reflections on the Revolution in France*, ed. J. C. D. Clark (Stanford, CA, 2001), 170.

9. P. N. Miller, *Defining the Common Good: Empire, Religion and Philosophy in Eighteenth-Century Britain* (Cambridge, 1994).

10. E. Burke, *Reflections on the Revolution in France*, 183–184. The literature on Burke, the *Reflections*, and the subsequent controversy is vast. F. P. Lock, *Burke's Reflections on the Revolution in France* (London, 1985) and S. Blakemore, ed., *Burke and the French Revolution* (Athens, GA, 1992) are good introductions. On the controversy, see G. T. Pendleton, "Towards a Bibliography of the *Reflections* and *Rights of Man* Controversy," *Bulletin of Research in the Humanities* 85 (1982): 65–103. A crucial topic in helping to understand terms is covered in J. T. Boulton, *The Language of Politics in the Age of Wilkes and Burke* (London, 1963).

11. I. Hampsher-Monk, "Edmund Burke and Empire," *Proceedings of the British Academy* 155 (2009): 133–34.

12. Burke, *Reflections on the Revolution in France*, 353.

13. Hatsell to Addington, November 6, 1790, Exeter, Devon CRO., D. 152M, C. 1790/oZ 25.

14. This is considered in M. Knights, *The Devil in Disguise: Deception, Delusion, and Fanaticism in the Early Enlightenment* (Oxford, 2011).

15. W. Coxe, *A Letter to the Reverend Richard Price* (London, 1790), 5–6.

16. F. Harris, "The Blenheim Papers and the Authorized Biography of John Churchill, 1st Duke of Marlborough," *Archives* 22 (1997): 22–29.

17. J. C. Weston, "Edmund Burke's View of History," *Review of Politics* 23 (1961): 228.

18. E. Breisach, *Historiography* (Chicago, 1983), 248.

19. S. Tomaselli, "Responses to the French Revolution," *Gender and History* 7 (1995): 316.

20. H. Butterfield, *Man on His Past* (Cambridge, 1955), 68–70.

21. D. Eastwood, "Robert Southey and the Meanings of Patriotism," *Journal of British Studies* 31 (1992): 271–72.

22. J. Bate, *Shakespearean Constitutions: Politics, Theatre, Criticism, 1730–1830* (Oxford, 1989).

23. S. Horsley, *Sermons*, ed. H. Horsley (London, 1816), 3:293–321; J. C. D. Clark, *English Society 1688–1832: Ideology, Social Structure and Political Practice during the Ancien Regime* (Cambridge, 1985), 230–33; R. Hole, *Pulpits, Politics and Public Order in England 1760–1832* (Cambridge, 1989), 164–65; F. C. Mather, *High Church Prophet: Bishop Samuel Horsley (1738–1806) and the Caroline Tradition in the Later Georgian Church* (Oxford, 1992), 228–30.

24. N. Aston, "Horne and Heterodoxy: The Defence of Anglican Beliefs in the Late Enlightenment," *English Historical Review* 108 (1993): 916–17.

25. Hole, *Pulpits, Politics and Public Order.*

26. G. C. White, *A Versatile Professor* (London, 1903); J. M. Black, "A Georgian Fellow of Merton: The Historian Edward Nares," *Postmaster* (1987): 53–59; J. M. Black, "A Regency Regius: The Historian Edward Nares," *Oxoniensia* 52 (1987): 173–78; J. M. Black, "A Williamite Reprobate? Edward Nares and the Investigation of his Failure in 1832 to Deliver His Lectures," *Oxoniensia* 53 (1988): 337–40.

27. E. Nares, *Burghley* (London, 1828), xx–xxii.

28. E. Nares, *A Sermon, Preached at the Parish Church of Shobdon* . . . (n.p., 1798), 1–18.

29. P. Ihalainen, "The Enlightenment Sermon: Towards Practical Religion and a Sacred National Community," in *Preaching, Sermon and Cultural Change in the Long Eighteenth Century*, ed. J. van Eijnatten (Leiden, UK, 2009), 233.

30. B. Melman, *The Culture of History: English Uses of the Past, 1800–1953* (Oxford, 2006).

31. H. Ben-Israel, *English Historians on the French Revolution* (Cambridge, 1968).

32. B. Coward and J. Swann, eds., *Conspiracies and Conspiracy Theory in Early Modern Europe: From the Waldensians to the French Revolution* (Aldershot, UK, 2004); P. R. Campbell, T. E. Kaiser, and M. Linton, eds., *Conspiracy in the French Revolution* (Manchester, 2007).

33. James, 1st Earl of Malmesbury, ed., *The Works of James Harris*, 2 vols. (London, 1801), 1:vi, xxv.

34. L. Colley, "The Apotheosis of George III: Loyalty, Royalty and the British Nation," *Past and Present* 102 (Feb. 1984): 94–129.

35. J. Cartwright, *The Trident: or, The National Policy of Naval Celebration, Describing a Hieronauticon or Naval Temple* (London, 1802). The Poet Laureate, Henry Pye, produced *Naucratia: or Naval Dominion* (1798), which was dedicated to George III.

36. G. Quilley, *Empire to Nation: Art, History and the Visualization of Maritime Britain, 1768–1829* (New Haven, CT, 2011).

37. S. J. Pratt, *Gleanings through Wales, Holland and Westphalia*, 3 vols. (London, 1795), 2:532.

38. J. Austen, *The History of England* (London, 1791).

39. Preface to second edition of *Oliver Cromwell and His Times* (London, 1822), v–vi. The first edition appeared the previous year.

40. *Oliver Cromwell and His Times*, 2nd ed., 479–87.

41. J. Milner, *The History Civil and Ecclesiastical, and Survey of the Antiquities of Winchester*, 2nd ed. (Winchester, 1809), 5.

42. W. Hutchinson, *The History and Antiquities of the County Palatine of Durham*, vol. 3 (Carlisle, 1794), iii–v.

43. W. Hutchinson, *The History of the County of Cumberland*, 2 vols. (Carlisle, 1794), 1:1–2.

44. Hutchinson, *The History of the County of Cumberland*, 1:2.

45. Hutchinson, *The History of the County of Cumberland*, 1:2–5. For the more general background, see S. Smiles, *Ancient Britain and the*

Romantic Imagination (New Haven, CT, 1994).

46. Hutchinson, *History of the County of Cumberland*, 1:5.

47. Hutchinson, *History of the County of Cumberland*, 1:9, 14.

48. Hutchinson, *History of the County of Cumberland*, 1:15.

49. J. Nichols, *The History and Antiquities of the Country of Leicester* (London, 1795), 1–2.

50. *Encyclopaedia Britannica* (Edinburgh, 1815), 8:44.

51. V. Green, *The History and Antiquities of the City and Suburbs of Worcester* (1764), dedication, i–ii.

52. Green, *History and Antiquities*, 90–91.

53. Green, *History and Antiquities*, 277.

54. Green, *History and Antiquities*, 284.

55. P. Baines, "The First Year of Printing in Colchester," *Factotum* 33 (Mar. 1991): 8–9.

56. W. Coxe, *An Historical Tour of Monmouthshire* (1801), ii.

57. Liverpool to Frederick, 4th Earl of Bristol, November 27, 1799, BL. Add. 38311 fol. 35.

58. Coxe, *Monmouthshire*, 5; J. Duncumb, *Collections towards the History and Antiquities of the County of Hereford* (Hereford, 1804), 1:33.

59. Coxe, *Monmouthshire*, 6.

60. S. Kliger, *The Goths in England, a Study in Seventeenth and Eighteenth Century Thought* (New York, 1972).

61. S. Turner, *History of England*, 4 vols. (London, 1799–1805), 1:12.

62. Duncumb, *Hereford*, 1:35.

63. A. Wawn, ed., *The Iceland Journal of Henry Holland 1810* (London, 1987).

64. Coxe, *Monmouthshire*, 9–10.

65. P. Jackson, *Education Act Forster: A Political Biography of W. E. Forster, 1818–1886* (Madison, WI, 1997); P. Yeandle, *Citizenship, Nation, Empire: The Politics of History Teaching in England, 1870–1930* (Manchester, 2015), 39.

66. R. Brackmann, *The Elizabethan Invention of Anglo-Saxon England: Laurence Nowell, William Lambarde and the Study of Old English* (Cambridge, 2012).

67. S. Nagle, *Histories of Nationalism in Ireland and Germany: A Comparative History from 1800 to 1932* (London, 2017).

68. H. Hoock, *Empires of the Imagination: Politics, War, and the Arts in the British World, 1750–1850* (London, 2010).

69. J. M. Black, *English Nationalism: A Short History* (London, 2018), passim.

CONCLUSIONS

BRINGING THE PAST
INTO THE PRESENT

"LET MODERN HISTORY BE BOTH YOUR STUDY AND AMUSEMENT; by modern history [I mean] from 1500 to your own time, from which era Europe took that colour which to a great degree it retains at this day, and let Alexander and Julius Caesar shift for themselves." Philip, 4th Earl of Chesterfield, a former diplomat, politician and ex-secretary of state, was characteristically clear when writing in 1771 to Robert Murray Keith, then preparing for what became a successful diplomatic career.[1] The utility of recent history was also the theme of James Hampton in his *Reflections on Ancient and Modern History* (1746): "The best source of civil instruction must be searched for in examples not altogether so remote from our own times. The grand business of the Roman policy was only to contain their own dominions in order and obedience: on the contrary, the interests of modern communities depend entirely on the management of many neighbouring states, equal perhaps in power to themselves."[2]

There could also be the argument that the past was being too influential. This view could be advanced from a variety of perspectives, including that of the curse of history in the shape of empowerment through past triumphs or disasters. From Ireland, a colonel complained in 1807: "A divided or distracted people like us are not calculated to meet such an invader as [Napoleon] Bonaparte ... the 12th of this month instead of lamenting over the fatal consequences of the battle of Friedland, the Orange Yeomanry of this kingdom were celebrating a battle fought upwards of 100 years ago, with every mark of triumph and exultation as if Ireland had no other enemy than its Catholic inhabitants."[3] Thus, a Napoleonic victory over Britain's principal ally, Russia, a victory that drove Russia from the war, appeared less significant than William III's victory over James II at the Battle of the Boyne in 1690. Patriotism had to make way for a divisive loyalism, or, alternatively, depending on the circumstances, was born from it.[4]

These utilitarian foci, however, were not to the fore as both historians and readers saw the resonance and value of more distant history, indeed of the very process of history. George, Lord Lyttelton, a onetime politician who devoted much of his life to his *History of the Life of Henry the Second* (1767), a king of England who ruled from 1154 to 1189, responded in 1772 to praise that "it may be useful to the highest interest of mankind, by inculcating a right sense of morality and religion, which indeed I had at heart, above any other work, and without the hope of which I could not have gone through the drudgery of it with any satisfaction."[5] This emphasis on morality and religion was not divorced from concern with improving historical accuracy and method but provided a context for the latter. Indeed, there was a parallel with the development of the novel and the birth of hermeneutics.[6]

At the same time, Lyttelton and the response to his work indicated developing public interest in the medieval period. Periodization was a longstanding practice, but there was also a tendency to see continuities, one in which the medieval was not necessarily outdated as Catholic and premodern.[7] Interest in the medieval was not simply that of a constitutionalism focused on the Magna Carta; nor did the politics of a partisan history drive out other subjects, themes, and approaches. In particular, there were already signs, possibly as a response to the triumph of the "moderns," of what would later be described as proto-Romantic, at least in so far as a commitment to landscape was concerned. This approach included an interest in history that was not that of the classical past or of its models. This interest was seen with the story of Edward I (r. 1272–1307) ordering the killing of the Welsh bards, a story that was a dramatic instance of the medievalism of the period. This Welsh tradition, later discredited, was mentioned in the second volume of Thomas Carte's *History of England* (1750), and that was the basis for Thomas Gray's poem *The*

Bard (1757). Gray wrote in powerful terms that linked the last surviving bard to the landscape:

> On a rock, whose haughty brow
> Frowns o'er old
> Conway's foaming flood,
> Robed in the sable garb of woe,
> With haggard eyes, the Poet stood;
> Loose his beard and hoary hair
> Stream'd like a meteor
> through the troubled air.[8]

Gray was inspired to complete the poem when he heard a Welsh harpist play at Cambridge. Gray's poem was the basis of *The Bard* (1774), a painting by Thomas Jones, which, in turn, was the basis for John Martin's dramatic painting *The Bard* (1817). Thus, there was a potent strand in the presentation of history in which what was written was but one aspect. Art should not be separated out from other forms, nor explicitly historical works abstracted from other writings. The interest in the bards was matched by that in Druids, although Carte's discussion of the latter was attacked by Samuel Squire, a Whig cleric, in his *Remarks on Mr Carte's Specimen of his General History of England* (1748).

The bardic craft was revived by Edward Williams, "Iolo Morganwg," (1747–1826), a stonemason, shopkeeper, forger of ancient manuscripts, charlatan, genius, and poet, akin to a William Blake on opium. His successful attempt at inventing traditions, including druidical ceremonies, eventually played a role in encouraging Welsh distinctiveness.

A somewhat different account of Henry II to that by Lyttelton was offered by Thomas Hull, a leading London actor, in his most successful play, the tragedy *Henry the Second, or the Fall of Rosamond*. First performed in 1773, the play appeared in four editions the following year, as did Hull's *Richard Plantagenet, a Legendary Tale*. His novel *The History of Sir William Harrington* had appeared three years earlier.

Medievalism was also seen in historians' criticism of Henry VIII's Dissolution of the Monasteries[9] and in the development of a Gothic style for architecture. In 1742, the first English book on Gothic architecture appeared, Batty Langley's *Ancient Architecture Restored and Improved by a*

Great Variety of Grand and Useful Designs, entirely new in the Gothic Mode for ornamenting of buildings and gardens. Henrietta Howard, Countess of Oxford, rebuilt Welbeck Abbey in the Gothic style from 1752, and Alnwick Castle was remodeled in a Gothic fashion in the same period. However, the Gothic was largely used for rebuilding, as at Arbury Hall and The Vyne, not new seats, and Horace Walpole's Gothic suburban villa at Strawberry Hill, Twickenham, was unusual in being a new house.[10] Gothic was not seen as a style equal to classicism, or, rather, neoclassicism, until the work of such architects as James Wyatt at the close of the century. Such work, however, led to an interest in buildings from the medieval past, as with George Cuitt the Younger's *Six Etchings of Saxon and Gothic Buildings now Remaining in the City of Chester* (1810–11) and his illustrations to the *History of the City of Chester* (1815).

In 1778, in occupied Philadelphia, the British army organized the Mischianza, an elaborate entertainment that included a pseudomedieval tournament. This was intended to display noble martial identity and to call on the allegorical potential of chivalric romance, one that provided an instance of loyalist Gothic.[11] Loyalist Gothic was also seen in other arts,[12] such as the paintings of Benjamin West, as well as in neo-Gothic novels, which became more fashionable in the 1790s, notably with the works of Ann Radcliffe and Matthew "Monk" Lewis.[13] The role of Gothic in culture in the late eighteenth century created a context more for artistic enterprise than for historical reflection. Yet the two should not be too abruptly separated. There were important links, both in content and tone. Indeed, the cultural dimensions of history need to be emphasized alongside the intellectual.

An engagement with the Gothic helped ensure a stronger interest in the Middle Ages and in medievalism than had been the case earlier in the century. George III's interest in the medieval period looked back to Bolingbroke's thesis of the Patriot King, an idea developed in his *The Idea of a Patriot King* (1749), and focused then on Frederick, Prince of Wales, before being adopted for George.[14] This was a theme readily located with Edward III and Henry V, monarchs who were easily recovered through accessible Tudor and Stuart histories. Other writers also looked to the Middle Ages, for example, Richard Hurd with his *Letters on Chivalry and Romance* (1757) and, somewhat differently, Thomas

Chatterton (1752–70), who invented, as a persona for himself when creating the medieval poetry he claimed to have found in a Bristol church, Thomas Rowley as a fifteenth-century Bristol poet. The long-lived and victorious Edward III, the founder of the Order of the Garter, proved especially valuable as an example, as with Clara Reeve's *Memoirs of Sir Roger De Clarendon* (1793) and George's sponsorship of West's historical paintings. West's *Edward III Crossing the Somme* (1788) showed how successful past monarchs could be portrayed in a dramatic (and colorful) fashion that reflected glory on their current successor.[15] Moreover, James Northcote, a protégé of Joshua Reynolds and a popular royal academician, helped form an impression of the national past from 1784 with paintings including *Sir William Walworth ... Killing Wat Tyler* and *The Murder of the Young Princes in the Tower*, events in 1381 and 1483 respectively. Alongside this general impression of the drama of the Middle Ages thus came potent individual images. As a reminder, however, that individual producers of culture, whether writers like Wesley or others, could comprehend, reflect, and reconcile different themes and traditions, West also produced such classical history paintings as *Agrippina Landing at Brundisium with the Ashes of Germanicus* (1768), as well as such religious paintings as *Christ Healing the Sick* (1811).

George Colman the Younger's play *The Surrender of Calais* (1791), a reference to English victory in 1347, not its loss under Queen Mary in 1558, contributed to the theme, closing with:

> Rear, rear our English banner high.
> In token proud of victory!
> Where'er our god of battle strides,
> Loud sound the trumpet of fame!
> Where'er the English warrior rides
> May luarelled conquest grace his name.

The Gothic was to become a theme linked to modern Catholicism,[16] but that was not a necessary linkage. Knowledge and understanding of the medieval period also benefited from the publication of sources, such as Thomas Rymer's *Foedera* (1704–13), Thomas Hearne's publication of major chronicles, and the publication, from 1767, of the Rolls of Parliament.

In historical terms, interest in the Middle Ages and in more obscure earlier periods could lead to a degree of antiquarianism,[17] but, more significantly, it ensured that national history was not solely a matter of the period from the Reformation or even the Glorious Revolution. This would have been the case had the relevance pursued been that of what was then held to be the origins of modern Britain. Equally, the focus on modernity encouraged a treatment of the Gothic and the medieval more generally in Romantic terms, one that was also to be evident in the Young England movement of the 1840s and its idealization of the medieval past. Both tendencies were readily apparent in historical writing at the close of the eighteenth century.[18] Romanticism in part represented an emotional, rather than intellectual, embrace of the past. The classic historical image, a ruined monastery presented a depopulated past. The relevance of this in terms of modern politics was less direct than for those aspects of the past that could be read in more complex terms. These tendencies were aspects of the uneasy compound that constituted the developing historical sense of nationalism and, both linked and separate, the reaction to other historical cultures.

HISTORICAL MORALITY

More talented and imaginative, though less politically experienced than Lyttelton, Gibbon, Hume, and other famous historians, as well as less famous counterparts, shared the peer's concern for morality. This concern was at once timeless and located in particular moments, both religious and secular, past and present. Thus, Charles, 11th Duke of Norfolk (1746–1815), a firm Whig, a lapsed Catholic, and a Unitarian, sought to commemorate the six hundredth anniversary of the Magna Carta by building an octagonal Great Hall at his seat of Arundel Castle, a hall dedicated to "Liberty asserted by the Barons in the reign of John." Norfolk also acquired and prominently displayed Mather Brown's painting *Thomas Earl of Surrey defending himself before Henry VII after Bosworth*, a 1797 work (still on prominent display in the castle) referring to a 1485 episode involving the later 2nd Duke. This was an instance of dynasticism on show. Norfolk supported the Reverend John Duncumb in his history of Herefordshire in which he owned land, including purchasing material for the history, which was stopped after the Duke's death, the third volume only appearing in 1882.[19]

The reference to the Magna Carta in 1215 provided an exemplary narrative, but there was a more general wish to place contemporary situations in historical contexts. Thus, for the Whigs of the early nineteenth century who pressed for parliamentary and other reform, it was possible to locate George III and George IV, both opponents of reform, as villains who were later versions of the dastardly Stuarts. Criticism of the Stuarts could thereby serve to justify criticism of the Hanoverians, which had not been the intention or means of the Whig writers under George I and George II.

The Whigs could also find heroes among their ancestors. In John, the 6th Duke of Bedford's Temple of Worthies at his stately home on his country estate at Woburn, a bust of Charles James Fox, the Whig leader, was present with those of Francis, the 5th Duke and the 6th Duke, as well as such figures of classical probity as the Elder and Younger Brutus, all serving as remembrances of heroic virtue. A pediment by John Flaxman depicted Liberty, and a frieze by Richard Westmacott, the march of heroic virtue. Liberty was thus asserted and carefully grafted onto Whig family trees. The third son of the sixth Duke, Lord John Russell, 1st Earl Russell (1792–1878), was to be a Whig prime minister (1846–52, 1865–66) and an eminent Victorian historian, including being a biographer of Fox.

Furthermore, the present was coined into historical myth, as with Fox, who, as soon as he died in 1806, gained iconic status, as seen in christening names as well as annual dinners in his memory. Then in opposition, Whigs wrote history as a vindication and as a point of catharsis, with every contemporary situation placed in a historical context: "the Whig account is a penny-dreadful story with virtue wrestling with wickedness, cliff-hanging crises and the ultimate triumph of good."[20]

At the same time, there was criticism of the Whigs not only from Tories but also from radicals, as in Catharine Macaulay's *History of England* (1763–83), which praised the execution of Charles I and criticized the Glorious Revolution, and in Francis Place's manuscript history of the Westminster constituency, one with a long tradition of radicalism, which was written in 1824. He claimed that "the end and aim of the Whigs was then, what it had always been, and still is, the establishment of an oligarchy in the hands of the aristocracy."[21]

EXAMPLES TO POSTERITY

More generally, the relevance of the past, the importance of history to identity and to politics, remained strong. Take an editorial in the *Exeter Weekly Times* of November 8, 1828, that began:

> The Gunpowder Plot
>
> The return of the Fifth of November calls forth all over the country, for Protestant execrations on Catholic bigotry, and the anniversary of a national deliverance is seized on, as a pretext for exciting by-gone prejudices for sowing dissentions and inflaming ancient animosities. Catholic intolerance is descanted on by Protestant bigots, and ready invectives supply the place of historical truth. To how few, even among the liberals, have the real features of this conspiracy been lain open; and among the vulgar, who knows the gunpowder treason by any other name than the Popish Plot?

In practice, the reference to the 1605 conspiracy to blow up Parliament was relevant, albeit also highly problematic, in 1828, as debate was then intense over Catholic emancipation with ultra-Tories unsuccessfully opposing the measure. In this case, the past did not shape the present, but the past was important to the debate over the present as the past provided a source of emotional resonance for one of the sides, that resisting emancipation.

There were also broader issues about how best to present individuals and, linked to that, whether history was appropriate as an education. In 1718, John Perceval wrote to his friend George Berkeley about the recently arrived *Mémoires* of Cardinal de Retz, a seventeenth-century French politician: "I could be angry with him for discovering so much of the corrupt nature of man, but that he pays you with good sense and useful instruction, and one thing appears through the whole work, that the greatest turns in state affairs are owing to minute and often accidental causes, and that men may talk what they please of the public, but their own private interest is the secret spring of their most gallant and popular actions."[22]

Those who wrote about history, unsurprisingly, were more positive about the value of their work. The *Protestor*, a London newspaper, expressed confidence on July 28, 1753: "when these fluctuating objects shall be ascertained, methodised and reposed in history, the reader, having none of the difficulties or diversions, which misled or confounded the spectator, will have the full and free use of his judgment, and will pronounce accordingly."

Many writers, especially in the press, commented on what could be learned, notably the role of individuals and contingencies. Another London newspaper, *Read's Weekly Journal*, in its issue of October 10, 1730, was skeptical about the likely success of optimistic "state chymists" because policies faced "the shortness and inconsistency of man's life and temper for the bringing any great project or design about, the emergency of undiscernible accidents that will be sure to interpose, the miscarriage of instruments that must be employed, [and] the competition and recounter of adverse parties. . . . Who can so play his game as to prevent all the blots that the dice of time and change may put the best gamester upon? . . . upon which miscarriages the historian concludes that men do not so much counsel things, as things do counsel men."

History and poetry were commonly contrasted, with the latter seen as inherently more fictional. Thus, Richard Rolt wrote:

> Historians have always an advantage over poets; these write to the passions, those to the judgement. The language of the poets, like the finest medals in the cabinets of the curious, is only to be understood, and enjoyed, by the selected few; the language of historians, like the best current coin, is intended for the general use of mankind; and the more diffusive it grows, the more benefit it conveys. Poets can inflame; historians must instruct. In the former, morality puts on her richest garments. In the latter, she is more plainly attired, more familiar, and at ease; truth should always accompany the historian; but eloquence is the best companion for the poet.[23]

An emphasis on the uplifting quality of true art led to a stress on the value of history. *The Way to the Temple of True Honour and Fame by The Paths of Heroic Virtue. Exemplified in the Most Entertaining Lives of the Most Eminent Persons of Both Sexes on the Plan Laid Down by Sir William Temple, in his Essay of Heroic Virtue* (1773) by William Cooke, an Oxford fellow (academic) and a chaplain to the widowed Marchioness of Tweedale, juxtaposed true art with fiction. The verse on the title page declared:

> Abhor'd the Tale, which vain amusement brings,
> Tempts the frail mind, and tickles till it stings,
> But blessed those lines, that in each faithful page

> Impart the fruits of far experienced age,
> Founded on truth, the youthful heart which mend,
> And precious use with various pleasures blend.

Criticizing "writings calculated to enflame the passions, and debauch the youth of both sexes," Cooke claimed that "real history, which imparts the knowledge of past events, affords the best instructions for the regulation and good conduct of human life." This approach was an aspect of a more general change from the idea of direct divine intervention in history (through the "hand of God" and miracles) to the alternative idea that the Almighty established moral values that worked themselves out in history through human inspiration and agency. Thus, the good struggled with the bad to do God's will. Wesley's career, among others, provided illustration of this shift to seeing divine agency as indirect rather than direct. This was but part of a more variegated pattern of change in society, culture, and politics, one that included, for example, the changing attitude toward the education of children, from driving out sin to molding and guiding a child positively.[24]

It is unsurprising that historians praised their vocation as well as their individual work. They were trying to win readers in a highly competitive context, and one in which the publishers expected these claims. At the same time, there is no sign of any cynicism or despair on the part of historians. Indeed, whatever the derivative processes by which most books or newspaper articles were written, there was a conviction of the value of historical work. Taking a longstanding view, the *Times* of May 26, 1790, argued that it was clear from history that the most harmful conflicts "originated in the injustice, the animosity, or the capricious passions of individuals." This very conviction of the significance of history encouraged these derivative processes, for value took a number of forms. In his *Journey from London to the Isle of Wight*, made in 1787, Thomas Pennant referred to the fraud over the Derwentwater estates, which led to the expulsion of two MPs from Parliament in 1732: "The reprimand itself, and the whole history of this iniquitous transaction, which is preserved in the seventh volume of the Debates in Parliament ... are most worthy of the attention of every Englishman, and ought to be an example to posterity."[25]

The emphasis on derivative accounts is one basis for criticism of the historical writing of the period. Such criticism is of a part with the argument that history as a subject really developed only in the nineteenth century. This approach, one seen far more widely in the traditional treatment of eighteenth-century government, institutions, ideology, society, and culture (for example, the often critical coverage of the Church of England), risks, however, downplaying the significance of eighteenth-century developments and castigating the character and tone of the situation then. It is clear from this book that there was a coherence and purpose to history writing, as well as plentiful use of archival research in the eighteenth century, and that the latter did not have to wait until the nineteenth and the professionalization of historical studies then.[26] Instead, in the eighteenth century, this use of archival research was linked to a commitment to accuracy and impartiality, although there was no single understanding of the latter,[27] any more than there was subsequently.

Taking the reader into confidence as an informed equal was a frequent aspect of the history writing of the period and one that captured the public and self-conscious nature of information and knowledge. The *Encyclopedia Britannica* helped make source criticism normative in ordinary encyclopedia entries, as in the following:

> The reign of Edgar [959–75] proved one of the most fortunate mentioned in the ancient English history. He took the most effectual methods both for preventing tumults at home and invasions from abroad.... The greatness of King Edgar, which is very much celebrated by the English historians, was owing to the harmony which reigned between him and his subjects; and the reason of this good agreement was that the king sided with Dunstan [Archbishop of Canterbury, 959–88] and the [Benedictine] monks, who had acquired a great ascendant over the people. He enabled them to accomplish their favourite scheme of dispossessing the secular canons of all the monasteries; and he consulted them not only in ecclesiastical but also in civil affairs. On these accounts, he is celebrated by the monkish writers with the highest praises; though it is plain, from some of his actions, that he was a man who could be bound neither by the ties of religion nor humanity.[28]

The conviction of the value of historical work led both writers and readers to devote much attention to the past even as Britain made a new world and, in part, particularly because it did so. This attention did not diminish and was not seen as in any way incompatible with the strong engagement with framing and molding the future.

NOTES

1. Chesterfield to Keith, August 4, 1771, BL. Add. 35503 fol. 197.
2. J. Hampton, *Reflections on Ancient and Modern History* (Oxford, 1746), 23.
3. Colonel Hawthorne to Henry Addington, July 17, 1807, Exeter, Devon Record Office, 152 M/C 1807/018.
4. I. McBride, *The Siege of Derry in Ulster Protestant Mythology* (Dublin, 1997).
5. Lyttelton to--, April, 5 1772, BL. RP 2377ii. The emphasis is very different in C. Harper-Bill and N. Vincent, eds., *Henry II: New Interpretations* (Woodbridge, UK, 2007), an academic volume.
6. F. Deconinck-Brossard, "England and France in the Eighteenth Century," in *Reading the Text: Biblical Criticism and Literacy Theory*, ed. S. Prickett (Oxford, 1991), 165.
7. G. McMullan and D. Matthews, eds., *Reading the Medieval in Early Modern England* (Cambridge, 2007).
8. Thomas Gray, *The Bard* (London, 1757).
9. P. Morant, *The History and Antiquities of the County of Essex*, 2 vols. (London, 1768), 1:xxii–xxiii; and, not so critically, J. Duncumb, *Collections towards the History and Antiquities of the County of Hereford*, vol. 1 (Hereford, 1804), 101.
10. M. McCarthy, *The Origins of the Gothic Revival* (London, 1987); M. Aldrich, *Gothic Revival* (London, 1994).
11. D. O'Quinn, "Invalid Elegy and Gothic Pageantry: André, Seward and the Loss of the American War," in *Tracing War in British Enlightenment and Romantic Culture*, ed. N. Ramsay and G. Russell (Basingstoke, UK, 2015), 41–42; J. Watt, *Contesting the Gothic: Fiction, Genre and Cultural Conflict, 1764–1832* (Cambridge, 1999).
12. P. N. Lindfield, *Georgian Gothic: Medievalist Architecture, Furniture and Interiors, 1730–1840* (Woodbridge, UK, 2016); K. Stevenson and B. Gribling, eds, *Chivalry and the Medieval Past* (Woodbridge, 2016).
13. R. Miles, *Gothic Writing 1750–1820: A Genealogy* (London, 1993).
14. D. Armitage, "A Patriot for Whom? The Afterlives of Bolingbroke's Patriot King," *Journal of British Studies* 36 (1997): 397–418.
15. B. Gribling, *The Image of the Black Prince in Georgian and Victorian England: Negotiating the Late Medieval Past* (Woodbridge, UK, 2017).
16. P. Nockles, "'The Difficulties of Protestantism': Bishop Milner, John Fletcher, and Catholic Apologetics against the Church of England," *Recusant History* 24 (1998–99): 193–236.
17. S. Piggott, *Ruins in Landscape: Essays in Antiquarianism* (Edinburgh, 1976); J. Cook, "The Discovery of British Antiquity," in *Enlightenment: Discovering the World in the Eighteenth Century*, ed. K. Sloan (London, 2003), 178–91.
18. W. A. Speck, "Robert Southey, Benjamin Disraeli and Young England," *History* 95 (2010): 193–206. For a different aspect, see M. S. Phillips, "Relocating Inwardness: Historical Distance and the Transition from Enlightenment to Romantic Historiography," in *The*

Modern Historiography Reader: Western Sources, ed. A. Budd (Abingdon, UK, 2009): 106–17.

19. J. Duncumb, *Collections towards the History and Antiquities of the County of Hereford*, 2 vols. (Hereford, 1804–12), preface to vol. 1; third volume, by William Henry Cooke, published in London in 1882.

20. L. Mitchell, *The Whig World, 1760–1837* (London, 2005), 150.

21. Place, history of Westminster, BL. Add. 27849 fol. 92.

22. Perceval to Berkeley, March 13, 1718, BL. Add. 47028 fol. 227.

23. R. Rolt, *Memoirs of the Life of James Lindesay, Earl of Crawfurd* (London 1753), 3–4.

24. A. Fletcher, *Growing up in England: The Experience of Childhood 1600–1914* (New Haven, CT, 2008).

25. T. Pennant, *A Journey from London to the Isle of Wight*, 2 vols. in one (London, 1801), 1:19.

26. G. Iggers, "Key Phases in the Development of Modern Western Historiography: A Retrospective View," *Storia della Storiografia*, 58 (2010): 4.

27. J. Smitten, "Impartiality in Robertson's *History of America*," *Eighteenth-Century Studies* 19 (1985): 56–77.

28. *Encyclopedia Britannica*, vol. 8 (London, 1815), 59–60.

SELECTED FURTHER READING

Aldrich, M. *Gothic Revival*. London: Phaidon, 1994.

Batchelor, J., and C. Kaplan, eds. *British Women's Writing in the Long Eighteenth Century: Authorship, Politics and History*. London: Palgrave, 2005.

Ben-Israel, H. *English Historians on the French Revolution*. Cambridge: Cambridge University Press, 1968.

Black, J. B. *The Art of History: A Study of Four Great Historians of the Eighteenth Century*. New York: Russell & Russell, 1965.

Black, J. M. *A Subject for Taste: Culture in Eighteenth-Century England*. London: Hambledon, 2005.

Bourgault, S., and R. Sparling, eds. *A Companion to Enlightenment Historiography*. Leiden: Brill, 2013.

Braudy, L. *Narrative Form in History and Fiction: Hume, Fielding, and Gibbon*. Princeton, NJ: Princeton University Press, 1970.

Brown, T., and G. Foard. *The Making of a County History: John Bridge's Northamptonshire*. Leicester: University of Leicester, 1994.

Browning, R. *Political and Constitutional Ideas of the Court Whigs*. Baton Rouge: Louisiana State University Press, 1982.

Bulman, W. *Anglican Enlightenment: Orientalism, Religion and Politics in England and Its Empire, 1648–1715*. New York: Cambridge University Press, 2015.

Cardwell, M. J. *Arts and Arms: Literature, Politics and Patriotism during the Seven Years War*. Manchester: Manchester University Press, 2004.

Champion, J. A. K. *The Pillars of Priestcraft Shaken: The Church of England and Its Enemies, 1660–1730*. Cambridge: Cambridge University Press, 1992.

Clark, J. C. D., and H. Erskine-Hill, eds. *Samuel Johnson in Historical Context*. Basingstoke: Palgrave, 2002.

Clark, J. C. D. *Samuel Johnson: Literature, Religion and English Cultural Politics from the Restoration to Romanticism*. Cambridge: Cambridge University Press, 1994.

Claydon, T., and I. McBride, eds. *Protestantism and National Identity: Britain and Ireland, c. 1655–c. 1850*. Cambridge: Cambridge University Press, 1998.

Clive, J. *Not by Fact Alone: Essays on the Writing and Reading of History*. New York: Knopf, 1989.

Damrosch, L. *Fictions of Reality in the Age of Hume and Johnson*. Madison: University of Wisconsin Press, 1989.

Dew, B., and F. Price, eds. *Historical Writing in Britain, 1688–1830: Visions of History*. Basingstoke: Palgrave, 2014.

Douglas, D. C. *English Scholars, 1660–1730*. London: Eyre and Spottiswoode, 1951.

Duke, A. C., and C. A. Tamse, eds. *Clio's Mirror: Historiography in Britain and the Netherlands*. Zatphen, Netherlands: Walburg, 1985.

Genuth, S. S. *Comets, Popular Culture, and the Birth of Modern Cosmology*. Princeton, NJ: Princeton University Press, 1997.

Gerrard, C. *The Patriot Opposition to Walpole: Politics, Poetry, and National Myth, 1725–1742*. Oxford: Clarendon, 1994.

Gordon, F., and G. L. Walker, eds. *Rational Passions: Women and Scholarship in Britain, 1702–1870*. Toronto: Broadview, 2008.

Gribling, B. *The Image of the Black Prince in Georgian and Victorian England: Negotiating the Late Medieval Past*. Woodbridge, UK: Boydell, 2017.

Grundy, I., and S. Wiseman, eds. *Women, Writing, History, 1640–1740*. London: Batsford, 1992.

Hanson, C. A. *The English Virtuoso: Art, Medicine, and Antiquarianism in the Age of Empiricism*. Chicago: University of Chicago Press, 2009.

Hay, D. *Annalists and Historians: Western Historiography from the Eighth to the Eighteenth Centuries*. London: Methuen, 1977.

Haywood, I. *The Making of History: A Study of the Literary Forgeries of James Macpherson and Thomas Chatterton in Relation to Eighteenth-Century Ideas of History and Fiction*. Rutherford, NJ: Fairleigh Dickinson University Press, 1986.

Hicks, P. *Neoclassical History and English Culture from Clarendon to Hume*. New York: St. Martin's Press, 2001.

Hill, B. *The Republican Virago: The Life and Times of Catherine Macaulay, Historian*. Oxford: Clarendon Press, 1992.

Hole, R. *Pulpits, Politics and Public Order in England, 1760–1832*. Cambridge, Cambridge University Press, 1989.

Hoock, H. *Empires of the Imagination: Politics, War and the Arts in the British World, 1750–1850*. London: Profile, 2010.

Johnstone, H., and F. W. Steer. *Alexander Hay, Historian of Chichester*. Chichester, UK: Chichester City Council, 1961.

Kelley, D. R., and D. H. Sacks, eds. *The Historical Imagination in Early Modern Britain: History, Rhetoric, and Fiction, 1500–1800*. Cambridge: Cambridge University Press, 1997.

Kramnick, I. *Bolingbroke and His Circle: The Politics of Nostalgia in the Age of Walpole*. Cambridge, MA: Harvard University Press, 1968.

Levine, J. M. *Humanism and History: Origins of Modern English Historiography*. Ithaca, NY: Cornell University Press, 1987.

Lianeri, A. ed. *The Western Time of Ancient History: Historiographical Encounters with the Greek and Roman Pasts.* Cambridge, Cambridge University Press, 2011.

Loftis, J. *The Politics of Drama in Augustan England.* Oxford: Clarendon Press, 1963.

Major, E. *Madam Britannia, Women, Church and Nation, 1712–1812.* Oxford: Oxford University Press, 2012.

Mandelbrote, G., and K. A. Manley, eds. *The Cambridge History of Libraries in Britain and Ireland, II, 1640–1850.* Cambridge: Cambridge University Press, 2008.

Marotti, A. *Religious Ideology and Cultural Fantasy: Catholic and Anti-Catholic Discourses in Early Modern England.* Notre Dame, IN: University of Notre Dame Press, 2005.

Melman, D. *The Culture of History: English Uses of the Past, 1800–1953.* Oxford, Oxford University Press, 2006.

Mendyk, S. A. E. *Speculum Britanniae: Regional Study, Antiquarianism and Science in Britain to 1700.* Toronto: University of Toronto Press, 1989.

Miller, P. N. *Defining the Common Good: Empire, Religion and Philosophy in Eighteenth-Century Britain.* Cambridge: Cambridge University Press, 1994.

Moore, J., I. M. Morris, and A. J. Bayliss, eds. *Reinventing History: The Enlightenment Origins of Ancient History.* London: University of London Press, 2008.

Neufeld, M. *The Civil Wars after 1660: Public Remembering in Late Stuart England.* Woodbridge, UK: Boydell and Brewer, 2013.

Nibelius, F. *Lord Bolingbroke and History.* Stockholm: Almqvist & Wiksell, 2003.

O'Brien, K. *Narratives of Enlightenment: Cosmopolitan History from Voltaire to Gibbon.* Cambridge: Cambridge University Press, 1997.

O'Brien, K. *Women and the Enlightenment in Eighteenth-Century Britain.* Cambridge: Cambridge University Press, 2009.

Okie, L. *Augustan Historical Writing: Histories of England in the English Enlightenment.* Lanham: University Press of America, 1991.

Phillips, M. S. *Society and Sentiment: Genres of Historical Writing in Britain, 1740–1820.* Princeton, NJ: Princeton University Press, 2000.

Piggott, S. *Ruins in Landscape: Essays in Antiquarianism.* Edinburgh: Edinburgh University Press, 1976.

Pocock, J. G. A. *The Ancient Constitution and the Feudal Law, a Study of English Historical Thought in the Seventeenth Century.* New York: Cambridge University Press, 1957.

Pocock, J. G. A. *Barbarism and Religion.* 6 vols. Cambridge: Cambridge University Press, 1999–2015.

Pocock, J. G. A. *Virtue, Commerce and History.* Cambridge: Cambridge University Press, 1985.

Price, F. *Reinventing Liberty: Nation, Commerce and the Historical Novel from Walpole to Scott.* Edinburgh: Edinburgh University Press, 2016.

Quilley, G. *Empire to Nation: Art, History and the Visualisation of Maritime*

Britain, 1768–1829. New Haven: Yale University Press, 2011.

Raven, J. *Publishing Business in Eighteenth-Century England.* Woodbridge, UK: Boydell, 2014.

Raven, J., H. Small, and N. Tadmor, eds. *The Practice and Representation of Reading in England.* Cambridge: Cambridge University Press, 1996.

Reid, J. P. *The Ancient Constitution and the Origins of Anglo-American Liberty.* DeKalb: Northern Illinois University Press, 2005.

Reill, P. H. *The German Enlightenment and the Rise of Historicism.* Berkeley: University of California Press, 1975.

Richard, C. *The Founders and the Classics: Greece, Rome, and the American Enlightenment.* Cambridge, MA: Harvard University Press, 1995.

Rivers, I. ed., *Books and Their Readers in Eighteenth-Century England.* Leicester: Leicester University Press, 2001.

Roberts, C. *Edward Gibbon and the Shape of History.* Oxford: Oxford University Press, 2014.

Seed, J. *Dissenting Histories, Religious Division and the Politics of Memory in Eighteenth Century England.* Edinburgh: Edinburgh University Press, 2008.

Shapiro, B. J. *A Culture of Fact: England, 1550–1720.* Ithaca: Cornell University Press, 1999.

Sharpe, K., and S. N. Zwicker, eds. *Writing Lives: Biography and Textuality, Identity and Representation in Early Modern England.* Oxford: Oxford University Press, 2008.

Sherman, S. *Telling Time: Clocks, Diaries and English Diurnal Form, 1660–1785.* Chicago: University of Chicago Press, 1996.

Simmons, J., ed., *English County Historians.* Wakefield, UK: EP Publishing, 1978.

Spadafora, D. *The Idea of Progress in Eighteenth-Century Britain.* New Haven, CT: Yale University Press, 1990.

Stauffer, D. A. *The Art of Biography in Eighteenth-Century England.* Princeton, NJ: Princeton University Press, 1941.

Staves, S. *A Literary History of Women's Writing in Britain, 1660–1789.* Cambridge: Cambridge University Press, 2006.

Sweet, R. *The Writing of Urban Histories in Eighteenth-Century England.* Oxford: Clarendon Press, 1997.

Taylor, C., and S. Buckle, eds. *Hume and the Enlightenment.* London: Pickering & Chatto, 2011.

Titler, R. *The Face of the City: Civic Portraiture and Civic Identity in Early Modern England.* Manchester: Manchester University Press, 2007.

Ucko, P. J., M. Hunter, A. J. Clark, and A. David, *Avebury Reconsidered: From the 1660s to the 1990s.* London: Unwin Hyman, 1990.

Vickery, A. *Behind Closed Doors: At Home in Georgian England.* New Haven, CT, Yale University Press, 2009.

Walkden, A. *Private Lives Made Public: The Invention of Biography in Early Modern England.* Pittsburgh: Duquesne University Press, 2016.

Wei, J. *Commerce and Politics in Hume's History of England.* Woodbridge, UK: Boydell and Brewer, 2017.

Weinbrot, H. D. *Britannia's Issue: The Issue of British Literature from Dryden to Ossian*. Cambridge: Cambridge University Press, 1993.

Williams, H. *Dean Swifts Library*. Cambridge: Cambridge University Press, 1932.

Williams, M., and S. P. Forrest, eds. *Constructing the Past: Writing Irish History, 1600–1800*. Woodbridge, UK: Boydell and Brewer, 2010.

Womersley, D., ed., *Edward Gibbon: Bicentenary Essays*. Oxford: Voltaire Foundation, 1997.

Worden, B. *Roundhead Reputations: The English Civil Wars and the Passions of Posterity*. London: Penguin, 2001.

Wright, D. *Bryan Faussett: Antiquary Extraordinary*. Oxford: Archaeopress, 2015.

Yale, E. *Sociable Knowledge: Natural History and the Nation in Early Modern Britain*. Philadelphia: University of Pennsylvania Press, 2016.

Young, B. W. *Religion and Enlightenment in Eighteenth-Century England: Theological Debate from Locke to Burke*. Oxford: Clarendon Press, 1998.

INDEX

abolition, 222
Abridgement (Tindal), 91
absolute monarchies, 123
Account of the Augustan Age in England, An (Goldsmith), 187
Account of the Discovery of the Body of King John in the Cathedral Church of Worcester, An (Green), 237
Act of Settlement, 48
Act of Succession, 86
Act of Union, 83
Adams, John, 237
Addington, Henry, 188
Addison, Joseph, 48, 53, 134, 195
Addison, Lancelot, 53
Advantages of Education, The (West), 69–70
Adventures of an Atom, The (Lloyd), 51
Adventures of David Simple, The (Fielding), 5
Adventures of Roderick Random, The (Smollett), 5
affective patriotism, 15
Africanus, Scipio, 151
Agrippina Landing at Brundisium with the Ashes of Germanicus (West), 249
Aix-la-Chapelle, 98
Aland, John Fortescue, 58
Alboin, 204
Aldrich, Henry, 133

Alexander the Great, 70, 111, 193
almanacs, 28, 68
Alnwick Castle, 248
American colonies, 34, 39, 53, 199. *See also* North America
American Revolution, 41, 53, 221–22
Anabaptists, 140–41, 163
Ancient and Modern Liberty Stated and Compared (Hervey), 194
Ancient and Present State of Glostershire (Atkyns), 59
Ancient and Present State of Gloucestershire (Wright), 45
Ancient Architecture Restored and Improved by a Great Variety of Grand and Useful Designs (Langley), 247–48
Ancient Constitution, 33–34, 93–94, 107, 109, 240
Ancient History (Rollins), 27
Andrew, John, 76, 215, 220–21
Anecdotes of Painting in England (Walpole), 186–87
Angers, 7
Angles, 163
Anglesey, Lord, 134
Anglicanism, 104, 105
Anglicans, 138, 139, 140, 142, 189
Anglicization, 96, 228, 241
Anglo-French conflict, 92
Anglo-French peace, 149

Anglo-Saxon tradition, 15, 20, 52, 62, 87, 92, 163, 239–40
Anglo-Scottish conflict, 92
Anjou, Margaret of, 14
Anne, Countess of Coventry, 113
anonymous works: Bowdler's collection of, 26; criticism of Rapin-Thoyras, 92; on Cromwell, 73; of Dissenters, 50, 130; future-oriented, 169; of Hume, 173; partisanship and, 83–85; *Sister Peg*, 173; *Answer to one part of a late infamous libel, An* (Pulteney), 94
anthems, 55
anti-Catholicism: Burnet and, 104; eighteenth century, 171; James II and, 38; Mary I and, 38, 48; national identity and, 132; progress and, 36–37; Rowe and, 48; anticlericalism, 149
anti-Jacobitism, 22, 171
antimonarchism, 129–32
antiquarianism, 37, 41–42, 49–50, 199, 235, 249–50
antiquities, 42, 46, 65, 66, 238
Antiquities of Surrey (Salmon), 66
Antiquities of the Christian Church (Bingham), 27
Antiquities of Warwickshire (Dugdale), 4
antislavery, 241
Apollo Belvedere, 75
apologists, 133
Appeal from the New to the Old Whigs (Burke), 225–26
Appleby Grammar School, 26
Aquitaine, Eleanor of, 14
Arabs, 202–3, 207–8, 210
Arbury Hall, 248
Arbuthnot, John, 89
archaeology, 19–21, 56–57
architecture, 196, 247–48
archival sources, 25–27, 58–76, 255
Argyll, John, 2nd Duke of, 76

aristocrats, private collections of, 50–51, 62
Arnauld, Antoine, 114
Arria, 16
artwork, 71–72, 196, 197, 223–24, 247, 248–49
Arundel Castle, 250
Ashmolean Museum, 42
Astell, Mary: authority and, 121–22; English Civil War and, 114, 115–21, 130; as historian, 13, 14, 30n32, 124–26; history and, 113–15; present-centered history, 122–24; on Puritans, 130; Astell, Ralph, 114
Astell, William, 114
Athalia (Handel), 55
atheism, 115, 213
Athens, 42, 213, 230
Atkyns, Sir Robert, 45, 59
atlases, 11
Atterbury Plot, 74
Atterbury, Francis, 62, 121, 124, 133–34
Aubrey, John, 30n38
Augustus, 194, 210
Aurelian, 203
Aurelius, Marcus, 104, 114, 209
Austen, Jane, 4, 12, 232
Austria, 39, 71, 151, 207, 211
authoritarianism, 99
authority: Astell on, 121–22; Burnet on, 113; past works and, 175; authorship. *See* historians
autobiographies, 5–6, 68, 69
autocracy, 183, 185, 221
Avars, 204
Avebury, 20

Bacon, Francis, 35, 66, 162
balance of power, 23, 97, 204, 205–8, 210–15
Bangor, 94
Bangorian Controversy, 94, 141

Index

Banks, John, 22–23, 71
Baptists, 140–41
barbarians, 198–99, 201–3, 204, 209, 213, 235
Bard, The (Gray), 246–47
Bard, The (Jones), 247
Bard, The (Martin), 247
Barnard, Edward, 221
Barnard, Toby, 2
baroque tradition, 34–35
Barrett, William, 42–43
Bath, 69
Bathurst, Edward, 85
Battle of Bosworth, The (Nichols), 235
Battle of Culloden, 177, 184
Battle of Minden, 185
Battle of Sedgemoor, 133
Battle of the Boyne, 246
Battle of the Boyne, The (West), 72
Battle of the Nile (Bowles), 231
Baxter, Richard, 136
Beckingham, Charles, 195
Bedford, John, 6th Duke of, 251
Belgrade, 207
Belsham, William, 227–28
Belshazzar (Handel), 55
Benevento, 207
Bengal, 214
Bentley, Richard, 200
Berkeley, George, 252
Berkshire, 54
Bertie, Albermarle, 84
bias, 50, 162, 165–66
biblical histories, 13–14, 54–55
biblicalism, 229
biblical tradition, 40, 175–76, 150
Bingham, George, 47
Bingham, Joseph, 27
Bingley, William, 44
Biographia Britannica, 57
Biographical History of England (Granger), 186

biographies: Banks', 22–23; Burnet's, 103, 109–10; Coxe's, 226–27; of foreign individuals, 51; genre of, 72; historical, 51; national history and, 50–51; Oldmixon's, 133; Rolt's, 149; Warner and, 166; Birmingham, 235
Bishop Burnet's Proofs of the Pretender's Illegitimacy (Salmon), 65
Blackall, Offspring, 85–86
Blackstone, William, 34
Blake, William, 247
Blenheim Palace, 75
"bluestocking theology," 14
Boadicea, 13–14, 68
Boadicea (Glover), 195
Bodleian, 62
Boleyn, Anne, 179
Bolingbroke, Henry, Viscount, 21–22, 23, 40, 63, 75, 91, 92, 159, 181, 196, 248
Bolingbroke or A Dialogue on the Origin and Authority of Revelation (Warner), 156, 159
Bonaparte, Napoleon, 231, 238
Book of Common Prayer, The (Burnet), 108
Book of Kings, 176
Book of Martyrs (Foxe), 103, 104, 146
bookselling market: criticism of, 67; female historians and, 13; growth in, 61, 155, 231; high-end works, 103, 155; historical writing forms and, 155; popular/mass, 67, 155, 174, 235; readership, 17–18, 114; republished works, 28, 49, 68–69, 88, 235; sensationalism and, 135; source criticism and, 61; subscriptions, 155; world histories, 54
Borgias, 46
Borlase, Edmund, 165
Borlase, William, 45, 59
Boughton House, 5
Bowdler II, Thomas, 26

Bowles, William, 231
Boyer, Abel, 52, 62–63, 71, 97
Boyle, Robert, 111, 112, 159
Bradshaw, John, 65
Brady, Robert, 34
Brecknock, Timothy, 171
Bridges, John, 45
"Brief Historical Relation of State Affairs from September 1678 to April 1714, A" (Luttrell), 25
Brigantes, 233
Bright, Richard, 239
Bristol, 3, 42, 43, 228
Bristol Journal, 222
Bristol Museum, 239
Britain: Cartagena defeat, 19; Catholicism as threat to, 7, 145–46, 171 (*see also* Catholicism); colonialism, 24, 210, 214, 225; constitution of, 228–29, 231 (*see also* English constitution); Denmark and, 95; Falkland Islands crisis, 19; foreign policy, 98–99, 146, 148, 184, 206, 209, 214; France and, 18, 96–98, 100, 123, 148–49, 169, 170, 177–78, 194, 197, 209, 211, 220–24; Hanover and, 38; histories of, 62, 227–28; imperialism, 169–72; international relations, 96–100; mid-century struggles and defenders, 145–47, 150–55; military victories of, 71–72; modernization, 204; national culture, 170, 228, 241; origin histories, 235–36; parallels with Rome, 55, 193–15; Romans in, 44; Russia and, 169, 246; Smollett on, 51; Spain and, 18–19, 148–49, 169, 186, 197; war with France, 145, 231; *See also* England; *Britannia* (Camden), 27, 49
British Biography, 24
British Museum, 24, 26
British Worthies, 196
Briton, 97–98

Brooke, Frances, 70, 75
Brooke, Henry, 193
Brown, Mather, 250
Buccleuch, 4th Duke of, 213
Buckingham, George, 1st Duke of, 73–74
Burges, James Bland, 39
Burgundy, Dukes of, 147
Burke, Edmund, 18, 23–24, 99, 186, 224–29, 232
Burlington Quay, 187–88
Burn, Richard, 45, 59
Burnet, Gilbert: Collier and, 162; contract theory, 103, 117; criticism of by contemporaries, 85; defense of new order, 103–6; Frederick and, 8; on monarchies, 85; nationhood and, 106–8, 157; popularity of, 27; on religious obligation of leaders, 108–13; on self-preservation, 105; on women's education and piety, 14; as Whig historian, 10, 100, 135; Wycliffe and, 141; Burton, John, 134
Bute, John, 3rd Earl of, 71, 74, 170, 198
Byron, George, Lord, 231
Byzantium, 203–4, 206, 209

Caesar, Julius, 111, 151, 199
Calamy, Edmund, 136
Caledonia, 202, 239
Calvin, John, 104
Calvinism, 69, 112, 135, 155
Cambridge, 8, 26, 50, 54, 57, 62, 64, 65, 66, 84–85, 166
Cambridge Castle, 54
Camden, William, 27, 43, 49
Campbell, Alexander Hume, 156
Campbell, John, 11, 65
Canonbury, 235
Capua, 207
Caribbean, 214
Carlisle, 62, 233

Index

Carmarthen, Francis, Marquess of, 214
Cartagena, 19
Carte, Samuel, 60
Carte, Thomas, 57, 153–55, 246, 247
Carter, Elizabeth, 14
Carter, Matthew, 237
Carteret, Edward, 85
Carthage, 151, 197, 200
Cartismandua/Cartimandua, 233–34
Castile, Eleanor of, 14
Castlehaven, Lord, 165
Castle of Otranto, The (Walpole), 5
Catherine of Aragon, 163
Catherine the Great, 211
Catholicism: Astell on, 115, 118, 119; Burnet on, 104–6, 107; Carte on, 155; Chandler on, 132; Charles II and, 21; Collier on, 104; criticism of, 36–37 (*see also* anti-Catholicism); Dissenters and, 87–88, 132; French Revolution and, 213; Gothic tradition and, 249; international relations and, 100; Ireland and, 164–65; Jesuit Order suppression, 64; Kennett and, 115–16; Neal on, 136; Protestantism and, 105, 112, 142, 150, 165–66; Royalist historians on, 34; Saxon tradition and, 149; as threat to Britain, 7, 145–46, 171; Warner on, 156–57, 161, 162; Wesley on, 183, 185
Cato, 9
Cato (Addison), 48, 195
Cecil, William (Lord Burghley), 57
Cellarius, Christoph, 11
Celtic tradition, 15, 163
Censors, 195
censorship, 193
Century of Eminent Presbyterian Preachers, A (Gray), 138–39
Chamberlain, Lord, 193
Chamberlaine, John, 51
Champion of Virtue, The (Reeve), 17

Chancery, 25
Chandler, Samuel, 132
chapbooks, 70
Chapel Royal, 55
Chapman, John, 146
Chapone, Sarah, 113
characters, genre and, 72
Characters of the Several Noblemen and Gentlemen that have died in the Defence of their Princes, The, 65 (Salmon), 65
Chardin, Sir John, 16
Charlemagne, 38, 205
Charles Dacres (anonymous), 70
Charles I: Astell and, 114, 116, 117, 119–20; Carte on, 154–55; execution of, 115, 137, 154–55, 223, 226, 229, 231, 237; France and, 115, 117; Gray on, 139; Lloyd on, 51; Lyttelton on, 93; Macaulay on, 15, 251; as martyr, 223; moralizing works on, 74; Neal on, 137, 139; Oldmixon on, 133; Oldmixon on, 133, 134; Palmer on, 131; Sanderson and, 48–49; trail of, 109; Warner on, 163, 165; Wesley on, 131, 180, 181; Whitelocke on, 134
Charles II: Carte on, 155; commemorations, 96; Green on, 236, 237; Louis XIV and, 21; moralizing works on, 74; Oldmixon on, 133; opposition to, 97; Royalist historians, 34; Rye House Plot against, 15–16; support of, 114; Warner on, 158, 163–64; Wesley on, 182–83
Charles III, 172
Charlett, Arthur, 113–14, 124
Charterhouse, 11
Charter of Manchester translated, The (Whitaker), 44
Chatterton, Thomas, 42–43, 248–49
Chauncy, Sir Henry, 57, 88
Chester, 37, 199

Chesterfield, Philip, 4th Earl of, 37, 245
children, histories for, 9
Chishull, Edmund, 84
chivalric romance, 248–49
Christ, biographies of, 22–23
Christendom, 207
christening, 3–4
Christ Healing the Sick (West), 249
Christian histories, 35, 36, 53–55
Christianity: Astell and, 116, 117–18; Christian persecution, 150; classical tradition and, 198; existentialism and, 204; French historians and, 36; French Revolution and, 223; Gibbon and, 200–1, 214; histories and, 175; Roman paganism and, 142; Rome and, 207; Warner on, 156–57; Wesley and, 175, 176–77
Christianity not Mysterious (Toland), 53
Christian Religion, As Profess'd by a Daughter of the Church of England, The (Astell), 124–25
chronicle writing, 175
Chronological Historian, The (Salmon), 65
Chronology, or the Historians' Vade Mecum, The Historians Guide (Trusler), 66, 67
Chronology: or, a Concise View of the Annals of England (Trusler), 66, 68
Chudleigh, Lady Mary, 113
church collections, 62
Church of England: Astell and, 115, 122–24; Burnet and, 104, 105; Chapman on, 146; deep history and schisms, 141–43; Dissenters and, 130–31 (*see also* Dissenters); Elizabeth I and, 148, 178; as Established Church, 207; Kennett on, 115–16; More and, 161; Oldmixon and, 135; Warner and, 161–63; Weston and, 7; Wycliffe and, 141–42
Cibber, Colley, 195

Cicero, 162, 195, 199
Cirencester Flying Post, 53
civic portraiture, 44
civilization: Gibbon on, 201–3, 204, 212; role of women in, 14–15
Civil War (England). *See* English Civil War
Clandon Park, 196
Clanricarde, Lord, 165
Clarendon and Whitlock Compar'd (Oldmixon), 133
Clarendon, 1st Earl of, 8, 10, 13, 88, 116, 124, 126, 133–34, 162, 183
Clarendon Code, 131
Clarke, Hewson, 231
Clarke, Laurence, 22
classical histories, 22, 54
classical republicanism, 223
classical tradition: Anglicization, 96, 196, 241; architecture and, 196; Burke and, 225; Burnet and, 105; Christian persecution, 150; Church vs. freethinkers and, 94; constitutionalism and, 51; contrasts with, 76; drama, 104; eighteenth-century histories, 171–72; emulation of, 35; national history and, 193–215; newspapers, 151; opposition works, 40; oratorios, 150; praise of, 72; presentation of rulers, 35; republicanism, 34; statuary, 75–76; world history and, 53
classicism, 248
Clavell, Robert, 130–31
clergy: as historians, 44–46; as sources, 58–59
Clifford, Sir Thomas, 74
Clio, 76
Clovis, 36
Cobham, Lord Richard, 196
Codrington, Christopher, 84

Index

Coke, Lady Mary, 11
Colbatch, John, 85
Coleridge, Samuel Taylor, 72
Collection of State Papers relating to Affairs in the Reigns of Henry VIII, Edward VI, Mary, and Elizabeth (Haynes), 57
collections, 25–27, 50–51
Collège des Ecossais, 155
College of Arms, 50, 62
Collier, Jeremy, 104, 141, 162
Collier, John, 41, 44
Colman, George, 249
colonialism: British, 24, 210, 214, 225; Portuguese, 24; Spanish, 24, 172
Colt Hoare, Sir Richard, 238
Columbus, Christopher, 125
Column and Statue of Liberty at Gibside, 196
Column of Victory, 75
commemorations, 96, 223–24
commercialism, 135
Common Law, 109, 113
Compassionate Enquiry into the Causes of the Civil War, A (Kennett), 115–16, 119–20
Compendious History of the House of Austria (Banks), 23, 71
Compendium of Sacred History, A (Trusler), 66
Compleat History of England, A (Brady), 34
Complete Body of Ancient Geography, Both Sacred and Profane, A, 11
Complete History of Algiers, A (Morgan), 54
Complete History of England, A (Hughes), 133
Complete History of England, A (Lloyd), 51
Complete History of Europe, A (Jones), 70–71
conciliar theory, 106–7

Concise History of England, from the Earliest Times, to the Death of George II, A (Wesley), 48, 73, 173–86
Concise History of Spanish America (Campbell), 65
Conduct of the Allies, The (Swift), 116, 183–84
Conference about the Next Succession to the Crown of England (Parsons), 118
Congregationalists, 130
Coningsby, Thomas Lord, 5
Conquest of Syria, Persia, and Egypt by the Saracens (Ockley), 54
conspiracy theories, 120–21, 231
Constantine, 205
Constantinople, 203, 207
constitutionalism, 51–52, 246
Continental Protestantism, 104
Continuation (Lloyd), 51
Continuation of Hume's History of England, A (Clarke), 231
contract theory, 103, 117
controversy, history as, 65, 134, 135
Convention of Klosterseven, 185
Convention Parliament, 84
Convocation of the Church of England, 105
Cooke, William, 253–54
copyright, 175
Copyright Act of 1710, 175
Cornish Antiquities (Borlase), 46
Cornwall, 45
Corporation Act, 139, 143, 136
correspondence, 4
cosmopolitanism, 11, 96, 170
Cottonian Library, 62, 239
Counter-Reformation, 35
county histories, 59
County Spectator, 52
Course of Hannibal over the Alps ascertained, The (Tytler), 41
Court of Honour, 42

Courtenay Earls, 50
courtly woman theme, 14
Cowley, Charlotte, 12–13
Cowper, Lady Sarah, 17
Cowper, William, 2nd Earl, 70, 194–95, 197
Coxe, William, 50, 56, 150, 226–27, 238–40
Cradock, Joseph, 11
Craftsman, 22, 40, 95, 195
Cranmer, Archbishop, 150
Crawford, John, 20th Earl of, 149
Critic, The (Sheridan), 1
Critical Examination, A (Tytler), 41
Critical History of England, The (Oldmixon), 133
Critical History of the Administration of Sir Robert Walpole (Ralph), 71
criticism: of American Revolution, 41; of Burke, 224, 227–28; of derivative accounts, 254–55; of ecclesiastical history, 146; *érudits*, 35; of French Revolution, 41; of Glorious Revolution, 41; of historians by contemporaries, 37, 41, 64, 134, 238–39; of Middle Ages, 36–37; *philosophes*, 35–36; of present, 33–41; of publishers and booksellers, 67; of religion, 36–37; of sources, 61–62, 255; theatrical works and, 99; of Whig historians, 251
Croft, William, 55
Croke, Lady, 15
Croke, Sir George, 15
Cromwell, Oliver, 22–23, 34, 49, 51, 73, 137, 138, 182, 184, 194, 232
Cromwell, Thomas, 51, 107, 232
Crosby, Thomas, 140–41
Crusader Acre, 207
Cuitt, George, 248
Culloden, 198–99
Cumberland, 45

Cumberland, Henry, Duke of, 49
Cumberland, William, Duke of, 71, 91, 149, 197
Cutbush, John, 27

D'Avenant, Charles, 123
Daily Courant, 3, 40
Daily Post, 38
Daily Post Boy, 71
Dalkeith, Charles, Earl of, 213
Dalrymple, Sir John, 16
Danelaw, 11
Danverian History of the affairs of Europe, The (Boyer), 71
Darwinism, 204
David, Jacques-Louis, 223–24
De Witt, Pensionary, 147
Death of Marat (David), 223
Deborah (Handel), 55
Declaration of Indulgence, 87, 137
Declaration of Rights, 225
Declaration of the French Republic, 223
Decline and Fall of the Roman Empire (Gibbon), 199–215
dedications, 155–66
deep history, 123, 141–43
Deering, George Charles, 61–62, 92
Defence of a Letter Concerning the Education of Dissenters in their Private Academies, A (Wesley), 131
Defence of English History Against the Misrepresentations of M. de Rapin-Thoyras (anonymous), 92
Defoe, Daniel, 70, 116, 123–24, 131–32, 134
deism, 104, 229
democracy, 106–7, 230
"Democrats Creed, The," 52–53
Denmark, 38, 95
Departure of Regulus from Rome, The (West), 197
Dering, Daniel, 7
derivative accounts, 254–55

Index

Derwentwater estates, 254
Descartes, René, 35, 114
Destruction of the French Fleet at La Hogue (West), 72
determinism, 69, 203
Devon, 50
dialogues, 155, 159, 166
diaries, 4, 11
dictionaries, 189
Dictionary of National Biography, 65
Dictionary of the English Language (Johnson), 189
didacticism, 214
Difference between an Absolute and Limited Monarchy, The (Macaulay), 58
Digby, Henry, 9–10
Diocletian, 142
Dionysius of Halicarnassus, 196
Discourse of the Contest and Dissensions between the Nobles and the Commons in Athens and Rome, A (Swift), 197
Dissenters: American Revolution and, 227–28; Astell and, 115–16, 120–21, 122–24; Charles II and, 163–64; deep history and schism, 141–43; Donatists and, 142–43; French Revolution and, 225–28; Good Old Cause, 129–32; Goodwin, 50; Gray and, 142–43; Hutton, 235; James II and, 87–88; Neal, 135–41; Oldmixon, 133–35; public office and, 122, 130–31, 136; Warner, 163–64, 166; Wesley, 130–31 (*see also* Wesley, Samuel); Wycliffe and, 141–42
Dissenting Deputies, 136
Dissertation on Juries, A (Nichols), 235
Dissolution of the Monasteries, 107, 247
divine will: Astell on, 121–22, 125; Blackall on, 86; Burnet on, 103–6, 109–11; Collier on, 104; Echard on, 90; history and, 36, 37, 254; Jacobitism and, 96; Nares and, 229–30; Wesley and, 175–76, 254

Dodwell, Henry, 54, 121
Dodwell, William, 54
Domesday Book, 43, 60, 235
Donaldson v. Becket, 175
Donatists, 142
Doncaster, 27
Donkin, Major Robert, 199
Doric architecture, 196
Dorset, 45, 46
Drake, Judith, 13
drama, 104. *See also* theatrical works
Droit le Roy (Brecknock), 171
Druids, 163, 214, 234, 247
Dublin, 158, 164–65
Dublin Society, 158
Dudley, John, 39
Dudley, Robert (Earl of Leicester), 57
Dugdale, Sir William, 4, 59, 134
Duncumb, John, 238, 239, 250
Durand, David, 91
Durham, 46, 233
Düsseldorf, 238
Dutch Republic: interventionism and, 39; Elizabeth I and, 23, 95, 178; Louis XIV and, 21; republicanism and, 182, 213; Wesley on, 182, 183; Whig ideology and, 97
Dutch tradition, 141
dynastic histories, 48, 175
dynasticism, 5–6, 250
Dyrham Park, 196

Earbery, Matthew, 141
East India Company, 215
Eastern Roman Empire, 211
ecclesiastical histories, 89, 103–4, 146, 157, 162–63. *See also* religious histories
Ecclesiastical History of England to the Eighteenth Century (Warner), 157
Ecclesiastical History of Great Britain (Collier), 103–4

Ecclesiastical History to the Eighteenth Century (Warner), 156, 158, 162–63, 165, 166
ecclesiastical patronage, 62–63
Echard, Laurence, 48, 57, 64, 73, 89–90, 133, 199
ecological imperialism, 214
economic progress, 215
Eden, Frederick, 75
Eden Treaty, 208–9
Edict of Nantes, 90
Edinburgh University, 172
editors, 133–34
education: Astell on, 115; Burnet on, 111; change in purpose of, 254; family/informal, 4–11; history and, 4–11, 252; secularization and, 223; sensationalism and, 62
Edward I, 246
Edward II, 49, 74
Edward III, 74, 146, 147, 148, 178, 248, 249
Edward III Crossing the Somme (West), 249
Edward IV, 170
Edward VI, 39, 108, 163, 179
Edward, James (Prince of Wales), 84
Edward the Confessor, 46
Elizabeth I: Astell on, 119, 123; Burnet on, 104, 106–7, 108; Carte on, 57; criticism of, 94; historian focus on, 177–78; Hume on, 173; interventionism and, 23; Lloyd on, 51; Lyttelton on, 92, 93–94, 95; Mary, Queen of Scots, and, 73, 94, 148, 173; Nares on, 229; Neal on, 136–38; Parsons on, 118; Queen Anne and, 16; Rolt on, 148; sources on, 57; Spain and, 18–19; Stephens on, 73; support of, 95, 147; Warner on, 163; Wesley on, 73, 177–78, 179–80, 184; women in history and, 14

Elstob, Elizabeth, 113
Ely, 26
emotionalism, 209
emperors, 204–5
empire, Gibbon on, 199–215
Encyclopaedia Britannica, 236, 255
England: Burnet's conception of, 113; Civil War (*see* English Civil War); dynastic histories, 48; eighteenth century partisan strife, 83–100 (*see also* partisanship); France and, 221; French Revolution and, 224–29; histories of, 24, 26, 49–53, 54, 58, 64–65, 68, 73, 75, 88–92, 133, 152, 153, 164, 165, 166, 172–73, 221, 239; Jesuit Order suppression, 64
English Bible, 107
English Civil War: Astell and, 114, 115–21, 130; Clarendon and, 162; Good Old Cause and, 129–32; Green on, 237; histories of, 88; lineage and, 5; Lyttelton on, 93; memorialization and, 38; Oldmixon and, 134–35; pamphleteering and, 25; Puritans and, 129–30; Warner on, 158; Wesley on, 180–81
English Common Law, 109
English constitution, 51–52, 94, 173, 225
English Historical Library, The (Nicolson), 62
Enlightenment, 15, 33, 62, 174, 176, 200, 231
Enquiries to be propounded (Plot), 42
Enquiry Into the Ancient and Present State of the County Palatine of Durham, An (Spearman), 46
Enquiry into the Foundations of the English Constitution, An (Squire), 52
Enthusiasm of Methodists and Papists Compar'd, The (Lavington), 146
environmental determinism, 203
Epicurus, 161

Index

episcopacy, 137
Epistolary Correspondence of Francis Atterbury (Nichols), 235
Errington, George, 114
Errington, Mary, 114
errors. *See* misinformation and errors
érudits, 35
Essai sur les moeurs et l'esprit des nations (Voltaire), 35
Essay Concerning Human Understanding (Locke), 98
Essay on Charters, in which are particularly considered those of Newcastle, An (Collier), 44
Essay on Criticism, An (Pope), 54
Essay on the English Constitution (Lloyd), 51
Essay towards an Abridgement of the English History (Burke), 23–24
Essay towards the History of the Late Ministry and Parliament Containing Seasonable Reflections on Favourites, An (Boyer), 71
Essay upon Government (Blackall), 86
Essays Upon Peace at Home and War Abroad (D'Avenant), 123
Essex, 45, 59, 66
Established Church, 183, 207
Esther (Handel), 55
Eugene, Prince, 22
Eurocentrism, 214
Europe: balance of power, 23, 97, 204, 205–8, 210–15; Burnet on, 105; divine will and, 105; expansionism, 213–14; France's domination of, 212; Gibbon on, 203–4; histories of, 23–24, 70; Jesuit Order suppression, 64; modernization, 204, 207
evangelism, 13
Evans, John, 136
Evelyn, John, 28
Evening Journal, 97

evidence: archival sources and, 62; Astell and, 124–26; debate on nature of, 43; factual errors and (*see* misinformation and errors); Hume on, 172; legal facts, 57; methodologies and, 55–58; Warner on, 162. *See also* sources
exceptionalism, 220, 221–22
Exclusion Crisis of 1679–81, 16, 25, 96, 118
"Exeter Queries," 87–88
Exeter Weekly Times, 252
Exeter, 3, 46
existentialism, 37, 204, 213–14
expansionism, 227

factionalism, 40
Fair Way with Dissenters and Their Patrons, A (Astell), 123–24
Falkland Islands, crisis of 1770–71, 19, 186
Fall of Mortimer, The, 74
Fall of Robespierre: An Historic Drama, The (Coleridge and Southey), 72
falsifications, 133–34, 249
Family Discourses by a Country Gentleman (Weston), 7
family histories, 47
Fausett, Bryan, 20
feast sermons, 42
feudalism, 88, 172–73, 223
fiction works, 13, 70, 253–54
Fielding, Henry, 17, 23, 69, 70, 71, 99, 194, 215
Fielding, Sarah, 5, 12, 69
Filmer, Sir Robert, 121
First Partition of Poland, 211
First State of Muhametism, The (Addison), 53
Flaxman, John, 251
Flitcroft, Henry, 196
Foedera (Rymer), 249

Fog's Weekly Journal, 38
Force of Truth, The (Croft), 55
foreign policy, 98–99, 146, 148, 184, 206, 209, 214
forgeries, 43, 71, 247
Fortescue, Sir John, 58
Foulis, Henry, 118
Fox, Charles James, 209, 232, 251
Foxe, John, 103, 104, 146, 141
France: Austria and, 211; autocratic political society of, 221; Britain and, 18, 96–98, 100, 123, 148–49, 169, 170, 177–78, 194, 197, 209, 211, 220–24; Burnet on, 106; Charles I and, 115, 117; England and, 221; future histories, 169; George II and, 146; George VI and, 169; Hanover and, 185; historians of, 36; histories of, 92; monasticism, 228; Napoleonic, 212, 223; revolutionary, 37, 212, 223 (*see also* French Revolution); Spain and, 169, 199; Spain and, 199; theatrical works portraying, 72; Tory ideology and, 96–98; war with Britain, 145, 231; Wars of Religion, 23; Wesley on, 184–85; Whig ideology and, 96–98
Franco-Spanish invasion, 1, 72
Frankish invasion, 207
Frederick, Prince of Wales, 147, 181, 248
Frederick II, 24, 145, 147, 151
Free Briton, 95
free will, 69, 72
freedom, 83, 106, 140, 160
French Canada, 184–85
French Ministry of War, 169
French Revolution: British radicalism and, 212–13; Burke and, 18, 224–29; criticism of, 41; Glorious Revolution and, 225–27; Margarot and, 152; Nares on, 229–32; national animosity and, 223; Tory ideology, 99
French Revolutionary War, 197, 212

French Wars of Religion, 23
Frowde, Philip, 195
Fumifugium (Evelyn), 28
funerary monuments, 76

Gallic Wars (Caesar), 199
Garrett, Daniel, 75–76
Gauls, 198–99
General History of England, A (Carte), 153–54
General History of Scotland (Guthrie), 187
General History of the World, from the Creation to the Present Time (Guthrie), 187
Generous Conqueror, The (Higgons), 100
Gentleman's Magazine, 235
Genuine History of the Britons, The (Whitaker), 41
Genuineness of Lord Clarendon's "History of the Rebellion," The (Burton), 134
Geographia Antiqua (Patrick), 11
geographies, 8, 17, 64
George I: Bangorian Controversy, 141; classical tradition and, 194; Echard and, 89–90; end of "royal touch," 36; Hanoverian interests, 147; Jacobites and, 235; narratives and, 47, 48; Wesley on, 181; Whig historians and, 251
George II, 8, 71, 146, 157, 184, 185, 251
George III: American Revolution and, 53; Burke on, 225; criticism of, 147, 149, 205; favored works of, 17, 48–49; Gibbon on, 205; Green and, 236; Hanoverian identity and, 169–70; Harcourt family and, 7; medievalism and, 248; moralizing works on, 74; Nichols and, 59–60, 235; piety and, 126; support of, 231; Tory ideology and, 186; Warner and, 156; Wesley and, 181; West and, 72; Whig ideology and, 251

Index

George IV, 9, 251
George VI, 169
Gepids, 204
Germany, 11, 147, 205, 212
Gibbon, Edward, 11, 15, 54, 63, 169, 172, 199–215, 230, 235, 239
Gibbon's 'History of the Decline and Fall of the Roman Empire' (Whitaker), 41
Gibson, Edmund, 49, 138
gloire, 35
Glorious Revolution: British identity and, 221–22; Burke and, 224–29; Burnet on, 104, 105; cosmopolitanism, 96; Coxe on, 226–27; criticism of, 41, 114–15; divine will and, 87, 90; Echard on, 90; French Revolution and, 225–27; George III on, 49; James II and, 43, 224; Lyttelton on, 93; Macaulay on, 251; modernization and, 204; national history and, 250; Neal on, 137; partisan strife, 83–89; radicalism and, 222; sense of possibilities and, 62; seventeenth-century historians and, 34; Wilkes on, 24; William II and, 99–100
Gloucester Cathedral, 49
Gloucester, William, Duke of, 49, 111
Glover, Richard, 193, 195
Godwin, William, 50
Goldsmith, Oliver, 6, 170, 174, 187, 200, 232
Good Old Cause, 129–32, 134
Goodman's Fields, 95
Gothic tradition, 14, 15, 247–50
Goths, 205
government: authoritarianism and, 99; Burnet on, 103, 117; church and state debates, 49, 94, 104; contract theory of, 103, 117; criticism of (generally), 33–41; divine authority and, 86; patronage, 62–63; representative, 112; urban histories, 50. *See also* Parliament

Gower, Humphrey, 84–85
Grand Tour, 46, 187, 197
Granger, James, 186
Gray, Thomas, 246–47
Gray, Zachary, 138–39
Great Britain. *See* Britain
Great Hall, 250
Great Historical, Geographical, Genealogical, and Poetical Dictionary, The (Collier), 104
Greece, classical, 22, 149, 196, 230. *See also* classical tradition
Greek Project, 211
Green, Valentine, 236–38, 240
Greene, Maurice, 55
Grisons, 112
Grub Street, 64, 69, 170, 235
Guardian, 69
Guide to Classical Learning, A (Tindal), 91
Gustavus, 151
Gustavus Vasa: The Deliverer of his Country (Brooke), 193
Guthrie, William, 21, 56, 64, 96, 152–53, 187, 199

Hadrian, 210
hagiography, 133
Hagley Hall, 196
Hague, The, 90, 147
Hainault, Philippa of, 14
Hale, Matthew, 109
Hampshire, 188
Hampton, James, 72, 179, 200, 245
Hampton Court, 5, 193
Handel, George Frederick, 55, 71, 150, 176
Hanover, 38, 98, 185
Hanover, Electress Sophia of, 47
Hanoverian dynasty, 47–48, 49, 104, 146–47, 184, 251
Hanoverian Succession, 24, 83, 97, 104

Harcourt, Simon, 1st Earl, 7, 8
Hardwicke, Philip, 2nd Earl of, 11–12
Harleian library, 62
Harleian Miscellany, 57
Harley, Edward, 26
Harley, Robert, 26
Harris, James, 36, 200, 231
Harte, Walter, 147, 150
Harvard, 136
Hasted, Edward, 47, 59
Hastings, Lady Elizabeth, 113
Hatsell, John, 225
Hawkesbury, Lord Charles, 152
Hay, Alexander, 37, 62
Hayes, William, 55
Haynes, Samuel, 57
Hearne, Thomas, 249
hegemony, 241
Henley, Sir Robert, 156
Henry Addington, 225
Henry I, 163, 247
Henry II, 48
Henry III, 170
Henry V, 147, 178, 248
Henry VI, 170
Henry VII, 66, 96, 106, 160, 162
Henry VIII: Astell on, 123; Bacon on, 66; Borlase on, 46; Burnet on, 104, 106, 107, 113; historian focus on, 177–78; Lewis on, 171; Lloyd on, 51; medievalism and, 247–48; moralizing works on, 73; Warbeck and, 96; Warner on, 163; Wesley on, 178; *Westminster Journal* on, 23
Henry IX, 49
Henry the Second, or the Fall of Rosamond (Hull), 247
Hensley, William, 58
Heralds' Office, 42
Herbert, Thomas, 174
Hereford, 22, 59, 61
Herefordshire, 5

hermeneutics, 246
Hermit's Tale, A (Lee), 17
Herring, Archbishop, 156
Hertfordshire, 45, 66
Hervey, John Lord, 194
heterodoxy, 229
Heywood, Samuel, 232
Hickes, George, 114, 121, 124
Higgons, Bevil, 100
High Church, 86, 104, 105, 115, 121, 122–24, 223, 137, 140, 141
Highlanders, 198–99
Hinckley, 235
Histoire des Ouvrages des Savans, 52
Historia Anglica (Vergil), 26
Historians Guide (Trusler), 67–68
Historia Regum Angliace (Rous), 62
historians: anonymous (*see* anonymous works); bias and, 50, 162, 165–66; clergy as, 44–46; criticism of by contemporaries, 37, 41, 64, 134, 238–39 (*see also* criticism); French, 36; Noncomformist, 59, 66; partisan, 89–90, 90–92, 92–94 (*see also* partisanship; Tory historians; Whig historians); politicians as, 231–32; pro-Hanoverian, 48; reputations of, 45; Royalist, 34, 134; seventeenth-century, 34; Tory (*see* Tory historians); unfinished works (*see* unfinished works); women as, 12–17, 58, 113–15, 124–26
Historic Doubts on the Life and Reign of King Richard the Third (Walpole), 73
Historical Account of the City of Hereford (Price), 37
"Historical Account of the Rise and Progress of the Arts and Sciences, An" (Smith), 176
Historical and Critical Remarks on Bishop Burnet's History of His Own Time (Higgons), 100

Index

Historical and Moral View of the Origins and the Progress of the French Revolution, An (Wollstonecraft), 227
Historical Antiquities of Hertfordshire, The (Chauncy), 57, 88
historical biographies, 51
Historical Collections (Dalrymple), 16
historical consciousness, 72
Historical Essay on the English Constitution (Hulme and Ramsay), 34
Historical Essay upon the Balance of Civil Power in England, An (Squire), 51–52
historical fiction, 13, 17–18
Historical Narrative of the Great and Terrible Fire of London, An (Webb), 43–44
historical narratives, 56, 193–215
historical relativism, 123
Historical Review of the Moral, Religious, Literary, and Political Character of the English Nation (Andrews), 221
Historical Revolutions (Rushworth), 188
historical romances, 17
Historical Tour of Monmouthshire (Coxe), 238
"historicisation of womanhood," 15
histories: anonymous (*see* anonymous works); archaeology and, 56–57; biblical, 13–14, 54–55; biographies (*see* biographies); Christian, 35, 36, 53–55; classical, 22, 24 (se also classical tradition); derivative accounts, 254–55; dynastic, 48, 175; ecclesiastical, 89, 103–4, 146, 157, 162–63 (*see also* religious histories); eighteenth century, 169–72; experimental forms, 155–56, 159, 166; family, 47; future, 169; local (*see* local histories); maps in, 11; maritime, 203; market for (*see* bookselling market); medieval, 92, 159, 205; methods, 55–58; military, 44; morality and, 10, 11, 17–18, 72–74, 250–51; narratives, 47–49; national (*see* national histories); national identity and, 33–34; newspapers and, 18–23; overview, 1–4; parish, 59; partisanship and, 39, 40–41 (*see also* partisanship); political, 33; politics in (generally), 16, 18, 33–41; pseudonymous works, 26; publishing world and, 23–28; purposes, 33–41; readership, 17–18; religion and, 12–13 (*see also* religious histories); republican, 42–43; republished works, 28, 49, 68–69, 88, 235; sales of (*see* bookselling market); Scientific Revolution and, 56; secret, 71; sources for (*see* sources); stadial, 176, 177; translated works, 24, 49, 51, 90, 91, 104, 195–96, 199; unfinished works (*see* unfinished works); urban, 42–43, 50; women and, 11–12; world, 53–55
historiography, 56, 63, 95, 175–76
history: as argument vs. chronicle, 35–36; Astell and, 113–15, 122–24; as controversy, 65, 134, 135; deep, 123, 141–43; education and, 4–11; female authors and, 12–17; influence on present, 245–50; morality and, 124, 125, 246, 250–51; national identity and, 252–55; national interest and, 40; newspapers and, 18–23; nineteenth century development, 255; overview, 1–4; politics and, 52, 252–55; present-centered, 122–24, 129, 136–37; religion and, 246; science and, 176; as term, 23, 52, 69–71; value of, 215, 253–55; women and, 11–12
History and Antiquities of the City and Suburbs of Worcester, The (Green), 236
History and Antiquities of the City of Bristol, The (Barrett), 42

History and Antiquities of the Counties of Westmorland and Cumberland, The (Burn and Nicolson), 59
History and Antiquities of the County of Dorset (Hutchins), 46
History and Antiquities of the County of Leicester, The (Nichols), 59–60, 235
History and Antiquities of the County of Rutland, The (Wright), 45, 58
History and Antiquities of the County Palatine of Durham, The (Hutchinson), 46, 233
History and Topographical Survey of the County of Kent (Hasted), 47, 59
History of America (Robertson), 172
History of America (Russell), 7
History of Autonos (anonymous), 70
History of Birmingham (Nichols), 235
History of Chichester (Hay), 37, 62
History of Derby, A (Nichols), 235
History of Emily Montague, The (Brooke), 70, 75
History of England (Carte), 246
History of England (Echard), 57, 73
History of England (Macaulay), 251
History of England by way of Question and Answer, The (Morant), 66
History of England during the Reigns of King William, Queen Anne, and King George I, A (Ralph), 153
History of England from the Accession of James I to that of the Brunswick Line (Macaulay), 188
History of England from the earliest period to the Norman Conquest (Turner), 239
History of England from the Invasion of Julius Caesar to 1688 (Guthrie), 21, 153
History of England in a Series of Letters from a Nobleman to his Son, A (Goldsmith), 6
History of England, during the Reigns of the Royal House of Stuart (Oldmixon), 133
History of England, from the Earliest Times to the Death of George II, The (Goldsmith), 174, 232
History of England, from the Invasion of Julius Caesar to the Revolution in 1688, The (Hume), 172, 173
History of England, from the reign of Henry 4th to the death of Charles 1st (Austen), 232
History of English Poetry (Warton), 187
History of Essex (Tindal), 91
History of France from the earliest period to the present time (Johnson), 9
History of Great Britain from the Revolution to the Accession of the House of Hanover, A (Belsham), 228
History of Great Britain to the Conclusion of the Peace of Amiens in 1802 (Belsham), 228
History of Greece (Nares), 230
History of Hertfordshire, The (Salmon), 66
History of Hindostan (Johnson), 214
History of Ireland to the Year 1171 (Warner), 156, 158, 164
History of James Lovegrove, The (Ridley), 69
History of John Bull (Arbuthnot), 89
History of Julia Mandeville, The (Brooke), 70
History of King William the Third (Boyer), 62–63
History of Late Warres in Denmark (Manley), 13
History of Manchester, The (Whitaker), 41, 44, 238
History of Mecklenburg (Goldsmith), 170
History of Modern Europe, in a Series of Letters from a Nobleman to his Son (Russell), 6–7
History of Mr Byron and Miss Greville (anonymous), 70

Index

History of My Own Time, 100
History of New England (Neal), 135–36
History of Ophelia, The (Fielding), 69
History of Our Own Times, The (Banks), 23
History of Rasselas, Prince of Abyssinia, The (Johnson), 69
History of Saguntum, The (Frowde), 195
History of Scotland, During the Reigns of Queen Mary and of King James VI (Robertson), 178
History of Sir William Harrington, The (Hull), 247
History of the British Dominions in North America (Rolt), 149
History of the City of Chester, 248
History of the Countess of Dellwyn, The (Fielding), 69
History of the County of Cumberland, The (Hutchinson), 233
History of the Cruel Sufferings of the Protestants and others by Popish Persecutions in Various Countries, A (Lockman), 152
History of the English Baptists, The (Crosby), 140
History of the Great Rebellion (Clarendon), 126
History of the Holy Bible (Walker), 22
History of the Hundred Courts, A (Nichols), 235
History of the Isle of Man (Rolt), 149
History of the Isle of Wight (Worsley), 46, 59
History of the Late War in North America (Mante), 169
History of the Life and Reign of William III (Banks), 22
History of the Life and Sufferings of the Reverend and Learned John Wickliffe, D.D. (Lewis), 141–42
History of the Life of Gustavus Adolphus (Harte), 150–51

History of the Life of Henry the Second, The (Lyttelton), 92–93, 246
History of the Life of the Late Mr Jonathan Wild the Great, The (Fielding), 70
History of the Life of William Pitt, The (Godwin), 50
"History of the Modern Patriots, The" (Boyer), 71
History of the Principal Events of the Reign of Frederic William II (Louis, Count of Ségur), 24
History of the Puritans (Neal), 136–37, 139–40
History of the Rebellion (Clarendon), 13, 133
History of the Rebellion (Manley), 13
History of the Rebellion and Civil War in Ireland (Warner), 156, 158–59, 164–66
History of the Rebellion and Civil Wars (Clarendon), 88
History of the Reformation (Burnet), 27, 103–4, 106, 109, 135, 141
History of the Reign of Charles V (Robertson), 55, 172
History of the Reign of Philip II (Watson), 51
History of the Reign of Queen Anne digested into Annals, The (Boyer), 71
History of the Revolutions of Denmark (Andrews), 221
History of the Rights of Princes in the Disposing of Ecclesiastical Lands (Burnet), 104
History of the Roman Wall, The (Nichols), 235
History of the Theatres of London and Dublin from 1730 (Victor), 187
History of the War with America, France, Spain, and Holland (Andrews), 221
History of the Wicked Plots and Conspiracies of Our Pretended Saints (Foulis), 118

History of the Works of the Learned, The, 52
History of the World (Oldys), 57
History of the World (Raleigh), 89, 200
History of Tom Jones, The (Fielding), 69
Hoadly, Benjamin, 86, 94, 141
Hoare, Henry, 196
hoaxes, 42, 43
Hodgson, John, 45
Hodgson, Solomon, 233
Holdernesse, Robert, 4th Earl of, 27–28
Holland, Henry, 239–40
Holland, Lord, 232
Holloway, Benjamin, 8
Holman, William, 59, 66
Hooke, Andrew, 42, 43
Horsley, Samuel, 228–29
Houghton, 196
House of Commons, 173, 197, 220, 223, 225
House of Lords, 123, 171, 175, 222–23, 228
Howard, Henrietta, 248
hubris, 17
Hughes, John, 133
Huguenots, 16, 23, 52, 71, 90, 91
Hull, Thomas, 247
Hulme, Obadiah, 34
humanists, 35
Hume, David, 15, 21, 23–24, 42, 63, 94, 169, 172–73, 174, 202
Hundred Years' War, 146–47
Huntingdon, 115
Huntingford, George, 188
Hurd, Richard, 159, 248
Hutchins, John, 45, 46, 47
Hutchinson, William, 46, 193, 233–35
Hutton, Henry, 29n13
Hutton, William, 235
hypocrisy, 99

Iceland, 239–40
Ickworth, 196
Idea of a Patriot King, The (Bolingbroke), 181, 248
ideology, 207–8, 212
Illustrations of British History (Lodge), 50
Imitations of Original Drawings by Hans Holbein (Chamberlaine), 51
Impartial Enquiry into the Causes of Rebellion and Civil War in this Kingdom, An (Astell), 115, 118
Impartial Examination of Bishop Burnet's History of his own Times, An (Salmon), 64–65
Impartial Examination Of The Third Volume Of Mr. Daniel Neal's History of the Puritans, An (Gray), 138
Impartial Representation of the Conduct of the Several Powers of Europe Engaged in the late General War, An (Rolt), 148
imperialism: British, 169–73; Gibbon and, 214–15; Roman, 183, 239; Spanish, 172
Independents, 134
Index to the Records, An (Somerset), 25
India, 214, 225
India Act of 1784, 214
Indian Antiquities (Maurice), 214
individuals: biographies and, 50; focus on in histories, 177–79; genre and, 75; Granger and, 186; Hume and, 173; role in histories, 252–53; Walpole and, 186–87; Wesley and, 177
indoctrination, 36–37
Indo-Persian works, 215
Inns of Court, 25
inscriptions, 58, 60
Institut National des Sciences et des Arts, 224
international relations, 96–100, 201–2, 204, 205–8, 210–25
interventionism, 23, 147, 151, 184, 198

Index

Introduction to Old English History, An (Brady), 34
Introductory Review of the Reigns of the Royal Brothers Charles and James (Ralph), 11
Introductory Sketches towards a Topographical History of Herefordshire (Lodge), 59
Invitation to Gentlemen to acquaint themselves with Ancient History, An (Dodwell), 54
Ipswich Journal, 21
Ireland, 24, 72, 90, 158–59, 164–66, 227, 240
Irish House of Commons, 158
Irish Privy Council, 164
Irish Rebellion, The (Temple), 165
irrationalism, 56
Islam, 175, 201, 202, 207–8, 213
Isle of Man, 149
Isle of Wight, 46, 59
isolationism, 95
Israel in Egypt (Handel), 55
Israel, 176
Italy, 104, 112, 196, 202, 205, 207, 212
Itinerarium Curiosum (Stukeley), 5

Jacobite's Journal, 194
Jacobitism: Astell and, 122; Battle of Culloden, 184; Carte and, 153, 155; classical tradition and, 194; Digby on, 10; dynastic histories and, 48; end of, 177, 181; Fausett and, 20; France and, 145; George I and, 235; Higgons and, 100; ideology of, 96; Jacobite invasion, 145; Jacobite rebellion, 156; Leslie and, 126; Lyttelton and, 171; morality and, 177; Oldmixon and, 133; partisanship and, 83, 84, 88, 96; Rolt and, 147–48; Rowe and, 195; as threat to Britain, 7; Wesley and, 177; Wright and, 45

James I, 47, 51, 83, 93, 95, 137, 181
James II: anti-Catholicism and, 38; Astell on, 117, 119, 120; Burke and, 224; Burnet and, 105; Carte on, 155; constitutionalism and, 51; Declaration of Indulgence, 87; Dissenters and, 137; French envoy and, 232; Glorious Revolution and, 43, 224; Neal on, 137; Oldmixon on, 133; opposition to, 84–85, 87–88, 96, 133; Plot and, 42; Rye House Plot and, 16; *State-Amusements* and, 83–84; Warner on, 164; Wesley and, 183; William III and, 246
James III, 49, 96, 104
Japan, 51
Jefferson, Thomas, 34
Jephtha (Croft), 55
Jesuit Cabal further opened, The (Chapman), 146
Jesuit Order, 64
Jewish naturalization, 28
Joan of Arc, 14
Joan of Arc (Southey), 228
John Gilpin (Cowper), 70
Johnson, Richard, 9
Johnson, Samuel, 18–19, 49, 69, 188–89, 214
Jones, David, 70–71
Jones, Lady Catherine, 113
Jones, Thomas, 247
Joseph and his Brethren (Handel), 55
Joseph Andrews (Fielding), 69
Joseph II, 39
Joshua (Handel), 55
journalism, 231, 94–96
journals, 6, 56
Journey from London to the Isle of Wight (Pennant), 187, 254
Journey from This World to the Next (Fielding), 99, 215
Judas Maccabaeus (Handel), 55, 71

Julian the Apostate, 209, 215
Justinian, 209
Juvenal, 18

Kames, Lord, 14
Kedleston, 196
Keene, Edmund, 85
Keith, Robert Murray, 245
Ken, Thomas, 85
Kennett, White, 115–17, 119–20, 123, 135
Kent, 59
Killerton, 196
King Arthur, 238–39
King David, 123, 132
King Egbert, 163
King Ina, 163
King John, 153
King Lear, 236
King Offa, 163
King's Band of Music, 55
King's Staircase, 193
Kirk, Colonel, 134
Kyd, Thomas, 1

Ladies History of England, The (Cowley), 13
Lady Jane Grey (Rowe), 48
Lambarde, William, 240
Lambeth, 235
Lambeth Palace, 164
Lancashire, 44
Langley, Batty, 247
language, 189
Latitudinarian, 141–42, 160, 166
Laud, Archbishop, 109, 163
Laudians, 141
Lausanne, 212
Lavington, George, 142, 146, 183
law, common, 109, 113
Lediard, Thomas, 88, 91
Lee, Sophia, 17
Lee, Thomas Ashe, 198–99

Leeds Mercury, 222
legal records, 25–26
legal rights, local histories and, 44
legal writing, 175
legitimism, 129–30
Leicester, 59–60, 235–36
Leicestershire, 235
Leighton, Robert, 110
Leominster, 5, 22, 37
Leonidas (Glover), 193
Le Siècle de Louis XIV (Voltaire), 35
Leslie, Charles, 124, 126
Letter from A Country Divine to his friend in London concerning the Education of Dissenters in their Private Academies in Several Parts of the Nation, A (Wesley), 130–31
Letter from a Gentleman in Worcestershire to a Member of Parliament, 38
Letters (Cato), 9
Letters from a Persian in England to his friends at Isaphan (Lyttelton), 93
Letters on Chivalry and Romance (Hurd), 159, 248
Letter to a Friend in the Country on the Publication of Thurloe's State Papers, A (Campbell), 65
Letter to a Member of the National Assembly (Burke), 226
Levellers, 135
Lewis, Edward, 171
Lewis, John, 141–42
Lewis, Matthew "Monk," 248
liberalism, 220
liberty, 136–37, 140, 149–50, 160, 239
libraries, 25–27, 62, 235
Licensing Act of 1737, 3, 99
Lichfield, 53
Life of Edward Seymour, Duke of Somerset, The, 39
lineage, family, 4–11

Lisbon earthquake, 201
Liverpool, Charles, 1st Earl of, 238
Lives (Plutarch), 72
Lives and Memorable Actions of many Illustrious Persons of the Eastern Nations, The (Morgan), 54
Lives of the Admirals and other Eminent British Seamen, The (Campbell), 65
Lives of the English Bishops from the Restoration to the Revolution (Salmon), 66
Lives of the Principal Reformers, Both Englishmen and Foreigners (Rolt), 150
Lloyd, Henry, 51
local histories: antiquarianism, 41–42; classical tradition and, 199; Coxe and, 238; criticism of, 41; eighteenth-century, 42, 233–41; partisanship and, 88; purposes and methods, 41–47; seventeenth-century, 42; sources, 58, 241
Locke, John, 98, 114, 133
Lodge, Edmund, 50–51
Lodge, John, 59
Lollards, 142
Lombards, 204, 207
London: air quality, 28; early historical publications, 11; earthquake (1692), 27; Glorious Revolution and, 224; histories of, 44, 59; newspapers, 38, 39, 52, 146–47, 253; opposition newspapers, 18, 22, 23, 40; press, 3, 21–22; progovernment newspapers, 100; publishing industry, 24
London (Johnson), 18–19
London Chronicle, 23, 147, 220
London Evening Post, 151
London Gazette, 84
London Journal, 22, 100
London's Flames Reviv'd, 88
Long, Thomas, 142
Lorrain, Claude, 196
Louis XI, 221

Louis XIV: autocratic political society and, 221; Bolingbroke and, 23; Burnet on, 105; Cabal support, 183; Charles II and, 21; Christian histories and, 53; opposition to, 145, 227, 228, 229; Philip II and, 16; *philosophes'* criticism of, 35; in theatrical works, 74; universal empire and, 204; Whig ideology and, 96
Low Church, 104, 115, 136, 140, 161
Low Countries, 145, 147, 212
loyalist Gothic, 248
Lucan, 195
Lucius: The First Christian King of Britain (Manley), 13
Luther, Martin, 104
Luttrell, Narcissus, 25
Lützen, 151
Lyme Park, 196
Lyttleton, Charles, 46
Lyttelton, Lord George, 92–94, 171, 246
Lyttelton, Thomas, 92–94

Macaulay, Catharine, 9, 14–16, 58, 139, 188, 227, 251
Macedon, Philip of, 51
Mackenzie, Sir George, 239
Macpherson, James, 170
Maddox, Isaac, 138
Magna Carta, 107, 225, 246, 250–51
Magnus, Donatus, 142
Maidstone, 26–27
Maitland, William, 59
Maldon, 26
Malmesbury, James, 1st Earl of, 231
Manchester, 44
Manley, Delarivier, 34
Manley, Sir Roger, 13
Manning, Lancelot, 85
Mante, Thomas, 169
manuscripts, private collections, 25–27, 50–51

maps, 11, 44, 47
Marden, 5
Margarot, Maurice, 152
Marian persecutions, 145
maritime histories, 203
maritime state, 42–43
Marlborough, John, 1st Duke of, 22, 75, 89, 183–84, 226–27
Marlborough, George, 4th Duke of, 230
Marlborough, Sarah, Duchess of, 8
Marlowe, Christopher, 74
marriage: Astell on, 121–22; between Crown and nobility, 49; Dissenters and, 109
Martin, John, 247
Mary, Queen of Scots: Burnet on, 104, 106; Collier on, 104; Elizabeth I and, 73, 94, 148, 173; Hume on, 173; polarized views of, 129; Wesley on, 73, 174, 178, 179–80; Whitaker on, 44; women in history and, 14
Mary I: anti-Catholicism and, 38, 48; Astell on, 121–22, 123; Burnet on, 104, 106–7; Collier on, 104; Protestantism and, 150; rebellion against, 108; Sancroft and, 121; *State-Amusements* and, 84–85; Warner on, 163; women in history and, 14
Mary II, 103, 112
Mary Queen of Scots Vindicated (Whitaker), 179–80
Matilda (daughter of Henry II), 48
Maurice, Thomas, 214
Maynard, Edward, 45
Medea (Glover), 195
medieval histories, 92, 159, 205
medievalism, 94, 179, 246–48
medieval tradition, 159, 173, 187, 228, 246, 248–50
Mehmed II, 203
Mémoire Justificatif (Gibbon), 199
Mémoires (Retz), 252
memoirs, 5

Memoirs . . . on the Turks and the Tartars (Tott), 24
Memoirs of Crawford (Rolt), 149
Memoirs of Europe towards the close of the Eighth Century (Manley), 13
Memoirs of Sir Roger de Clarendon, The (Reeve), 17, 249
Memoirs of the Kings of Great Britain of the House of Brunswick-Luneburg (Belsham), 227
Memoirs of the Life and Negotiations of Sir William Temple, The (Boyer), 97
Memoirs of the Life and Reign of Frederick the Third (Towers), 24
Memoirs of the Life of Sir Thomas More (Warner), 156, 160
Memoirs of the Reign of George III, 227–28
memorialization, 38
Memorials of Affairs of State in the Reigns of Queen Elizabeth and King James I (Sawyer), 58
Memorials of the English Affairs (Whitelocke), 134
Memorials of the English Affairs from the beginning of the Reign of Charles I to the happy Restoration of King Charles II (Whitelocke), 188
memory, individual and collective, 5
Mercia, 11
Messiah (Handel), 55
metempsychosis, 99, 215
Methodists, 142, 146
methodology, 41–47, 55–58, 226–27
Mexico, 169
Middle Ages, 35, 221, 228, 239, 248–50
Military Collections and Remarks (Donkin), 199
military histories, 44
Military History of the late Prince Eugene of Savoy and the late John, Duke of Marlborough (Campbell), 65

Milles, Jeremiah, 46
Minorca, 145
miracles, 36, 107
Miscellaneous State Papers from 1501–1726 (Philip, 2nd Earl of Hardwicke), 12
Miscellanies (Fielding), 99
Mischianza, 248
misinformation and errors: Burke and, 227; Carte and, 246–47; Clarendon and, 133–34; D'Avenant and, 123; Defoe and, 124–26; Neal and, 138, 140–41; Trusler and, 68–69
Mist's Weekly Journal, 18, 100
Mitchell, Andrew, 27–28
Mitford, William, 230
Modena, Queen Mary of, 84
Moderation a Virtue (Owen), 122
Moderation Truly Stated (Astell), 122–23
modern classicism, 196
Modern History (Salmon), 27
Modern History, or the Present State of all Nations (Salmon), 65
Modern Universal History (Campbell), 65
modernity, 5, 250
modernization, 204
monarchies: absolute, 123; as defender of the Church, 35; Astell on, 118–19, 123; Burnet on, 85, 104; classical tradition and, 194; divine will and, 86, 121–22; female, 16; focus on in histories, 177–79; France and, 223; Gibbon on, 205; glorification in artwork, 249; morality and, 73; parliamentary, 205; Parsons on, 118; Warner on, 157, 163; Wesley and, 176–82, 185–86. *See also* rulers
monasticism, 104, 228
Monasticon (Dugdale), 59
Monck, General George, 182
Mongols, 201, 210
Monitor, 74, 147, 151, 170
Monmouth, James, Duke of, 85–87

Monmouthshire, 238
monogamy, 14
monotheism, 200
Montagu, Edward Wortley, 171
Montagu, Elizabeth, 11–12, 171
Montagu, Lady Mary Wortley, 113
Montagu, Ralph, 4–5
Montesquieu, 213, 210–11
Montgau, Edward Wortley, 34
Moore, Bishop John, 26
Moral and Political Dialogues (Hurd), 159
morality: Andrews and, 221; Astell on, 120, 125; biographies and, 50; civilization and, 14; classical tradition and, 200; genre and, 70; Gibbon and, 209–10, 214–15; histories and, 10, 11, 17–18, 72–74, 250–51; history and, 124, 125, 246, 250–51; novels and, 12; in oratorios, 150; politics and, 73, 178; Wesley and, 174, 177–78, 180
Morant, Philip, 66
More, Hannah, 13
More, Sir Thomas, 156–57, 160–61
More Short Ways with Dissenters (Defoe), 123, 131–32
Morgan, John, 54
Mortimer, Roger, 74
Mosaic injunctions, 108
Mosheim, Johann Lorenz, 142
Most True Relation of That as Honourable as Unfortunate Expedition of Kent, Essex, and Colchester, A (Carter), 237–38
multipolarity, 203–4, 207–8, 211
Murder of the Young Princes in the Tower, The (Reynolds), 249
Murdin, William, 57
Musée des Monuments Française, 224
music, 54–55
Muslims, 207

Nalson, John, 134, 188
naming, 3–4
Naples, 207
Napoleonic Wars, 212, 232, 241
Nares, Edward, 6, 9, 229–30, 238
Narrative of what passed at the Revolution House at Whittington, A (Rooke and Pegge), 224
narratives, 47–49
national culture, 170, 228, 241
national histories: ancient vs. modern debate, 96; classical tradition and, 199; Echard's, 89–90; eighteenth-century, 169–72; French Revolution and, 223; local histories and, 46; maps and, 11; medieval tradition and, 250; partisanship and, 88–89; purposes and methods, 49–53; religion and, 87; travel and, 187–88; world history and, 53
national identity: anti-Catholicism and, 132; histories and, 33–34; history and, 252–55; religion and, 87
national interest, 40, 96–100
nationalism, 1, 36, 186, 241
nationhood: Burnet and, 106–8; Rolt on, 147–50; women and, 13–14
Natural History of Oxfordshire, The (Pennant), 42
Natural History of Religion (Hume), 94
Natural History of Staffordshire, The (Pennant), 42
natural history, 42, 46
Naval and Military History of the Wars of England (Mante), 169
Naval History of England, The (Lediard), 88–89
Naval, Military, and Political Events in Europe (Clarke), 231
navies/naval power: Britain, 145, 169; classical tradition and, 197–98; cosmopolitanism, 96; eighteenth century, 38; Gibbon and, 203, 213, 215; Glorious Revolution and, 89; republican histories and, 42–43; Spanish Armada, 1, 180, 197
Neal, Daniel, 129, 135–42, 143
neoclassicism, 196, 248
neo-Gothic tradition, 9, 248
Nero, 105
Netherlands, 135, 145
New Abridgement and Critical Review of the State Trials and Impeachments for High Treason, A (Salmon), 65
New and Accurate History of South America, A (Rolt), 149
New England, histories of, 135–36
New History of England, A (Lockman), 152
New History of France, A (Rolt), 149
New Survey of England wherein the Defects of Camden are Supplied, A (Salmon), 65
New Theatre, 95
New World history, 172
New, Impartial and Complete History of England, The (Barnard), 221
Newcastle, 114
Newcastle, Thomas, Duke of, 52, 98, 151, 177
Newcastle Chronicle, 233
Newcastle Courant, 21
Newcastle Journal, 19
Newgate prison, 38, 131
newspapers: advertising, 21–22; culture of print and, 3; historical works and, 18–23; history and, 94–96; opposition, 40–41, 98; politics and, 23; progovernment, 40–41, 42, 95, 100, 198; provincial presses, 3; religious works, 22
Newtonian science, 36
Nichols, John, 59, 60, 235–36

Index

Nicolson, Joseph, 45
Nicolson, William, 62
"noble savage," 202
Nonconformist historians, 59, 66
Nonjurors, 54, 104, 115, 121–22, 126, 141, 142, 150, 153
Norfolk, Charles, 11th Duke of, 250
Norman Conquest, 25, 87, 88, 93, 207, 228, 239, 240
North America: British colonization of, 24 (*see also* American colonies); France and Spain war in, 199; French and British war in, 145; histories of, 172, 221; Portuguese colonization of, 24; Puritans and, 139; republicanism, 213; Spanish colonization of, 24, 148; Wesley on, 184–85
Northampton Mercury, 19–20
Northamptonshire, 45
Northanger Abbey (Austen), 4, 12
Northcote, James, 249
Northumberland, 45
Northumberland, Duke of, 156
Northumberland, Wilfred of, 163
Norway, 38, 239
Norwich, 3
Nottingham Vetus et Nova (Deering), 61
Nottingham, 3, 62, 224
novels, 12, 17–18, 71, 72, 75, 246
Nowell, Laurence, 240

Oath of Supremacy, 108, 160
Observations on the Reflections of the Right Hon. Edmund Burke on the Revolution in France (Macaulay), 227
"Observations on the Reign and Character of Queen Elizabeth" (Lyttelton), 93
Occasional Conformity, 122–24, 125
Ockley, Simon, 54
Okie, Laird, 56
Old Corps Whigs, 52, 97

Old England, 23, 98–99, 146
Old English Baron, The (Reeve), 17
Old Etonians, 50
Oldmixon, John, 64, 129, 132–35
Old Testament, 132, 176
Oldys, William, 57
opposition newspapers, 40–41, 98
opposition Whigs, 23, 71, 93, 147–48, 194
oral traditions, 4
Orange, William of. *See* William III
oratorios, 55, 71, 150, 176
Order of the Garter, 249
Orientalism, 16
Originals physical and theological, sacred and profane (Holloway), 8
Ormonde, James, Duke of, 89
Ormonde, Earl of, 134
Ossian cult, 202
Osterley Park, 196
Ostrogoths, 205
Otto IV, 48
Owen, James, 122
Owen's Weekly Chronicle, 151
Oxford, 6, 49, 64, 72, 75, 84–85, 150, 229
Oxford editors, 133–34
Oxfordshire, 171
Oxford University Library, 62, 166

paganism, 15, 142
paintings, 9, 71–72, 196, 197, 223–24, 247, 248, 249
Palaeographia Britannica (Stukeley), 20
Palatinate, 95
pamphlets, 25, 94
Pantheon at Stourhead, 196
Parcel Post, 67
Paris, 11, 212, 213
parish histories, 59
parish libraries, 26–27
Parker, Samuel, 130–32, 142

Parliament: Act of Settlement, 48; Astell on, 114, 118–20, 121, 122; Blackall on, 86; Burnet and, 103; classical tradition and, 193; Elizabeth I and, 93; factionalism, 40; Lyttelton on, 93; Neal and, 136; Oldmixon on, 135; opposition to, 51; political speeches, 100, 105; Rapin-Thoyras on, 90; rise of, 56; Warner on, 160; Wesley and, 130–31
Parlement of Paris, 18
Parliamentarians, 49, 109, 114, 118, 118, 125, 183
parliamentary monarchy, 205
parliamentary records, 25, 62, 153
parody, 1, 232
Parsons, Robert, 110, 118
partisan historians: Echard, 89–90; Lyttelton, 92–94; Rapin-Thoyras, 90–92. *See also* Tory historians; Whig historians
partisanship: bias and, 50; contentious issues, 96–100; education and, 10; eighteenth-century, 170; histories and, 39, 40–41; journalism, 94–96; local histories, 88; national histories and, 88–89; religion and, 86–87; Revolution Settlement, 83–89; scholarship and, 64
partworks, 65
party identity, 40–41
Patriarcha (Filmer), 121
Patrick, Samuel, 11
Patriot Gothic, 92
Patriot King, 91, 171, 183, 248
Patriot King, The (Lewis), 171
Patriot opposition, 92
patriotism, 186, 229, 240, 246
patronage, 62–63, 155–66
Peace of Aix-la-Chapelle, 75
Peace of Amiens, 232
Peace of Utrecht, 97–98

Peasants Revolt, 222, 226
Pegge, Samuel, 224
Pelham, Henry, 98
Pelhamite system, 145
Pennant, Thomas, 42, 187–88, 199, 254
Perceval, John, Viscount, 7, 252
Percy, Thomas, 170
periodization, 246
Perolla and Izadora (Cibber), 195
Persia, 149, 209, 215
Peter the Great, 22
Peter, Heylyn, 141
Petition of Right, 225
Pharsalia (Lucan), 195
Philadelphia, 248
Philip II, 16, 23, 204
Philip III, 51
Philip V, 149
Phillipps, Sir Thomas, 58
philosophes, 34, 35–36, 210
Philosophical Arrangements (Harris), 36
philosophy, 172, 196
piety, 14, 16, 108–9, 112, 126, 160
Pilgrimage of Grace, 107
Pitt, William the Elder, 71, 93, 147, 173, 197
Pitt, William the Younger, 209, 220
plagiarism, 59
Plain Dealer, 94–95
Plan of the Dictionary (Johnson), 189
Plato, 114
plays. *See* theatrical works
Plot, Robert, 42
Plume, Thomas, 26
Plumptre, Anne, 172
Plutarch, 9, 72
Pocket Companion for Members of Parliament, A, 85
poetry, 71, 84–85, 195, 246–47, 249, 253
Poland, 211
polemics, 33, 34, 104, 126, 171
political histories, 33
Political History of the Devil (Defoe), 70

Index

political ideology, 119
political rhetoric, 97
political satire, 89
political tracts, 25
politicians, as historians, 231–32
politics: Burnet on, 103–6; constitutionalism and, 52; eighteenth century, 170; in histories (generally), 16, 18, 33–41; history and, 52, 252–55; international relations, 96–100, 201–2, 204, 205–8, 210–15; morality and, 73, 178; newspapers and, 18–19, 20–21, 23; Tory (*see* Tory ideology/politics); Whig (*see* Whig ideology/politics)
poll taxes, 27
Polybius, 72
polygamy, 14
Pomfret, Louisa, Countess of, 11
Poor Law, 122
Pope, Alexander, 54, 187
Pope Pius II, 207
Popery, 118, 119, 156–57, 183, 223
Popery the true Bane of Letters (Chapman), 146
Popish Plot of 1678, 16, 25, 104, 183
populism, 174
Port Royal earthquake (1692), 27
portraiture, 6, 44
posterity, 252–55
posthumous works: of Bridges, 45–46; of Fox, 232; of Rolt, 149; of Watson, 51; of Whitelocke, 134
Poussin, 196
power, balance of, 23, 97, 204, 205–8, 210–15
Pratt, Samuel, 231–32
Predictions for the Year 1708 (Swift), 28
pre-Romantic period, 5
Presbyterians, 34, 118, 130
"Present History of Europe" (Banks), 23
Present State of the Jews, The (Addison), 53

press: newspapers, 18–23 (*see also* newspapers); provincial, 3, 21–22. See *also* publishing industry
Pretyman, George, 223
Price, John, 22, 37, 47, 58–59, 61
Price, Richard, 225, 226
Priestley, Joseph, 212, 225
Primitive Christians, 146
Primitive Physick (Wesley), 174
"primitive" cultures, 201–3
print, culture of, 2–3
private collections, 50–51, 59
Private Life of Mary Queen of Scots, The (Whitaker), 44, 180
probability theory, 172
profiteering, 116
progovernment newspapers, 42, 95, 100, 198
Progress of Romance through Times, Centuries and Manners, The (Reeve), 9
progress: French Revolution and, 224; Gibbon on, 203, 215; religion and, 36–37
pro-Hanoverian historians, 48
property, ownership of, 135
proselytism, 227
prosopography, 100
Protestant Dissenters, 87–88, 105, 122–24. See *also* Dissenters
Protestant Reformation, 156
Protestantism: anti-Catholicism, 36–37; Astell on, 115; Burnet on, 108; Catholicism and, 105, 112, 142, 150, 165–66; Collier on, 104; Elizabeth I and, 148, 178; forms of, 140; Harte and, 150–51; James II and, 137; Lockman and, 152; More and, 161; Nares and, 229; Protestant virtue, 14, 48, 179; Rolt and, 147–50; Russell and, 16; Wesley and, 183
Protestor, 252–53
proto-Romanticism, 178, 246
Providence. *See* divine will

providentialism, 174, 229
provincial presses, 3, 21–22
Prussia, 145, 211
pseudonymous works, 26
pseudopatriotism, 40
public records, 25–26, 59
publication, posthumous. *See* posthumous works
publishing industry: criticism of, 67; financing, 47, 62–63; history and, 23–28; London and, 24; partworks, 65; republished works, 28, 49, 68–69, 88, 235; sales (*see* bookselling market); speculative, 155; subscriptions, 46, 47, 155, 166, 57
Pulteney, William, 94
Punic Wars, 151, 197
Purcell, Henry, 55
Puritans: Dissenters and, 129–30; as Donatists, 142; Neal and, 135–41; Oldmixon and, 134–35
Pym, John, 117

Quakers, 136
Queen Anne: Abjuration Oath, 45; Astell on, 120; Northumberland and, 39; opposition to, 86, 96; religious iconography, 125; sources on, 63; *State-Amusements* and, 85; theatrical works and, 74; Wesley on, 186; Whig ideology and, 226; Wilkes on, 24; women in history and, 16
Queen Charlotte, 170
Queen Henrietta Maria, 119
Queen Isabella (wife of Edward II), 74, 125
Quincy, Josiah, 34
Quintilian, 199

Rackett, Thomas, 47
Radcliffe, Ann, 248
radical republicanism, 129–32
radicalism, 212–13, 225–26
Raleigh, Sir Walter, 57, 89, 200
Ralph, James, 11, 24, 56, 64, 71, 96, 135, 153
Ramsay, Allan, 34
Rapin-Thoyras, Paul de, 9, 10, 27, 52, 88, 90–92, 135, 174
Rational Defence of the English Reformation and Protestant Religion, A (Warner), 156
rationalism, 56
Read, Katherine, 14
Read's Weekly Journal, 100, 253
Reading Mercury, 21
reading, 17–18, 114
realism, 36
reason, 37, 214, 229
Recess, The (Lee), 17
Reduction of Ireland to the Crown of England (Borlase), 165
Reeve, Clara, 9, 17, 249
reference works, 68
Reflections on Ancient and Modern History (Hampton), 72, 179, 245
Reflections on the Revolution in France (Burke), 224–29
Reflections on the Rise and Fall of the Ancient Republics (Montgau), 34, 171
Reformation: Astell on, 120; Burke on, 226; Burnet on, 103–4, 105–6, 107–8; debates on, 94, 96; Green on, 237; Hume on, 173; monarchy and, 35; national history and, 250; Warner on, 156–57, 163; Wesley on, 177
Regicide: Or, James the First of Scotland, The (Smollett), 51
Reign of George VI, The (anonymous), 28, 169
Reign of Terror, 229
religion: Astell on, 122–24; Burnet on, 103–6, 108–13; church and state issues, 49, 104; criticism of,

36–37; deep history and schisms, 141–43; divine will and. *See* divine will; female historians and, 13–14; freethinkers vs., 94; histories and, 12–13, 33 (*see also* religious histories); history and, 246; Hutchinson on, 234; iconography, 125; local histories and, 46; national, 35; newspapers and, 22; partisanship and, 86–87; progress and, 36–37; world histories and, 53–55

religious histories: Burnet's, 103–4; local historians, 46; music and, 55; Nares and, 229–32; Neal's, 135–41; sources, 62

religious liberty, 136–37, 149–50, 158, 163, 165–66, 180

Reliques of Ancient English Poetry (Percy), 170

Remarks on Mr Carte's Specimen of his General History of England (Squire), 247

Remembrancer, 52

Renaissance, 56

Reply to Mr Palmer's Vindication of the Learning, Loyalty, Morals . . ., A (Wesley), 131

representative government, 112

reprintings, 237–38

Republic of Letters, 64

republican histories, 42–43

republicanism, 23, 34, 183, 213, 223

republished works, 49, 68–69, 88, 235

Repulse of the Spaniards before the Rock of Gibraltar, The, 72

research. *See* methodologies; scholarship; sources

Restoration, 90, 224

Retz, Cardinal de, 252

Review of Dr Zachary Grey's Defence of our Ancient and Modern Historians, A (Oldmixon), 133

Review of Mr. Daniel Neal's History of the Puritans, A (Gray), 138

Review of the History of England, A (Salmon), 64

Revocation of the Edict of Nantes, 90

Revolution House, 224

Revolution Settlement, 83–89, 106, 125, 149, 226

Revolution Society, 222

Reynolds, Joshua, 249

Richard II, 38, 170

Richard III, 73, 94, 129, 178–79

Richard Plantagenet, a Legendary Tale (Hull), 247

Richelieu, Cardinal, 220, 220–21

Richmond, Charles, 3rd Duke of, 214

Ridley, James, 69

Rienzi, Cola di, 40

Rights of the Kingdom (Sadler), 34

Rinnuccini, Giovanni, 165

Ripperda, Jan Willem van, 11

Robertson, William, 21, 55, 63, 169, 172–73, 174, 178, 201, 204, 206

Rochester, John, Earl of, 103, 109–10

Roderick Random (Smollett), 71

Rollins, Charles, 27

Rolls of Parliament, 249

Rolt, Richard, 64, 87, 147–50, 209, 223, 253

Roman Catholicism, 104. *See also* Catholicism

Roman Conquest, 173

Roman Empire, collapse of, 194, 200–1, 210. *See also* Rome

Roman History from the Building of the City to the Perfect Settlement of the Empire by Augustus Caesar, The (Echard), 89, 199

Roman History, from the Foundation of the City of Rome to the Destruction of the Western Empire (Goldsmith), 200

Roman matron theme, 14–16

Romanticism, 16, 178, 195, 239, 241, 250
Rome: architecture, 196; artifacts of, 19–20; artifacts/remains, 60, 65, 187, 199; Carthage and, 151, 197, 200; Christendom, 207; Christian persecution, 150; classical histories, 22, 24; criticism of, 156, 234–35; defiance of, 40, 239; Gibbon on, 193–215; histories of, 44; histories of, 8, 22, 72; Hutchinson on, 233–34; imperialism, 183, 239; as model, 15; paganism, 142; parallels with Britain, 55, 193–215; religious persecution, 163; republicanism, 183
Rooke, Hayman, 224
Rotherham, 27
Rous, John, 62
Rowe, Nicholas, 48, 74, 195–96
Rowe, Thomas, 135
Rowley, Thomas, 249
Royal Academy, 170
Royal Magazine, 176
Royal Navy, 145, 230
Royal Society, 8, 42, 166
Royal Supremacy, 160–61
"royal touch," 36
Royalist historians, 34, 134
Royalists, 109, 116, 135, 188, 237
rulers: divine will and, 109–10; dynastic histories, 48; Gibbons and, 209–10; historians' focus on, 177–79, 209–10; morality and, 73; religious obligation of, 108–13
Rushworth, John, 188
Russell, Lord John, 251
Russell, Lord William, 6–7, 15, 16, 24, 133
Russell, Rachel, 15–16
Russell papers, 16
Russia, 38, 169, 210, 246
Rye House Plot, 15, 16
Rymer, Thomas, 249

Sacheverell, Henry, 85, 124, 226
Sackville, Lord George, 185
Sacred History of the World as displayed in the Creation and subsequent events to the Deluge (Turner), 239
Sadler, John, 34
Salerno, 207
Salmon, Nathanael, 45, 65–66
Salmon, Thomas, 27, 64–65
Samson (Handel), 55
Sancroft, Archbishop William, 121
Sanderson, Robert, 48–49
satire, 1, 4, 70, 88, 89, 99, 131, 173
Satirist, 231
Saul (Handel), 55
Sawyer, Edmund, 58
Saxon histories, 62
Saxon tradition, 90, 149, 163, 238–39, 240
Scarborough, 83
scholarship: antiquarianism and, 37; archival sources and, 58–76; archival sources and, 63; methodologies, 55–58; partisanship and, 64
science, 176, 203, 229
scientific history, 55–56
Scientific Revolution, 33, 56
Scilly Isles, 46
Scipio Africanus (Beckingham), 195
Scotland, 59, 83, 106, 198–99, 227, 240
Scott, Sir Walter, 5
Second Punic War, 195
Secret History of Queen Zarah and the Zarazians, The (Manley), 13
Secret History of White Hall from the Restoration of Charles II down to the Abdication of the late King James (Jones), 71
Secret Memoirs and Manners of Several Persons of Quality, of both Sexes. From the New Atlantis (Manley), 13
Secret Treaty of Dover, 97, 31n57

Index

sectarianism, 23, 34
secularism, 33, 72
Sedgemoor, 134
Sejanus, 73, 198
Sellwood, Thomas, 16
sensationalism, 62, 135
sentimentalism, 74–75
September Massacres, 213
serialization, 22
Serious Proposal to the Ladies for the Advancement of their True and Greatest Interest, A (Astell), 115
sermons, 17, 54, 73, 85–86, 115–16, 156, 225–26
Serres, Dominic, 71–72
Seven Years' War, 98, 145, 148, 150, 169, 170
Seville, 98
Seymour, Edward, 39
Shaftesbury, Anthony, 3rd Earl of, 69, 133, 159
Shakespeare, 73, 178–79, 228
Shakespeare Jubilee, 170
Shakespeare Ladies' Club, 12
Sharp, Archbishop, 86
Shebbeare, John, 198
Sheffield, John, 1st Earl of, 208, 220
Sheridan, Richard Brinsley, 1, 172, 214
Sherlock, Bishop, 138, 139
Short Account of Domesday Book, A (Webb), 43
Short Critical Review of the Political Life of Oliver Cromwell, A (Banks), 23
Short History of the Donatists. With an Appendix, A (Gray), 142–43
Short History of the Parliament, A (Boyer), 71
Short View of the English History, A (Higgons), 100
Short View of the Families of the present English Nobility, A (Salmon), 65
Shortest Way With Dissenters, The (Defoe), 123–24, 131

Sicily, 207
Siege at Fort Royal, Martinique, The (Serres), 71–72
Sinclair, Sir John, 233–34
sinfulness, 121, 125, 126
Sinners saved by Jesus Christ as preached in Scripture (Lewis), 171
Sir William Walworth ... Killing Wat Tyler (Reynolds), 249
Sister Peg (anonymous), 173
Six Etchings of Saxon and Gothic Buildings now Remaining in the City of Chester (Cuitt), 248
skepticism, 188
Sketches of the History of Man (Kames), 14
slavery, 152, 202, 222
Smalridge, George, 133
Smart, Christopher, 70
Smith, Adam, 176, 178
Smith, Thomas, 174
Smithson, Sir Hugh, 76
Smollett, Tobias, 5, 51, 71, 97–98, 169, 174
Society of Antiquaries, 43, 45, 60, 235
Society of Arts (FSA), 11
Solemn League and Covenant, 49
Solomon (Handel), 55
Somerset, 25, 133, 134
Somerset, Duke of, 163
Song of Deborah and Barak, The (Croft), 55
sources: archival, 25–27, 58–76, 255; Burke on, 226; Carte on, 153–54; clergy as, 58–59; conforming views and, 188; criticism of, 61–62, 255; Hume on, 172; Hutchinson on, 233; local histories, 241; methodologies, 55–58; Warner on, 164
South America: British colonization of, 24; histories of, 149, 172; Portuguese colonization of, 24; Spanish colonization of, 24
South, Robert, 121
Southey, Robert, 72, 228

Spain, Isabella of, 14
Spain: Britain and, 18–19, 148–49, 169, 186, 197; colonialism, 172; Dutch rebellion against Philip II, 23; Falkland Islands crisis of 1770–71, 19, 186; France and, 169, 199; imperialism, 172; North America and, 19, 172, 199; Roman conquest, 202; war with Britain (1738), 18–19
Spanish Armada, 1, 180, 197
Spanish Tragedy, The (Kyd), 1
Spearman, John, 46
Spencer, John, 1st Earl, 8
Spencer, Lady Charlotte, 230
Squire, Samuel, 52, 247
St. Augustine, 163
St. Botolph's Church, 115
St. Dunstan's Church, 86
St James's Chronicle, 198
St. Mary's Colchester, 66
St. Paul, 123
St. Paul, Horace, 17
St. Paul's Cathedral, 55
St. Paul's Churchyard, 26
St. Stephen's Walbrook, 14
stadial histories, 176, 177
Stafford, Thomas, Earl of, 109
Staffordshire, 66
Stanhope, George, 85
Stanwick Hall, 76
State of the Poor, The (Eden), 75
State Songs, 96
State-Amusements, Serious and Hypocritical, fully exemplified in the abdication of King James the Second, 83–85
statuary, 75–76, 196
Steele, Richard, 134
Stephens, William, 73
Sterne, Laurence, 4
Stow, John, 26
Strachey, John, 25–26

Strawberry Hill, 248
Stuart dynasty, 23, 49, 121, 126, 133, 183, 224, 248, 251
Stuart, James "Athenian," 196
Studley Royal House, 196
Stukeley, William, 5, 20
Subject's Duty, The (Blackall), 86
subscriptions, 46, 47, 155, 166, 57
Suetonius, 68
Summary (Tindal), 91
Surrender of Calais, The (Colman), 249
Surrey, 45, 66
Survey of London (Stowe), 26
Susanna (Handel), 55
Sweden, 151, 193
Swift, Jonathan, 17, 28, 97, 116, 183–84, 187, 197
Switzerland, 112, 212
Syon House, 196
Syria, 207
System of Divinity and Morality (Warner), 155–56

Tablet of Memory, The (Trusler), 66, 68
Tacitus, 177, 195
Talbot, Catherine, 14
Talmud, 175
Tamerlaine, 209
Tamerlane (Rowe), 74
Tangier, 53
Tanner, Thomas, 26
Tartars, 201
Tatler, 195
"Taunton Letters," 87
Tauntons, 87
Temple, Sir John, 165
Temple, Sir William, 147
Temple of Ancient Virtue, 196
Temple of Bacchus at Painshill, 196
Temple of Theseus, 196
territorial expansion, 210

Test (newspaper), 146
Test Act, 122, 136, 138, 139, 143
thalassocracy, 42–43
Thanksgiving Sermon (Stephens), 73
theatrical works, 51, 71–75, 99, 172, 193, 195, 247
Theodora (Handel), 55, 150
Theodoric, 204–6
theological works, 48, 54, 155–56
Thirty Years' War, 95
Thomas Earl of Surrey defending himself before Henry VII after Bosworth (Brown), 250
Thomas, Elizabeth, 113
Thomason, George, 25
Thomason tracts, 25
Thomson, William, 51
Thoughts on Education (Burnet), 111
"Thoughts on Levelling with an Account of the Insurrection of Wat Tyler" (anonymous), 222
Thoughts on the Late Transactions respecting Falkland's Islands (Johnson), 188–89
Thraseas, 105
Thucydides, 196
Thurlow, Lord Edward, 39
Tiberius, 73
Times, 254
Tindal, Nicholas, 90–92
Toland, John, 53
Toleration Ac, 87t, 104, 137
Tom Jones (Fielding), 71
Topographical Account of the Hundred of Bosmere, The (Bingley), 44
Torbay, 90
Tory historians: Astell (*see* Astell, Mary); Atkyns, 45; Atterbury, 62; Carte, 153; Clarendon, 126; criticism of, 86; Echard, 89–90; Hume, 15; Manley, 13; midcentury, 155; pessimism and, 189; Plot, 42; seventeenth-century, 34; "Taunton Letters," 87; Walpole and, 50; Wright, 45
Tory ideology/politics: church and state independence, 104; commercialism and d, 135; contentious issues, 96–100; English Civil War and, 122–24; Hume and, 173; Neal on, 137; War of the Spanish Succession and, 39; Wesley and, 183–84, 186
Tott, Baron François de, 24
Toulmin, Joshua, 135, 140
Tour in Scotland (Pennant), 187, 199
Tour in Wales (Pennant), 187
Tower of London, 25
Towers, Joseph, 24
Trajan, 205, 210
transcription, of reading material, 17
translated works, 24, 49, 51, 90, 91, 104, 195–96, 199
travel, 46, 47, 112, 134, 187–88
travel literature, 187, 189
Travels in Iceland (Mackenzie), 239–40
Treaty of Nonsuch, 95
Trevor, John, 212
Trinitarian Dissenters, 140
Trinitarian Protestants, 136
Tristram Shandy (Sterne), 4
Troy, 235–36
True Briton, 39–40, 177
Trusler, John, 66–69, 81n103
Tudor Age, 178
Tudor histories, 248
Turkish Empire, 207, 211
Turner, Francis, 85
Turner, Sharon, 239
Turner, Thomas, 17
tutors, 7–8
Twelve Maps of Ancient Geography Drawn by the Sieur d'Anville, 11
Twickenham, 248

Two Extracts from the sixth Book of the general history of Polybius (Hampton), 200
Two Sermons on the Doctrine of Divine Visitation by Earthquakes, 54
Tytler, Alexander Fraser (Lord Woodhouselee), 41

unfinished works: Bolingbroke, 23; Holman, 59; Hume, 23–24; local histories, 44, 45, 66; Raleigh, 200; Warner, 158; Whitaker, 180
Union of 1707, 173
Unitarianism, 37, 140, 212, 232
United Provinces, 42, 232
United States, 106. *See also* American colonies; North America
universal frameworks, 36, 205–6
Universal History, 27
Universal Magazine, 76
Universal Visiter and Memoralist, The, 148
University of Leiden, 135
Upper Boddington, 45
urban histories, 42–43, 50
utilitarianism, 35
Utopia (More), 161

Venice, 27, 42, 145, 209, 213
Venutius, 233–34
Vergil, Polydor, 26
Verrio, Antonio, 193
Victor, Benjamin, 187
Vienna, 38, 98
Vikings, 38, 239
Vindication of Mr Fox's History of the Early Part of the Reign of James II (Heywoord), 232
Vindication of the Government, Doctrine and Worship of the Church of England during the Reign of Queen Elizabeth, A (Maddox), 138

Vindication of the Learning, Loyalty, Morality and Most Christian Behaviour of the Dissenters towards the Church of England, A (Palmer), 131
Virgil, 114
virtue, 179, 214
Vollocatus, 234
Voltaire, 35–36
Vota Non Bella (Astell), 114
Vyne, 196, 248

Wake, William, 132
Wales, 240
Wales, Frederick, Prince of, 8, 91, 92
Walker, Robert, 22
Wallington, 196
Walpole, Horace, 5, 73–74, 186–87, 248
Walpole, Sir Robert, 18–19, 38, 40, 50, 195, 196, 226
Wanley, Humphrey, 26
Warbeck, Perkin, 96
war commentaries, 231–32
Ward, Edward, 134
Wareham, 46
Warminster, 188
Warner, Ferdinando, 24, 155–66
War of American Independence, 72, 199, 208–9, 221
War of the Austrian Succession, 1740–48, 23, 71, 145
War of the Bavarian Succession, 211
War of the Spanish Succession, 39, 97, 116, 149, 183
Wars of the Roses, 49
Warton, Thomas, 187
Waterland, Daniel, 114
Watson, Robert, 51, 52
Way to the Temple of True Honour and Fame by The Paths of Heroic Virtue, The (Cooke), 253–54
Wealth of Nations, The (Smith), 176, 178
Webb, Philip Carteret, 43

Weekly Journal: or, The British Gazetteer, The, 95–96
Weekly Register, 99–100
Welbeck Abbey, 248
Weldon, John, 55
Weller, Miss, 27
Welsh bards, 246–47
Wesley, Charles, 84
Wesley, John: *Concise History of England, from the Earliest Times, to the Death of George II, A*, 173–86; defense of Mary, Queen of Scots, 73, 174, 178, 179–80; didactic purpose of, 87; as Dissenter, 130–31; on divine will, 175–76, 254; on Elizabeth I, 73, 148; focus on rulers, 73; on Hanoverian succession, 48; influence of, 129; Palmer and, 130–32; Shakespeare and, 73; use of previous works, 174–75; Wycliffe and, 142
Wesley, Samuel, 84
West, Benjamin, 72, 197, 248, 249
West, Jane, 69–70
West Barbary (Addison), 53
West Country, 87, 133
Westmacott, Richard, 251
Westminster, 251
Westminster Abbey, 76, 228
Westminster Assembly of Divines, 137
Westminster Hall, 25
Westminster Journal, 23
Weston, Edward, 7
Weymouth, Thomas, 3rd Viscount, 199
Whalley, Peter, 45–46
Whig historians: anonymous works, 83–85; Astell on, 117; Banks, 23; Boyer, 97; Burnet, 135; criticism of, 86, 251; eighteenth century, 187; Gibson, 49; Hooke, 42; Kennett, 115, 117, 135; Macaulay and, 15; moderate, 135; morality and, 251; Neal and, 136; Nicolson, 62; Oldmixon, 133–35;

Puritans and, 139; Rapin-Thoyras, 88, 90–92, 135; Rowe, 48; seventeenth-century, 34; Walpole and, 50
Whig ideology/politics: church and state linkage, 94; contentious issues, 96–100; Dissenters and, 132; Eden Treaty, 209; English Civil War and, 122–24; expansionism, 210; Gibbon and, 205; Hume and, 173; James II and, 133; Manley and, 13; opposition Whigs, 23, 71, 93, 147–48, 194; radical, 251, 225–26; Warner and, 159
Whitaker, John, 41, 44, 179–80, 238
Whitbread, Samuel, 210
Whitefield, George, 142
Whitehall Journal, 198
Whitelocke, Bulstrode, 134, 188
Whittington, 224
Wickliff, Lollard John, 37
Wilkes, John, 24, 51
William Borlase, 46
William I, 228
William III: Astell on, 120, 121–22; Burke on, 226–27; Burnet and, 111, 112; Coxe on, 226; Elizabeth and, 178; James II and, 246; monarchial destiny and, 194; Neal on, 137; opposition to, 87, 96, 99–100; Sancroft and, 121; sources on, 62–63; *State-Amusements* and, 84–85; support of, 99–100, 193, 226–27; in theatrical works, 74; Wesley on, 183; Wilkes on, 24
William the Conqueror, 125, 163
Williams, Edward ("Iolo Morganwg"), 247
Willis, Richard, 84
Wilson, Thomas, 15
Wilton House, 196
Winter's Tale, The (Shakespeare), 179
Woburn Abbey, 16
Wolfe, James, 71, 185

Wollstonecraft, Mary, 227
Wolsey, Cardinal, 73
women: gender roles and, 30n32, 233–34; as historians, 12–17, 58, 113–15, 124–26; historicisation of womanhood, 15; history and, 11–12
Wootten, Sir Henry, 151
Worcester, 22, 235, 236
world histories, 53–55
Worsley Richard, 46, 59
Wright, James, 45, 58
Wyatt, James, 248
Wyatt's rebellion, 108
Wycliffe, John, 141–42, 143

Wynne, John, 84

xenophobia, 149, 209

York, 3
York, Prince (Duke) Edward of, 8–9
Yorke, Philip, 145
Yorkshire, 187–88
Young England movement, 250
youth, cult of, 5

Zelmane: or The Corinthian Queen, 193
Zenobia, 203
Zurich, 112

JEREMY BLACK is Professor of History at the University of Exeter. He is author of many books, including *Plotting Power: Strategy in the Eighteenth Century*; *Clio's Battles: Historiography in Practice*; *War and Technology*; and *Geographies of an Imperial Power: The British World, 1688–1815*. Black is a recipient of the Samuel Eliot Morison Prize from the Society for Military History.

www.ingramcontent.com/pod-product-compliance
Lightning Source LLC
Chambersburg PA
CBHW030335240426
43661CB00052B/1635